costa rica

FODOR'S TRAVEL PUBLICATIONS
NEW YORK • TORONTO • LONDON • SYDNEY • AUCKLAND

WWW.FODORS.COM

Contents

KEY TO SYMBOLS

✚ Map reference
✉ Address
☎ Telephone number
🕐 Opening times
💷 Admission prices
🚌 Bus number
🚆 Train station
⛴ Ferry/boat
🚗 Driving directions
ℹ Tourist office
🍂 Tours
📖 Guidebook
🍴 Restaurant
☕ Café
🏬 Shop
🚻 Toilets
🛏 Number of rooms
🚭 No smoking
❄ Air-conditioning
🏊 Swimming pool
🏋 Gym
🅿 Parking
❓ Other useful information
🏬 Shopping
🎭 Entertainment
🍸 Nightlife
🏅 Sports
⭐ Activities
💗 Health and beauty
👣 For children
★ Walk/drive start point
▷ Cross-reference

HOW TO USE THIS BOOK

Understanding Costa Rica is an introduction to the country, its geography, economy and people. **Living Costa Rica** gives an insight into Costa Rica today, while **The Story of Costa Rica** takes you through the country's past.

For detailed advice on getting to Costa Rica—and getting around once you are there—turn to **On the Move**. For practical information, from weather forecasts to emergency services, turn to **Planning**.

Out and About gives you the chance to explore Costa Rica through walks and drives.

The **Sights**, **What to Do**, **Eating** and **Staying** sections are divided geographically into seven regions, which are shown on the map on the inside front cover. These regions always appear in the same order. Towns and places of interest are listed alphabetically within each region.

Map references for the **Sights** refer to the atlas section at the end of this book or to the San José street map. For example, Dominical has the reference ✚ 239 K9, indicating the page on which the map is found (239) and the grid square in which Dominical sits (K9).

UNDERSTANDING COSTA RICA

Costa Rica's headline act is its incomparable natural diversity. The country might be small—less than 290km (180 miles) wide and 400km (250 miles) north to south—but it is home to twice as many bird species as North America and more species of butterfly than all of Africa. One quarter of it is protected land, ranging from cloud-covered mountains to steamy rainforests pulsating with vitality. But this peaceable Central American nation isn't a one-hit wonder. Further down the bill, a trio of live volcanoes provide consistently fiery entertainment. And visitors are drawn to Costa Rica's jungle-backed beaches: You can find surf and sunshine on both coasts. Costa Rica, a country that pioneered ecotourism, is now also a thrilling adventure travel destination. Gold-seeking conquistadors largely bypassed this gem of a country. Don't make the same mistake.

GEOGRAPHY

Costa Rica owes at least part of its biological variety to its position in the narrow isthmus linking North and South America. Flora and fauna from both continents meet and flourish in the country's exceptionally varied habitats. Visitors will find chilly cloud forests, sultry lowland jungle and highland plains. Volcanoes are thrust skyward as tectonic plates beneath Costa Rica crumple together: the country has seven active volcanoes in three cordilleras (ranges). You can even get a crater-side view at Volcán Poás and Volcán Irazú.

The highest ground in Costa Rica is the Talamanca mountain range in the south of the country. The highest peak here, Cerro Chirripó, is 3,818m (12,526ft) and swathed in impenetrable forest. But most of Costa Rica's population lives at the more moderate altitude of 1,525m (5,000ft) in the Central Highlands. The capital, San José, sprawls across a fertile, temperate valley, the Meseta Central, with beaches, rainforests and volcanoes no more than a couple of hours' drive away. To the east, the Caribbean lowlands are a mix of forest and fruit plantations. Jungle also extends to the Pacific coast, but towards the northwest of the country, the Gaunacaste region, the landscape changes to a hot, dry savanna. Travel south down the Pacific coast and the climate becomes progressively wetter until you reach the remote Osa Peninsula, a challenging environment for humans and a sanctuary for jaguars and rare macaws.

The perfect cone of Volcán Arenal rises above the cloud forest

SOCIETY

Ticos (the name Costa Ricans give to themselves) are Central America's best-educated, wealthiest people. Education is free and compulsory up to the age of 15, with the result that the literacy rate tops 95 percent. Three state universities produce 18,000 graduates per year. Costa Rica's comprehensive social security system also provides effective health care to 95 percent of the population. Infant mortality rates—at 9.7 deaths per 1,000 a year—are some of the lowest in the region, and life expectancy is 77 years, as opposed to a Latin American average of 70. But the best education and health service in the region costs money and Costa Rica's rapid annual population growth of 2.9 percent means that some see the current welfare system as unsustainable. The welfare system is very important to Costa Ricans and the government's proposals to fund reforms by privatizing some state-owned organizations face stiff opposition.

PEOPLE

Costa Rican people may seem enviably egalitarian on the surface, but they are as divided as any other society. The principal divisions are racial and regional. The 94 percent majority of Costa Rica's population of about 4 million are considered to be white of mixed Spanish descent. The next largest single group is Afro-Caribbeans, representing 3 percent, followed by Amerindians,

Chinese and others at 1 percent each. There are also as many as 400,000 refugees and economic migrants from Nicaragua in Costa Rica. Following Hurricane Mitch in 1998, the Costa Rican government announced a general amnesty to all illegal Central American immigrants living in the country. By June of 2000, 156,000 people had qualified for legal residency papers, the majority of them from Nicaragua. Fair-skinned Costa Ricans of Spanish descent tend to look down upon dark-skinned Costa Ricans of African descent and the indigenous tribal peoples. There are eight indigenous tribes in Costa Rica: Huetar, Bribrí, Cabécar, Guaymí, Chorotega, Boruca, Guanacaste, Heredia, Limón, Puntarenas and San José. Since the creation of Costa Rica's Constitution in 1949, the country has had no standing army, hence its reputation as "the Switzerland of Central America." The nation's neutrality has enabled it to take a prominent role in negotiating for peace in turbulent Central America.

ECONOMY

The single largest factor affecting Costa Rica's economy is its colossal national debt. In 1981 the country was the first in the world to default on its loans; by 1989 it had amassed a US$5 billion

Totally tropical: Between the sun-baked beaches on Costa Rica's Caribbean and Pacific coasts you can explore rainforests packed with unusual plants and animals

Guatuso and Térraba, with land protected in 22 reserves. It was only in 1994 that tribal people were granted the vote and often they feel marginalized, while the Comisión Nacional de Asuntos Indígenas (National Commission for Indigenous Affairs; CONAI) is considered ineffective. Most tribal groups have opened up to ecotourism in recent years.

POLITICS

Power alternates between the two main national parties, the left-wing National Liberation Party (PLN) and the right-leaning Social Christian Unity Party (PUSC). Elections are often close-run events and bribery, corruption and cronyism are major concerns. In 2006 Oscar Arias Sánchez, of the PLN, became the first president elected for a second term after he initiated a constitutional amendment permitting multiple terms. The 57 members of the Legislative Assembly, based in a Moorish building in San José's Plaza de la Democracía, represent Costa Rica's seven provinces: Alajuela, Cartago,

Heredia's fortress: The flawed window design let bullets in easily and made it hard to fire out of the slits

national debt. A period of austerity has trimmed this sum to about US$4 billion. Economically, the country has been undergoing a slow revolution, with every year bringing a shift away from traditional agricultural production and growth in manufacturing, the service sector and tourism, the country's largest source of foreign income. The economy experienced strong growth in the late 1990s and early 2000s, with gross domestic product (GDP) averaging a 5 percent year on year increase. However, two of Costa Rica's most important crops, bananas and coffee beans, are suffering, respectively, from falling quotas and plummeting prices, and inflation, at approximately 14 percent, is also hurting economic forecasts. Unemployment, low by the standards of the region, is on the rise, topping 6 percent in 2006.

LANGUAGE

Costa Ricans speak Spanish, with a Tico twist. It's based on Castilian Spanish but there are several minor differences; there are no soft "*c*"s or "*z*"s, for example, and Costa Ricans use the more formal versions of "you," "*vos*" and "*usted.*" Local slang is easy to pick up and includes such common words and phrases as "*tico*" and "*pura vida.*" The suffix "*tico,*" used to indicate something in the diminutive, has been adopted by Costa Ricans as a self-deprecating way of referring to themselves. "*Pura vida*" means "pure life," a prized Costa Rican concept often used as a salutation. An influx of Westerners means that increasing numbers of people speak or understand English outside the capital, but in rural areas don't expect to find many English-speakers, except in Puerto Limón, where settlers from Jamaica prefer English.

COSTA RICA'S REGIONS AT A GLANCE

San José The Costa Rican capital is not one of the world's great cities, but it benefits from a provincial scale, a compact downtown area easily explored on foot, and a mild climate. If you spend a day or two here, the Mercado Central and the Museo de Oro make go d diversions.

Central Highlands You don't have to go far from San José to arrive in some spectacular scenery. The Central Highlands surround the capital, with the colossal crater Volcán Poás to the north and Costa Rica's highest volcano, Irazú, to the east. Tapirs and jaguars reside in the primary forest of Parque Nacional Braulio Carrillo, while Heredia is a coffee-growing heartland.

Northern Region The Cordillera de Tilarán mountain range sweeps north through this region, where dairy farmers have carved out settlements among the mountains, lakes and wildlife parks. Volcán Arenal is a classically conical volcano and may be either spitting lava, fuming quietly or shrouded in cloud. Monteverde is a world-renowned nature reserve.

Guanacaste This is ranching country, with a rugged but welcoming regional identity. There's little rainfall here, offering a respite from the humid, insect-infested jungles farther south, but tracts of tropical dry forest survive in Guanacaste's popular national parks.

Central Pacific and Nicoya Head west to the remote and relatively undeveloped Nicoya Peninsula and you will find some of Costa Rica's finest beaches and bays, with Pacific swells attracting surfers from around the world. The low-lying Central Pacific region continues the sun, sand and surf theme and is the principal region for sportfishing.

Southern Region As the Central Pacific coast heads south, it gets steadily more tropical and humid, until conditions become extremely demanding in the steamy rainforest of the Osa Peninsula. Inland, the Southern Region claims Costa Rica's highest point, Cerro Chirripó, and some of the country's remaining indigenous communities.

The Caribbean Lowlands The culturally diverse Caribbean coastline stretches from the inaccessible sea turtle breeding grounds of Tortuguero, past banana plantations to the laid-back charms of Puerto Limón and the beautiful beaches farther south of the regional capital.

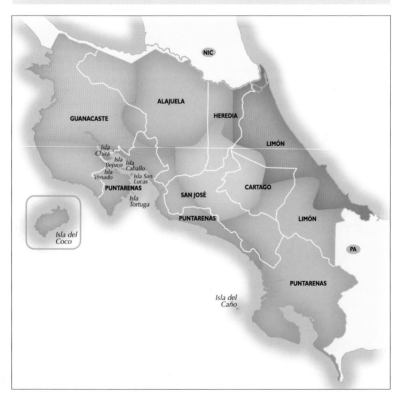

Learn to surf (▷ 134–135) at a surf camp at one of Costa Rica's world-class west coast beaches, but leave the big waves to the experts.

Watch turtles hatch at Parque Nacional Tortuguero (▷ 122–124) the most important breeding site for green turtles in the Caribbean.

Climb Cerro Chirripó (▷ 119); the country's highest point is in the Cordillera de Talamanca

Go sportfishing (▷ 133) for marlin, dorado, tuna and sailfish in the Pacific and snook, tarpon or hard-fighting bonefish in the Caribbean.

Witness a nighttime eruption at Volcán Arenal (▷ 198)—if you're lucky and your timing is good, you might catch Arenal throwing glowing lava into the night skies.

Hike to the Blue Lagoon in Parque Nacional Rincón de la Vieja (▷ 98)—and wallow in the park's hot springs.

Hike to the Montezuma Falls (▷ 103). There are waterfalls throughout Costa Rica, but those on the Montezuma River are among the most impressive.

Take a yoga class (▷ 151) at one of the New Age lodges springing up across the Central Pacific and Nicoya region.

Watch the macaws fly home to roost in Parque Nacional Carara (▷ 104)—it's late afternoon and time for the park's noisy macaws to fly back to their trees for the night.

Track a jaguar in Parque Nacional Corcovado (▷ 112–115). During the turtle breeding season the big cats venture onto the beach to hunt turtles.

String up a hammock on a beach Pick a beach (Manuel Antonio is a good choice, ▷ 106–107). Find two trees about 2.5m (8ft) apart. Attach hammock. Relax.

Go white-water rafting (▷ 132) through virgin rainforest on the Pacuare River. Other rivers, such as the Sarapiquí, are less turbulent.

Take a canopy tour (▷ 131). Several are now offered in different areas and are a great way to understand the rainforest ecosystem.

Rent a mountain bike (▷ 132) because there's no better way of experiencing Costa Rica's countryside than cycling through it on jungle trails and the rough tracks that pass for roads in some areas.

Go scuba-diving among hammerhead sharks at Parque Nacional Isla del Coco (▷ 104) where great concentrations of the predators feed on smaller fish.

Top, surfing at Dominical.
Above, sportfishing
for snook at
Río Parismina Lodge

Start the day with a coffee, Costa Rica's finest commodity. Café Britt (▷ 69), an excellent, nationally available brand, is made from 100 percent arabica beans.

Finish the day with a chilled local beer Imperial is the most widespread brand, while Bavaria Gold is equally highly regarded.

Watch the sunset from a Pacific-facing restaurant (▷ 202–204) for one of the most romantic sights of all, but reserve early because the best restaurants fill up fast in the high season.

Rent a four-wheel drive and explore the hill country (▷ 47). A rugged four-wheel-drive vehicle is the only way to travel in some of the remote regions and every trip has the potential to become an adventure.

Take a day-trip to Granada (▷ 42). It's a short hop from Daniel Oduber Quirós airport to Central America's grandest and oldest colonial city in neighboring Nicaragua.

A jaguar (top). Costa Rican beer is the perfect sundowner (above). Enjoy the sunset at Playa Grande in Guanacaste again and again (right)

THE BEST OF COSTA RICA

SAN JOSÉ

Mercado Central (▷ 139) Bargain hunt or just browse the stands at the biggest market in the country.

Museo de Oro Precolumbino (▷ 65) Contain your avarice at this astounding display of gold artifacts dating from AD500.

Galería Namú (▷ 138) Get your gifts at the best souvenir shop in San José.

Museo del Jade (▷ 64) Don't miss this fascinating collection of hundreds of jade artifacts, the best in Latin America.

Teatro Nacional (▷ 67) The most handsome, and interesting, building in the Costa Rican capital is the national theater in the Plaza de la Cultura.

Grano de Oro (▷ 183) Treat yourself to a meal at one of San José's top eateries.

A collection of tools at the Museo del Jade (above). A fruit seller at the Mercado Central in San José (top left)

CENTRAL HIGHLANDS

Barry Biesanz (▷ 141) Wood-carver Biesanz is Costa Rica's top craftsman, designing furniture and other items at his workshop in Escazú.

Poás Volcano Lodge (▷ 143) Go horseback-riding at this English-owned eco-lodge on the outskirts of Parque Nacional Braulio Carrillo.

Fábrica de Chaverri (▷ 143) Buy your Sarchí oxcart here and they'll mail it home for you.

Volcán Poás (▷ 75) Close to San José, this colossal crater attracts plenty of visitors hoping for a glimpse of it through the clouds.

Volcán Irazú (▷ 76) Arrive early at the closest volcano to San José to avoid clouds and crowds.

Parque Nacional Braulio Carrillo (▷ 72–74) A highway runs conveniently straight through this relatively unexplored park.

Cerutti (▷ 184) Treat yourself at the top Italian restaurant in the Highlands.

The crater of Volcán Irazú (above). The wheel of an oxcart from Sarchí (left)

NORTHERN REGION

Monteverde (▷ 84–89) Renowned for its diversity, this compact cloud forest reserve is right at the top of most sightseers' lists.

Volcán Arenal (▷ 78–81) Brooding over the surrounding area, Arenal is a classically conical volcano, prone to fiery eruptions.

Pizzeria de Johnny (▷ 186) The best restaurant in the region? Pizza lovers think so.

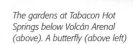

The gardens at Tabacon Hot Springs below Volcán Arenal (above). A butterfly (above left)

GUANACASTE

Sueño del Mar (▷ 201) Stay at this charming bed-and-breakfast on Playa Langosta.

Playa Grande (▷ 99) Watch the surfers catch the rolling waves by day, then return to watch leatherback turtles nest by night at this magnificent sweeping beach location.

Parque Nacional Rincón de la Vieja (▷ 98) Hot springs, turquoise bathing pools and waterfalls, verdant Rincón de la Vieja is made for water lovers.

Surf at Playa Grande (above). A jay from Guanacaste (left)

THE BEST OF COSTA RICA

CENTRAL PACIFIC AND NICOYA

Loma Del Mar Surf Camp (▷ 151) Beginners can learn to surf at this popular women-only camp at Playa Hermosa.

Parque Nacional Manuel Antonio (▷ 106–107) String up a hammock at the beach or take a walk along the popular trails.

Flying Crocodile (▷ 204) This imaginatively decorated hotel offers ultra-light flying lessons.

Barba Roja (▷ 189) Watch the sunset from the cocktail bar at this hilltop restaurant overlooking Manuel Antonio.

Parque Nacional Carara (▷ 104) If you can't wait to get to the forest, this is the closest park to San José.

Parque Nacional Isla del Coco (▷ 104)—uninhabited desert island and a UNESCO world heritage site famous for shoals of hammerhead sharks.

The Festival of the Virgin of the Sea (▷ 152) A parade of brightly painted boats sails out from Puntarenas during this festival.

Horseback-riding at Manuel Antonio (above). A strawberry poison arrow frog (right)

SOUTHERN REGION

Parque Nacional Corcovado (▷ 112–115) Sweltering in the southwest corner, Corcovado repays the hardiness of its visitors with extraordinary wildlife spotting opportunities.

Parque Nacional Chirripó (▷ 118–120) Costa Rica's second-largest park is home to its highest mountain and high-altitude plains called *páramo*.

Lapa Ríos Lodge (▷ 205) Chill out at this highly rated eco-lodge, with its own nature reserve, in Matapalo.

Pavones (▷ 116) This surf spot has one of the world's longest waves.

Finca Eddie Serrano (▷ 153) Haven't seen a quetzal yet? Then visit this reserve for an almost guaranteed sighting.

Crossing a river in the Osa Peninsula (above). A bird-watcher at Lapa Ríos (right)

THE CARIBBEAN LOWLANDS

Parque Nacional Tortuguero (▷ 122–124) Watch turtles laying their eggs on the beaches of this national park, where boat trips along the canals and lagoons offer spectacular wildlife encounters.

Puerto Limón Carnaval (▷ 156) It's noisy, chaotic and even edgy, but Costa Rica's biggest street party is also a lot of fun.

Miss Edith's (▷ 192) A legend in Cahuita, Miss Edith's restaurant serves good, inexpensive Caribbean food to queues of eager diners.

Tortuga Lodge and Gardens (▷ 208) Splash the cash at this fashionable resort in Tortuguero, with economical package deals also available.

A green turtle seen on a Deep Blue Diving Adventure (above). The Caribbean coast (right). Kayaks on Río Tortuguero (below)

THE NATIONAL PARKS AND ECOSYSTEMS

The relationship between temperature, altitude and rainfall creates Costa Rica's variety of ecosystems. National parks may cover one or more category, depending on location. Find out whether you're standing in tropical lowland, tropical premontane, lower montane or dry forest, with this brief guide.

Welcome to the jungle: left to right, a Swiss cheese plant; a ceibo tree; giant ferns at Monteverde

LOWLAND WET FORESTS

Lowland wet forest is found in the northern and southern Caribbean lowlands and in the southern Pacific lowlands. Protected areas containing this forest include La Selva Biological Reserve, Cahuita National Park, Manuel Antonio National Park and Corcovado National Park.

These are the classical tropical forests. Tall, semi-deciduous and evergreen trees reach to a height of 40–55m (130–180ft) and even taller, emergent evergreen trees soar above this canopy. A subcanopy of lower trees is often present, while the ground may be bare or have a sparse shrub layer. While walking through the forest, one of the most commonly seen plants in the understorey and shrub layer are members of the genus **piper**. There are more than 90 species in this genus within Costa Rica. All are small trees or shrubs characterized by their erect, candle-like flowering structures, which are generally pollinated by bats. Buttress and stilt roots are common features in these forests. Buttress roots appear as broad ridges attached to the side of a tree trunk and acting as support for the tree, accounting for the minimal sub-surface root system. Stilt roots come off the side of a tree trunk, growing down and entering the earth some distance from the trunk to anchor the tree more firmly in the soil.

Palms are common in this type of forest and one species you may well see is *Welfia georgii*, which bears its fruit on its trunk. Vines are also numerous; quite common is the **passion flower** (*Passiflora foetida*), with bright red flowers, and the **Swiss cheese plant** (*Monstera deliciosa*), a large-leafed climber in these wet forests and commonly seen as a house plant in European and North American homes. **Epiphytes**, plants that grow on other plants, are frequent in the lowland wet forests and large trees such as the **kapok** (*Ceiba pentandra*) are often heavily laden with them. This tree is massive, often emerging above the surrounding canopy, with a broad, flat crown and a seed that produces a fibrous material often used to stuff cushions and furniture. Epiphytes include mosses, ferns, orchids and bromeliads. The orchids, with more than 1,000 species in Costa Rica, can be spectacular when in flower–indeed Costa Rica's national flower is an orchid, the **guaria morada** (*Cattleya skinneri*). **Bromeliads** typically have fleshy, often spiky, leaves formed into a rosette with a central "well" that holds water, which is often used as a small pond by a host of animals including snails, worms, insects and even frogs and tadpoles.

The driving force for change in the lowland wet forest is forest gaps. Clearings created by a tree fall produce a sudden availability of light and various plant species rush to colonize the area, before being gradually replaced by more mature, slower-growing species. Within the lowland forest, pioneer species such as the **balsa tree** (*Ochroma lagopus*), grow rapidly in these gaps to reach a height of 30m (98ft). Its light, soft wood is used for making many of the wooden souvenirs available to tourists in Costa Rica. *Cercropia obtusifolia* is another pioneer species, frequently found in lowland forests. Thriving on the light of forest gaps, it has large, umbrella-like leaves, which sloths love to eat.

Also found in disturbed areas of the forest, in clearings and along streams are species of *Heliconia*, which have large leaves resembling those on banana trees and striking red, orange and yellow flowers, shaped rather like lobster claws, pollinated by hummingbirds.

LOWLAND DRY FOREST

This type of forest once covered extensive areas of Costa Rica's northern Pacific coastal plain, but most has now been cleared for agriculture. The rainy season in this region is only six months in length (May to October). By comparison, rain falls year-round in the Caribbean lowlands hence the difference in forest type. The dry forest is semi-deciduous, with a canopy at 20–30m (65–100ft), an understorey of trees 10–20m (33–65ft) tall and a 2–5m (6.5–16ft) high, dense shrub layer. Vines are present, but epiphytes are generally rare. Common or

Mists of cloud or fog enshroud the forest canopy for much of the time, hence the name "cloud forest" which is often used to describe them. Light levels tend to be reduced at higher elevations and the foliage drips with water that condenses out of the atmosphere. These forests are less diverse than those in the lowlands, but they are often home to species that are found nowhere else in the world. These forests occur on the slopes of Costa Rica's mountains. In the lower areas the cloud forest is mixed deciduous and evergreen, while at higher elevations it is uniformly evergreen. There are frequent strong

Left to right, dry tropical forest at Santa Rosa; fresh coffee beans; timber at a logging station

conspicuous plants include the **gumbo limbo tree** (*Bursera simaruba*), which is recognizable by its smooth, red/orange bark. The *Crescentia alata*, a fairly common large, shrub-like tree, has conspicuous hard fruits or gourds growing from its trunk which are eaten by rodents and also used for decoration. *Corteza* trees, in the genus *tabebuia*, are commonly seen but stand out most when in flower as all members of a species flower simultaneously towards the end of the dry season, though for only four days, so you'll have to be lucky to catch them. The flowers are either yellow or pink. **Palms** are not as frequent in the dry forests as they are in the wetland forest, but one palm, *Acrocomia vinifera*, is fairly common; it has long, sharp spines on its lower trunk and occurs particularly in swampy areas and along roads.

Wildlife is often easier to see in these more open, less dense forests than in the thicker, wetter forests, though biodiversity is lower.

PREMONTANE AND MONTANE FOREST

In the forests at higher elevations, the hot stickiness of the lowland forest areas is replaced by a cooler dampness. The cooler climate is due to the temperature dropping, on average, by 0.5°C (33°F) for every 100m (330ft) gained in altitude.

winds in the higher forests so the tops of the trees become flatter than those of lowland trees. In addition, the trees tend to become gnarled, twisted and multi-stemmed and the leaves are much smaller, narrower and leathery. Canopy height at lower levels is around 30–40m (100–130ft), declining as elevation increases. There is usually a subcanopy and dense undergrowth. **Vines** and **epiphytes** grow profusely, especially in the evergreen cloud forests; indeed **lichens** can be seen hanging in curtains from trees. Though also found at lower elevations, **tree ferns** are especially common in the

The Guanacaste tree: shaped like an umbrella

higher forests. Quite a number of the trees and shrubs at these higher elevations may be found in temperate regions, such as **oaks** (*Quercus*), **buddleia** (*Buddleja*) and **magnolia** (*Magnolia*). Also found in these high forests is the **Winter's bark** (*Drimys winteri*). Growing to about 15m (50ft) in height, it has aromatic bark, large, leathery, oval yellow-green leaves and clusters of fragrant, small, white flowers and purple berries.

PÁRAMO

This treeless, subalpine habitat predominates at the highest elevations in Costa Rica. Only grasses and shrubs are found in these areas. Chirripó National Park contains some areas of *páramo*.

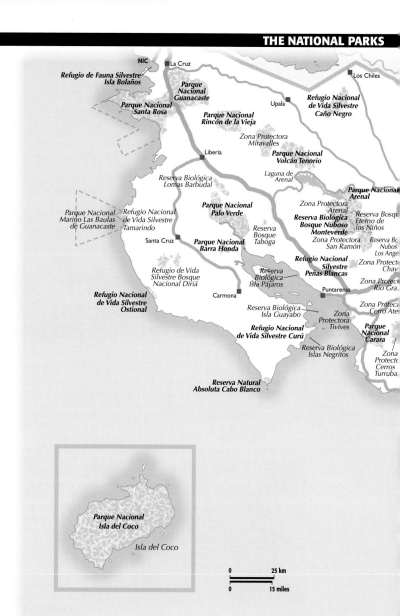

Refugio de Fauna Silvestre
Isla Bolaños

NIC La Cruz

Los Chiles

Parque Nacional
Guanacaste

Upala

Refugio Nacional
de Vida Silvestre
Caño Negro

Parque Nacional
Santa Rosa

Parque Nacional
Rincón de la Vieja

Zona Protectora
Miravalles

Liberia

Parque Nacional
Volcán Tenorio

Laguna de
Arenal

Parque Nacional
Arenal

Reserva Biológica
Lomas Barbudal

Parque Nacional
Palo Verde

Zona Protectora
Arenal

Reserva Biológica
Bosque Nuboso
Monteverde

Reserva Bosqu
Eterno de
los Niños

Parque Nacional
Marino Las Baulas
de Guanacaste

Refugio Nacional
de Vida Silvestre
Tamarindo

Reserva
Bosque
Taboga

Zona Protectora
San Ramón

Reserva Bo
Nubos
Los Ange

Santa Cruz

Parque Nacional
Barra Honda

Refugio Nacional
Silvestre
Peñas Blancas

Zona Protect
Chay

Refugio de Vida
Silvestre Bosque
Nacional Diriá

Reserva
Biológica
Isla Pájaros

Puntarenas

Zona Protec
Río Gra

Refugio Nacional
de Vida Silvestre
Ostional

Carmona

Reserva Biológica
Isla Guayabo

Zona Protec
Cerro Ate

Zona
Protectora
Tivives

Parque
Nacional
Carara

Refugio Nacional
de Vida Silvestre Curú

Reserva Biológica
Islas Negritos

Zona
Protecto
Cerros
Turruba

Reserva Natural
Absoluta Cabo Blanco

Parque Nacional
Isla del Coco

Isla del Coco

0   25 km

0   15 miles

NATIONAL PARKS

Costa Rica is promoted as a model of conservation with national parks protecting 12 percent of the country and just over one quarter of the national territory falling within a protected status category of some kind.

The country has undergone a dramatic turnaround in recent decades. From the 1940s to the 1970s the country had some of the highest rates of deforestation in the world, clearing at a rate that would have stripped the entire country by the 21st century. Fortunately, the efforts of a dozen or so national and international individuals and groups–among them such guiding lights as

Mario Boza, Archie Carr, Leslie R. Holdridge and the Organization for Tropical Studies (OTS)–have been successful in highlighting Costa Rica's extraordinary flora and fauna. Coupled with timely falls in commodity prices, the government moved away from state-sponsored land clearance for ranching and agriculture, preferring instead the creation of the national parks system.

The evolution of protected parks began in 1970 with the creation of the National Parks Service (SPN). The latest reorganization completed in 1995 divided the entire country into 11 regions, creating a National System of Protected Areas (SINAC–Sistema Nacional de Areas de

NIC

Refugio Nacional
de Vida Silvestre
Barra del Colorado

Zona Protectora
Tortuguero

eserva Bosque
Cordillera
Volcánica

Zona Protectora
La Selva

Parque Nacional
Tortuguero

Reserva Bosque
Matina

que Nacional
n Castro
nco
que Nacional
olcán Poás

Parque
Nacional
Braulio
Carrillo

Guácimo

Reserva
Bosque
Grecia

Reserva Bosque
Central Cordillera
Volcánica

Zona
Protectora
Pacuare

Puerto Limón

Alajuela

Heredia

SAN JOSÉ

Parque Nacional
Volcán Irazú

Parque
Nacional
Barbilla

Zona
ectora
Rodeo

Zona
Protectora
Cerros de
Escazú

Zona Protectora
Carpintera

Zona Protectora
Río Banano

Parque Nacional
Cahuita

na Protectora
Cangreja

Zona
Protectora
Río Navarro y
Río Sombrero

Parque Nacional
Tapantí-Macizo
de la Muerte

Zona Protectora
Cuenca del Río Tuis

Reserva
Biológica
Hitoy Cerere

Bribrí

Refugio Nacional
de Vida Silvestre
Gandoca-Manzanillo

Zona Protectora
Caraigres

Reserva Bosque
Río Macho

Parrita

Zona Protectora
Cerro Nara

Reserva
Bosque
Los Santos

Parque
Nacional
Chirripó

Parque Internacional
La Amistad

que Nacional
anuel Antonio

San Isidro de
El General

Reserva
Biológica
Durika

Parque Nacional
Marino Ballena

Palmar
Norte

Zona Protectora
Las Tablas

Reserva Biológica
Marenco

Reserva Bosque
Golfo Dulce

Parque
Nacional
Piedras Blancas

Ciudad
Neily

PA

Reserva Biológica
Isla del Caño

Parque
Nacional
Corcovado

Refugio Nacional
de Fauna Silvestre
Golfito

Reserva Bosque
Golfo Dulce

The entrance of Rincón de la Vieja National Park

Conservación), which is administered as part of the Ministry for the Environment and Energy (MINAE–Ministerio del Ambiente y Energía).

In addition to national parks, the National System protects land within a range of categories including biological and forest reserves, wildlife refuges and a few smaller categories. Its goals are to consolidate and guarantee the conservation of the protected areas and the national biodiversity, and to manage their sustainable use. Many of the national parks have a combined purpose of protecting watersheds which feed the country's essential hydroelectric power system and protecting areas of particular biological interest.

THE ANIMALS AND BIRDS OF COSTA RICA

Costa Rica, for its size, contains more species of plants and animals than any other country in the world, with around 10,000 plant species, 875 bird species, 205 species of mammals, 215 reptiles, 160 amphibians, and some 360,000 insects. It is home to around five percent of the world's terrestrial species.

Sloths, such as this female three-toed sloth and its young, move so slowly that algae can grow on their coats (left). A white-faced capuchin monkey (middle). A tamandua feasting on termites (right)

Costa Rica's amazing biodiversity is partly due to its geographical situation linking two huge continental masses, the fact that it is a barrier between two oceans, and its wide variety of landscapes, including mountains, valleys, coastal plains and prairies. In addition, though wholly within the tropics, Costa Rica has a climatic diversity.

Much of the country's wildlife remains only in the small, but numerous, national parks and reserves which protect 25 percent of the country. Elsewhere, most of the forest, home to the majority of the animals, has been cut down and replaced by farmland.

PRIMATES

Costa Rica has four of the seventy or so species of New World monkey. The three larger ones are common in many protected areas, while the squirrel monkey is found in only a few lowland wet forests of the southern Pacific slope of the country.

Red-backed squirrel monkeys (*Saimiri oerstedii*) are small monkeys, with a golden orange back, hands and feet, a black crown and muzzle and white mask. Moving in groups of 10 to 20 individuals, they run and jump through the trees feeding on fruits, seeds, leaves and insects. The groups contain several adult females and males, with juveniles and infants. This species is only found in Panama and Costa Rica and is considered to be in danger of extinction.

White-faced capuchin monkeys (*Cebus capucinus*), are medium-sized monkeys with a white throat, head and shoulders, while their back and prehensile tail are black. They forage in wet forests, including mangroves, and may even be seen on the ground. Their diet is mostly fruit, but also includes leaves, nuts, flowers, insects, small birds, reptiles and young mammals. Group size is around 10 to 20, consisting of males and females. These monkeys are probably the most commonly seen in Costa Rica as they occur in dry and wet forests and are active and noisy during the day; their threat display involves jumping up and down and shaking branches.

Geoffroy's spider monkeys (*Ateles geoffroyi*) are the most elegant Costa Rican primates. Their coat varies from light buff to black, with black hands and feet. They use their prehensile tail as a fifth limb, swinging, climbing and hanging in the upper canopy of the forest, preferring the wet, evergreen forests to the dry forests. They eat mainly fruit, but add seeds, flowers, leaves and insects to their diet. Groups usually have twice as many females as males, though the number of monkeys moving together is variable as the troop divides into small foraging parties. Spider monkeys are active during the day.

Mantled howler monkeys (*Alouatta palliata*) are black except for a fringe of long gold hairs on their sides. Even if not seen, these large monkeys will certainly be heard by anyone visiting lowland evergreen forests or the dry forests, though they are also present in montane forests. The males, in particular, give loud roaring vocalizations at dawn and in the late afternoon. Howlers move slowly and deliberately high in the forest and may well be passed by unnoticed. Leaves are the main component of their diet, along with flowers and fruits. Group size is usually 10 to 20, made up of adult males and females and offspring.

OPOSSUMS

There are nine species of these marsupials in Costa Rica, occupying most habitats. The **common possum** (*Didelphis marsupialis*) resembles a large rat with yellowish face, gray-black body, black ears and a long, hairless, prehensile tail. They are nocturnal, but may be seen during the day foraging on the ground for fruits, eggs, invertebrates and small vertebrates.

The smaller gray **four-eyed opossum** *(Philander opossum)* is found in rainforest regions; it has a black face mask with large white spots over its eyes. The **water opossum** *(Chironectes minimus)* is also seen quite commonly, often by or in water. This species has a grey body with broad black or brown stripes.

ANTEATERS
Costa Rica has three species of anteater. The most commonly seen is the **northern tamandua** *(Tamandua mexicana),* which has a brown or yellow-ish head and legs with a black vest on its belly and back. It can be found in trees and on the ground in

A howler monkey (above). An ocelot in Braulio Carillo National Park at nighttime (right)

wet and dry forests and in savanna habitats, feeding mainly on termites at night. The **giant anteater** *(Myrmecophaga tridactyla)* is up to 2m (7ft) long and extremely rare, while the tiny **silky anteater** *(Cyclopes didactylus),* standing 17cm (6.5in) tall, is arboreal, nocturnal and unlikely to be spotted.

ARMADILLOS
Two of the world's 20 species of armadillo live in Costa Rica. The more common species is the **nine-banded armadillo** *(Dasypus novemcinctus)*. It has a gray to yellowish, armor-plated body, a long snout, large ears and scales on its head and legs, and is found on the ground in all but the most arid habitats. Its diet is variable, including insects and small vertebrates, fruit, fungi, tubers and carrion. It, and Costa Rica's other species, the **naked-tailed armadillo** *(Cabassous sp.)*, are nocturnal. Uniquely among mammals, the nine-banded and other armadillos may give birth to four genetically identical offspring.

SLOTHS
Costa Rica has two of these strange, slow-moving, upside-down creatures: **Hoffman's two-toed sloth** *(Choloepus hoffmanni)* and the brown-throated **three-toed sloth** *(Bradypus variegates)*. The for-mer is generally a tan color and has no tail, while the latter is grayish brown with a distinctive gray and white mask and a small, stumpy tail. In moist condi-tions, the coats of both species may be suffused with green, the tint coming from the blue-green algae that live on their fur and help camouflage them in the trees. Both have three curved claws, or "toes," on their hind feet, while it is the claws on the forefeet that give them their common names. The three-toed sloth is active day and night and may

move through four or five trees in two days, whereas the two-toed is nocturnal and is often in the same tree for two consecutive nights. Both species eat only leaves and it may take a month for a full meal to be completely digested. As a result, they need to defecate only once a week and descend to the base of a tree to do so. Young are born throughout the year and are carried by their mother for six to nine months, so it is worth looking for an extra, smaller head when you see an adult.

CATS
All six species of the cat family in Costa Rica are noc-turnal and rare, which makes it unlikely that they will be seen. The smallest, spotted species is the **oncilla** *(Felis tigrinus)*, which is the size of a small domestic cat; next in size is the **margay** *(Felis wiedi)*, followed by the medium dog-sized **ocelot** *(Felis pardalis)*, and then the large **jaguar** *(Panthera onca)*. The two unspotted cats are the smaller **jaguarundi** *(Felis yagouaroundi)*, and the **puma** *(Felis concolor)*, which is almost the same size as a jaguar. All species are found in forest, though some also occur in scrubland and even savanna. The diet of the smallest, the oncilla, includes large insects, frogs, birds, lizards and small mammals, while even the largest, the jaguar, is not averse to small prey such as fish and frogs; it also takes deer, tapirs, monkeys and peccaries. Most climb trees as well as hunting on the ground and both the jaguar and ocelot are excellent swimmers. Nocturnal activity is most com-mon, though the jaguar and jaguarundi may also be active during the day. Walking at night along trails cleared in the forest will give you the best chance of seeing one of these cats. Wear a headlamp, rather than carry a torch, as then their glowing eyeshine is reflected back to your eyes.

PECCARIES

The **collared peccary** (*Tayassu tajacu*) and the **white-lipped peccary** (*T. pecari*) both travel in groups of up to 50 individuals in the case of the collared peccary and 100 or more for the white-lipped. They tend to divide into smaller family groups of adult males, females and their offspring, and are pig-like, in both activity and appearance. With a diet of roots, seeds and fruit, signs of their rooting activities are often seen, as well as their dung piles, which are used as territory markers, and their mud wallows. The collared peccary is black or gray with a band of lighter hair around its neck. It is the more widespread species, occurring in all forest types at low and mid elevations, in shrublands and agricultural areas, and it is active during the day. The white-lipped peccary lives in forests and is active day and night.

DEER

The **white-tailed deer** (*Odocoileus virginianus*) is the largest of Costa Rica's two deer species, standing 1m (3.3ft) high at the shoulder, and is seen more commonly. It is a light-, dark- or grayish-brown deer, with a white belly and white under the tail. Males over a year old have branched antlers, which are shed and regrown each year. The smaller red **brocket deer** (*Mazama americana*) is reddish brown, with white under the tail. The males have small, straight

White-lipped peccaries can be aggressive if confronted

antlers. The white-tailed deer lives in open drier forests and on forest edges, while the brocket deer tends to be in thicker, wet forests. Both are active day and night. The deer graze on grass and browse on leaves and twigs from trees and shrubs, with the brocket deer also eating fruit and flowers. Brocket deer live singly or in very small groups, while the white-tailed deer form larger, usually single-sex, groups. When alarmed, both species flee with their tail raised, displaying its white underside. A disappearing rump is the most frequent sighting of the deer.

TAPIRS

Baird's tapir (*Tapirus bairdii*) is the only tapir living in Costa Rica. The coat of this large, stocky animal is sparsely furred with reddish brown hair and it has a short, bristly mane extending along the back of its neck. The tapir has a short, fleshy trunk, derived from the nose and upper lip, which is used to pull leaves and shoots into its mouth. Its sense of smell is excellent, its hearing is good, but its vision is poor. Found in wet forests and swampy areas, it is active mostly at night, feeding on leaves, twigs, fruit and grass. The most likely clue to its presence is its characteristic three-toed track, but tapirs are uncommon and rarely seen.

RACCOONS

Of the six species of raccoon found in Costa Rica, the

white-nosed coati (*Nasua narica*) is most likely to be seen; also quite common are the **northern raccoon** (*Procyon loctor*) and the **kinkajou** (*Potus flavus*). The **crab-eating raccoon** (*Procyon cancrivorous*), the **olingo**, (*Bassaricyon gabbi*) and the **cacomistle** (*Bassariscus sumichrasti*) are also present. All but the coati are nocturnal and all are omnivorous. Generally, these species have pointed muzzles, short legs and long tails. The northern and crab-eating raccoons have a striped tail and a black face-mask; the coat of the former is grizzled gray, while that of the latter is brown. The northern raccoon is more widespread in Costa Rica, the crab-eater being confined to the Pacific lowlands. Both are seen

RODENTS

There are about 50 rodent species in Costa Rica, including mice, rats, gophers, squirrels and others such as the **Mexican hairy porcupine** (*Coendou mexicanus*), **paca** (*Agouti paca*) and **agouti** (*Dasyprocta punctata*). The agouti, a reddish brown creature resembling a large, long-legged guinea pig, searches the forest floor for fallen fruit and seeds. The paca is similar in shape, but twice the size and nocturnal. Mexican hairy porcupines spend most of their time in trees, using their prehensile tails to get around. Their diet consists of leaves, fruits, seeds, roots, insects and small vertebrates.

Of Costa Rica's five squirrel species, the **red-tailed**

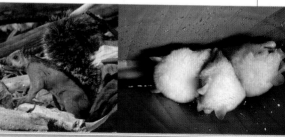

Far left, a Baird's tapir in Corcovado National Park. Above, left to right, a white-nosed coati; a variegated squirrel at Cabo Blanco Nature Reserve; white tent bats roosting in a tent made from Heliconia *leaves*

mostly living near water. Unlike the other species, coatis are very sociable, with females and offspring living in groups; adult males are solitary. They have a long, ringed tail that is often held erect above the body, and a mobile, upturned and elongated snout.

The kinkajou is uniformly grayish or reddish brown and without a ringed tail; it also has a shorter muzzle than the others. Its tail is prehensile, and it has a long tongue used for probing nectar from flowers and obtaining honey from bees' nests. The olingo is similar in behaviour, but is smaller with indistinct rings on its bushier (non-prehensile) tail and faint gray markings on its more pointed face; it is also rarer. The cacomistle, found in drier forests, has a fox-like face, larger ears than the other species in this group and a bushy, ringed tail.

DOGS

The **coyote** (*Canis latrans*) and the **gray fox** (*Urocyon cinereoargenteus*) are Costa Rica's two species from the dog family. The coat of the former, the larger species, varies from grizzled gray to brownish yellow, while that of the latter is silver gray with tawny legs, feet and ears. Both are active during the day and night and both are found in forest or, more commonly, open areas of the northern Pacific lowlands. Both species tend to eat whatever is available, from fruit and insects to small mammals or even deer. The howl of the coyote—high-pitched staccato yelps followed by a long wail—is likely to be heard.

RABBITS

Two or three species are found in the country, including the **eastern cottontail** (*Sylvilagus floridensis*) and the **forest rabbit** (*S. brasiliensis*). The former is found on forest edges and in open areas, while, as you'd expect, the latter lives in forests.

squirrel (*Sciurus granatensis*) and the **variegated squirrel** (*S. variegatoides*) are the ones most likely to be seen. The former tends to be in wet forests, while the latter is found in drier forests and more open areas. Both are diurnal, foraging for food in the trees.

WEASELS

Costa Rica's three species of skunk are more likely to be smelled than seen. The **striped hog-nosed skunk** (*Conepatus semistriatus*) is black, with a white stripe on its head and along its back and a white, bushy tail. The **spotted skunk** (*Spilogale putorius*) and the **hooded skunk** (*Mephitis macroura*) are less common. All three are nocturnal and omnivorous.

The **tayra** (*Eira barbara*) is a long, slender animal with a black or brown body and a tan head. They are often seen in pairs, foraging for birds, small mammals and fruit. Other species found in Costa Rica are the **grison** (*Galictis vittata*), which has a gray back and tail, with black legs and face and a white stripe on its forehead; the **long-tailed weasel** (*Mustela frenata*); and the **neotropical otter** (*Lutra longicaudis*).

BATS

With more than 100 species in the country and all just glimpsed as they swoop past at night, it is often very difficult to identify the species seen. The smallest bat in Costa Rica, the **black myotis** (*Myotis nigricans*) has a wingspan of 5cm (2in), while the largest, the **false vampire bat** (*Vampyrum spectrum*), has an 80cm (30in) wingspan. Foods include pollen, nectar, fruit, insects, small vertebrates (such as fish, frogs, birds, rodents or other bats) and blood, with different species focusing on different items. Daytime roosting sites are hollow trees, caves, tree branches, rock crevices, under bridges and in buildings, or even in rolled up plant leaves.

BIRDS

Though the mammals in Costa Rica might be elusive, you can guarantee that you will see birds, and lots of them. They vary from "little brown jobs" (LBJs for short) to comparatively massive, eye-catching macaws and toucans. For anyone with more than a superficial interest, a good bird book is a must.

SEA AND SHOREBIRDS

Very obvious by the sea is the magnificent **frigatebird** (*Fregata magnificens*), a soaring, black bird with a 2m (7ft) wingspan and forked tail. Males have red throat pouches that they inflate during courtship displays. Seeing these frigatebirds stealing fish from

MARSH AND STREAM BIRDS

Among Costa Rica's marsh and stream birds are such species as the jacana, several rails, crakes, gallinules, coots and the sunbittern. The **northern jacana** (*Jacana spinosa*) is often seen walking on top of lily pads or other floating vegetation, its long toes spreading its weight. It feeds on insects, snails, frogs, fish and vegetable matter. Adults have a black head, neck and chest with bright brown wings, belly and back and a yellow beak, forehead and unmistakable yellow under the wings. The **purple gallinule** (*Porphyrula martinica*), found in marshes and around lakeshores, has a purple head, neck and chest, green wings, red and yellow beak, light blue forehead and yellow legs.

People come from all over the world to see some of Costa Rica's 600 resident bird species and 170 migrant species: the purple gallinule (left); a pelican (middle); white ibis at Palo Verde National Park (right)

other seabirds and eating sea turtle hatchlings makes you realize that their habits do not live up to their elegant appearance. **Brown pelicans** (*Pelecanus occidentalis*) are sturdier birds, easily recognizable by their throat pouches, which they use as a net to scoop up fish underwater. Ungainly on the ground, a group of them flying slowly in formation low over the water or beach is an impressive sight.

WATERBIRDS, HERONS AND EGRETS

Also seen by the sea, as well as in freshwater areas, are anhingas and cormorants–quite similar looking birds, very often observed standing with their wings spread out to dry in the sun. The **olivaceous cormorant** (*Phalacrocorax brasilianus*) is a black or brown bird with a wingspan of 1m (3.5ft), a long tail and a down-curved bill. The **anhinga** (*Anhinga anhinga*) has a longer neck and a long, pointed bill without a hook; the female has a brown neck. Many other birds, including storks, ibis, herons, egrets and spoonbills can be seen in aquatic habitats. The **roseate spoonbill** (*Ajaia ajaja*) is a large, pink wading bird with a white neck and distinctive spoon-shaped beak that it opens and swings about underwater, snapping it shut when it feels a frog, fish or other such prey. Also distinctive is the **jabirú stork** (*Jabiru mycteria*), a very large, white wading bird standing 1.4m (5ft) high, with a huge black beak and a red area on its neck.

    Cattle egrets (*Bubulcu ibis*) precede any river safari through open savanna, taking to the air in flocks in a blaze of feathers only to settle elsewhere. The **bare-throated tiger-heron** (*Tigrisoma mexicanum*) is a far more impressive bird, standing 80cm (31in) tall. The juvenile has tiger-like stripes that blend perfectly against the alternating shade and sunlight, eventually growing out at adulthood.

DUCKS

Costa Rica's 15 or so species of duck includes the **muscovy** (*Cairina moschata*); it is mostly greenish-black, with white patches on its wings and the male has a feathered crest and red warts on his face and beak. It is no longer very common due to hunting pressure and habitat destruction.

KINGFISHERS

There are six species of kingfisher in Costa Rica, often seen perching on branches while they scan the water beneath them for fish. All have large heads, with long, straight, sturdy bills and stubby bodies, but they vary in size. The bigger species eat larger prey to avoid competition with the smaller ones. They lay their eggs in burrows dug in the banks of rivers or streams. The **ringed kingfisher** (*Ceryle torquata*), a blue-gray bird, with a brownish front, white neckband and throat, is the largest kingfisher in the country. The smallest is the **American pygmy kingfisher** (*Chloroceryle aenea*). It has a green back and head, a reddish brown neck-band and throat and chest with a white lower front. The female has a green bar across her chest.

MOTMOTS

The motmots, relatives of the kingfisher, are handsome birds, with distinctive, long tails. Perhaps the most attractive of the country's six species is the **turquoise-browed motmot** (*Eumomota superciliosa*), a brownish green bird, with a black throat, a black mask around its eye and a turquoise bar above the eye, and turquoise tail and wings. Motmots are more common in low and mid-altitude forests, but they can also be seen in parks and orchards. Like the kingfishers, they tend to sit and wait for their prey, mostly insects, then swoop down, grab it and return to their perch to beat it to death.

VULTURES

Not beautiful, but conspicuous and commonly seen, are Costa Rica's vultures. There are four species in the country. The more sociable **black vulture** (*Coragyps atratus*) and **turkey vulture** (*Cathartes aura*) are a frequent sight around towns and villages. Both are large black birds, the former with a bare, red head and neck and the latter with a featherless, black head and neck. Larger than either of these, with a wingspan of 2m (7ft), is the **king vulture** (*Sarcoramphus papa*), which is white with black wings and tail and has a featherless, black, orange and yellow head. It usually hunts over forest and wooded areas. Least common and smallest is the **lesser yellow-headed vulture** (*Cathartes burrovianus*). All are carrion eaters, though the king and black vulture do sometimes take live prey.

RAPTORS

Also known as birds of prey, raptors hunt mostly living animals, usually other vertebrates. They include birds such as hawks, kites, eagles, falcons and caracaras; there are about 50 species in Costa Rica. Though often quite difficult to identify as they soar far overhead above all types of habitats, some more conspicuous ones can be picked out. The **osprey** (*Pandion haliaetus*) is unusual in that it feeds on fish, grabbing them with its sharp claws from fresh or saltwater. White below and brown above, it is found more or less worldwide. The **American swallow-tailed hawk** (*Elanoides forficatus*) can be distinguished from other raptors by its deeply forked, long black tail. It feeds on the wing, grabbing flying insects and snatching small prey such as lizards from trees. The **harpy eagle** (*Harpia harpyja*) used to be widespread in Costa Rica, but is now very rare and seen only in Corcovado National Park and the Talamanca mountains. It is a large, spectacular bird standing around 1m (3.5ft) tall that can grab small monkeys and other mammals from the tree tops as it flies above them. The **crested caracara** (*Polyborus plancus*) is a large black bird, with a barred black and white neck, a black, white and red head and yellow legs, that is found over open areas and quite commonly seen in groups eating carrion.

OWLS

You might be lucky and see one of Costa Rica's 15 species of owl during the day, especially if a local guide knows a roosting site that a particular owl regularly uses, but, as they are mostly nocturnal hunters, you are more likely just to hear them.

However, both the **spectacled owl** (*Pulsatrix persicillata*) and the **ferruginous pygmy owl** (*Glaucidium brasilianum*) can sometimes be seen hunting in the day or at dusk. The former is a large owl, 46cm (18in) high, with a dark brown head and back with a lighter chest and, as its name indicates, white "spectacles" and white on its throat. It is found in forest and in more open areas. The diminutive **pygmy owl** is just 16cm (6in) high and

The enormous, monkey-eating harpy eagle is an awe-inspiring but extremely rare sight

A spectacled owl roosting at Hacienda Barú, near Dominical

commonly hunts during the day. It is a reddish or grayish brown owl with white streaks on its front.

GOATSUCKERS OR NIGHTJARS

Nine species of these nocturnal birds are found in Costa Rica, the most common being the **pauraque** (*Nyctidromus albicollis*). They inhabit open areas such as farm- and parkland, thickets and forest edges, but are most commonly seen as they fly up directly in front of your car. Indeed, their Spanish name means "common road blocker." Their mottled brown, black and white color is an excellent camouflage, ensuring that they are almost impossible to spot roosting (on the ground or along tree branches) during the day. The **common potoo** (*Nyctibius griseus*), unlike most other nightjars, adopts a vertical roosting posture, often perching during the day in the open on a dead tree stump, looking much like an extension of it.

SWIFTS AND SWALLOWS

There are 12 species of swallow and 11 swifts in Costa Rica. Though not closely related groups, they do superficially resemble each other being slender streamlined birds, which can be seen swooping through the air catching insects while on the wing. This group will be familiar to most visitors, indeed the **barn swallow** (*Hirundo rustica*) is a common species more or less worldwide.

TROGONS

Of the 10 trogon species found in Costa Rica, the resplendent quetzal is the one most people want to see. However, all species are spectacular, particularly the males. They have metallic green, blue or violet heads and chests, with contrasting bright red, yellow or orange underparts. They usually sit erect in the forest with their distinctive tails (long, with horizontal black and white stripes on the underside and a squared off end) pointing downwards. The impressive male **resplendent quetzal** *(Pharomachrus mocinno)* is a bird of the cloud forests with an emerald green head, a crest of green feathers and long trailing green plumes extending 45cm (17.5in) or

A resplendent quetzal arrives at its nest hole with food (left). A black guan at Monteverde (above)

HUMMINGBIRDS

Hummingbirds are wonderful little creatures that are a delight to watch and Costa Rica has more than 50 species of them. Though easy to recognize as a group, they are actually quite difficult to identify as they dart past at high speed or hover briefly at a flower extracting its nectar. So tiny are some of the species, mostly weighing between 3–6g (.12–.24oz), that they can become entangled in spiders' webs or be eaten by praying mantises and frogs. The major part of their diet is nectar, but they also feed on insects to obtain protein. The largest hummingbird in Costa Rica is the **violet sabrewing** *(Campylopterus hemileucurus)*, which is 15cm (6in) in length with a down-curved bill and white patches at the end of its tail. The male has a violet head and front with a dark green back and wings, while the female has a violet throat but a gray front. Although the **long-tailed hermit** *(Phaethornis superciliosus)* also measures 15cm (6in) in length, much of this is, indeed, its tail. It is a greenish brown hummingbird, with a long white tipped tail, a down-curved bill, black and light colored eye stripes and a light brown front that is found in forests and on forest edges. Most "hummers," including the **crowned woodnymph** *(Thalurania colombica)*, are less than 10cm (4in) long. The male of this species has a glossy green throat, chest and rump, with a purple head and belly and a dark forked tail and dark wings; the female is greenish with a light gray throat and chest. Both have a straight bill, only slightly curved at the tip. Many hummingbirds act as pollinators for flowers, the flowers generally being red, pink or orange, thereby indistinguishable to insects, and scentless so they don't attract nectar-feeding insects. The flowers also tend to be shaped into long thin tubes, adapted to fit the birds' beaks.

more beyond its white tail. In spite of their bright colors, trogons can be quite difficult to spot in forests as they blend into the dark green foliage and tend to sit silently waiting to catch passing insects. They feed on small lizards and frogs, as well as fruit, especially figs. Other trogons found in Costa Rica are the **slaty-tailed trogon** *(Trogon massena)* and the **violaceous trogon** *(Trogon violaceus)*, the latter being found in dry as well as wet forests at low elevations.

TOUCANS

The toucans, all sporting large, bright bills, are an unmistakable group. There are six species in Costa Rica—two toucans, two aracaris and two toucanets. The **chestnut-mandibled toucan** *(Ramphastos swainsonii)* is the largest. Both it and the slightly smaller **keel-billed toucan** *(Ramphastos sulfuratus)* are mainly black with a yellow face and chest and red under the tail. The former has a bicolored bill, chestnut below and yellow above, while the latter has an amazing multicolored one, red, orange, green and blue. The **collared aracari** *(Pteroglossus torquatus)* and **fiery-billed aracari** *(Pteroglossus frantzii)* look somewhat alike, but the former is found on the Caribbean side of the country and in the Guanacaste region, and the latter on the south Pacific. Both have a black head and chest, a dark green back and a yellow belly with a central black spot; the bill in both is black below, but is bright orange red above in the fiery-billed and pale yellow in the collared. The **yellow-eared toucanet** *(Selenidera spectabilis)* and **emerald toucanet** *(Aulacorhynchus prasinusare)* are smaller birds, the latter only 30cm (12in) in comparison with the 56cm (22in) of the chestnut-mandibled toucan. The emerald toucanet is mostly green, but has a blue throat and is chestnut below its tail. Its bill is black below and yellow above. All species are forest-dwelling, fruit eaters, and tend to be seen in small groups, high up in the canopy. Toucans nest in hollow trees, often using holes that have been made by woodpeckers.

PARROTS

Many of Costa Rica's 16 species are small and green and quite difficult to tell apart unless seen very clearly, but quite unmistakable and very spectacular is the **scarlet macaw** (*Ara macao*). It is a large bird, 84cm (33in) long, with a bright red body, yellow and blue wings, a long red tail and a white face. Sadly, this species has become quite rare, devastated by habitat destruction and hunting for the pet trade. It is found

a reddish one. The male Hoffman's has red on the top of his head, while both sexes of the red-crowned have red backs to their necks and the male has a red crown. Both species prefer open, wooded sites and are found on the Pacific slope, but Hoffman's occurs in the north and the red-crowned in the south.

CURASSOWS

This group of 13 species, related to partridges, contains the quans and chachalacas, as well as curassows, with the larger members weighing up to 4kg (9 lb). Unfortunately, they taste so good that several species, including the **black guan** (*Chamaepetes unicolor*), **crested guan** (*Penelope purpurascens*)

Some of Costa Rica's birds, such as the macaws and toucans make a point of being conspicuous: the endangered green macaw (left), the lineated woodpecker (middle), the keel-billed toucan (right)

mostly on the southern Pacific side of the country. The similarly sized **green macaw** (*Ara ambigua*) is found on the Caribbean side. It, too, is endangered in Costa Rica. Most parrots are noisy and sociable, feeding on fruits and seeds that they tear apart with short, powerful, hooked beaks. Breeding usually occurs in hollow trees, with the young of the large macaw species remaining in the nest for three to four months and those of smaller species for three to four weeks. They are vulnerable at this time as many nestlings are taken and sold as pets. Typical of the smaller species is the **white-fronted parrot** (*Amazona albifrons*), a green bird with red around its eyes, a white forehead, blue on top of its head and red and blue patches on its wings.

WOODPECKERS

Two of Costa Rica's 16 woodpecker species, the **lineated woodpecker** (*Dryocopus lineatus*) and the **pale-billed woodpecker** (*Campephilus guatemalensis*), have crested heads with red markings, large black bodies with white markings and banded, black and white fronts, but only the lineated has white on its head. Both are found in wet forests. Though insects make up most of the woodpeckers' diet, fruits, nuts and nectar are also eaten. The smallest of the woodpeckers in Costa Rica is the **olivaceous piculet** (*Picumnus olivaceus*), which may be spotted in gardens as well as woodland. It has a dull green back and lighter front. The male has orange streaks on its head. Medium-sized members of the species, around 19cm (7.5in) in length, include **Hoffman's woodpecker** (*Melanerpes hoffmannii*) and the **red-crowned woodpecker** (*Melanerpes rubricapillus*). Both have black and white bars on their backs and wings and light brown chests; the former has a yellowish belly and the latter

and the **great curassow** (*Crax rubra*) are rare outside protected areas. Bulky birds, with sturdy legs and often a long tail, they tend to be brown, black, gray or olive. Some have bright patches, such as a red dewlap in the crested guan or yellow knobs on the bill of the male great curassow. Guans and curassows live in forests, the former living in the trees and the latter on the ground.

TINAMOUS

The five species of **tinamou** look like partridges, with chunky bodies, short tails and legs and a small head. All are terrestrial, feeding and sleeping on the ground, except for the **great tinamou** (*Tinamus major*), which roosts in trees. Their flight is clumsy and they are more likely to run than fly from danger. Tinamous are brown, gray or olive, with darker spots or bars, so they are well camouflaged as they forage in the forest for fruit and seeds. Females lay their eggs, under a bush, but it is the male that incubates them and looks after the chicks. They feed themselves as soon as they hatch, but he leads them around the forest and protects them from predators.

CUCKOOS AND ANIS

Most commonly seen among the 11 species in this group are the **squirrel cuckoo** (*Piaya cayana*), the **smooth-billed ani** (*Crotophaga ani*) and the **groove-billed ani** (*Crotophaga sulcirostris*). None of them lays their eggs in other species' nests. The secretive squirrel cuckoo, a large reddish brown bird, with a long tail with black and white stripes on its underside, is found in wooded areas. In contrast, the anis are noisy, gregarious birds. Both species are black with a parrot-like gray bill. The smooth-billed is found on the southern Pacific slope and the groove-billed in the northern Pacific and the Caribbean.

PASSERINES

The groups mentioned earlier include fewer than half of Costa Rica's birds. All the others are passerines, with feet specialized to grasp and perch on tree branches. They tend to be small land birds; many are LBJs ("little brown jobs") but some are very bright and conspicuous.

Included among them are 16 species of **wood-creeper**. They are slender brown birds, with longish beaks and stiff tails, most often seen moving up and down tree trunks. The **antbirds** (30 species) are not seen often as they are inclined to skulk in the forest shade. Their name comes from their habit of following marching columns of ants and eating insects disturbed by the ants.

The 22 species of **wren** are all small and mostly brown or reddish brown. Their distinguishing feature is their tail–usually held stiffly upright. They are found in forests, thickets, grassland and marshes.

Many of the 50 species of **warbler** are migrants from North America. These small birds are commonly found in gardens. They can be brightly colored, usually yellowish or greenish with amounts of black, gray and white, and patches of red, orange or blue.

The thrushes, 11 species breeding in Costa Rica, also tend to be rather drab birds, but you will see the sooty robin (*Turdus nigrescens*), as it looks and acts much like Europe's blackbird. One group member, the **black-faced solitaire** (*Myadestes melanops*) is famed for its singing: its numbers have declined as it is caught for the pet trade.

Another diverse group are the **blackbirds** and **orioles**, including **caciques**, **cowbirds**, **grackles**, **meadowlarks** and **orpendolas**. Around 20 species occur in Costa Rica, distributed through all elevations and most habitats. They vary in size, color, ecology and behaviour. The most spectacular is

Montezuma's orpendola (*Psarocolius montezuma*), which has a large brown body, with a black head and chest, a yellow-edged tail, an orange tip to its large black bill and a blue patch under its eye. Orpendolas breed in colonies, weaving large bag-like nests, which hang from tree branches. Montezuma's orpendola is unusual in that 3 to 10 males establish a colony in a single tree and then defend the 10 to 30 females that join them to mate and nest there.

Jays are some of the largest passerines. Most are brightly feathered, such as the **white-throated magpie-jay** (*Calocitta formosa*), from the northern Pacific slope. This species is brilliant blue above and white below with a conspicuous crest and a long blue tail. Jays are omnivorous and eat eggs, nestlings, carrion, insects, fruit and nuts. They live in small groups and jointly defend a territory. The oldest pair mates; the others help to nest build and feed the young.

The American flycatchers number about 75 species in Costa Rica. Many of the small, drab varieties are difficult to identify but the **scissor-tailed flycatcher** (*Tyrannus forficatus*) is handsome and easily seen as it adopts the typical flycatcher technique, perching motionless on a fence to dart out and grab a passing insect and then return to the same perch to eat it. This medium-sized flycatcher is found in open areas on the northern Pacific slope. It is a silver-gray bird with a long black, forked tail, black wings with reddish patches under them and a white chest.

Some of the gaudiest of Costa Rica's passerines are the 50 species of **tanager**, including **honeycreepers** and **euphonias**. They are found in shrubby areas over a wide range of elevations and are often seen feeding near human habitation. Most tanagers are arboreal and eat small fruits and berries. Honeycreepers eat nectar, making holes at the base of a flower and sucking out the liquid. The **blue-gray** tanager (*Thraupis episcopus*) is found in abundance over most of the country. As its name implies, it is a blue-gray bird, with a darker blue back and bright blue wings and tail. The male **scarlet-rumped tanager** (*Ramphocelus passerinii*) is black with a red rump and pale blue-gray beak. Many male honeycreepers are dressed in brilliant hues, such as the **red-legged honeycreeper** (*Cyanerpes cyaneus*), a bright blue bird with a black back, wings, tail and eye-stripe, a turquoise patch on its head and red legs.

Though they are small, stocky birds, male **manakins** are noted for their bright plumage and elaborate courtship diplays. They are active, forest dwelling birds, foraging for fruits and insects. One attractive

reddish yellow, to bright golden yellow with or without markings on the body. Its name comes from the horny spine-like scales that jut out above each eye. Another eye-catching, poisonous snake is the **Central American coral snake** (*Micrurus nigrocinctus*), which may be found on the floor in forests, but also in more open areas. It is vividly patterned, with a small, black and yellow head and red and black rings along its body, which may or may not have narrower yellow rings as well. At a glance, it is easy to confuse the nonpoisonous **harlequin snake** (*Scolecophis atrocinctus*) and the **tropical kingsnake** (*Lampropeltis triangulum*) with the coral snake. Both have bodies with bands of yellow, red and black,

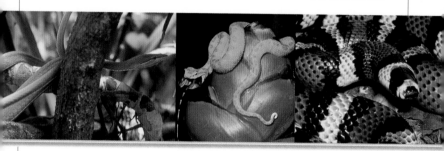

A blue-gray tanager (far left). The innocuous green vine snake (above left); a delicate eyelash viper consuming a lizard (middle); a harmless tropical kingsnake mimics a venomous coral snake (right)

species is the **long-tailed manakin** (*Chiroxiphia linearis*), which is found in forests on the northern Pacific slope. The male is black with a bright blue back, a red crest on his head and two long, black tail feathers. During the February to July breeding season, several manakin males display at special sites, trying to attract females with visual and vocal displays. In some species several males do a coordinated dance on the same perch; once the female has selected the most spectacular and has mated with him, she goes off to nest build and rear the young on her own.

Closely related to the manakins are the **cotingas**. This diverse group contains **bellbirds**, **umbrella birds**, **phias** and **fruitcrows**. The male **three-wattled bellbird** (*Procnias tricarunculata*) is a medium-sized, brown bird with a white head and three odd-looking appendages or wattles, hanging from its beak.

SNAKES

Costa Rica's reptiles comprise 127 snake species. The best place to see snakes is in a zoo or snake farm –they are not often seen in the wild. Indeed, there are some of them you will be very glad not to encounter. The **bushmaster** (*Lachesis muta*), for instance, is the New World's largest venomous snake, reaching 3.5m (11ft) in length. It is an aggressive, slender, large-headed snake with a yellowish to tan body with black or brown blotches along it. Another large (up to 2.5m, 8ft), poisonous snake to be avoided is the **fer-de-lance** (*Bothrops asper*) as it too can be aggressive. It has a triangular head and a patterned olive, beige, black and brown body. Both this species and the bushmaster tend to be found on the ground, though young fer-de-lance may be found in trees. The **eyelash viper** (*Bothriechis schlegelii*) is much smaller, reaching only 75cm (30in) in length and is arboreal. It is varies from gray, olive and

mimicking the coral snake, perhaps in an attempt to deter predators. It should be noted that the majority of Costa Rica's snakes, such as the **green vine snake** (*Oxybelis aeneus*), are harmless. Those that are venomous tend to be nocturnal and secretive, so don't worry unduly about being bitten. However, it is not advisable to poke under rocks and logs or into bushes, and pay attention to where you are walking.

LIZARDS

Perhaps most conspicuous and certainly largest of Costa Rica's 68 lizard species are the **green iguana** (*Iguana iguana*) and **black iguana** (*Ctenosuara similes*). The green iguana is more widespread, found in wet forests at low elevations and along streams and rivers in drier areas on both the Caribbean and Pacific slopes. It can often be seen sunbathing high in trees, especially early in the morning. The black iguana is found only on the Pacific slope, often in drier areas and on the beach, but also in forests. Considerably smaller, but very commonly seen at night in houses are **geckos**, usually gray or brown with large eyes, and toes that appear to have little pads on them. Unlike most lizards, they make quite audible squeaks.

Of the two crocodilians, the smaller **spectacled caiman**, (*Caiman crocodiles*), is more common, but the **American crocodile** (*Crocodylus acutus*) is also found in the country. The crocodile has a longer, more slender and more pointed snout than the caiman and also, unlike the caiman, has a tooth on each side of its lower jaw, projecting upwards, that is visible when the mouth is closed.

TURTLES

Freshwater turtles (there are eight freshwater and six marine species), such as the **white-lipped mud** turtle (Kinosternon leucostomum) are quite a common sight, sunning themselves on logs along rivers. Six types of marine turtles nest on Costa Rican beaches and with luck and planning you may get to see one or two come ashore to nest on either the Pacific or Caribbean beaches. The small **olive ridley turtle** (Lepidochelys olivacea) arrives at Playas Nancite and Ostional in spectacular arribadas with many thousands nesting over a few consecutive nights at certain times of the year. The hook beak of the **hawksbill turtle** (Eretmochelys imbricata) is a distinctive characteristic of the species, as is the treasured tortoise-shell carapace once prized for its subtle patterns. Green turtle soup is fortunately on fewer

visitors is the beautiful **red-eyed leaf frog** (Agalychnis callidryas). This is 5–7cm (2–3in) long with a pale or dark green back, blue-purple patches both on the underside of its limbs and vertical bars on its side, orange fore and hind feet and blood red eyes. When resting or dormant, only the green coloring shows, making the frog virtually invisible. The vivid poison-dart and poison arrow frogs are also much sought after. These include the **strawberry poison-dart frog** (Dendrobates pumilio), which is bright red with varying quantities of black flecks on its body and with red, blue, green or black limbs; the **orange and black poison-dart frog** (Phyllobates vittatus), which is small and black with a wide pair of orange stripes on its back and

The variety of spectacular creatures that can be seen in Costa Rica is staggering: a tiny green poison-dart frog (left), an olive ridley turtle hauls itself ashore (middle), a large, blue morpho butterfly (right)

menus, improving the survival rates of the **green turtle** (Chelonia mydas). The largest reptile in the world is the **leatherback turtle** (Dermochelys coriacea) which can grow to 2m (7ft) in length and weigh more than 500kg (1,100 lb). All marine turtles are endangered and protected, along with their nest sites and eggs, by international law.

AMPHIBIANS

Around 35 salamanders, 3 caecilians, 14 toads and some 105 frogs are found in Costa Rica. **Salamanders** look rather like wet lizards and tend to be nocturnal and secretive, hiding in damp places. **Caecilians**, which are legless and resemble earthworms, are even less commonly seen as they live underground mostly. The largest toad in the country is the huge marine or **cane toad** (Bufo marinus), which reaches up to 20cm (8in) in length and 1.2kg (2.5 lb) in weight. These toads can be found in forests, in more open areas and in and around buildings. In contrast, Costa Rica's **golden toad** (Bufo periglenes) is only 6cm (2.3in) in size; the males are golden while the females are black with red spots ringed with yellow. These toads were found only in the Monteverde Cloud Forest Reserve, but the last sighting was in 1990 and they are now believed to be extinct (▷ 27). Their demise, and that of many other amphibian species in Costa Rica, is due principally to an infectious fungal disease. The amphibian that is probably the best known and most sought after by

turquoise mottling on its limbs; and the **green poison-dart frog** (Dendrobates auratus). This species can be up to 4cm (2in) in size and patterned in bright blue, turquoise, green or dark green with brownish or black patches. It is found on the forest floor or in low vegetation, mostly in forests at lower elevations. While the vivid warning colors of poison-dart frogs and their sensational name suggest otherwise, there is no evidence that their toxic secretions have ever been used to tip darts for hunting by indigenous tribes in Costa Rica, unlike the Choco Indians of western Colombia and southern Panama.

INSECTS

There is no space in this guide to cover Costa Rica's inumerable invertebrates, but try, at least, to visit a butterfly farm and keep your eyes open to search out these smaller creatures in the forests. You might well, for instance, see long marching columns of **leaf-cutter ants** (Atta spp), each carrying a piece of leaf back to the nest. These can be very large structures—a mound of leaf mulch surrounded by a considerable area of forest floor cleared of all green vegetation. Probably most impressive of the many butterfly species is the **morpho** (Morpho peleides), which has a 15cm (6in) wingspan. The upper side of its wings are bright, shiny blue with a brown edge marked with white, but once it settles and closes its wings, the dull brown underside ensures that it is almost invisible.

Leaf-cutter ants: an essential part of the rainforest ecosystem

Living
Costa Rica

A hecales longwing butterfly (above).
Janine Licare (right)

Leatherback turtles (below) use Costa Rica's beaches to incubate their eggs. Mangroves (right)

Wildlife and Conservation

Turtle Trouble

Time is running out for the leatherback and other turtles. Protection has reduced the poaching of eggs from Costa Rica's Playa Grande, but the global picture does not bode well for these magnificent creatures. Causes of the decreasing numbers include modern fishing techniques, disorientation from lighting at beach resorts, and plastic bags, which they mistake for their principal food—jellyfish. In 2000, six nations, including Costa Rica, signed the Inter-American Convention for the Protection and Conservation of Sea Turtles.

The isthmus of Costa Rica links North America and South America and separates the Caribbean and the Pacific ocean. As a result, the country has an unparalleled biodiversity: for its area, there are more species in Costa Rica than anywhere else in the world, living in a wide variety of landscapes, including mountains, valleys, coastal plains and prairies. In addition, the country has great climatic diversity, from the impossibly lush jungles of the Caribbean coast to the chilly, windswept reaches of its highest peaks.

Today, Costa Rica is revered globally as a model for conservation, which is something of a dramatic turnaround following periods of widespread deforestation between 1940 and 1970. International and national figures including Mario Boza and Leslie Holdridge have been the great torchbearers for conservation initiatives and the National Parks have achieved their intended goals of consolidating and protecting the area's biodiversity.

A bird of paradise flower at Lankester Botanical Gardens (left)

Large iguanas are a common sight on the coast

Recycling water at Monteverde (left). A green macaw (right). An angelfish (below)

Cachí Dam (right). Missing in action: the golden toad (below)

What a Waste

What happens to the waste we flush down the toilet? In Monteverde it gets recycled back into the environment. Stewart Dallas, a research engineer at the Monteverde Institute, installed an ecological sanitation system in the grounds of the Monteverde Community Arts Center. Solid waste goes into a composting toilet to be broken down by bacteria and micro-organisms before being used as an organic fertilizer. 'Graywater'—from showers, kitchens and laundry—goes through a reed bed system that removes the pollutants, before flowing to a small pond where sunlight and aeration further improve the quality.

Dallas has installed a similar project at a four-house site in Santa Elena. The water authority is keeping an eye on the project for its potential to be used elsewhere, and the early signs are promising.

Right, squirrel monkey. Left, agriculture puts pressure on the land

Education in Manuel Antonio

Finding a balance between rainforest conservation and economic growth is a complex task, but children will keep things simple. Kids Saving the Rainforest is a non-profit association founded by two school-children, Janine Licare and Aislin Livingstone, in the town of Manuel Antonio, who want to protect the local jungle and save its remaining community of endangered squirrel monkeys. The leading causes of death of the squirrel monkeys are cars and electrocution. Funds they have raised have purchased 120 monkey bridges to help them cross the busy main road without dodging traffic on the ground or using the dangerous electric cables which straddle the road.

Goodbye to the Golden Toad

They're 5cm (2in) long, a bright orange-gold (or black with red spots if female) and have been described as jewels scattered on the forest floor. At least they were: nobody has seen a golden toad (Bufo periglenes) since 1990. Their habitat was, remarkably, just a small area high in Monteverde's cloud forest. Each April, the rare toads would congregate in pools of rainwater for a brief spell of mating. But suddenly the toads disappeared. In 2004, the World Conservation Union added them to its list of extinct species. Reasons for the toad's demise include climate change, with hotter, drier seasons at Monteverde, pollution, a deadly fungus and deforestation.

Laguna Angostura —a new Arenal?

Being self-sufficient in energy is the goal of most nations and Costa Rica is no different. Hydroelectric power has the greatest potential here. There are several large projects dotted around the country. South of Turrialba, Angostura Dam was completed in 2000, but not without controversy. Blocking the Río Reventazón, the dam has created the 256ha (632-acre) Lake Angostura and inundated farmland and world-class sections of white water that attracted international kayakers to Costa Rica. It has the country's largest hydroelectric generator, which will produce 177 megawatt hours and has created local employment. But critics say most of the power will be exported to Panama, and archaeological studies have revealed 42 new sites of pre-Columbian cultures that have now been flooded.

Neatly dressed schoolchildren in San José (above). Relaxing, Caribbean-style (right)

An Easter Sunday procession on the Route of the Saints (left). Children playing in Puerto Limón (right). A rancher in Guanacaste (below left)

People and Society

La Danza de los Diabolitos

Each year on the last day of December and the first two days of January the hardships of agricultural life are discarded by the Boruca tribe in the celebrations of *La Danza de los Diabolitos*: the Dance of the Devils. Dosed with *chicha*, a traditional corn liquor, and dressed as devils, men come down from the hills to play an elaborate game of tag with a "bull," also a man in costume. Three days of fiestas culminate in the symbolic killing of the bull. The bull represents the colonization and persecution of the lands and indigenous people by the Spanish, and the centuries-old dance offers the hope that, one day, the Indian communities will be victorious.

Costa Ricans, regardless of descent, use the self-deprecating term *tico* (*tica* for women) to describe themselves. It's thought to have its origin in the Costa Rican suffix "-tico" which changes a word into its diminutive form.

Most Ticos are descended from Spanish settlers, but there are three other important groups: Afro-Caribbeans on the east coast, the Chinese, who migrated to Costa Rica to work, and indigenous peoples.

Today, Costa Ricans have the highest literacy rate in Central America and the highest life expectancy. About 60 percent of the total population of 4 million live in the Central Valley, with ever-increasing numbers attracted to San José's suburban sprawl. But outside the capital there are distinctive regional differences. The cultural foundations of Guanacaste lie close to the land in ranching and rodeos. Take a short flight east to the Caribbean and the laidback lifestyle is accompanied by calypso and reggae.

Indigenous Indian communities are generally high in the Talamanca mountains or deep in the jungles of the south. A more pervasive influence on society comes from the large number of Western expatriates retiring or setting up businesses in the country.

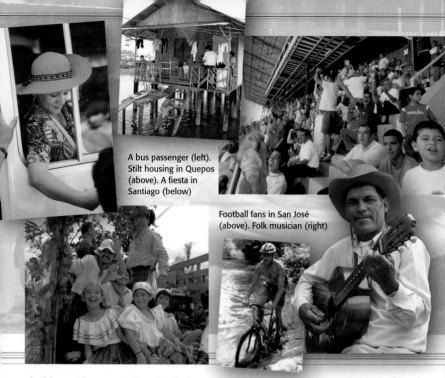

A bus passenger (left). Stilt housing in Quepos (above). A fiesta in Santiago (below)

Football fans in San José (above). Folk musician (right)

Caribbean Charm

In Costa Rica, the Afro-Caribbean population is concentrated on the Caribbean coast, in particular in Puerto Limón. Most Costa Rican Afro-Caribbeans are descended from people who arrived from Jamaica to build the Atlantic railroad in the 19th century and later found work on banana plantations. Subjected to social and political marginalization, they were granted citizenship only in the middle of the 20th century. Poor transport links between the capital and the Caribbean isolated the region, causing underdevelopment, but it has preserved a rich Afro-Caribbean heritage, a world apart from the Latin culture in the rest of Costa Rica. The most exuberant expression of Caribbean culture is Carnaval, a parade of floats, dance groups and calypso bands, held to celebrate the arrival of Christopher Columbus.

Right, a *tica*.
Left, traditional dancing

Switzerland of Central America

By fortune or disinterest, Costa Ricans have never really got the hang of conflict. Instead, they have a strong pride in their democratic traditions, renowned health care and excellent education system.

As far back as the 1930s one commentator named Costa Rica "The Switzerland of Central America." The lack of any army, which was abolished after the civil war in 1948, contrasts with the military factions in other Central American countries.

But Costa Rica also resembles the neutral European nation in another respect: it has become a tax-free banking haven.

La Ruta de los Conquistadores

With such a challenging climate and such difficult terrain, Costa Ricans have had to be adventurous; none more so, perhaps, than local athlete Roman Urbina. In 1991, retracing the steps of conquistador Juan de Caballón across Costa Rica, he realized that the route would be the world's toughest mountain bike race. La Ruta de los Conquistadores race was soon inaugurated and is now held annually in November. Racers face riding 483km (300 miles) from the Pacific Ocean to the Caribbean coast in three days, with 7,300m (24,000ft) of altitude gain in 90 percent humidity and sweltering temperatures. The 300 riders start in Jacó, with only a handful making it all the way across Costa Rica's volcanoes, jungles and rivers. If you're not that masochistic but would like an adventure, Urbina offers guided cycling tours along the route; taking ten days instead of three.

Soccer Star

In soccer-mad Central America, Costa Ricans are some of the game's most fervent fans. One man, though, inspires more passion than any other: Paulo Wanchope. Arguably the most famous Costa Rican, and certainly the country's biggest sports star, the striker left for the English League in 1997 and went on to play for Manchester City for four seasons. British tourists could expect to be frequently quizzed on the soccer player's progress, until his move to Malaga in 2004. Born into a soccer family in Heredia–his three brothers are also soccer stars in Costa Rica–Wanchope has played for his country in more than fifty matches. He scored both goals in Costa Rica's 4–2 loss to Germany in the opening game of the 2006 FIFA World Cup, after which he signed with Argentina's Rosario Central club.

A life-size sculpture of peasants in San José by Fernando Calvo

An oxcart artist at work (above) and, an example of the finished product (right)

Arts and Crafts

Sarchí's Oxcarts

Sarchí's painted oxcarts, decorated with floral motifs, are not an old tradition. Wooden oxcarts were introduced from Nicaragua in the mid-1800s to haul coffee, but it was not until 1903 that an inspired *campesino* decided to decorate the wheels. Soon after, metal axles and sectioned wheels led to even more elaborate designs, while preserving the original star-shaped motif. In 1915, painting spread to the body of the cart and hues evolved from grays and greens to today's orange. When motorized transport took over in the 1960s, Sarchí's oxcart painters turned to the tourist trade, but some carts are still used in San Antonio de Escazú.

Contemporary arts and crafts flourish in Costa Rica, particularly in the capital. The first Costa Rican sculptors emerged in the 19th century and, using wood, worked mainly on religious themes. Francisco Zuñiga (1912–98) was the best known artist in this field. Painting blossomed from the 1930s and by the 1960s was influenced by Western abstract painters. Some painters, including Manuel de la Cruz González, Loda Fernández and Juan Luis Rodríquez, achieved international recognition. The Bocaraca school of painting, influenced by Francis Bacon and informal Catalan art, arrived in the 1980s.

Literature in Costa Rica is still young and lacks the struggles that inspired many Latin American writers. A thriving theatrical and contemporary dance scene has much to offer visitors. Some of the best productions are performed by the Companía Nacional de Teatro, but smaller amateur productions tackle every subject. Theaters are required to perform at least two plays a year written by local playwrights.

Costa Rica's distinctive handicraft tradition includes the pottery from Guaitíl produced by the Chorotega Indians, the balsa-wood masks of the Boruca tribes and the omnipresent oxcarts.

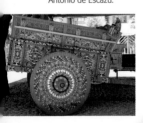

Left, a painted oxcart from Sarchí
Right, handpainting a pottery bowl in Guaitíl

A Boruca Indian woodcarver. A scene from *Endless Summer II* (right)

Barry Biesanz in his workshop (left) and a set of three wooden bowls by him (above). Tiles in San José (right)

AL MERCADO

¿QUÉ LE VENDO, CHOLITA?... ¿QUÉ QUIERE, ENCANTO?
¡MIRE QUÉ CEBOLLITAS, ESPÍ QUÉ NABOS!

Barry Biesanz

Craft in Costa Rica reaches its peak in the expert work of Barry Biesanz (born 1948). Originally employed as a furniture designer, producing highly individualistic pieces, Biesanz has extended his repertoire to create a stunning array of decorative bowls and ornate boxes handcarved from Costa Rica's exotic woods, including rosewood, tigerwood, satinwood and purpleheart. With a conservationist philosophy, Biesanz works with the natural beauty of the wood: knots, grooves, stains and other perceived flaws become artful features of individual pieces. Biesanz has gained international fame and visiting dignitaries often come to his Escazú studio, where he employs more than 20 people. Biesanz takes his inspiration from the harmonious and sensual qualities of traditional Japanese bowls.

A Chorotega woman shapes a pottery bowl

Chorotega Pottery

The Chorotega Indians, one of eight indigenous groups in Costa Rica, are the flagbearers in a revival of pre-Columbian traditions. The dusty roads of Guaitíl are lined with urns, pots and vases in eye-catching black-and-white designs. In the pre-Columbian period, the distinctive Chorotega pottery was valued highly and it was often traded with the Zapotecs, Aztecs and Panam. Traditionally, the women of the town made and sold the pottery, which was originally more practical than ornamental in nature; pots to cook beans or to ferment *guaro*, the local alcohol. The old techniques are still used: First the clay is shaped then dried before being fired in large kilns. Traditional dyes are used to hand-paint each piece.

In Search of an Endless Summer

Costa Rica's film industry is as hard to spot as the elusive quetzal. The country isn't renowned for producing great directors, actors or films. But its beaches have played a very important role on celluloid, starring in the classic surf movie from 1966 *Endless Summer*, and the 1994 sequel, *Endless Summer II*. The story of two Californian surfers searching for the perfect wave, the first movie was filmed in 1964 when surfing was still a relatively unknown sport. Director Bruce Brown introduced the world to Costa Rica's Witches Rock surf spot, now one of the world's most famous breaks. In 1994 he reprised the movie and returned to Costa Rica to film two more surfers at Playa Negra and Ollie's Point (supposedly named after Colonel Oliver North), this time putting Tamarindo on the global surf map.

Corazones Valientes

The vibrant natural beauty of Costa Rica is expressed through *campesino* folk art. In 1994, the Peace Corps established a program in Costa Rica aimed at harnessing the talents of impoverished groups, ranging from street children to women in the countryside, who traditionally had no outlet for their creative impulses. Corazones Valientes is one of several cooperative art groups in Costa Rica producing a kaleidoscopic array of art in a variety of different media from oil and canvas paintings to papier-mâché mirrors, picture frames and ornamental tiles. The women of Corazones Valientes range in age from 12 to 50 years, and live in a down-at-heel area close to Volcán Arenal. Idiosyncratic, evocative and unselfconscious, the paintings are very personal representations of the natural landscape around the artists.

Modern buildings in San José (top left). Fresh papaya (above). Coffee beans (left)

A truck on the Pan-American Highway (above).
A technician at the Intel factory in Belén (left)

Bananas are a key export (below)

The
Economy

Tourism is Top

In recent years tourism has superseded coffee and bananas as a source of foreign currency for Costa Rica. More than 1.5 million people visited the country in 2005, an increase of 4 percent on 2004. These visitors spent almost $1.6 million, compared to $1.5 million in 2004. This income accounted for 8.7 percent of the GDP and 23 percent of export revenue, more than three times the money earned from bananas and eight times the income from coffee. The sector directly employs more than 90,000 workers and up to 500,000 workers indirectly. Since the construction of the first private hotel in 1930, tourism has taken over the economy, but clearly it will need careful management if it is not to become a victim of its own success.

Costa Rica is part of the Central American Common Market (CACM) and also has free trade agreements with Canada, Mexico, Panama, Chile and the Dominican Republic. Economically, the country has been undergoing a slow revolution, with every year bringing a steady shift away from traditional agriculture and towards manufacturing, the electronic economy services and tourism.

The national economy experienced strong growth in the last years of the 1990s, taking the average increase of gross domestic product (GDP) during the decade to a steady 5 percent a year. In 2005, GDP was US$11,100 per head.

Thrills and spills: adventure tourism is booming

Going Bananas

Bananas are key to the Costa Rican economy. In 1994, Costa Rica signed up to the Banana Framework agreement which gave it a quota of 23.4 percent of all bananas imported to Europe from Latin America, but this expired in 2006.

The certain losers in the global market for greater competition are the independent growers of Costa Rica, who sell to the multinational companies. Hard-won, and reluctantly given, concessions have slowly improved working conditions and job security for banana industry workers.

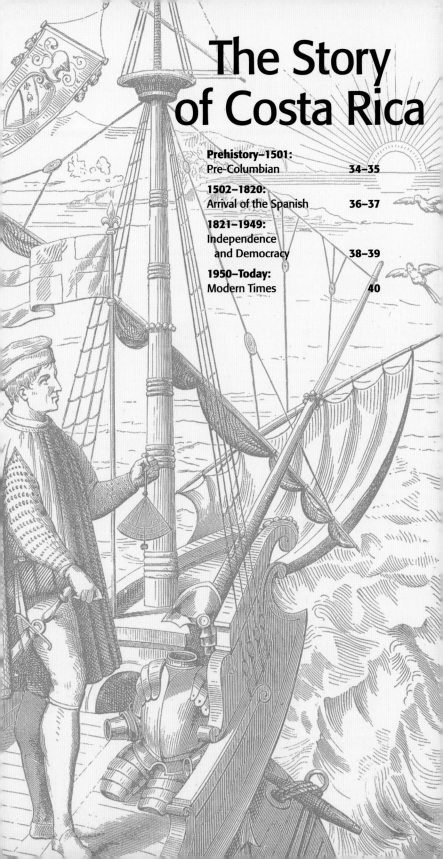

The Story of Costa Rica

Pre-Columbian

Humankind first arrived in the Americas somewhere between 40,000 and 15,000 years ago, when people crossed the Bering Strait from Asia. A slow southerly migration steadily occupied the continent, and evidence suggests that humans first appeared in what is now Costa Rica roughly 10,000 years ago. Early human settlement developed in this intermediate zone without a single dominant cultural group. Each group was characterized by its own distinct craft traditions and by its trading with other Mesoamerican cultures. The region was at a north–south divide, influenced by both the Maya civilizations of modern-day Mexico and several smaller groups in South America. Farming began in earnest around 1000BC, and with increased food supplies, social organization and hierarchy developed to manage the larger populations.

Population estimates prior to the arrival of the Spaniards in 1502 vary dramatically. Early studies put it as low as 27,000, but these are almost certainly estimates made after the first wave of imported diseases had ravaged the region. More recent studies put the figure somewhere between 250,000 and 400,000.

Cortahega gold work in the Museo Nacional (top right). Some of Costa Rica's indigenous people live on protected reserves (right)

Chorotega Indians

The Chorotega Indians arrived from Chiapas in southern Mexico early in the 14th century and settled on the Nicoya Peninsula, in present-day Guanacaste. As the largest and most advanced tribe in the country at the time, they cultivated beans and maize and produced ceramics influenced by the Mesoamerican cultures of the Maya. Crops were traded and other foods were obtained by fishing and hunting. Evidence suggests that slaves were often sacrificed and war was common. In recent decades, tombs have been excavated to reveal valuable artifacts.

An Indian child from a reserve near Suretka

Prehistory

A petroglyph site in Guanacaste National Park

A detail from a jade carving in the Museo del Jade in San José (left)

Rincónde la Vieja National Park (right)

Cacicazgos

Regions of Costa Rica were divided into *cacicazgos,* which were the basis for exchange of goods within the country and further afield. The political leader was the *cacique,* a chief who exerted absolute power through the supernatural beliefs of the social strata beneath him. War was commonplace and usually based on the expansion of the *cacique,* protection of trade routes or for the acquisition of slaves. Each *cacicazgo* was distinguished by its own language, culture, religious beliefs and political structures. Most *cacicazgos* were animistic and the shaman played a large role in communicating with supernatural entities.

Mysterious Jade

Inhabitants of Costa Rica were carving jade as far back as 500BC, but experts today are puzzled about the source of the jade. None has ever been found in the country, yet thousands of exquisite jade carvings have been discovered in Greater Nicoya and the Atlantic watershed.

One idea is that the stone could have been brought by the Mayas or the Olmecs, tribes native to Mexico and Guatemala to the north, or traded through intermediaries. Olmec influence has also been traced in "baby-face" sculptures that possibly followed the same route. Another theory is that the scant sources of jade could have been used up in prehistoric times.

Whatever the truth, it is clear that jade was highly prized at the time, more so even than gold.

Guayabo National Monument

The largest single pre-Columbian site in the country is the Guayabo National Monument, close to Turrialba, which is believed to have been ruled by a *cacique* or shaman. Guayabo was inhabited from 1000BC to AD1400, flourishing around AD800, the period when many of the stone structures that remain were constructed. The economy of Guayabo was based on agriculture, hunting and fishing. Stone roads stretch for considerable distances with mounds of different sizes and heights thought to have been constructed as bases for housing. Petroglyphs have been etched on to many of the stones, their meaning undeciphered, and centuries-old aqueducts still carry water to the reservoirs. The reasons for abandoning the site remain a mystery.

The Diquis Stone Spheres

Found in the southern region around Palmar Sur, Buenos Aires and Golfito, the Diquis stone spheres are one of Central America's most intriguing archaeological phenomena. Believed to be around 2,000 years old, thousands of stone spheres, from 10cm (4in) to 2.5m (8ft) in diameter, were uncovered in the 1940s. How they were created and what purpose they served is a mystery. Many of the stones were close to grave sites, aligned in straight and curved lines, triangles and parallelograms. Considerable mechanical and mathematical skill was required to produce such precise shapes. They were most likely constructed by the ancestors of the Boruca, Térraba and Guaymí. Were they ceremonial symbols or did they denote a chief's rank?

A jade object from the Museo del Jade

A petroglyph from Guanacaste

A Diquis sphere at the Museo Nacional

1501

Paddling a traditional dugout canoe (left). Washing in the river at Bribrí (below left). Excavating a Diquis stone sphere (bottom)

Arrival of the Spanish

From the day Christopher Columbus (left) anchored off the Costa Rican coast in 1502, it took almost 60 years of half-hearted attempts on the part of the Spanish to settle the region. The conquest of Central America was launched from Panama to the south, and, following Cortés' successful defeat of the Aztecs, from Mexico to the north, but it was hampered by difficulties. Despite some successes, a pattern of exploration, settlement and desertion continued as Spanish attempts to colonize through coercion met with resistance. Not until 1561 was an attempt at conquest successful, when Juan de Cavallón moved through the territory from east to west for the first time.

The relatively small indigenous population and the absence of mineral wealth in any substantial quantity denied the Spanish landholders many of the comforts afforded landlords in other parts of the Spanish empire. Most were simple farmers, forced to work the land themselves. For a brief time in 1709, money was so scarce that the cacao bean was temporarily used as currency.

The absence of a workforce, the growth in cacao production and trade with the Caribbean brought the first wave of Afro-Caribbean migration as slaves were imported from Jamaica. However, by the 1750s, the demand for cacao and consequently slave labor had fallen owing to increased competition from regions throughout the Caribbean.

Fools' Gold

The Genoese explorer Christopher Columbus introduced European influences to Costa Rica when he dropped anchor off the coast of Puerto Limón at Isla Uvita on September 18 1502—his fourth voyage to the New World. His initial intention was merely to repair his storm-ravaged vessels. After 17 days exploring the coastal area, teased by the prospect of welcoming Indians draped in glittering gold jewelry and ornamentation, Columbus and his men moved south calling the section of coast Costa Rica de Veragua—the rich coast of Veragua. "I saw more signs of gold in the first two days than I saw in Española during four years," he optimistically recorded in his diary, referring to the region as La Huerta (the Garden). But the precious metal never materialized in significant quantities.

Gold coast: an exhibit at the Museo de Oro

1502

Christopher Columbus arrives by ship in 1502 (above)

Ruins in Cartago, Costa Rica's former capital (left)

Coffee cultivation (below) brought wealth and trade to Costa Rica

Bringing Disease

The lack of workers in Costa Rica was partly the Spaniards' own doing. The indigenous population, with no immunity, succumbed rapidly to the microscopic killers of smallpox, measles, influenza, typhoid and the bubonic plague introduced to the New World by the Europeans. Terrible epidemics swept the country in 1519, then again between 1545 and 1548, reducing an already small Indian population to next to nothing. Within a century of Columbus's arrival in Costa Rica, the tiny indigenous population had been severely depleted. Modern estimates suggest that up to 400,000 native Costa Ricans were killed by smallpox, an extremely contagious virus. The global eradication of smallpox was finally confirmed in 1980.

Small but deadly: the smallpox virus

Juan Vásquez de Coronado

Spanish conquistador Juan Vásquez de Coronado established the first truly permanent settlement in Costa Rica. Forging temporary alliances and utilizing rivalries between different indigenous groups—a technique that proved successful for Cortés in Mexico and Pizarro in Peru—he founded Cartago in 1563. Here, in the Central Highlands, there was plenty of fresh water and fertile volcanic soils for agriculture. Despite Vásquez de Coronado's less bellicose approach to settlement, he too faced problems of indigenous uprisings. The energy and resources of the governor were all but depleted and the city nearly abandoned in 1568, when the next governor, Perafán de Ribera, arrived with more supplies, manpower and enthusiasm for the conquest. Still searching for precious metals, Ribera attempted to pacify the Indians of the Talamanca region, but they resisted, and attempts at settling the region were quickly abandoned.

Pirates of the Caribbean Coast

During the 17th century, the Caribbean coast became the target of swashbuckling pirates and privateers of the Spanish Main: French and Dutch buccaneers, but, above all, the notorious English pirates, including Sir Henry Morgan and Edward Mansfield. The Miskito Indians of the coast of Honduras and Nicaragua became allies with the English, looting various targets, including the cacao plantations of Limón. Raids were so successful that by 1779 the Miskitos were able to demand tribute from Costa Rica, a tradition that continued until 1841. During this time there was also a flourishing black market between the pirates and the settlers.

Pirate of the Caribbean, Sir Henry Morgan

Diego de Nicuesa

Diego de Nicuesa was appointed governor of Veragua (the Panamanian coast) by the Spanish in 1508. Soon after, he launched the first attempt to establish a settlement on Costa Rica's Caribbean coast, using Panama as a base. But his expedition floundered off the coast of Panama. Ground troops who attempted to march north endured sickness, hunger and encountered hostile tribes who denied the Spaniards food and slaughtered the invaders when the opportunity allowed, eventually forcing them to retreat.

The ruins of Ujarrás church

1820

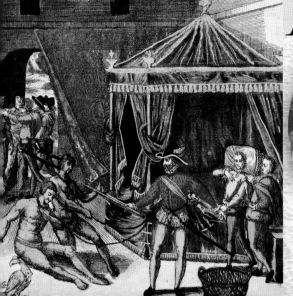

Sir Francis Drake (above)

The Spanish governor extorting gold in 1540 (left)

Independence and *Democracy*

Independence for the nations of the Central American isthmus was granted on September 15 1821. Mexico declared independence a few weeks before the Central American provinces, and General Agustín de Iturbide invited the other nations to join a Mexican Empire. Heredia and Cartago wanted to join with Mexico, but San José and Alajuela preferred the Central American Federation. With the collapse of the Mexican Empire in 1821, Costa Rica joined the Central American Federation. Conflicts ensued until the forceful leader Braulio Carrillo Colina established San José as the capital in 1837. When he declared himself dictator for life in 1841, his opponents sought out Honduran General Francisco Morazán Quesada. Morazán was briefly popular until he imposed direct taxes with the aim of funding a Costa Rican army and relaunching his ideal of the regional federation. He was overthrown and later executed in San José's Central Park.

Economic hardship between the two world wars, culminating in the depression of the 1930s, led to social conflict as Costa Rican politics became ideological. The Communist Party was founded in 1931 and strikes paralyzed the banana plantations in 1934. Despite the problems, government continued to invest in health and education, while reforms in the 1940s drained power from social elites.

1821

The Golden Bean

Coffee was introduced to Costa Rica at the end of the 18th century and by 1829 it had overtaken cacao, tobacco and sugar as the nation's major source of foreign revenue. When Braulio Carrillo Colina became head of state in 1835, he encouraged cultivation of coffee, donating publicly owned land to anyone who would plant it with coffee trees. He also built roads to bring coffee to market. The breakthrough for Costa Rica occurred in 1843, when an English captain took sacks of coffee beans as ballast for his return journey back to Liverpool. The cargo was well received in England.

Golden ballast: roasted coffee beans

A statue of Juan Mora Fernandez in San José (above)

The bridge to Alajuela's Customs building (above). The fort in Heredia's square (right)

The Atlantic Railroad

In 1870, when General Tomás Guardia Gutiérrez instigated the building of the railroad link from the Central Valley to the Atlantic coast, the logic was to facilitate the shipping of coffee to Europe's markets. Guardia contacted Henry Meiggs who had experience railroad building in Chile and Peru. The first tracks were laid in 1872, but mismanagement and corruption meant frequent delays. Meiggs's nephew, Minor Cooper Keith, completed the line in 1890, having managed to secure some generous concessions—a 99-year lease on the railroad, land for banana cultivation alongside the track—in return for taking on the debts of the railroad. During construction more than 4,000 people died and workers from China, Italy and Jamaica were recruited to finish the railroad.

The Walker Affair

In 1855, American William Walker tried to reunite Central America and extend slavery to his new "empire". Arriving in Nicaragua, he declared himself President, and set about implementing his plans. News reached President Porras that Walker had taken La Casona ranch in Guanacaste and he gathered the army, swelled by volunteers. After a victorious battle in March 1856, the Costa Rican forces marched on to Rivas in Nicaragua where Walker's troops were defeated in a bloody battle which saw the young Alajuelan drummer boy Juan Santamaría become a national hero by torching the mercenary's headquarters. Walker was sentenced to death by firing squad in 1860 by the Honduran authorities. For Costa Rica, the Battle of Rivas kindled a sense of nationalism in what was a young state.

Don Pepe's Day

The elections of 1940 were won by Rafael Angel Calderón Guardia of the Partido Republican Nacional (PRN). One vocal critic of Calderón was José Figueres Ferrer who was exiled to Mexico. In 1944, when talk of a coup pushed Calderón into the arms of the Communist Party, Figueres returned from Mexico and called for a military uprising in support of democracy. The five-week civil war caused 2,000 deaths before government troops surrendered in April 1948. Don Pepe, as Figueres was known, became head of state. The Junta nationalized the banks, and created public health and utility bodies, and social security. The army was abolished and the constitution granted suffrage to women, Afro-Caribbeans and Indians. Figueres handed power peacefully to elected president Ulate in 1949.

Carlos Luis Fallas 1909–1966

A notable Costa Rican writer of the 20th century, Carlos Luis Fallas examined social progress in his 1940 work, *Mamita Yunai*, an account of life on United Fruit Company banana plantations. Born in Alajuela, Fallas worked on the railways before moving to Limón where he experienced the hard realities of plantation life. He became active in the National Workers Movement and was jailed several times for organizing strikes. In Limón, he was involved in the Gran Huelga Bananera del Atlantico (Great Atlantic Banana Strike) in 1934, mobilizing more than 15,000 workers. In 1944, he was elected to the National Congress, but it was as a writer that he found his true metier. In 1962, he won the Premio La Novela Iberomericana for *Marcos Ramírez*, a book of children's adventures.

The facade of the old Atlantic Railway station

Juan Santamaría, the heroic drummer boy

Indians got the vote in the new constitution

The banana strike of 1934 shut plantations

José Figueres Ferrer, in the dark suit, surrounded by armed followers in 1949 (left)

A locomotive near San José's Parque Nacional (right)

The Chinese community's cemetery (below)

1949

COLONIA CHINA

Modern Times

The post-1949 era was defined by the acceptance of public involvement in the economy, centrist politics and the introduction of democratic elections.

Through the 1960s and 1970s, despite economic growth, governments battled to balance the books that funded the welfare and social security system. Banana and coffee exports provided higher tax revenues.

The oil crisis of 1973 deflated the economy. The drop in commodities' prices and the global recession exacerbated the shortfall in income By 1987, the national debt had risen to US$4.7 billion—more than the gross domestic product. Governments in the 1990s had to reduce public spending and reschedule debt repayments while managing to hold on to the education, health and social security benefits that made Costa Rica stand out from most countries in Latin America.

The Nicaraguan Border Dispute

Relations between Costa Rica and her northern neighbor have periodically been difficult. Prior to 1979's revolution in Nicaragua, Sandinistas were alleged to be launching attacks from bases in Costa Rica. After the revolution, the region was used as a base by Contras fighting against the Sandinistas's government. Tension mounted again in the late-1990s when Costa Rican police began patrolling the San Juan river to prevent illegal immigration. The Los Chiles border crossing was closed and the situation was just short of outright conflict in 1998 when Costa Rican police using the river were judged to be threatening Nicaraguan sovereignty.

Francisco Zuñiga and the Ancient Goddesses

Costa Rican sculptor Francisco Zuñiga (1912–98) has achieved considerable international fame. Born in San José, he left for Mexico in 1936 where he began to develop sculptural skills including metal smelting and stone carving and polishing. Zuñiga was influenced by modern European masters such as Brancusi, Giacometti and Moore. Like the Mexican Diego Rivera, Zuñiga drew and sculpted individuals as symbols of the strength of the human spirit, notably in the sculptures of women portrayed as resilient mother-earth figures. Each female form has the serenity of an ancient goddess. They are staunch and monumental females, handmade madonnas with Indian features.

Docks near Puerto Limón

1950

Plaza de la Libertad Electoral in San José

Today

Nobel Peace Prize

Oscar Arias Sánchez was born in Heredia in 1941. After studying at the University of San José, in the United States and earning his doctorate in Great Britain, he entered the political arena. He was elected president in 1986, and gained a reputation as an idealistic and charismatic leader. In a turbulent time in Central America, Sánchez negotiated a peace plan between Nicaragua, El Salvador, Guatemala, Honduras and Costa Rica. The plan made big steps towards stability in the region, calling for an end to guerrilla war, amnesty between warring factions and the suspension of military aid. It seems appropriate for a country that disbanded its army almost 40 years before to be the seedbed for regional peace. Sánchez received the Nobel Peace Prize in 1987. After campaigning successfully to lift a restriction limiting presidents to one term, he was reelected in 2006.

On the Move

ARRIVING

Arriving by Air

ON THE MOVE

Most visitors will arrive by air at the Juan Santamaría International airport. The opening of Daniel Oduber Quirós airport in Guanacaste has led to competitively priced tickets from the US and direct flights from Miami, Houston, Atlanta, Phoenix, Dallas, Newark, Chicago and Charlotte.

Juan Santamaría International airport (SJO), tel 506 443 2622, is 16km (10 miles) northwest of San José on the outskirts of Alajuela. For arrivals the airport is laid out with immigration, baggage reclaim and customs following one after the other. After customs,

Waiting for a flight at Juan Santamaría International airport

but before leaving the customs hall, there is a tourist desk which can provide maps and information, as well as make hotel reservations and organize transportation to San José and other areas. In the same area is a branch of Banco Nacional, which opens to meet international flights, and the car rental desks.

For departures, you will find currency exchange, bank ATMs, a few shops, a restaurant and café close to check-in and the departure gates. Beyond passport control there are cafés, a newsagent and gift store, and perfume and liquor stores.

Confirm flight details at least 24 hours in advance. The departure tax is US$26, payable in dollars, colones or a mixture.

This must be paid at the desks immediately to the right as you enter the main terminal. You will need to show your receipt before you can check in. Arrive at least two hours before departure.

Daniel Oduber Quirós International Airport (LIR), tel 506 668 1010, in the northwest of the country, 13km (8 miles) from Liberia along Highway 21, is a smaller airport, but more convenient if you are heading for the Guanacaste beaches and national parks. Renovation and expansion continues, but the modern terminal, which reopened in 1995, has full customs and immigration services, a small café, bank and car rentals.

GETTING TO THE CITY FROM THE AIRPORT		
AIRPORT (CODE)	**JUAN SANTAMARÍA (SJO)**	**DANIEL ODUBER QUIRÓS (LIR)**
TAXI	Outside, the swarms of greeting taxis will compete for your business. A pre-pay fixed-fare system operates at the booth to the right as you exit the terminal. The standard fare is US$12 to downtown San José but outside the microcenter, you may pay in the region of US$10–15, the legal maximum fare.	A taxi from outside the terminal building to Liberia will cost approximately US$8.
BUS	The cheapest option for getting to downtown San José is by bus. Buses on the Alajuela to San José route stop to the right of the main exit. Services run between 5am and 11pm, every ten minutes, fare: 210 colones (US$0.50).	Empreso Alfaro local buses heading in the direction of Nicoya or the northwestern Guanacaste beaches stop at the entrance road to the airport terminal, a 1.5km (1 mile) walk from the main terminal. Only recommended if you have very light luggage.
CAR	When you exit the airport, head east on the Pan-American Highway, and follow the signs for San José, 16km (10 miles).	The airport is 13km (8 miles) west of Liberia, along Highway 21.

COSTA RICA'S AIRPORTS

NIC

Los Chiles

Upala

Daniel Oduber
Quirós International

Liberia

San Rafael

Barra del Colorado

Puerto Viejo de Sarapiquí

Tortuguero

Playa Tamarindo

Tilarán

Puerto Moreno

San Isidro

Ciudad Quesada (San Carlos)

Guácimo

Nicoya

Zarcero

Sarchí

Siquirres

Heredia

Puerto Limón

Carmona

Puntarenas

Alajuela

SAN JOSÉ

Nosara

Sámara

Puerto Carrillo

Playa Naranjo

Tambor

Paquera

Juan Santamaría International

Cartago

Bribrí

Jacó

Isla del Coco

Quepos

San Isidro de El General

PA

Palmar Sur

Drake

Golfito

Puerto Jiménez

Ciudad Neily

This map shows ferry and cruise ship terminals and domestic airports

AIRLINES AND PRICE INFORMATION
From the US and Canada

Daily flights leave various cities in the United States and Canada for Costa Rica. There are direct daily flights from Atlanta, Chicago, Dallas, Fort Worth, Houston, Los Angeles, Miami, Newark, New York, Orlando and Phoenix with American Airlines, Continental, Delta, United Airlines and US Airways. In addition, Martinair, a low-cost subsidiary of KLM, provides services from Orlando three times a week and Miami four times a week. Indirect flights offer a broader range of departure points, but normally stop in one or more Central American capitals en route. Flights from Los Angeles via Guatemala City and/or San Salvador are provided by United Airlines and Grupo Taca airline. From Chicago, United Airlines has a flight via Guatemala City, and Grupo Taca has flights via Guatemala City and/or San Salvador and Managua. Scheduled flights from Canada leave Montreal and Toronto for San José. Air Canada and Grupo Taca offer direct flights from Toronto.

Prices vary, but start from as little as US$269. While they tend to be more expensive, there are direct flights to Daniel Oduber Quirós International airport in Guanacaste with American Airlines (twice weekly from Dallas and three times weekly from Miami), Continental (twice weekly from Houston, once weekly from Newark), Delta (daily from Atlanta), United (once weekly from Chicago) and US Airways (twice weekly from Charlotte). Prices start from $678.

From the UK and Ireland
There are no direct flights to Costa Rica from the United Kingdom or Ireland. You will have to make at least one stopover. American Airlines, Continental, Delta and United Airlines connect through Miami, or any of their direct services from the US. Alternatively, travel via Europe: Iberia flights connect in Madrid. Martinair connects in Amsterdam.

AIRLINE CONTACT INFORMATION		
AIRLINE	**WEBSITE**	**TELEPHONE**
Air Transat	www.airtransat.com	800 388 586
American Airlines	www.aa.com	800 433 7300 (US)
Avianca	www.avianca.com	800 284 2622 (US)
British Airways	www.british-airways.com	0870 850 9850 (UK)
Continental Airlines	www.continental.com	800 523 3273 (US)
Delta Airlines	www.delta.com	800 221 1212 (US)
Grupo Taca	www.grupotaca.com	800 400 8222 (US)
Iberia	www.iberia.es	0870 609 0500 (UK)
Martinair	www.martinair.com	800 627 8462 (US)
United Airlines	www.united.com	800 864 8331 (US)

For a long trip you can go via Bogotá, Colombia, with Avianca.

Prices start from US$885 with Martinair in the low season, about US$2,000 with Iberia via Madrid in the high season. The low season corresponds to winter in the northern hemisphere.

Direct options from Europe are encouraging but varied. Iberia has direct daily flights from Madrid. Martinair has direct flights from Amsterdam and LTU from Dusseldorf. The frequency of Martinair and LTU flights varies every year.

From Australia, New Zealand and South Africa
Routes from Australia and New Zealand go through Los Angeles and then south, picking up one

of the North American airlines to Costa Rica. Expect to spend from US$2,685 flying via Los Angeles.

From South Africa, the situation is even worse, with flights going via Europe and possibly the United States to reach San José. Prices can be about US$3,000.

From Latin America
Regular daily flights are available from Panama and Nicaragua and every Latin American capital city with Grupo Taca.

PRICES AND DISCOUNTS
Hard and fast rules are difficult to establish, but a few general guidelines can be helpful. Fares vary seasonally and from destination to destination. If you have flexibility, check with a local agent for the cheapest time to travel. The high (popular) season in Costa Rica (December–April) does not correspond with the high (expensive) season for airline tickets (July–September) from the northern hemisphere. The busiest seasons are 7 December–15 January and 10 July–10 September.

There are generous discounts for students, the young (under-26s) and, increasingly, teachers.

Apex or excursion (return) fares purchased in advance normally provide a healthy discount off the full economy fare. Flexibility is typically restricted, but you can change details for a fee.

Discounted fares that come and go with the popularity of a particular flight are sold through discount firms or consolidators with the aim of filling up the plane, but restrictions normally apply. The internet offers opportunities to pick up a bargain with online auctions and sales.

Yearly fares are simply return tickets with a return date set to a year or several months from departure, or left open. You are required to fix the route in advance and are normally charged a fee to make changes.

BAGGAGE ALLOWANCE
European carriers usually restrict passengers to two bags of checked luggage weighing up to 20kg (44 lb) for economy class. One piece of hand luggage is permitted. If you are taking specialist equipment such as a surf board, confirm the cost of transport in advance. Some airlines have greater allowances so check before purchasing your ticket. Excess luggage is often permitted if your weight or size allowance is exceeded.

A Nature Air plane flying over Manuel Antonio National Park

Arriving overland and by sea

BY CAR, BUS OR SHIP

Traveling overland to Costa Rica is possible from North America and all countries in Central America. Whether you travel by bus or private vehicle, allow plenty of time for the trip.

Many American cruise ships dock in Costa Rica, letting passengers disembark and spend a day on shore.

BY PRIVATE VEHICLE

Driving overland requires advance planning and a prepared vehicle. You will need vehicle registration documents, your driver's license, an international driver's license (not essential, but can be useful) and insurance. On entering Costa Rica you will be required to buy insurance (three months: US$30) and road tax (US$10 per month).
● Drive with caution: potholes, animals and people are some likely hazards. Avoid driving at night, and choose when and where to park very carefully.
● A detailed map is essential. International Travel Maps publish a good series on the region: Maps: (ITM), 530 West Broadway, Vancouver BC, V5Z 1E9, Canada, tel 604-879 3621 www.itmb.com

BY LONG-DISTANCE BUS

The most direct service to San José is with Tica Bus, starting in Tapachula, Mexico at 6am daily. The journey involves staying overnight in Managua, Nicaragua; book accommodation in advance and take a taxi to your hotel.
Contact details
Tica Bus, in Mexico: 17 Oriente y 3ra Norte, Col. Centro, Tapachula, tel 529 626 2880 www.ticabus.com
In Costa Rica: Avenida 4, Calle 9–11, tel 506 221 8954.

BORDER POSTS
Peñas Blancas–Nicaragua
On the western side of the

It's a bumpy bus ride on the dirt road to Monteverde

isthmus, Peñas Blancas is the only road crossing between the two countries. It takes the traffic of the Pan-American Highway. There is a US$1 fee for entering the border crossing area, and a US$2 fee for having your passport checked. After the formalities at the immigration office on the Nicaraguan border, head to the Costa Rican border post. The immigration office is open Monday to Friday, 6am– 8pm, daily. Pedestrians will need to purchase a *cruz roja*; fill out an immigration card and get both stamped and checked. All cars are fumigated at a cost of US$4.

Paso Canoas–Panama
On the western side of Costa Rica, Paso Canoas marks the frontier with Panama and the Pan-American Highway. Immigration and customs are open 24 hours on the Panama side; Costa Rica provides services from 6am to 10pm.

CRUISE LINERS
Luxury cruise liners departing from Los Angeles and Fort Lauderdale stop at Puntarenas on the Pacific coast and Limón on the Caribbean coast. Excursions are offered on shore, ranging from visits to Manuel Antonio National Park, Cahuita National Park or white-water

rafting on the Río Sarapiquí. Cruises from the US run from September to May. A better option is to explore Costa Rica by boat with Cruise West. The company uses small ships, allowing for a more intimate experience on multi-day tours.
Contact details
Cruise West
2301 Fifth Avenue
Suite 401
Seattle
Tel 888 851 8133 (US)
www.cruisewest.com/costarica

A Cruise West ship anchored at Manuel Antonio

GETTING AROUND

Transport within Costa Rica is simple and straightforward by air or road, whether in a private or rented vehicle or on public buses. Judicious use of hotel-provided transport to get to out-of-the-way places like Tortuguero or Corcovado National Park, combined with a rented vehicle, provides the freedom to explore a bit of the country at your own pace. An efficient and generally effective network of buses will get you to all major destinations and most smaller towns. You may find that occasionally you have to go via one town to make a connection for your destination, but the extra time taken is rarely excessive. Two national airlines, Sansa and Nature Air, provide scheduled services to numerous destinations across the country.

By Car

The road network throughout Costa Rica is generally very good, with most destinations of interest accessible by paved road. As a whole the roads are better than most in Central America, but worse than those in North America and are still liberally sprinkled with potholes. The majority of roads in the Central Highlands are paved, creating a warren-like network that is poorly signposted and very confusing.

Beyond the Highlands, paved roads link most regions in the country, apart from the north-eastern Caribbean lowlands.

Moving between major destinations is easy, but as soon as you want to deviate slightly, the roads deteriorate from hard-packed stony roads which allow a fair speed, if a somewhat juddering ride, to wash-board bone-shakers–loosely packed, rutted sandy shales which become quicksand in the rain–or

rocky roads more like dry-stream beds. It may not be possible to assess the quality of a road when you start out, so the only solution is to take advice from locals and try to be flexible about your travel plans.

Renting a vehicle in Costa Rica is extremely popular and provides the most freedom of movement. You choose when to start, stop, dally and deviate.

BRINGING YOUR OWN CAR

● Most vehicles from the United States arrive in Costa Rica by sea. The principal port is Puerto Limón on the Caribbean side.
● Import taxes are very high, and you will be charged CIF (cost, insurance and freight)
● Shipping time for a vehicle from the US varies from five to ten days.
● Tourists are legally permitted to drive their vehicles for three months, after which they will be required to pay road taxes, of around US$90. The three months starts when you, and not your vehicle, arrive in Costa Rica.

CAR RENTAL

● Most international companies have an office in San José. Check opening hours to ensure you don't miss the drop-off time.
● If you do rent, make sure you are going to use the vehicle. In some locations you won't need it, and it is pointless to have a car sitting around doing nothing. You can get round this problem to a certain degree by arranging drop-offs and pick-ups from different locations around the country. There is normally a charge for this service, but it can work out cheaper than driving back to the original rental office.
● To drive in Costa Rica you have to be over 21 (although some rental companies insist that drivers are over 23) and have a full driving license from your home country. In order to rent a car you will need your passport

One-horse town: a bus arrives at San Gerardo de Rivas in Chirripó

the vehicle, stay with the assistant and agree on paint chips, dents and damage. Check the amount of fuel in the tank. Likewise when returning it stay with the assistant and agree on any charges to be paid before you leave the office. If the car is very dirty, it may be worth getting it cleaned before returning it to the rental company.

● A few roads, mainly in the Central Highlands, have road tolls with minimal charges.

Heavy traffic in San José can be daunting for first-time visitors

and be able to pay a deposit, normally by credit card, of up to US$1,500 against any possible damage.

● Think about where you are likely to want to go; the general recommendation is to get a four-wheel drive with high clearance, but if you only intend to stay on good roads and visit the main areas then you'll be paying for more fuel and vehicle than you need. If you are thinking of moving around the quieter areas of the Nicoya Peninsula, heading for Santa Elena, Monteverde or the Osa Peninsula, driving in the rainy season, or just striking out to see where a road goes then four-wheel drive is a must.

● Vehicles available for rent are normally Japanese. They are mainly Toyotas, with some Suzukis and other makes, ranging from simple sedans like the Toyota Tercel, through mid-size four-wheel drives like the Suzuki Sidekick or Toyota Rav 4, up to the Toyota Land Cruisers. Most cars will have air-conditioning, a good radio and cassette and locking system.

● Prices vary from around US$30 a day for the cheapest cars. A Suzuki Sidekick is around US$55, a Rav 4 US$60 and a Toyota Land Cruiser between US$80 and US$120. The weekly rate is normally priced at seven days for the price of six. The

monthly rate is the weekly rate times 3.5. To this you need to add insurance—from US$12 to US$25 a day.

● There are many car rental firms in San José. The main international companies have offices in the city and at the airport, or you can go with a local company, or companies that specialize in using lower quality vehicles. Beyond San José, there are few rental companies, although Liberia (near Daniel Oduber Quirós airport), Tamarindo and Jacó have several.

● The level of integrity of many car rental companies is questionable. When checking out

DRIVING IN COSTA RICA

Costa Rican drivers, despite a propensity for tail-gating and dangerous overtaking maneuvers, are generally observant, and this is the best advice for prospective drivers. Look out for other drivers, for potholes, poorly signposted roads and unmarked speed restrictions. Beyond that, here are a few tips:

● Signposting is generally appalling. Most people will start their journey in San José, and you could end up driving round the city for a couple of hours before you've got anywhere. Instinct is useful, a compass is better, local knowledge is best.

● Driving in the rain has an added danger, especially in torrential downpours. Be

River crossings are a fact of life in Costa Rica's backcountry

Dirt roads are common and may be impassable after storms

especially careful when roads are drying out. Overhanging trees mean the roads dry out in patches, particularly in and approaching the Central Highlands, where twisting roads make driving dangerous at the best of times.

● In less populated areas, be aware that some vehicles do not always put their lights on at night. Don't drive at night unless it is essential.

● Gas stations in parts of the country are few and far between. Fill up when you get the chance.

● Driving off-road creates new hazards, apart from the fact that your rental company may stipulate you are not allowed to do so. If you've ended up in difficulty unintentionally, re-trace your route and find another way through. If you come across a landslide, mudpools or a ford, get out and walk the route first: if you can't walk through, round or over the obstacle it's unlikely the vehicle will make it.

THE LAW

● On highways and secondary roads the speed limit is 80kph (50mph). In urban areas the limit is 40kph (25mph). Around schools, hospitals and clinics the limit is 25kph (15mph).

● Driving under the influence of alcohol and/or drugs is strictly prohibited.

● Wearing a seatbelt is a legal requirement.

● You must pull over if requested to do so by a police officer. Your personal documents and the vehicle registration are private property and may not be retained by a police officer for any reason. If the police officer insists on retaining your documents ask him to escort you to the nearest police station to clear up the problem. If you believe a police officer has acted inappropriately telephone 506 295 3273.

● If you are involved in an accident, do not move your vehicle until a police officer has arrived and prepared a report. The accident can be reported on 911 or direct to the transport police on 117. You should also call the car rental company.

● If you are fined for an infringement of the law, do not

	Alajuela	Bribrí	Carmona	Ciudad Neily	Guácimo (Heredia)	Heredia	Jacó	Liberia	Los Chiles	Nicoya	Nosara	Palmar Norte	Puerto Limón	Puerto Viejo de Sarapiquí	Puntarenas	Quepos	San Isidro de El General	San José	San Rafael (Alajuela)	Tilarán
Bribrí	220																			
Carmona	297	498																		
Ciudad Neily	368	536	633																	
Guácimo (Heredia)	86	144	377	415																
Heredia	12	209	305	338	78															
Jacó	75	295	282	207	157	92														
Liberia	190	428	116	523	286	209	166													
Los Chiles	166	386	397	511	258	178	223	289												
Nicoya	260	461	37	596	340	268	245	79	360											
Nosara	295	496	72	631	375	303	280	114	395	35										
Palmar Norte	297	465	562	71	344	267	136	452	440	525	560									
Puerto Limón	156	64	434	472	80	145	237	364	322	397	432	401								
Puerto Viejo de Sarapiquí	93	201	390	422	57	66	168	293	151	353	388	351	137							
Puntarenas	98	298	243	416	181	90	68	133	200	206	241	345	234	191						
Quepos	138	358	345	150	220	155	63	229	286	308	343	79	300	231	131					
San Isidro de El General	153	321	418	215	200	123	109	308	296	381	416	144	257	207	201	52				
San José	20	210	311	349	66	12	91	220	192	274	309	278	146	73	115	154	134			
San Rafael (Alajuela)	139	365	217	504	221	146	214	101	122	180	215	433	295	125	142	277	289	155		
Tilarán	156	367	181	521	238	163	139	65	158	144	179	450	312	161	106	202	306	172	36	
Upala	175	401	253	540	257	182	183	95	158	174	209	469	331	161	150	246	325	191	36	82

CAR RENTAL COMPANIES		
COMPANY	**WEBSITE**	**TELEPHONE**
Adobe	www.adobecar.com	506 258 4242
Alamo	www.alamocostarica.com	800 570 0671 (US)
Avanti	www.avantirentacar.com	506 430 4647
Avis	www.avis.com	506 293 2222
Budget	www.budget.co.cr	506 223 3284
Dollar	www.dollar.com	506 443 2950
Economy	www.economyrentacar.com	506 299 2000
Europcar	www.europcar.com	506 257 1158
Hertz	www.hertzcostaricarentacar.com	506 221 1818
National	www.natcar.com	800 227 7368 (US)
Payless	www.paylesscr.com	506 257 0026
Thrifty	www.thrifty.com	506 257 3434
Toyota	www.toyotarent.com	506 258 5797
Tricolor	www.tricolorcarrental.com	800 949 0234 (US)

The road to Braulio Carrillo

give money directly to the police. Pay the fine, which is subject to 30 percent tax, at the nearest Banco Nacional.
● Driving on beaches is prohibited everywhere, except when there is no other route connecting two towns.

PARKING
● Parking in San José is not that difficult, with several *parqueos* dotted around the city.
● 24-hour parking is available but may be harder to find. Reserve a space in a secure parking area.
● For early starts ensure access to the parking area is 24 hours.

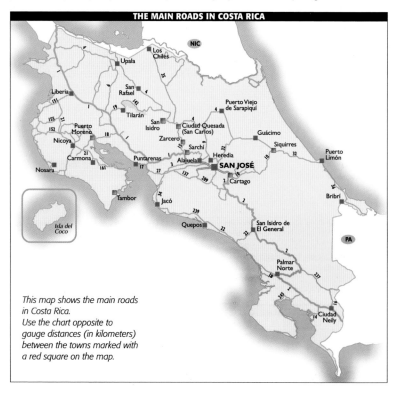

THE MAIN ROADS IN COSTA RICA

This map shows the main roads in Costa Rica.
Use the chart opposite to gauge distances (in kilometers) between the towns marked with a red square on the map.

GETTING AROUND

By Air

Two companies provide a scheduled service to destinations throughout the country: Sansa and Nature Air. If you have limited time and tolerance for bone-shaking bus and car journeys, go by air; services are regular and cost-effective, especially if you are visiting the more remote parts of Costa Rica. It is worth bearing in mind that packages offered by agencies in San José may well work out to be even more economical. Lodges in the Southern Region often have their own landing strips and will arrange flights. Charter flights also operate out of Tobías Bolaños airport, in Pavas, 5km (3 miles) west of San José, and helicopter charters are available.

AIRLINES

● Sansa (tel 506 221 9414; www.flysansa.com) flies out of the domestic terminal at Juan Santamaría International airport near Alajuela. Flights are in Cessna Caravans and have a reputation for being late, frequently cancelled or overbooked. Sansa has a Costa Rica Airpass offering unlimited air travel for one week for US$199, two weeks for US$249.

● Nature Air (tel 506 299 6000 and 800 235 9272 (US); reservations@natureair.com and www.natureair.com) operates out of Tobías Bolaños airport. They use 15-seater Lets and 7-seater Britten-Norman Islanders. In addition to internal destinations, Nature Air flies to Granada, a beautiful colonial city in Nicaragua, from Liberia and San José, and to Bocas del Toro in Panama from San José. Nature Air also provides a charter service to all their scheduled destinations from Tobías Bolaños airport. Reservations can be made in advance and Nature Air works with Adobe Rent a Car to arrange for a rented vehicle to be picked up or dropped off at the airport.

Local airfields mean that regular internal flights are affordable

● Aerobell has a fleet of single-engine Cessnas and twin-engine Cessnas and Pipers operating out of Tobías Bolaños airport (tel 506 290 0000; www.aerobell.com). Paradise Air utilizes Gippsland Airvans from both Tobías Bolaños airport and Juan Santamariá International airport (tel 506 231 0938; www.flywithparadise.com).

● Working out of Tobías Bolaños is Alfa Romeo Aero Taxi (tel 506 296 4344), which operates mainly between the capital and the southwest.

● Aerodiva offers sky tours and air charters using helicopters (tel 506 296 7241; www.aerodiva.com).

● You can charter a helicopter with Helisa (tel 506 231 6867) from Tobías Bolaños airport.

TICKETS AND FARES

● Children under two years old travel free, from two to twelve, there is a 25 percent discount.

● Weight allowances are minimal at 12kg (25 lb) with a US$0.45 surcharge for every pound.

● Flights must be paid for when you make the reservation, which can be done online, and tickets are non-refundable.

● Always confirm that the flight is direct.

● Services are less frequent in the low season.

FLYING WITHIN COSTA RICA				
DESTINATION	**NATURE AIR**		**SANSA**	
	FREQUENCY	PRICE (US$) (ONE WAY / RETURN)	FREQUENCY	PRICE (US$) (ONE WAY / RETURN)
Barra del Colorado	1 per day	70/140	1 per day	66/132
Drake Bay	2 per day	92/184	3 per day	84/186
Golfito	3 per day	84/168	5 per day	82/164
Granada (Nicaragua)	3 per week	120/240		
Liberia	3 per day	88/176	1 per day	71/142
Nosara	1 per day	86/172	2 per day	82/186
Palmar Sur	1 per day	80/160	2 per day	75/150
Puerto Jiminez	3 per day	92/184	3 per day	82/164
Punta Islita	1 per day	90/180	1 per day	82/164
Quepos	3 per day	54/108	8 per day	49/96
Sámara			2 per day	82/164
Tamarindo	2 per day	88/176	12 per day	82/164
Tambor	1 per day	69/138	4 per day	65/130
Tortuguero	1 per day	70/140	1 per day	66/132
Toro (Panama)	3 per week	100/200		

DOMESTIC AIR, BUS AND FERRY ROUTES

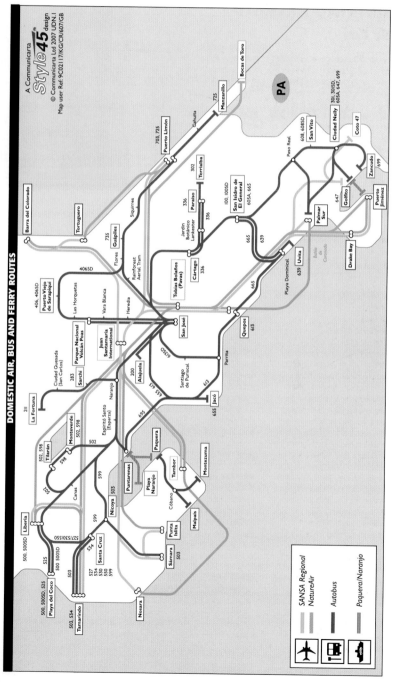

SANSA Regional
NatureAir

Autobus

Paquera/Naranjo

GETTING AROUND

By Bus

Nationwide services are provided by about 20 private companies which are dotted around San José in clusters. A few services have grouped together and the Coca-Cola Terminal is the hub for Central Highland services, with a few offices in surrounding streets and to the north providing many other services. All Caribbean destinations are neatly served from the Gran Terminal del Caribe. Beyond the capital, a few towns act as regional hubs.

There are alternatives to using public buses. Comfortable air-conditioned private shuttle buses run by Interbus and Grayline will collect you from your hotel and drop you at your destination. You can also rent a bus from Coach Costa Rica if you are traveling in a group (up to 22 people).

PUBLIC BUSES
● Buses tend to depart promptly so arrive on time.
● If your bus is scheduled to arrive late in the day, particularly in popular areas such as Montezuma and Tamarindo, it is always advisable to reserve your tickets in advance. Buses are prone to break down, which means sending a replacement bus from San José, adding several hours to the journey time.
● On services longer than five hours, there will invariably be a fifteen-minute stop midway. Always take your carry-on bags off the bus with you.
● Services tend to be reliable if the weather and conditions have been kind to the road.
● The cost of travel is cheap, working out at roughly between US$1 and US$1.50 an hour.
● The longest journey in Costa Rica is currently from San José to Puerto Jiménez on the Osa Peninsula (eight hours), and will cost you about US$6.50.
● Local buses exist in the larger towns, but tend to be of limited use to the passing visitor outside San José.
● Always keep on eye on your belongings, both in the bus terminals (especially Coca-Cola in San José) and inside the bus.

TRANSPORT HUBS
● To the west, Puntarenas is a good stop-off point, negating the need to return to the Highlands and linking to services down the Pacific coast and up to Santa Elena and Monteverde.
● Farther north, Cañas is the point to break from the Pan-American Highway and head inland to Tilarán and from there to Fortuna or Monteverde.
● Liberia offers similar, but lesser opportunities with links to the Nicoya Peninsula.
● Heading south, San Isidro de El General is a useful place to change buses, as is Palmar Norte where you can link with the southern section of the coastal road (costanera) and travel north to Dominical, Quepos and Manuel Antonio.
● On the Caribbean, Limón is the main transport hub, but it is possible to get buses traveling all the way down the coast from San José so you don't have to change, unless you're stopping over in Limón.

PRIVATE BUSES
● The Fantasy Bus by Grayline operates hundreds of services connecting most towns, cities and tourist attractions. Prices range from US$29 to US$38; call or check the website for full details of the schedule.

A proud driver and his tourist bus in Puntarenas

● Interbus offer a similar service with hundreds of daily trips on 44 established routes from San José. Prices range from US$19 to US$39; or see the website for the full schedule
● Always reserve seats at least 24 hours in advance, especially for services to the northwestern Guanacaste beaches and the Nicoya Peninsula.
● Montezuma Expeditions provide bus services from San José to Montezuma, connecting with the Paquera ferry, and to other locations on the Nicoya Peninsula from Montezuma.
● Many services pick up passengers from several hotels and if you are picked up first and dropped off last you are unlikely to gain much time.

COACH HIRE
● Coach Costa Rica's rates are for each destination on a daily basis, or for US$125 a day with a chauffeur, if rented for more than three days.

BUS AND COACH CONTACT INFORMATION		
COMPANY	**WEBSITE**	**TELEPHONE**
Coach Costa Rica	www.coachcostarica.com	506 229 4192
Fantasy Bus Grayline	www.graylinecostarica.com	506 220 2126
Interbus	www.costaricapass.com	506 283 5573
Montezuma Expeditions	www.interbusonline.com	506 642 0919

ON THE MOVE

GETTING AROUND COSTA RICA BY BUS

Company	Pick-up point	Telephone	Route
CENTRAL HIGHLANDS			
TUASA	Ave. 2 Calle 12–14, San José	506 442 6900	San José to Alajuela, airport, Heredia, Volcan Poas
Microbuses Rápido	Calle1, Ave. 7–9, San José	506 238 8392	San José to Heredia
Lumaca	Calle 3, Ave. 4, San José	506 537 2320	San José to Cartago
Auto Transportes Mata	Behind Cartago convent	506 533 8001	Cartago to Orosí valley
TUAN	Ave. 3, Calle 16–18, San José	506 258 2004	San José to Grecia, Sarchí; Alajuela to Naranjo
Transportes Palmarenos	Calle 16, Ave. 1–3, San José	506 453 3808	San José to Palmares
Empresarios Unidos	Calle 16, Ave. 10–12, San José	506 222 0064	San José to San Ramón
Coopacaraires	Calle 8, Ave. 10–12, San José	506 410 0015	San José to San Ignacio de Acosta
Transtusa	Calle 13, Ave. 6–8, San José	506 556 4233	San José to Turrialba
Buses Metropoli	Ave. 2, Calle 1–3, San José	506 530 1064	San José to Volcán Irazú
Transportes Zarcero	Calle 16, Ave.1–3, San José	506 451 4080	San José to Zarcero
NORTHERN REGION			
Autotransportes San José	Calle 12, Ave. 7–9, San José	506 255 4300	San José to Ciudad Quesada, Fortuna, Pital, La Guatuso
Transportes Pital	Plaza San Carlos, Ciudad Quesada	506 460 2596	Ciudad Quesada to Pital
Coopetrack	Ciudad Quesada bus terminal	506 460 5032	Ciudad Quesada to Fortuna
Empresarios Guapilenos	Ciudad Quesada bus terminal	506 766 6740	Ciudad Quesada, San José to Puerto Viejo de Sarapiqui
Transportes Upala	Calle 12, Ave. 3–5, San José	506 221 3318	San José to Bagaces, Fortuna, Guayabo, Aguas Claras, Upala
Autotransportes San Carlos	Calle 12 Ave. 7–9, San José	506 255 4318	San José to Los Chiles
GUANACASTE			
Pulmitan	Calle 10–12, Ave. 5–7, San José	506 222 1650	San José to Liberia, Playa del Coco
Alfaro-Tracopa	Calle 14, Ave. 5, San José	506 222 2666	San José to Santa Cruz, Tamarindo
Tralapa	Calle 20, Ave. 3, San José	506 221 7202	San José to Brasilito, Flamingo, Panama
Transportes Tilaran	Calle 20, Ave. 3, San José	506 256 0105	San José to Tilarán
Trans Cañas	Calle 18, Ave. 1, San José	506 222 3006	San José to La Cruz, Peñas Blancas
CENTRAL PACIFIC AND NICOYA			
Alfaro-Tracopa	Calle 14, Ave. 5, San José	506 222 2666	San José to Nicoya, Sámara, Nosara
Empresa Rojas	Nicoya bus terminal	506 685 5352	Nicoya to Sámara, Carrillo, Nosara, Garza, Guiones
Empresarios Unidos	Calle 16, Ave. 10–12	506 222 8231	San José to Puntarenas
Transportes Delio Morales	Calle 16, Ave 1–3, San José	506 223 5567	San José to Quepos, Manuel Antonio
Transportes Blanco	Perez Zeledon, Quepos	506 771 4744	Perez Zeledon to Dominical
Transportes Jacó	Calle 16 Ave, 1–3, San José	506 223 1109	San José to Jacó
SOUTHERN REGION			
Empresa Los Santos	Ave. 16, Calle 19–21, San José	506 221 7070	San José to Los Santos
MUSOC	Calle Central, Ave. 22–24	506 222 2422	San José to San Isidro de El General, Chirripó
Transportes Blanco	San Isidro de El General	506 771 4744	San Isidro to Uvita, Dominical
Transportes Blanco	Calle 12 Ave. 7–9, San José	506 771 4744	San José to Puerto Jiménez
Tracopa-Alfaro	Ave. 5, Calle 14, San José	506 222 2666	San José to Ciudad Cortes, Palmar Norte
Tracopa-Alfaro	Ave. 5, Calle 14, San José	506 221 2666	San José to Paso Canoas, Golfito; San Vito
THE CARIBBEAN LOWLANDS			
Empresarios Guapilenos	Calle Central, Ave. 13, San José	506 222 0610	San José to Cariari, Tortuguero, Guápiles, Braulio Carrillo, Puerto Limón, Siquirres
Boats Ruben Bananeros	Calle Central, Ave. 13, San José	506 709 8005	San José to Moín; boat to Tortuguero
Empresarios Guapileños	Calle Central, Ave. 13, San José	506 222 0610	San José to Puerto Limón
Transportes Mepe	Calle Central, Ave. 13, San José	506 257 8129	San José to Cahuita, Puerto Viejo, Sixaola

GETTING AROUND

CHILDREN

On long-distance buses children generally pay half or reduced fares. For shorter trips it is cheaper, if less comfortable, to seat small children on your knee. Often there are spare seats, which they can occupy after tickets have been collected. On city and local excursion buses, small children do not generally pay a fare, but are not entitled to a seat when paying customers are standing.

On sightseeing tours always bargain for a family rate—often children can go free. Note that a child being carried free on a long excursion is not always covered by the operator's travel insurance; it is advisable to pay a small premium to arrange cover.

Airlines charge a reduced price for children under 12 and less for children under 2. Check the child's baggage allowance; some are as low as 7kg (15.5 lb).

BICYCLING

Costa Rica is generally bicycle friendly, with less traffic than many other nearby countries. However, thin paving on roads soon deteriorates, especially at the shoulders, so look out for cracks and potholes, which bring

Mountain bikes are a practical and fun way to travel short distances

traffic to a crawl. Paved highways are also narrow and winding and pose many hazards. Many bicycle routes require negotiating unpaved roads. Much of the terrain is exceedingly hilly, although following the coast roads is flatter. The prevailing wind is from the northeast, so if you plan a long tour, going from Nicaragua to Panama is slightly easier. The Nicoya Peninsula is particularly bad for bicyclists; a mountain bike is best for the terrain and the poor road state.

TAXIS

Taxis offer an alternative way of exploring San José and the Central Highlands. A realistic price for a trip in a cab to Volcán Irazú is 10,000 colones, (US$32). With a group of four, this becomes a remarkably affordable way to travel without the trouble of driving yourself. If taking a long-distance ride, you may have to pay part of the fare in advance. Most red cab drivers have a list of recommended prices for various destinations.

VISITORS WITH A DISABILITY

Costa Rica could be much more accessible to the visitor with a disability, but progress is being made. Vaya con Silla de Ruedas (Go with Wheelchairs) is a specialist organization that offers day tours for cruise ship passengers and other trips. Tel 506 454 2810; www.gowithwheelchairs.com

FAUNA (Fundacion para el Acceso Universal a la Naturaleza) PO Box 217-8000, San Isidro de El General, Perez Zeledon, tel 506 771 7482, provides information and organizes tours of Costa Rica for those with physical disabilities.

For long-distance trips, agree a fee with your taxi driver in advance

San José City Transport

WALKING

Central San José is easy to explore on foot—most places of interest are close to downtown. Joining the general mêlée, you can struggle your way through the chaos or stroll at leisure, stopping at will for caffeine fixes and nibbles. With the simplicity of the street layout, if you're lost just head back towards the lower numbered streets and you end up in the center.

But hazards do exist. The streets of capital cities are rarely paved with gold, but in parts of San José they are barely paved at all. This is not a warning to watch out for the occasional raised or cracked paving slab; it is serious advice to look where you are walking. Slabs stick up at shin-cracking angles and in some places they're missing completely, revealing precipitous drops to the drainage system below. Keep your eyes down while walking; stop when you want to look around.

A second hazard is the traffic. Crossing the roads is safest at pedestrian crossings which conform to the standard green light code. Arguably Tico drivers are no less jumpy than any other Latin nation, which means you'll be pushing your luck if you leave the curb on anything but green. A complicated one-way system adds to the confusion, so when crossing roads the simple rule is to watch the vehicles. While courtesy does exist, few drivers at the lights hang around unnecessarily.

BUS

An extensive service covers the surrounding districts and suburbs of the city. Once you get the hang of a few basic routes, judicious use of buses can be very convenient, but as a general rule unless weighed down with luggage, or late for an appointment (in which case consider a taxi), it's probably worth walking any distance up to 20 blocks or so.

One benefit of catching a bus is to share the experience of commuting, San José style. All but the very wealthiest travel by bus and you'll be elbow-to-elbow with a broad cross-section of Joséfinos. As ever, warnings related to busy places hold true. Pickpockets and bag-snatchers love cramped settings, so take extra care.

The urban bus system is extensive and efficient enough, traffic congestion permitting. Buses run from around 5am until 11pm or so at night. Urban buses cost 150 colones (US\$0.30) payable to the driver on boarding. It's a little more (220 colones, US\$0.40) for towns on the outskirts, such as Escazú, Alajuela and Heredia. Buses get very crowded at rush hours, and luggage space is limited at the best of times.

Destinations are marked on the front of the bus. Officially, buses stop only for passengers to board and alight at official stops. Far from obvious, the cunningly disguised metal posts doubling up as stops are found through chance not design. Labelled on one side with the destination, the bus stop blends in perfectly with the pavement furniture. The clearest indication is a neat line of people patiently waiting.

A few general routes that may be of interest to visitors: Heading west towards Parque Sabana down Paseo Colón from the middle of town, buses leave from along Avenida 3. Returning from Parque Sabana buses travel down Paseo Colón before joining Avenida 2. With these two routes you can move through the heart of the city.

An inexpensive tour of San José can be made on the bus marked "periférico" from Paseo Colón in front of the Cine Colón, a 45-minute circle of the city. A smaller circle is made by the "Sábana/Cementerio" bus going along Paseo Colón out to Parque Sábana and then returning along Avenida 10. Pick it up on Avenida 2, at Parque Morazán or on Avenida 3.

A few starting points for stops and destinations: Desmaparados, Avenida 4, Calle 5–7; Escazú, Avenida Central–1, Calle 16; Moravia, Avenida 3, C 3–5; Sabana Cementerio, Avenida 2, Calle 8–10; Sábana Estadio, Avenida 2, Calle 2–4; San Pedro, Avenida Central, Calle 9–11.

Buses in San José are modern, but elsewhere they may be basic

DRIVING

Few would advise driving in San José as a way of seeing the city, but given that most car rental journeys will start and end in the capital, you may find yourself behind the wheel in the city at some point.

The combination of an unfamiliar vehicle, new road layouts, street signs and traffic flow systems, and uncertainty about where you may be going and how to get there, make driving in Costa Rica a challenge. Add heavy traffic loads and the urgency found in capitals throughout the world, and the best advice is simply to be cautious. One-way systems are poorly signposted, lane discipline is nonexistent and pedestrians appear from nowhere. Stay alert; a helpful passenger can be a godsend. Parking in the day is not that difficult, with several *parqueos* dotted around the city; 24-hour parking is available but

A woman cycling past a single-floor house in Liberia

may be more difficult to find. If you are planning an early start make sure access is 24-hour. One specific word of warning. Most car rental firms have offices along Paseo Colón, one of the busiest and fastest stretches of

San José, and it is a test to start your driving career in the city here. Added to that, traffic flows change at rush hour when the road becomes one-way, eastbound, heading into the middle of town, on weekdays between 6.30am and 8.30am.

TAXIS

With more than 7,000 cabs cruising the streets, taxis are a quick and efficient way of moving around the city. Official red cabs are marked with a yellow triangle on the side and equipped with meters or *marías* that should be used for all journeys within the metropolitan district. Although meters are generally used if you're traveling with a Tico, visitors often find them "broken" which does little to enhance the universal suspicion that taxi drivers rip you off given half the chance. But the other universal truth holds true: taxi drivers know their patch and once you've made friends, they're an invaluable asset. On the whole, drivers are fair, but get a rough idea of the cost before setting off. The meter starts at 350 colones and advances 32 colones every 100m (110 yards) or so. A cross-town journey will be in the region of 1,000–1,200 colones (US$2–2.30).

San José is a busy city with one main road through the middle

This chapter is divided into seven regions, which are shown on the map in the inside front cover. Places of interest are listed alphabetically in each region. Major sights are listed at the start of each region.

The Sights

SAN JOSÉ

San José may seem chaotic but its cosmopolitan diversity and compact manageability soon exert their charm on visitors. Here, history, art and architecture draw your attention, rather than the scenery and wildlife that are supreme elsewhere in the country.

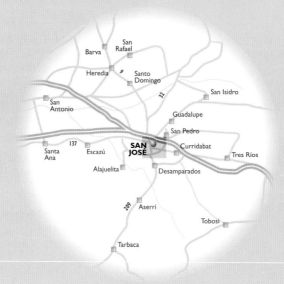

MAJOR SIGHTS

San José

✚ 239 J6

ℹ Below Plaza de la Cultura, tel 506 222 1090; Mon–Fri 9–1, 2–5

www.visitcostarica.com

HOW TO GET THERE

✈ Airport

Juan Santamaría International airport, 20km (12 miles) west of city.

Other transport

The city is served by buses and taxis, and a limited commuter railway service. Car rental agencies can be found at the airport.

SEEING SAN JOSÉ

Central San José is best explored on foot; most places of interest are in the heart of the city. Downtown San José conforms to the extended grid system moving outwards from two main streets that cross in the heart of the city—Avenida Central and Calle Central. Avenues run west to east, with the odd numbers north of Calle Central and even numbers to the south. Streets, or calles, are numbered odd to the east of the city and even to the west. The central reference point is Plaza de la Cultura. An extensive bus service covers the surrounding districts, but buses barely move beyond second gear; they are only worth taking for longer distances. Taxis are marked with a yellow triangle. When walking, watch out for the poor condition of the sidewalks.

A fruit vendor at a San José street stall (below) and customer (above)

BACKGROUND

In the 18th century, San José was a ramshackle collection of barely 400 farms. By the end of it, a monopoly in the tobacco trade had given San José a slight prominence over the other towns of the region, fuelling the development of an urban economy and early signs of civic pride. When the shoots of a promising coffee industry began to appear, the entrepreneurial spirit of the emerging agricultural élite created a conflict between the towns of the Central Valley. The youthful, energetic cities of San José and Alajuela were pitted against the more traditional forces of Cartago and Heredia who preferred annexation by Mexico to becoming a member of a Central America Federation.

The dispute was settled in 1823 at the Battle of Ochomongo but skirmishes continued for a further 20 years. San José's victory set a path for the nation's growth. A flurry of activity promoted trade in mining and lumber, but it was coffee from the Central Valley that provided a stable market. The emerging merchant classes or *cafetaleros* took control of the manufacture and export of coffee, and when Juan Rafael Mora Porras rose from the coffee aristocracy to become president in 1849, the role of the coffee elite in society and the economy was established.

The shipment of the golden bean to Europe brought a return trade in European goods and new ideas to the capital.

The high-rise heart of San José

TIPS

• The street layout and numbering is simple: If you're lost just head towards the lower numbered streets and you end up in the middle.

• The tourist office is efficient and helpful and can provide general information, maps and bus schedules, as well as assisting with specific inquiries and problems.

• Because of the heavy traffic, it's probably quicker to walk any distance up to 20 blocks or so, unless you are weighed down with luggage.

• An economical 45-minute circular route of San José can be made on the bus marked "periférico" from Paseo Colón, in front of Cine Colón.

• The best time to visit San José is from December to April when clear skies and very little rain are almost guaranteed.

DON'T MISS

Shopping at the **MERCADO CENTRAL** (▷ 139), the heart of the city.

Descending into the **MUSEO DE ORO PRECOLUMBINO** (▷ 65), to find spectacular pre-Columbian gold artifacts below the Plaza de la Cultura.

Visiting the Plaza de la Cultura for the **TEATRO NACIONAL** (▷ 67), the grandest building in the city.

Admiring the ancient jade carvings at the **MUSEO DEL JADE** (▷ 64), the most important jade collection on the continent.

Visiting the **MUSEO DE ARTE COSTARRICENSE** (▷ 64), a gallery in Parque Sabana, once San José's airport and now its largest green space.

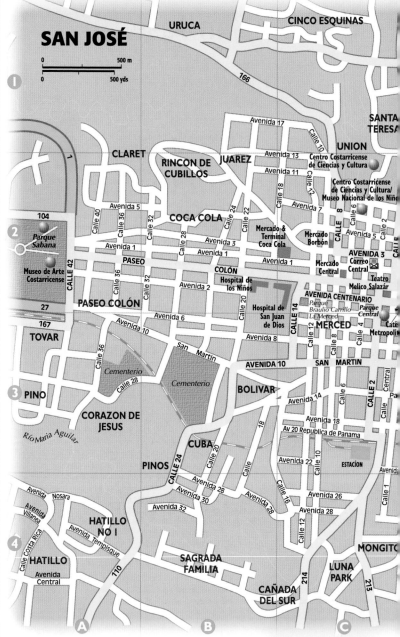

SAN JOSÉ

URUCA
CINCO ESQUINAS

0 ——— 500 m
0 ——— 500 yds

1

SANTA TERESA

166

CLARET
JUAREZ
UNION

RINCON DE CUBILLOS

Avenida 17
Avenida 13
Centro Costarricense de Ciencias y Cultura

Avenida 11
Calle 10

Centro Costarricense de Ciencias y Cultura/ Museo Nacional de los Niños

Avenida 5
COCA COLA
Avenida 7

104

2

Parque Sabana

Museo de Arte Costarricense

Calle 40
Calle 36
Calle 32
Calle 24
Calle 22

Avenida 1
Avenida 3
Mercado & Terminal Coca Cola
Mercado Borbón

Mercado Central

Avenida 5
Calle 6
Calle 8
Calle 2

PASEO
COLÓN
Hospital de los Niños

AVENIDA 3
Correo Central
Teatro Melico Salazár

27
PASEO COLÓN
Avenida 6
Hospital de San Juan de Dios

AVENIDA CENTENARIO
Parque Braulio Carrillo
La Merced
Parque Central

167
TOVAR
Avenida 10
Avenida 8

MERCED
Calle 14
Calle 12
Calle 8
Calle 4

Cat...
Metropoli...

San Martin
AVENIDA 10
SAN MARTIN

Cementerio
Cementerio

3

PINO
CORAZON DE JESUS
Río Maria Aguilar
Calle 36
Calle 28

BOLIVAR
Avenida 14
Avenida 18
Av 20 Republica de Panama
18

Calle 6
Calle 2
Calle Central
Pa...

CUBA
PINOS
Calle 24
Calle 20
Calle
Avenida 22
Avenida 26

ESTACION
Avenid...

Calle 10
Calle 1

4

Avenida Nosara
Avenida Villanea

Avenida 28
Avenida 30
Avenida 32
Calle 16
Avenida 28
Calle 12

MONGITO

HATILLO NO I
Avenida Tempisque

Calle Costa Rica

HATILLO
Avenida Central
710

SAGRADA FAMILIA

CAÑADA DEL SUR

LUNA PARK
214
215

A   **B**   **C**

The cultural landscape had been redefined. The University of Santo Tomás opened in 1843 and the Teatro Nacional was inaugurated in 1897. Standing in the heart of the capital, it was a monument to the extravagant style and tastes that now dominated the lives of rich Joséfinos.

The strength of the coffee oligarchy ensured San José remained the capital, but the air of opulence was dispersed by the depression of the 1930s. After a couple of decades drifting through depression, economic and social reform and civil war, San José's extravagance became a distant memory until industrialization ushered in a second wave of prosperity in the mid-20th century. With the city's growth, colonial majesty was usurped by functionality. Today Joséfinos are broadly indifferent about their capital.

A statue in the Museo Nacional

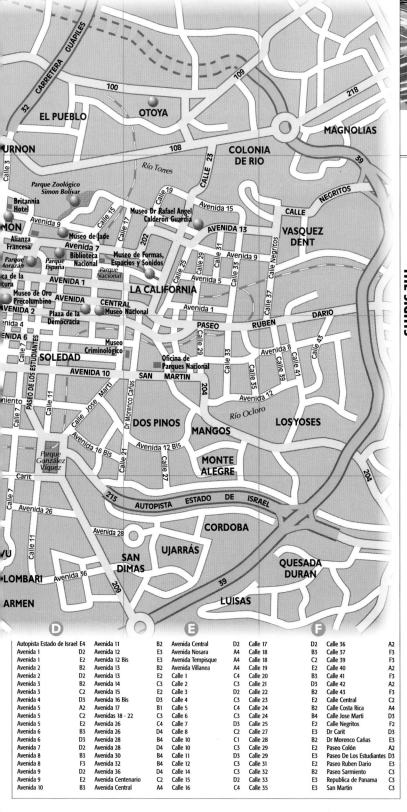

SAN JOSÉ STREET PLAN **61**

Amón and Otoya

Amón and Otoya districts testify to San José's bygone wealth and style. Colonial grandeur and contemporary bohemia fuse among leafy streets dotted with hotels, fine restaurants, art galleries and embassies.

The battlements of El Castillo, once home to a bishop

A jaguar in the Simón Bolívar Zoo and, top, a spider monkey

Colonial architecture: the Alianza Francesa building on Avenida 7

RATINGS	
Cultural interest	● ● ●
Photo stops	● ● ●
Walkability	● ● ● ●

SEEING AMÓN AND OTOYA

Northeast from Plaza de la Cultura lie the two historic districts of Amón and Otoya, a neighborhood built on coffee wealth where colonial buildings now stand as monuments to grand living and architectural extravagance. From Avenida Central, walk north along Calle 5 and on to Amón, past the leafy retreats of Parque Morazán and Parque España, where traffic noise gives way to bird chatter. On Avenida 9, between Calle 3 and 7, alongside Hotel Don Carlos, the walls lining the street are decorated with ceramic tiles. These districts are good places for a stroll, past colonial houses with low-slung eaves shading broad balconies.

HIGHLIGHTS

PARQUE MORAZÁN
✚ 61 D2
The largest of central San José's parks is Parque Morazán. With soaring araucaria trees, serpentine benches and an aging bandstand, more poetically known as the Music Temple, the park is an ideal spot to rest after visiting the shops on its south and west sides. It is named after General Francisco Morazán who tried to unite Central America in 1842; he was executed shortly afterwards in Parque Central. To the west of the park is the Edificio Metálico, made of cast iron in Belgium and shipped from France in the 1890s; today it is a school.

PARQUE ESPAÑA
✚ 61 D2
East of Parque Morazán, bisected by the hazardous Calle 9, is Parque España, a verdant square with Moorish-style, mosaic-tiled fountains and an old pergola. On Sunday it hosts a market. In the middle are the statues of Juan Vázquez de Coronado and Simón Bolívar. Coronado became governor of Veragua in 1562, and he is renowned for his compassionate treatment of the indigenous tribes.

COLONIAL ARCHITECTURE
A stroll around Amón and Otoya reveals fine examples of colonial architecture. To the northeast of Parque España, the ornate Casa

The Edifico Metálico has been a school since it was assembled

Amarilla (Yellow House) is home to Costa Rica's Ministry of Foreign Affairs. The ceibo tree at the front was planted by John F. Kennedy in 1963; his visit coincided with the last eruption of Volcán Irazú on March 19 of that year. One block east of the Casa Amarilla, a dazzling white building houses the Mexican embassy. The peppermint-green Alianza Francesa building (tel 506 222 2283), on the corner of Calle 5 and Avenida 7, was built in 1949. Other treasures in the area are the pastel-pink Hotel Britannia, on Calle 3 and Avenida 11, and the turrets of El Castillo, on Avenida 11 and Calle 3.

ART GALLERIES

In keeping with the area's artistic vigour, a clutch of art galleries can be found along undulating streets, including Galería Namú (▷ 138), an excellent introduction to Costa Rica's arts and crafts.

PARQUE ZOOLÓGICO SIMÓN BOLÍVAR

➕ 61 D2 ✉ Avenida 11, Calle 7 ☎ 506 256 0012 🕐 Mon–Fri 9–3.30, Sat, Sun 9–4.30 💵 US$2, donations welcome 🚌 Go north on Calle 7 until you reach Avenida 11

At the northern reaches of Amón is the Simón Bolívar Zoo, which has a small number of native species. The zoo is popular at weekends but it isn't the best kept place. Conditions have been improving slowly.

BACKGROUND

The colonial-style architecture of Barrio Amón and Otoya memorializes San José's glorious belle epoque. The boom in coffee exports to Europe funded development during the 19th century. With the rise of the coffee elite—*cafetaleros*—infrastructure in the capital improved. Ships brought back European goods, and fashion, architecture and culture all took their lead from Europe.

Economic growth stimulated expansion in the late 1950s and promoted new prosperity. San José grew at the expense of the surrounding rural communities and its rapid growth quickly destroyed its European charm. A world apart from much of the unprepossessing capital, Amón and Otoya remain the most aesthetically pleasing and fashionable districts for visitors to explore.

The domed Temple of Music in Parque Morazán

● The areas around Parque Morazán and Parque España are best avoided at night. They are notorious red-light districts where robbery is not uncommon.

● If you are staying at a hotel in Barrio Amón or Barrio Otoya, a taxi (US$1.50–2) to and from the downtown area, or to El Pueblo in Barrio Tournón, is recommended for safety reasons.

No entry: The Yellow House is not open to the public

Buying tickets to the Costa Rican Center of Science and Culture

CENTRO COSTARRICENSE DE CIENCIAS Y CULTURA

🗺 60 C2 • Calle 4, beyond Avenida 9 ☎ 506 258 4929 ◷ Tue–Fri 8–4.30, Sat, Sun 9.30–5 💲 Tue–Fri adult US$2, child US$1.30, Sat, Sun adult US$1.75, child US$1.25 🚌 Join Calle 4 and head north, or catch a cab ❓ See *La Nación* newspaper for exhibition details www.museocr.com

The yellow facade of the Costa Rican Center of Science and Culture, a former penitentiary just beyond comfortable walking distance from downtown San José, hides a blend of art, history and fun. The Children's Museum occupies a couple of wings. The National Gallery uses the vaulted ceilings and spaces to display art exhibitions. In the Carlos Luiz Saénz Library prisoner accounts describe life inside the prison. Completing the mix, the National Auditorium is a performance venue. The transformation of what was an unpleasant place is impressive even if the contents don't overwhelm.

MUSEO DE ARTE COSTARRICENSE

🗺 60 A2 • Calle 40, Avenida 2 ☎ 506 222 7155 ◷ Tue–Fri 9–5, Sat, Sun 10–4 💲 US$5, free on Sun 🚌 To Sabana Cementerio from Avenida 2, 80 colones; taxi from Parque Central US$1.50 www.musarco.go.cr

One of the capital's more memorable museums, the Museum of Costa Rican Art, is in the old airport terminal in Parque Sabana. Architect José María Barrantes's conversion, opened in 1940, is the minimalist backdrop to a small but absorbing collection of 19th- and 20th-century art and sculpture by national and international artists. Limited by space, the most representative collection of Costa Rican contemporary art is exhibited chronologically and thematically. Perhaps the

An exhibition of jade tools at the Museum of Jade

MUSEO DEL JADE

The city's most absorbing museum houses the largest collection of jade in the Americas and provides a cultural insight into this precious stone.

BASICS	RATINGS		
🗺 61 D2 • 11th floor of INS building, Avenida 7, Calle 9–11 ☎ 506 287 6034 ◷ Mon–Fri 8.30–3.30, Sat 9–1 💲 US$2 www.ins-cr.com			
	Cultural interest	● ● ● ●	
	Good for kids	● ● ●	
	Historical interest	● ● ●	

North of Parque España is the Instituto Nacional de Seguros (INS) which houses the Fidel Tristan Jade Museum on the ground floor. In addition to the stunning collection of jade carvings with hundreds of beautifully worked pieces, there are displays of pre-Columbian art, pottery and sculpture. All of the museum's jade was recovered from archaeological digs in Costa Rica and sheds light onto the different indigenous cultures. A significant part of the exhibition derives from the private collection of archaeologist Carlos Balser, who came to Costa Rica in 1921.

For the Maya and Aztec cultures, jade was more important than gold and was believed to have medicinal powers. Beyond its beauty and its intrinsic value for those who traded it, the jade collection reveals the increased social stratification in the period between 100BC and AD700. Many of the pieces would have been worn by chiefs or shamans as status symbols. Most of the jade in the collection was recovered from the northwest province of Guanacaste. Outcrops of jade are not known in the region, suggesting that either they were exhausted in prehistoric times or that raw jade was imported to the Chorotega area, perhaps from the Montagua Valley in Guatemala (the only site in the hemisphere where jade is now found), to be distributed to craftsmen.

Considered among the finest jade carvings of the ancient Americas, there are many examples of polished axe forms, revealing shamans disguised as zoomorphic deities, including eagles, jaguars, crocodiles, ocelots and even the resplendent quetzal. The pottery and sculptures displayed include *metates* (tripods for grinding corn) and ceramic tables. The final room, often referred to as the Sala Exotica, contains many examples of fertility goddesses, believed to have religious significance.

Don't miss "La Familia," a sculpture outside the entrance by renowned Costa Rican artist Francisco Zúñiga, is an elegant contrast to the institutional INS building.

Cannon stationed outside the National Museum, a fortress which was a soldiers' barracks during the Civil War of 1948

Gold star: the Gold Museum has 1600 items in its collection

most compelling work in the museum, and reason enough for visiting, is the Salón Dorado, on the upper level. In 1940, French sculptor, Louis Férron, created an epic bronze-painted stucco mural relief that depicts Costa Rica's history from the pre-Columbian period to the airport's inauguration. You'll find work by Francisco Zuñiga (1912–98, ▷ 40) in the splendid sculpture garden.

MUSEO DE FORMAS, ESPACIO Y SONIDOS

✚ 61 E2 • Avenida 3, Calle 21 ☎ 506 223 4173 ⏰ Mon–Fri 9–2 👤 US$1

One block east from Parque Nacional, the old Atlantic Railway station is now the Museum of Form, Space and Light. The station, constructed in 1907 and now a national monument, combines neoclassical and baroque architecture. It was the final stop on the San José to Limón line that linked the Central Valley to the Caribbean lowlands, and the site is more interesting for conjuring images of past glories than for the museum displays. The old coaches contain a photographic history of the railway and memorabilia. The museum has been designed for visitors with disabili-

Pre-Columbian art at the National Museum

ties to experience the exhibits via tactile and aural displays. In 2006 plans were announced to move the museum to an undetermined location.

MUSEO NACIONAL

✚ 61 D2 • Calle 17, Avenida Central 2 ☎ 506 257 1433 ⏰ Tue–Sat 8.30–4.30, Sun and holidays 9–4.30 👤 Adult US$4 www.museocostarica.go.cr

Some six blocks east of Plaza de la Cultura, the muscular Bellavista Fortress lines the eastern flank of Plaza de la Democracia. The bullet scars of battle from the 1948 civil war (▷ 39) are clearly visible. The converted barracks now house the National Museum. A mixed bag of displays looks at Indian life pre-colonization and the introduction of Catholicism in Costa Rica, with a few rooms given over to lifestyle in the colonial era and art. Highlights are the large collection of pre-Columbian stone spheres and metates, and a separate room exhibiting pre-Columbian gold. Downstairs, a small exhibition leads through the quarters and prison cells of the fortress explaining events leading up to the civil war. One block north of the National Museum, on Calle 17, Avenida Central 2, is the Palacio Nacional (Mon–Fri from 4pm) where the Legislative Assembly sits.

MUSEO DE ORO PRECOLOMBINO

✚ 61 D2 • Plaza de la Cultura ☎ 506 243 4202 ⏰ Daily 9.30–5 www.museosdelbancocentral.org

Buried like treasure below the Plaza de la Cultura, accessible through a gated entrance on the eastern side, is the Pre-Columbian Gold Museum. Delicate figurines of frogs, spiders and other creatures glisten in the museum. The displays

show the development of metallurgical techniques in the Diquís region of southwest Costa Rica, demonstrating a fine degree of craftsmanship. Gold work grew steadily in importance from around AD500, marking a move away from the north's Mayan influences that preferred jade, to the southern influences of Panama and Colombia, which gave greater importance to gold.

Within the same three-floor underground complex, the small Numismatic Museum displays a selection of notes, coins and bills reflecting Costa Rican history from the 16th century to the present day. An open area is used for temporary exhibitions. While you're here, you can pop into the ICT Tourist Office, which is in the same complex.

MUSEO DR. RAFAEL ANGEL CALDERÓN GUARDIA

✚ Off map • Avenida 11, Calle 25 ☎ 506 222 6392 ⏰ Mon–Sat 9–5 👤 US$0.50 www.mcjdr.co.cr

In Barrio Escalante, a 20-minute walk from central San José close to the Iglesia St. Terente, this museum is recommended for visitors who want to learn more about Costa Rica's political background. There are displays on the life of Rafael Angel Calderón Guardia, the reformist Partido Republican Nacional (PRN) president who laid the foundations for the Costa Rican welfare state in the 1940s. Early reforms proposed were unsuccessful but raised the suspicions of landowners, and stimulated thought in modernizing liberals who suggested that it was the institutions of government that needed to be changed, not just the policies. Set in the beautiful, old Calderón family mansion, the museum also has monthly art exhibitions.

Watch out for the uneven steps up to the park's bandstand

PARQUE CENTRAL

Imbued with a bubbling energy, Central Park may have little in the way of sights, but it reveals the vibrant mosaic of Costa Rican daily life.

BASICS	RATINGS	
⊞ 61 C3 • Calle 2–Calle Central, Avenida 2–4 🕐 24 hours 🚌 Buses from La Sabana run along Paseo Colón and stop alongside the park, 80 colones	Cultural interest	● ● ●
	People-watching	● ● ● ●
	Transport links	● ● ● ●

TIPS

● The area immediately west and south of the park is a seedy red-light district and should be avoided.
● Pickpockets are very common in Parque Central. Try to leave all valuables locked up in your hotel and be mindful of camera thieves.

At the heart of downtown San José, a couple of blocks west of the Plaza de la Cultura, bordered by Avenida 2 and Calle Central, Central Park provides plenty of people-watching opportunities. The park is noted for the grandiose bandstand in the middle; the eyesore was kindly donated by Nicaraguan dictator Anastacio Samoza. Add to this uneven steps and the serious need of some new paint, and there is very little to endear the monument to you. Although there is no street café, you can normally buy an ice cream. At weekends, Sundays in particular, this is a popular spot with locals who saunter through the temporary stalls and stop to admire the lifelike bronze figures.

Dominating the eastern side of the square is the slightly cramped Catedrál Metropolitana (tel 506 221 3826), visited by the now deceased Pope John Paul II in 1983 on his first visit to Central America. The original structure was destroyed by a powerful earthquake, and the 19th-century replacement has been renovated. Inside the cathedral there are eye-catching, stained-glass windows and the Capilla de Santíssimo Sacramento is adorned with flowers. Gone are the sooty candles, replaced instead with a neat line of electric ones—25 centavos will light your bulb for a few minutes, 50 centavos and you can brighten two.

North of the plaza on Avenida 2 is the Teatro Melico Salazar, Costa Rica's most important theater after the Teatro Nacional. Performances and shows at the Melico have a broad appeal, ranging from pop and jazz concerts through to ballet and orchestral works.

A rock concert being held in the Plaza de la Democracía

PARQUE SABANA

⊞ 60 A2 • Paseo Colón and Highway 1 🕐 24 hours 🚌 Buses marked Sabana Estadio or Sabana Cementerio run from Parque Central along Paseo Colón to the park, 80 colones

West of downtown, Avenida Central becomes six-lane Paseo Colón. At the western end of Paseo Colón, Parque Sabana was the city's airport until the middle of the 20th century. The transformation has created a vast park 30 minutes' walk from central San José. On the western side is the National Stadium, where the national soccer team plays in front of crowds of 20,000, a running track, a sports complex and a lake. Inside the park, there is the Museum of Costa Rican Art (▷ 64). La Salle Natural History Museum (Mon–Sat 8–4.30, Sun 9–5), southwest of the park, contains stuffed animals to help you identify the different species that you see wild in the national parks.

PLAZA DE LA DEMOCRACÍA

⊞ 61 D2 • Avenida Central, Calle 13–15 🕐 24 hours ❓ At the middle of town, head east, down Avenida Central. A taxi from Parque Central costs US$1

Plaza de la Democracía is dominated by the Bellavista Fortress, now the National Museum (▷ 65), which was created in 1989 to celebrate the centenary of Costa Rican democracy. A bronze statue of José Figueres stands in the quiet plaza. Along the western side of the square is a small craft market (daily 8–6). To the park's southwest, Museo Para La Paz (tel 506 223 4664; Mon–Fri 8–4.30) is dedicated to peace and displays President Oscar Arias Sánchez's Nobel Peace Prize. Three blocks west and one block south is the Iglesia Soledad.

The Opera House is the backdrop to the Plaza de la Cultura

PLAZA DE LA CULTURA

Plaza de la Cultura is the heart of the city where the sublime Teatro Nacional stands, a graceful reminder of San José's opulent days. The Pre-Columbian Gold Museum is oneof the city's best museums.

On Avenida Central and Calle 3–5, Plaza de la Cultura is a vibrant hub of pedestrian activity, where clusters of locals and visitors, and a few hundred pigeons, gather around to watch the constant flow of people from all walks of life. There are plenty of street cafés, but the Hotel Gran Costa Rica offers the best vantage point for the urban anthropologist. In the drier months, the Plaza de la Cultura is the focus of evening performances of anything from classical orchestras to jazz, blues and cultural events, often with international artists. On the weekend, a small market, selling everything from textiles to herbal remedies, opens up in front of the Gran Hotel. On Tuesday and Saturday, late in the afternoon, a Peruvian panpipe band makes its appearance, in front of Costa Rica's ice cream über-parlour, Pops.

ALL THAT GLISTENS
One of San José's glittering highlights, the Museo de Oro Precolombino (▷ 65), lies beneath the square but is accessed through an entrance on the east side.

DRAMA
Back at ground level, on the southern side of the plaza is the neoclassical Teatro Nacional (National Theater), one of the most impressive buildings in the city, and a source of considerable pride (tel 506 221 9417; Mon–Sat 10–5; US$3). It was funded by a coffee tax in the late 19th century when the country's social elite realized the city was lacking a theater suitable for world-class performances; opera star Adelina Patti evidently omitted the Costa Rica leg of her tour as there was not a venue she deemed sufficiently glorious.

Construction of this national treasure called on the skills of European artisans, including Belgian architects and Italian artists. The colonnades of the exterior are complemented by a lavish interior with a balance of extravagance and detail in the mahogany furniture, crystal chandeliers, gold-leaf murals and paintings, including the acclaimed image of Marielitos smiling out of the dockside scene *Alegoría a Las Exportaciones*, referring to the coffee exporters. The carrara marble staircase is adorned with Costa Rica's most renowned painting, *Una Alegoria* by Italian artist Aleardo Villa, which depicts the coffee harvest. The painting is reproduced on the back of the 5,000 colones bank note. The theater opened with a production of *Faust* in 1897. Check the website for the monthly program.

An exhibit at the Pre-Columbian Gold Museum

RATINGS	
Cultural interest	●●●○
Historical interest	●●●○
People-watching	●●●●○

BASICS
✚ 61 D2 • Calle 3–5, Avenida Central

TIPS
● San José has little in the way of geography to help you get your bearings. Running along the northern flank of Plaza de la Cultura, Avenida Central is a useful navigator, forming a neat horizontal line through the city map.
● A coffee stop in the Café del Teatro (▷ 182) grants access to the theater's toilet, providing a sneak view of the glorious interior of the Teatro Nacional.
● Many museums and attractions are closed on Sundays or Mondays, including the Pre-Columbian Gold Museum and National Theater, so plan accordingly.

TEATRO NACIONAL
✉ Avenida 2, Calle 3 ☎ 506 221 1329
🕐 Mon–Sat 10–5 💲 US$3
www.teatronacional.go.cr

CENTRAL HIGHLANDS

Blessed with one of the balmiest climates in the world, the Central Highlands are the cultural, agricultural and civic hub of the nation. Most of Costa Rica's major towns are here and dense traffic can be a problem. But each of the region's highlights, from coffee plantations to volcanoes, can be explored in a day.

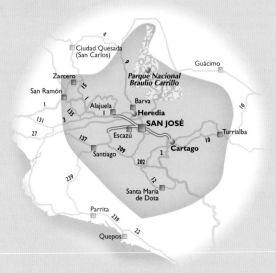

MAJOR SIGHTS

The exterior of Alajuela's 19th-century cathedral

ALAJUELA

✚ 239 H6 🚌 Frequent, from San José

The capital of Alajuela province, this market town, 2km (1.25 miles) from the airport, is a more relaxing base than San José for exploring the Central Valley. Small enough to walk around, the town focuses on the Central Plaza, shaded by huge mango trees. The domed cathedral, damaged by an earthquake in 1990, is one of the 19th-century buildings on the square. A more interesting church is the baroque-style La Agonía, five blocks east of the plaza. National hero Juan Santamaría was born in Alajuela and saved the country in the battle of 1856 (▷ 39). One block north of the plaza, at Avenida 3, Calle 2, is the Museo Histórico Juan Santamaría (Tue–Sun 10–5.30), which describes the war.

CAFÉ BRITT COFFEE PLANTATION TOUR

✚ 239 J6 ☎ 506 260 2748 🎫 Adult US$20, child (under 12) US$15; with transport US$27 🚌 From pick-up points in San José. Public buses leave from Parque La Merced to Heredia, every 10 min; short taxi ride from Heredia, US$2.50, or 40-min walk 🕐 Dec 15–Apr 30, 3-hour tours run at 9, and 3; May 1–Dec 14 at 9 only 🚗 Take the Barva road from Heredia; at first stop sign turn left, right, then left www.coffeetour.com

As one of the largest coffee processors in the country, Café Britt offers tours of the whole coffee-making process. Professional actors guide you through every stage of the process and the result is informative and enjoyable. The tour has been so successful that Café Britt combine it with other Central Valley activities. For the true caffeine addict there is a Coffee Lover's Tour with visits to the coffee mill (Adult US$45, child US$40).

Las Ruinas: earthquakes repeatedly destroyed Cartago's church

CARTAGO

Cartago, dominated by Volcán Irazú, is the provincial capital and gateway to the Central Valley's southeast corner.

BASICS
✚ 239 J6 ☎ 506 556 0073 🚌 Buses leave San José from Calle 5 and Avenida 18–20 every 10 min 🚗 From Avenida 2 in San José head east and follow the signs. There's a small toll on Highway 2

RATINGS	
Cultural interest	●●○
Historical significance	●●●
Walkability	●●●

Once the ruling quarter of Costa Rica, Cartago's dominant position was frequently tested and finally faltered in 1823 when San José acquired the capital seat after a series of minor civil scuffles. Since then, nature has challenged the city with many tremors and two devastating earthquakes, first in 1841 and again in 1910, which finally finished off the architectural heritage of the town. Today, the town bustles with the energy of a local market and transport hub (it is just over 20km/12 miles from San José,) and has little to detain the visitor beyond the Basílica de Nuestra Señora de Los Angeles, one of the finest churches in the country, 1km (0.6 miles) to the east of the central park. It holds the diminutive La Negrita, an Indian image of the Virgin Mary less than 15cm (6in) high, which draws pilgrims from throughout the country and from all over Central America because she is believed to have great healing powers. Having arrived at the Basílica, pilgrims take to their knees, inching their way down the aisle towards La Negrita. It's easy to overlook the finery of the Basílica itself. Destroyed by an earthquake in 1926, it was rebuilt in Byzantine style. The interior is ornately decorated with gold leaf and fine carvings and always has fresh flowers. To the side of the church, pilgrims fill La Negrita-shaped plastic containers and soda bottles with holy water from a spring. Pilgrimages to the Basilica take place throughout the year, but August 2 is the most important date in the pilgrim's calendar.

Cartago's other attraction, La Parroquia, locally known as Las Ruinas, was the city's first parish church, founded in 1575. Frequent tremors meant the church had to be reconstructed several times. Almost completely destroyed in 1841, it was rebuilt only to be destroyed again in 1910, in an earthquake estimated to measure around 6.4 on the Richter scale. What stands now is what remained then. A small ornamental garden fills the space within, but it is closed for much of the time. In front of the ruins, the central park is a large expanse of pavement, but despite the blandness, it makes for good people-watching.

Oxcart drivers turn up for the Día del Boyero festival in Escazú

THE SIGHTS

ESCAZÚ

239 J6 🚌 Buses leave San José from Calle 16, Avenida Central every 10 min 🚗 From San José, take the main highway west for 10 min, until turn-off signs on the right, then continue driving to the La Cruce intersection

Just outside the city limits to the west of San José, the fashionable suburb of Escazú has little in the way of sights, but bags of charm. Many expatriates living in Costa Rica don't spend a night in the capital, preferring to stay in one of Escazú's characterful hotels. Each of the three smaller towns that make up Escazú—San Rafael, San Miguel and San Antonio further up the hill—has a church. Up in San Antonio de Escazú, adobe houses around the central plaza create the effect of a village. Facing the square, the modest church of San Antonio de Escazú has a beautiful setting overlooking the valley of San José. **Don't miss** El Día del Boyero (Day of the Oxcart Driver) takes place in March (▷ 143).

LA GUÁCIMA BUTTERFLY FARM

238 H6 • PO Box 2132-4050, La Guácima, Alajuela ☎ 506 438 0400 🕐 Daily 8.30–5 💵 Adult US$15, child (5–12) US$7, under 5 free 🚌 The farm offers direct bus services daily from the main hotels in San José at 7.20, 10 and 2, US$25 including tour 🕐 Two-hour tours at 8.30, 11, 1, and 3 www.butterflyfarm.co.cr

One of the most popular day trips from San José is a visit to La Guácima Butterfly Farm, the world's second largest exporter of butterflies. Set up in 1984 by Joris Brinckerhoff, a former Peace Corps volunteer, the Butterfly Farm was opened to the public in 1990 and gives a fascinating insight into the life cycle of the butterfly. After a video explains the life cycle, the tour proceeds

Built to last: the resilient Basílica de la Inmaculada Concepción

HEREDIA

On the lower slopes of Volcán Barva, 11km (7 miles) north of San José, is Heredia, whose history is entwined with that of coffee cultivation in the Central Highlands.

BASICS	RATINGS		
239 J6 🚌 From San José every 10 min from Avenida 2, Calle 12–14 (La Merced Church), Avenida 2, Calle 10–12	Bars and nightlife	● ● ●
	Cultural interest	● ● ●
	Walkability	● ● ● ●

TIPS
● A taxi to Heredia from San José is about 4,000 colones (US$8); from the airport, expect to pay US$10–15. ● The town offers the best access to Volcán Barva , the main goal of trekkers in Parque Nacional Braulio Carrillo ▷ 72–74.

Founded in 1706, the town fought for dominance of the country alongside Cartago against Alajuela and the eventually victorious San José at the time of independence. Today, though, the quiet town is in danger of losing its position as the fourth city of the republic to more vibrant growth areas such as Liberia or Turrialba. However, Heredians don't seem to be too concerned—traces of colonial heritage and the youthful energy of the Universidad Nacional (National University) give the town a busy grace. This "City of Flowers" has a quiet charm.

The sights of Heredia can be seen from one spot through judicious positioning; in the northeastern corner of the central plaza, face north. Over your right shoulder is the Basílica de la Inmaculada Concepción, with a short squat design that has helped the structure survive several earthquakes since completion in 1797. External weathering has taken its toll, but the inside is a complete contrast, starkly crisp and bright white. Looking north is El Fortín, a single turret complete with gun slots overlooking a small park. Unfortunately the tower is closed to the public. On the northern side of the plaza is the Casa de la Cultura (tel 506 261 4485), a beautifully restored colonial house that was once the residence of President Alfredo González Flores (president 1914–17). Today, this fine example of period architecture houses exhibitions and concerts. Keep an eye out for events or just turn up and see what's going on.

Barva, 2km (1.5 miles) north of Heredia, is a lovely colonial village with a fine church and many historic red-tile-roofed houses. President González Flores's former home is today the Museo de Cultura Popular (Mon–Fri 8–4, Sat, Sun 10–4), furnished with period pieces.

A Cheliorchis Ampliata orchid at Lankester Botanical Gardens

Watch butterflies hatch at La Guácima Butterfly Farm

The ruins at the heart of the Guayabo National Monument

to the export office to see where the pupae are packed. Then guides lead you to tropical gardens, where they point out some of the 120 native species. The climax of the 90-minute tour is the caterpillar room.

After visiting the laboratories you can wander through the gardens at a more leisurely pace. Visiting in the morning, especially during the green season, is recommended as the insects take shelter when it is raining. Early morning tours can watch butterflies emerging from chrysalises.

INBIO PARQUE

✚ 239 J6 ☎ 506 507 8107 ⏰ Tue–Sun 8–6 💷 Adult US$15, child (5–12) US$8, under 5 free 🍴 🛍 🏫 🚌 North and west of the Shell gas station in Santo Domingo. Pick-up from hotels in San José possible www.inbio.ac.cr/inbioparque

South of Heredia, 15 minutes from San José on the road to Santo Domingo, is INBio Parque, a private educational establishment that explains Costa Rica's biological diversity and its national parks. Excellent tours begin with an audiovisual presentation, before you are taken through four Costa Rican ecosystems. You can experience the Central Highland forest, dry forest, humid forest and wetland. In addition to 51 bird species, there are 538 native plant species, as well as mammals and reptiles. Along the well-marked trails, you can see many species, which may remain elusive during visits to the national parks: white-tailed deer, three-toed sloths, Hoffman's woodpeckers and many others. Interactive exhibits provide insights into poison-dart frogs, tarantulas, ants, orchids and bromeliads. Recent additions to INBio include a butterfly garden and a lagoon with underwater viewing gallery, plus a traditional farm.

JARDÍN BOTÁNICO LANKESTER

✚ 239 K6 ☎ 506 552 3247 ⏰ Daily 8.30–4.30 💷 Adult US$5, child US$0.50 🚌 From Cartago take a bus towards Paraíso, ask to get off at the entrance to "Jardín Botánico Lankester" and from there walk south for 500m (545 yards), turning right at the sign ❓ Taxi from Cartago around US$3

Some 5km (3 miles) east of Cartago on the road to Paraíso, Lankester Botanical Garden, an overgrown hobby founded by the British naturalist Charles H. Lankester in the 1950s, has grown to be an internationally renowned collection of epiphytic flora, in particular the orchids, of Costa Rica. The gardens have around 800 species of national and exotic orchids laid out in the 10.7ha (26.5 acres) of tranquil gardens. These flowers reach peak blooming from February to May.

Besides the orchids, the gardens have bromeliads, ferns and cacti, as well as heliconia, palm and bamboo. More than 100 species of birds visit the gardens. It's a calming place, and respectful noise levels are requested. Short courses cover the care and cultivation of orchids, plant recognition and nature photography. Tour operators in San José offer tours to the gardens, normally as part of a trip to Volcán Irazú (▷ 76), costing from US$55.

LOS ANGELES CLOUD FOREST RESERVE

✚ 233 G5 ☎ 506 461 0300 ⏰ Daily 8–4 💷 US$12 or $24 with guide 🚌 Buses every 30 min from San José, Avenida 12, Calle 16, and frequent buses from Alajuela 🚗 Villablanca Cloudforest Hotel can arrange tours 🚌 From San Ramón, follow the road to La Fortuna until the town of Los Angeles Norte, follow signs for Villablanca Cloudforest Hotel www.villablanca-costarica.com

The Los Angeles Cloud Forest Reserve lies 20km (12 miles) north of San Ramón. A privately owned reserve of 800ha (1,976 acres), it is owned by the former President of Costa Rica, Rodrigo Carazo. The diversity of plants and animals here is astounding—equal to that of Monteverde, without the crowds and bone-shaking journey. At the entrance, the Villablanca Lodge provides the ideal base for exploring the park and offers various activities in the reserve, including a canopy tour. There are a couple of short trails, with a longer one, requiring about eight hours and an overnight stop at the lodge. One-day visits from San José can be arranged directly or by tour operators in San José.

MONUMENTO NACIONAL GUAYABO

✚ 239 K6 ☎ Information office 506 559 1220 ⏰ Daily 8–4 💷 US$4 🚌 Buses from Turrialba 🍴 ❓ Taxi from Turrialba about US$20 one-way

Some 18km (11 miles) from Turrialba lies Costa Rica's top archaeological site, the Indian ceremonial complex of Guayabo National Monument. Excavation at the site only began in 1968, though it was discovered at the end of the 19th century by Anastasio Alfaro. It remains underfunded and rarely visited.

Over 3,000 years old, the site was occupied from 1000BC to 1400, flourishing around AD800, the period when many of the stone structures were constructed. Petroglyphs have been etched on to many of the stones, their meaning undeciphered. Centuries-old aqueducts still carry water to the reservoirs. Today only a fraction of the protected area has been excavated, although Guayabo does not compare to the great ruins of Guatemala and Mexico.

THE SIGHTS

Parque Nacional Braulio Carrillo

Vast, wild and majestic, Parque Nacional Braulio Carrillo is a world of plummeting waterfalls and abundant wildlife. Trail walks and the Rainforest Aerial Tram provide closer encounters.

Cloud forest foliage has to cope with chilly, windy conditions

A white-tailed deer and its young

The best way to see life in the trees is to take a canopy tour

RATINGS	
Adventure activities	●●●○
Photo stops	●●●○
Wildlife spotting	●●●○

BASICS

✚ 233 J5 • Zurquí entrance station
☎ 506 233 4533
🕐 Daily 8–3.30
💵 US$6
🚌 Buses heading east from the Gran Terminal de Caribe in San José pass the park entrance (Quebrada González sector)
🚗 Take Highway 32 San José–Guápiles heading northeast. Toll booth US$0.20. A taxi from San José will cost about US$30

Mind your step: This boa is harmless but look out for snakes

SEEING PARQUE NACIONAL BRAULIO CARRILLO

Only 20km (12 miles) from San José, Braulio Carrillo National Park protects some of the country's most rugged landscapes. Steep-sided gorges, eroded by rivers, lie concealed in forested valleys laced with drifting clouds, which rise to the volcanic peaks of Barva (2,906m/9,532ft) and Cacho Negro (2,150m/7,052ft) where they deposit annual rainfall of around 4,500mm (177in). The result is some dramatic waterfalls, most of which are hardly ever seen by human eyes. The park is divided between the Quebrada González Sector and the Barva Volcano Sector. The main entrance is about 1km (0.6 miles) beyond the Zurquí tunnel, about 20km (13 miles) northeast of San José. You can walk the trails on your own, but a guided walk is best as the guides will point out far more than you will see by yourself. Spend a whole day in the park if you can.

The San José–Guápiles–Limón Highway travels through the park, so you still get a good impression of the topography as you travel to the Caribbean. Despite its proximity to San José, groups entering the park do get lost, so go prepared.

HIGHLIGHTS

TRAILS

Three trails lead out from the rangers' station at Quebrada González. Las Palmas is a 1.6km (1-mile) trail taking about 1.5 hours, and provides excellent birdwatching. El Ceibo is even shorter, taking just an hour and leading to some ceibo trees. The Botarrama Trail, an extension of El Ceibo, leads to the Río Sucio and gets deeper into the rainforest; it stretches for 3km (2 miles) and takes about two hours. A list of animals to look out for including, monkeys, toucans, peccaries, tarantulas and snakes, makes for an interesting read before and after your trek; it's available from the rangers' station. Other trails begin at the Barva ranger station (tel 506 261 269) and wind through cloud forest inhabited by quetzals and tapirs.

FLORA AND FAUNA

Estimates suggest that more than 90 percent of the park is primary forest and contains some 6,000 species of plants. While the

higher altitudes struggle to support life, profuse humid rainforest dominates, reaching its greatest diversity at the lower altitudes. More than 500 species of birds have been logged, including quetzals in the higher altitudes, toucans, king vultures and the national bird—the sooty robin. Mammals include three species of monkey, as well as tapirs, pacas, jaguars, pumas and ocelots. To complete the list, reptiles include two of the deadliest snakes in the world, the fer-de-lance and the bushmaster. The best chance of seeing mammals is by hiking one of the short trails that lead through the 450ha (1,112 acres) of the private reserve used for research.

RAINFOREST AERIAL TRAM

Reservations office behind the Aurola Holiday Inn in San José, or 150m (160 yards) west of INS building ☎ 506 257 5961 🕐 Daily 6.30–4 (most tours arrive after 9) 🎫 Park entrance and tram ride: adult US$49.50, child (under 11) US$24.75 🚌 Take any bus heading towards Guápiles from Gran Caribe bus terminal in San José 🚐 Package tour from San José, including pick-up from most hotels, tram fees, meal and hike: adult US$78.50, child (under 11) US$53.75 🍽 Daily 7–6 🏧 🅿 www.rainforesttram.com

Moving silently through the forest at canopy level is the best way of seeing the complexity of the rainforest. Fortunately, the unique attraction of the Rainforest Aerial Tram, the brainchild of Dr. Donald Perry and John Williams, is that it gives you the chance to do pre-cisely that. Open-air cable cars, with protection from the sun and rain, glide slowly through the forest rising from ground level to drift below, in and above the canopy for a close-up view of life above the forest floor. Each car has a bilingual guide who will point out interest-ing fauna. As with all good guides, their practised eyes will spot birds and animals long before the casual observer does, and you will see the sheer density of plant life and insects found in the upper sec-tions of the rainforest. At the half-way point, a short walk leads to a vista stretching to the Caribbean lowlands, with views as far as Tortuguero on a clear day. The return journey flies just above the canopy, before coming back to land—an unforgettable experience. In addition to being a fascinating ride, the story of the creation of a successful green tourism experience on such a large scale is equally interesting.

Jungle-clad hills are home to chestnut-mandibled toucans

TIPS

● Highway 32 is one of Costa Rica's busiest roads, but driv-ing conditions are dangerous and extreme caution is required.
● The weather can change dramatically. Take maps, com-pass, food and water for all trekking in the park.
● Another option for hikers is Monte de la Cruz Reserve (daily 8–4), on the southern slopes of Volcán Barva, with cloud forest that's good for spotting quetzals.

White-crowned parrots

A green tropical parrot

VOLCÁN BARVA

Hiking to the summit of Barva Volcano (2,906m/9,532ft) is one of the best ways to see some of the less explored parts of Parque Nacional Braulio Carrillo. The hike to the top passes through the chilly and moist climate of the cloud forest, with moss-covered trees heavily laden with epiphytes and bromeliads. On a clear day in the dry season, the scenery is unforgettable and the climate exhilarating. In the pine forests on the upper slopes, lodges, hotels and mountain resorts are hidden away. The area is popular with birdwatchers who flock here to catch a glimpse of quetzals, king vultures and three-wattled bell birds, as well as countless hummingbirds. Monkeys, reptiles and poison-arrow frogs can also be seen. Trails lead to three water-filled craters. From the summit, magnificent views stretch across the Central Valley over densely forested valleys shrouded in swirling mist.

Access to Barva requires hiking or use of a rugged four-wheel-drive vehicle. For the serious hiker there is a trail heading north from the top of Barva down to La Selva Biological Station near Puerto Viejo de Sarapiquí. The trip takes about four days, covers 65km (39 miles) and requires planning. Three daily buses travel to Porrosatí from San José de la Montaña and Heredia, from where a poorly marked trail leads to the summit and then out through the park headquarters. The 4km (2-mile) trek takes a little over one hour. A more common route leaves from the ranger station, 3km (2 miles) beyond Sacramento.

BACKGROUND

A great achievement in tropical conservation, Braulio Carrillo National Park extends from Volcán Barva down to the Caribbean lowlands abutting La Selva. It was created in 1978 to protect the region against damage caused by the construction of a new highway to the Caribbean in 1977. When plans were announced to build a highway to Limón, through prime, virgin rainforest, vocal campaigning by conservationists persuaded the government to declare the area a National Park. It was the republic's third president, Braulio Carrillo, who identified the need for a road to link the coffee-producing Central Valley with the Caribbean, to speed the transportation of beans which could reach Europe much more quickly from the Caribbean ports.

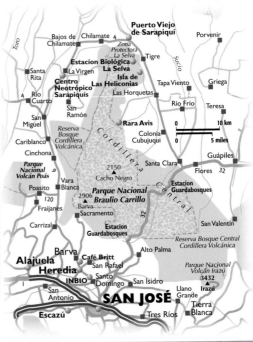

There are 500 bird species in Braulio Carrillo National Park

You have to arrive very early to beat the clouds at Volcán Poás, the most popular national park in Costa Rica

The oxcarts of Sarchí have hand-painted designs

PARQUE NACIONAL TAPANTÍ-MACIZO DE LA MUERTE

239 K7 ☎ 506 551 2970 ⏰ Daily 7–5 💲 US$6 🚌 Buses run as far as Río Paloma, from where it is a 9km (5-mile) walk 🚌 Follow signs to Orosí then take road to the park headquarters ℹ Small information center with trail maps and slide show 🎬

Approached from Orosí and just 30km (18 miles) from Cartago, Tapantí-Macizo de la Muerte National Park is packed with interest. It is one of the country's newest national parks and is also in one of the wettest parts of the country, reportedly receiving as much as 8,000mm (312in) of rain a year. Covering 58,000ha (143,260 acres), Tapantí-Macizo includes the former Tapantí National Park and much of the Río Macho Forest Reserve. The park incorporates a wide range of life zones, from lower montane wet forest to montane rainforest with altitudes rising from 1,220m (4,000ft) to more than 3,000m (9,840ft) at the border with Chirripó. The diverse altitudes and relative seclusion of the park have created an impressive species list. Tapir, pacas, racoons, and white-faced monkeys are some of more than 45 species of mammal in the area, which include the elusive jaguar and ocelot. The quetzal nests in late spring and can be found near the entrance on the western slopes. In total 260 bird species have been spotted. Frogs love the wet conditions.

Three trails lead off the principal road providing walks ranging from 30 minutes to two hours, but don't forget a raincoat. There are several waterfalls that are good for swimming and picnic spots. Tour operators in San José can arrange guided trips, and horseback riding to the park from Orosí is also an option (▷ 142).

PARQUE NACIONAL VOLCÁN POÁS

233 H5 ☎ 506 482 2165 ⏰ May–end Nov daily 8–3.30, Dec–end Apr Fri, Sat 9–3.30 💲 US$7 ℹ A good information center is the final stop for visitors, from where it's a short walk uphill to the look-out 🍴 🅿 ❓ Road access almost to the summit for visitors with disabilities and those unable to walk at this altitude

Only 37km (22 miles) north of Alajuela, Volcán Poás National Park is the most popular national park in the country. Standing at a lofty 2,708m (8,882ft), the park focuses on the vast crater of Poás Volcano, 1,320m (4,330ft) wide with sloping sides descending for 300m (984ft). Currently filled with a simmering turquoise lake, the crater dries out in more active periods, sprinkling the landscape with sulfur. The most notorious eruption in the 20th century blew an ash cloud skyward some 8km (5 miles). Poás erupted between 1952 and 1954, with more explosions in 1989, 1994 and 2006. Today, volcanologists believe the magma chamber is just 400–500m (1,300–1,640ft) below the lake. Whenever there is a risk to visitors, the park is closed.

Beyond the drama of the volcano, 79 bird species, including quetzals, reside in the park's dwarf cloud forest and a short trail of just over 1km (0.6 mile) leads to a second crater. Last entry to the trail is at 2.30 and free rambling around the park is not permitted for safety reasons.

Try to arrive early—clouds often hang low over the crater above 1,000m (3280ft) obstructing the view. But with strong winds throughout the year, gaps in the clouds often offer brief glimpses. The best time of year for good views is between December and April. On a clear, windless day, you can wear shorts and T-shirts, but when the clouds arrive, the

temperature plummets. Add a dousing of rain and you can get cold, so take a rain jacket.

SAN GERARDO DE DOTA

🚌 Regular daily buses from San José (Calle 16, Avenidas 1–3) to San Isidro will drop you at Km80, from where it's a 9km (5.5 mile) downhill hike to San Gerardo 🚌 Follow the Pan-American Hwy south from Cartago to Km80, then turn right

This small community is tucked into a lovely valley carved by the waters of the Río Savegre, and enjoys a springlike climate year-round. Mists sift through orchards and forests, adding to the surreal beauty, and quetzals are as numerous here as anywhere in Costa Rica. The Quetzal Education Research Center pursues research into the birds' ecology. Hiking trails lead into the cloud forest, which drips with epiphytes and mosses.

SARCHÍ

233 H5 🚌 Regular daily buses from San José's Coca-Cola Terminal take 1hr ❓ Taxis in Sarchí make quick journeys between the north and south towns if you want to look around before buying

The small craft village of Sarchí owes its fame to the painted *carretas* (oxcarts) produced locally. Originally distinctive to the area, they are now sold across the country. Sarchí is actually two towns—Sarchí Sur and Sarchí Norte—set among hills offering views across valleys. The heart of the town is to the north, where a tiered plaza leads to a wedding-cake church of lime green which glows at sunset.

The oxcarts and other wooden furniture, including rocking chairs, are mass-produced by hand in factories and *mueblarías* (furniture shops), and the town has done everything it can to relieve you of your cash: goods can be flat-packed and shipped home.

THE SIGHTS

Vegetation colonizes the harsh volcanic slopes of Volcán Irazú

Surreal topiary in front of Zarcero's church

Cetanos birds wait for release from the Zoo Ave rescue facility

THE SIGHTS

VOLCÁN IRAZÚ

🏳 239 K6 ☎ 506 200 5025 🕐 Daily 8–3.30 💲 US$7 🚌 One bus daily at 8am from Avenida 2, Calle 1–3, from Gran Hotel Costa Rica 🅿 US$2.50 🚐 Most tour operators in San José have day-trips to Irazú costing US$35 per person ❓ Taxi, US$35

Easily reached on a day-trip from San José, Irazú is the highest volcano in Costa Rica at 3,432m (11,257ft). A road reaches to the edge of the dramatic lagoon-filled craters, making this one of the busiest parks. Whether buffeted by icy winds, or basking in sunlight, the volcano is worth visiting for the stupendous views. Visit as early in the day as possible for the best chance of a clear view; even if the lower slopes are cloudy, it is possible that the summit is above the clouds.

This "mountain of quakes and thunder," has a lively history. The first documented eruption was recorded by Cartago's governor, Diego de la Haya Fernández, in 1723. Violent eruptions began in 1963, damaging the crater and showering San José with ash—a dramatic welcome to President John F. Kennedy who was visiting the city at the time. Fumaroles, small lava flows and tremors are proof that the mountain still quakes and thunders today.

Once at the top, there are pockets of fragile vegetation on the inhospitable, lunar landscape.

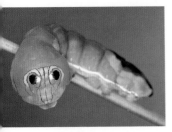
You might see a silkmoth caterpillar in Zarcero's gardens

The temperature range of -3°C to 17°C (27°F to 63°F) and the poor soil supports a hardy scrub with thick leaves and stunted growth to cope with the winds. Three of the five craters can be visited. The main crater is a cube, 1,050m (3,444ft) wide, 300m (984ft) deep, blown out of the earth. Playa Hermosa crater is a good birdwatching spot, where you may see the ubiquitous volcano junco bird. Otherwise, little survives in this hostile desert.

VOLCÁN TURRIALBA

🏳 234 K6 🚌 From Cartago to San Gerardo north of Turrialba, then walk to Finca la Central in the saddle between Irazú and Turrialba. Also from Turrialba to Santa Cruz and walk up to Finca la Central 🚐 Daytrips can be organized through tour operators in San José

Volcán Turrialba is the least visited and smallest of the Central Highland volcanoes to merit its own national park, which was established back in 1955. The lack of interest means there is no entrance fee—or at least no one to collect it, officially you get a permit in San José—and no services are provided. At 3,328m (10,916ft), Volcán Turrialba sits next to Volcán Irazú on the eastern flank of the Cordillera Central, and on a clear day can be seen from the San José–Limón road. Three craters show evidence of lava flows, but the last eruptions occurred between 1864 and 1865.

If you want to stay overnight you can camp. Alternatively, a good base is Volcán Turrialba Lodge (tel 505 273 4335), 2km (1.2 miles) from Finca la Central. Tour options include treks and horseback riding to the crater floor; Turrialba is the only volcano where this is possible.

ZARCERO

🏳 233 H5 🚌 Regular buses from San José Coca-Cola Terminal

At the north side of the Central Valley, Zarcero draws crowds to the bizarre Daliésque topiary that fills the town's square. These creations are the work of Zarcero's most famous son, Evangelista Blanco Breves. Given the job of maintaining the plaza in 1964, he set about the task with a few simple shrubs that have grown, been clipped, grown and clipped again. Breves has created animals, couples dancing, a helicopter and other works.

Zarcero has an exhilarating, mountain climate where dairy cattle fuel the local economy. A local specialty is *palmito*, a white, moist cheese like mozzarella. Fruit jams are another regional product for sale.

ZOO AVE

🏳 238 H6 ☎ 506 433 8989 🕐 Daily 9–5 💲 US$9 🚌 Bus from Alajuela to La Garita 🚗 Follow the signs to Zoo Ave from the Pan-American Highway heading west from Juan Santamaría airport ❓ Taxi from Alajuela around US$7 www.zooave.org

Owned and operated by the Nature Restoration Foundation, this government-recognized wildlife rescue facility is set in landscaped gardens. Zoo Ave educates visitors about Costa Rican wildlife through interactive exhibits and rehabilitation and release programs. Zoo Ave's breeding efforts are focused on endangered species such as the macaw and the squirrel monkey. Captive breeding programs have successfully introduced 28 birds as part of the Scarlet Macaw Restoration Program.

While visiting, you'll see more than 100 species of native and exotic birds including toucans, parrots, black swans, eagles and the resplendent quetzal, as well as all four types of monkey that live in Costa Rica, and other mammals and reptiles.

NORTHERN REGION

The region here is dominated by Arenal's volcano and the cloud forest of Monteverde. One stands fuming menacingly against the sky, the other is one of the world's best loved ecotourism destinations. Rafting, climbing and wildlife-watching are some of the activities to be experienced in the Northern Region.

MAJOR SIGHTS

Arenal

●

The perfect cone of Volcán Arenal is one of the world's most active volcanoes. This breathtaking spectacle crowns a region that abounds with natural wonders and exhilarating activities.

Hot tub time: Tabacón hot springs are volcanically heated

Saddle up! You can take horseback tours of Lake Arenal

Bats, snakes and spiders live in Venado's limestone caves

RATINGS	
Adventure and activities	●●●●
Pampering and relaxation	●●●●
Photo stops	●●●●●

MORE TO SEE

● For a completely natural hot spring experience follow the road for 1.5km (1 mile) to Quebrada Cedeña. It can be difficult to find as there are no signs, but it's completely free; look for local parked cars.

● On the north shore of Lake Arenal is the delightful Arenal Botanical and Butterfly Gardens (tel 506 694 4273; daily 9–4, closed Oct; US$8) with many flowers, birds and butterflies.

SEEING ARENAL

Rising from the western plains of the San Carlos valley, three hours by car from San José, Volcán Arenal stands symmetrical, clear and tall against the horizon, puffing fumes and exploding against a fine blue sky (if you are lucky) with the expansive Lake Arenal in the foreground. A steady supply of people has changed the once-sleepy backwater of La Fortuna, 6km (3.7 miles) away, to an occasionally lively focus of activity, providing a good base for excursions to the volcano and other activities. All trips to the volcano can be done independently or with a tour operator. While there are variations on a theme, most trips to the volcano leave in the late afternoon to get you to the best viewing spot for dusk. Several hotels on the shore of Lake Arenal providing memorable nighttime views of the hot plumes and red lava of Arenal. Friendly Fortuna provides time to relax and unwind with pools, waterfalls and luxury at the romantically kitsch Tabacón hot springs. Other activities in the area include visits to spectacular waterfalls, and tours of the area by foot, on horseback or by bicycle.

HIGHLIGHTS

PARQUE NACIONAL VOLCÁN ARENAL

Dominated by the conical peak of the volcano, Arenal Volcano National Park (tel 506 461 8499) covers 12,106ha (29,902 acres). Upgraded from a reserve to a national park in 1994, it protects the watershed that maintains water levels in Lake Arenal and sustains the volcano's micro climate.

A trip to see the lava flows and eruptions of Arenal Volcano is one of Costa Rica's most popular excursions. As darkness cloaks the region, the dust plumes that skirted down the bare slopes through the day reveal themselves to be glowing lava tumbling, crashing and smashing down the volcano slopes in a spray of natural fireworks. The sight is spectacular and the sound decidedly eerie. Arenal is a classic Stromboli-type stratovolcano, with a symmetrical cone formed by layers of volcanic material. It is the youngest of the stratovolcanoes in Costa Rica with no rock more than 2,900 years old. Research from the Arenal Observatory Lodge has produced a wealth of data, including the mind-boggling

notion that the magma chamber that feeds the eruptions is just 5km (3 miles) below the surface. You will be permitted to visit safe areas—the current spot used by groups is El Silencio, 2km (1.25 miles) west of Tabacón Resort—but heed warnings. After viewing the volcano, groups head down to one of the nearby thermal baths for a relaxing soak before returning to Fortuna at 9pm. Beyond the volcano the park has five interesting (and safe) trails starting at the park entrance. The walks take from 25 minutes to a couple of hours and provide the chance to see heliconias, birdlife and howler monkeys. Las Coladas trail involves a bit of scrambling over old lava flows, but provides good views of the lake and Volcán Chato. While trekking solo is permitted, hikes and treks can be arranged by tour operators in Fortuna. Opposite the park entrance is a camping area.

HOT SPRINGS

Hot baths in the area offer the chance for serious rest and relaxation. Some 4.5km (3 miles) north of town, the closest hot springs to Fortuna are Baldi Thermae (tel 506 479 9652, daily 10–10, US$10). It has a number of pools starting at a comfortable 37°C (98°F) rising to an egg-poaching 63°C (145°F). Some 12km (8 miles) from Fortuna, and much more fancy, is the Tabacón Resort (tel 506 519 1900; daily 7am–10pm; adult US$45, child under 9 US$25, under 4 free). The focus of the resort is a series of mineral pools at a variety of temperatures. While the geothermally heated waters are totally natural, the rest is pure kitsch (▷ 199).

VENADO CAVES

The small community of Venado, about an hour away, is home to the labyrinth of the Venado Caves (tel 506 478 9081). Formed during the Miocene period, 20 million years ago, the limestone was brought to the earth's surface by tectonic movements. Eight caverns can be visited, each eroded in the limestone by acidic waters. Linked by narrow passages, the caves' stalactites and stalagmites form Gaudí-esque shapes. There are dried-out river beds, waterfalls and, of course, bats. Tarantulas, snakes, crickets and frogs are also present. Dress accordingly and be prepared to get wet and dirty. Showers are available, so take a change of clothes. Not recommended for the claustrophobic.

Looking deceptively quiet, Volcán Arenal at dawn

BASICS

➕ 232 F4

🕐 Parque Nacional Volcán Arenal: daily 8–4; Venado Caves: daily 7.30–4

💲 Parque Nacional Arenal: US$6; Venado Caves: US$10

🚌 Daily to Fortuna via Ciudad Quesada from Terminal Atlántico Norte, San José (tel 506 255 4318), 3.5hr. Daily from Ciudad Quesada, 1hr. Daily to Venado, Guatuso from Ciudad Quesada

🚗 Trips to Arenal can be reserved through tour operators in Fortuna, cost US$25 if visiting Baldi Thermae, US$60 if going to Tabacón Resort. All-inclusive trips to the Venado Caves cost US$39–45 depending on hotel pick-up location

ℹ️ In Fortuna on the south side of the main square

🚍 From the south leave the Pan-American Highway near San Ramón; a good road leads north for 73km (47 miles). An alternative and longer route passes through Zarcero and Ciudad Quesada. Arriving from Tilarán to the west, a pot-holed road follows the north shore of Lake Arenal with views across the lake to the volcano. From Arenal to Venado, a dirt road leaves the north shore of the lake. Another route goes north from Tanque heading west close to Jicarito www.arenal.net

LAKE ARENAL

Ringed by lushly forested hills and under the gaze of Volcán Arenal on its eastern side, Lake Arenal provides a superb setting for watersports. In 1974, it was flooded to form a basin that now supplies the country with 75 percent of its electrical power. In addition to the shoreline hotels, and the hydroelectric power from the Tronadora dam, the wind that blows the length of the lake has created world-class boardsailing conditions with winds reaching 97kph (60mph). A mostly paved road twists around the northern shore of Lake Arenal, leading to Tilarán via Nuevo Arenal, making for a scenic drive. Boat trips are arranged with tour operators or by talking to local boatmen at the northern end of the dam. Fishing for rainbow bass (*guapote*) and *machaca* is possible during the year, with March to July being the best time for bass.

Man-made Lake Arenal, above and right, is a playground for windsurfers

FORTUNA

With a football pitch in the middle and a church to the west, sights in Fortuna are limited. Farther east, Arenal Mundo Aventura (tel 506 479 9762) has waterfall rappelling, zipline tours and other adventures. Heading south, Río Fortuna waterfall (US$6) plunges 70m (230ft) from lush forest to the pool below, creating a hazy mist. Wear good shoes: it is a steep and slippery path. Below the falls there are good swimming spots. You can walk or drive to the falls from town following the road for 1.7km (1 mile) before taking a 4km (2.5-mile) bumpy road through yucca and papaya plantations. Alternatively take a half-day horseback-riding tour (US$25).

BACKGROUND

Volcán Arenal was a sleeping giant until 1968 when a massive eruption devastated the western flank of the volcano, killing 78 people. That event reignited a pattern characterized by periods of explosive activity and lava flows followed by dormancy for hundreds of years. Since 1968, Arenal has been erupting almost continuously. The most recent major eruption in August 2000 caused the deaths of two people. As the lava flows increase, volcano viewing has been subject to a more cautious approach.

Lake Arenal was formed in 1974 to provide hydroelectric power for the country. The wall damming the River Arenal is at the eastern end of the lake near Fortuna, but the generating plant is at the western end at Tronadora close to Tilarán. East to west trade winds from the Caribbean are channeled through the narrow gap between the Cordillera de Tilarán to the south and Cordillera de Guanacaste to the north. As the winds rise, they dump 4,500mm (175in) of rain each year on Arenal Volcano National Park at the eastern end of the lake but when they reach the western limits of the lake, rainfall is down to 1,500mm (60in) annually. One final push over the western hills and the drained winds pass over Guanacaste with little moisture left in them, creating conditions ideal for the dry tropical forests of Santa Rosa National Park.

THE SIGHTS

TIPS

● If seeing the volcano is the main reason for your visit, the skies are most reliably clear between December and April. Otherwise take into account greater rain between August and November—the waterfall will be more impressive, but walking trails will be muddier.
● Take a flashlight, good shoes and rainproof attire for visiting the volcano, and swimming gear and towel for visiting the thermal springs.
● For the budget conscious, across the road from the Tabacón hot springs is a less expensive option at just US$6 (Mon–Fri 10–9.30, Sat–Sun 8am–9.30pm).
● If you have your own transport, Toad Hall (tel 506 692 8020), on the scenic paved road between Fortuna and Nuevo Arenal, is an excellent café for a meal and drink in a prime spot over the lake. It is also one of the best souvenir craft shops in the country.

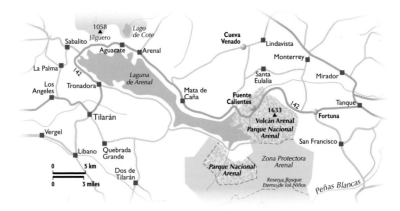

A breadfruit tree at the Centro Neotrópico Sarapiquís

Crossing a bridge at La Selva Biological Station

Spot flowers and butterflies at Isla de las Heliconias

THE SIGHTS

CENTRO NEOTRÓPICO SARAPIQUÍS

➕ 233 J4 • La Virgen de Sarapiquí, Heredia, PO Box 86-3069 ☎ 506 761 1004 🅿 US$19, or US$12 museum only 🚌 From San José to Puerto Viejo de Sarapiquí (▷ 83), pass La Virgen 🚌 85km (53 miles), a 90-min drive, from San José. Head west from Puerto Viejo de Sarapiquí toward San Miguel www.sarapiquis.org

The non-profit Centro Neotrópico Sarapiquís is more an ecological experience than a hotel, and has become a model for sustainable development. The complex emphasizes the theme of Man and Nature and includes a museum of contemporary indigenous cultures, botanical gardens, an archaeological park and the 350ha (865 acre) Tirimbina Biological Reserve. In addition to providing a setting for exploring the lowland Caribbean rainforest, the Centro aims to be a place to learn and be challenged physically and mentally. The museum uses state-of-the-art technology, including audiovisual and animated displays.

The Alma Alta archaeological park, set amid the Centro's orange grove, includes a reconstructed pre-Columbian 15th-century village and an eco-friendly hotel using solar energy. In 1999, after the construction of the Centro, pre-Columbian tombs were discovered and excavation work is continuing.

A macaw at the Centro Neotrópico Sarapiquís

CIUDAD QUESADA (SAN CARLOS)

➕ 233 G4 🚌 Regular buses to and from Atlántico Norte Terminal, San José. The terminal in San Carlos is 1km (0.6 miles) north of the plaza

Just 24km (15 miles) from Zarcero, Ciudad Quesada, also called San Carlos, is the transport hub for the northern lowlands. The town is of little interest to the visitor, but it is a useful junction between Fortuna, Los Chiles and Puerto Viejo de Sarapiquí.

By Costa Rican standards Ciudad Quesada is a large town, but it has a distinctly small-town feel. There is little need to move more than a block or two from the main plaza, which is densely packed with trees and palms. To the east is a cavernous church with an impressive sculpture of Christ hanging above the altar. East of town, Termales del Bosque (tel 506 460 4740, US$8) has a botanical garden, forest trails, mineral springs, and a zipline canopy tour (US$45).

ESTACIÓN BIOLÓGICA LA SELVA

➕ 233 J4 ☎ 506 766 6565 🕐 Daily 6–4 🅿 US$28, including guided walk; US$85 overnight 🚌 From San José to Puerto Viejo de Sarapiquí, at 6.45am and 12.15pm, to an intersection; walk the kilometer (half mile) to the entrance 📷 3.5-hour Experience La Selva tour leaves at 8 and 1.30 🚌 The Station is 3km (2 miles) south of Puerto Viejo de Sarapiquí. Watch carefully for the sign www.ots.ac.cr

Some 3km (2 miles) south of Puerto Viejo de Sarapiquí, adjoining Braulio Carrillo National Park at its northernmost boundary, La Selva Biological Station is a renowned research station with astonishing species diversity. Over half of the 875 bird species found in Costa Rica have been sighted on the 1,513ha (3,737 acres) of old growth and tropical wet forests. Toucans, parrots, trogons, monkeys, agoutis, peccaries and coatis are regularly seen. There's even a warning to look out for the seven venomous snakes out of the 56 species found at the station.

Owned by the Organization for Tropical Studies, the facility welcomes guests, usually as part of a day-trip from San José or Puerto Viejo de Sarapiquí. Half-day and three-day birdwatching courses provide a great introduction to the subject.

ISLA DE LAS HELICONIAS

➕ 234 J4 • Apd 48-3069 ☎ 506 397 3948 🕐 Daily 8–5; call ahead to check 🅿 US$12 🚌 From Puerto Viejo de Sarapiquí (▷ 83) to Montero 🚌 Montero is 8km (5 miles) south of Puerto Viejo de Sarapiquí. Take the right turn 1km (0.6 miles) south of Río Isla Grande bridge and the Isla Grande petrol station. A right turn, followed by another right turn leads down a grassy track that should be signposted www.heliconiaisland.com

Heliconias Island is a fantastic collection of 80 types of heliconia from across the world, which flower all year round. You can also find other botanical species, including a type of ornamental banana and graceful palm trees. Throughout the gardens, bamboo, ferns, orchids and bromeliads grow with untamed abandon, and birdlife is abundant, with long-tailed hermit hummingbirds and orange-chinned parakeets making an appearance. The eye-catching blue morpho butterfly can also be seen. Rarely will you see such variety and diversity in so small an area. Tim Ryan, the owner, is a knowledgeable, self-taught botanist. Camping on the 2ha (5-acre) island is allowed and the price includes entrance.

Don't fall in: a local resident of the River Sarapiquí

Wood storks at Caño Negro National Wildlife Reserve, one of the last remaining wetlands in Central America

MONTEVERDE

See pages 84–89.

PUERTO VIEJO DE SARAPIQUÍ

⊞ 233 J4 🚌 Almost hourly from San José Gran Terminal del Caribe (tel 506 257 6854), 3.5hr 🚤 Launch to Tortuguero is US$300–350 for 1 to 10 people, 5hr. Daily launch service to Trinidad on the San Juan River, leaving at 12.30, returning the next day at 10am 🚗 Take the San José–Limón Highway, and after passing through the Braulio Carrillo National Park, take Highway 4 north at Rancho Robertos for 33km (20 miles). A longer, scenic route heads north to Heredia and Vara Blanca, then east via La Virgen to Puerto Viejo

It is difficult to believe that Puerto Viejo de Sarapiquí, 97km (60 miles) north of San José, was once a flourishing port. Today's laid-back community is a couple of roads linking the riverside dock with the bus station and not much of interest in between. But the road west to La Virgen and the road south to the highway have plenty of lodges, reserves and river-rafting operations.

A few kilometers west towards La Virgen, set in 500ha (1,235 acres) of lowland rainforest, the Selva Verde Lodge (tel 506 766 6800) is more accessible than other lodges in the region. It's a good spot for birding and river trips. You can take walks along the multitude of trails—focusing on botany, birding or butterflies—with a resident naturalist. The Río Sarapiquí, which bisects the property, is here a scenic boat journey or, upstream, an adrenalin-pumping challenge. The lodge arranges guided hikes (US$15), boat tours (US$20) and horseback riding (US$25). Next door, the Sarapiquí Conservation Learning Center (tel 506 766 6482) works to ensure that the local community benefits from the rainforest's secrets.

RARA AVIS

⊞ 233 J4 ☎ 506 764 1111 📷 From US$55 inclusive package 🚌 The 6.30am from San José reaches the hut at Las Horquetas in time to catch the tractor that leaves at 9.30am for the 3hr journey to Rara Avis. Tractors leave Rara Avis at 2pm to catch the bus back to San José 🚗 From San José, take the Guápiles–Limón Highway through Braulio Carillo National Park. Follow signs for Puerto Viejo de Sarapiquí. Las Horquetas is 16km (10 miles) farther on www.rara-avis.com

Reached through Las Horquetas, around 16km (10 miles) north of the San José–Limón road, Rara Avis is a private reserve (an overnight stay is required owing to transport logistics) perched on the eastern flanks of Braulio Carillo National Park at an altitude of 700m (2,296ft). The reserve's faunal diversity is staggering. More than 360 birds have been recorded, including the green macaw. You will probably see monkeys, coatis and anteaters. The really lucky may spot tapirs and jaguar. At the reserve, reached by a bone-shaking 15km (9-mile) journey in a tractor-pulled cart, a network of trails leads through primary forest. Some are rough and muddy, so go prepared. You can hike them with a guide or enjoy the solitude and silence on your own. Booking accommodation at the reserve in advance is essential especially in the dry season.

REFUGIO NACIONAL DE VIDA SILVESTRE CAÑO NEGRO

⊞ 232 F2 ☎ 560 471 1309 🕐 Daily 8–4 💲 US$6 🚌 2 daily from San José Terminal Atlántico Norte to Los Chiles 🚗 Take the road north through Santa Rosa towards Los Chiles, then follow the signposted turnoff to Caño Negro, several kilometers (a couple of miles) before Los Chiles. Four-wheel-drive vehicle is required

Close to the Nicaraguan border, the Caño Negro National Wildlife Reserve covers 10,171ha (25,122 acres). The reserve draws birds and wildlife to one of Central America's most important wetlands. At its heart is Lake Caño Negro, covering 800ha (1,976 acres) but no more than 3m (10ft) deep, which evaporates at the end of the dry season in May. Swamps, forest and marshes attract a wide range of migratory birds. The reserve is home to Costa Rica's largest colony of Neotropical cormorants and is the country's last refuge for the Nicaraguan grackle. The roseate spoonbill with its spatulate bill is a common sight, and you may glimpse the huge jabirú standing 1.5m (5ft) tall—Central America's largest bird and critically endangered. Floating safaris in canoes leave Los Chiles and follow the Río Frío through primary forest. You may see howler, spider and white-faced monkeys, along with sloths and caiman. Most people take the eight-hour tour from Fortuna, which costs around US$50. Tours organized from Los Chiles are less expensive at US$20, and pick-up can be organized with tour operators in Fortuna. Sportfishing for tarpon is available from lodges in the village of Caño Negro.

Stalking fish, great egrets dine in safety at Caño Negro's lake

Monteverde

Majestic and remote, Monteverde encapsulates the essence of Costa Rica—diversity of wildlife, seclusion and at times exhilaration. One of the world's outstanding tropical plant and wildlife sanctuaries, it encompasses eight ecological zones.

Walking in a wet wonderland at Monteverde (left and above) *Venture into the canopy on a Sky Walk bridge. Top, a coati*

SEEING MONTEVERDE

One of the world's premier nature destinations, the secret hideaway that was Monteverde Reserve in the 1970s when it was founded, is now a well-trodden path. With its head often shrouded in mist, Monteverde Cloud Forest Reserve will keep you (literally and metaphorically) on the edge of your seat in anticipation. But before you curse the poor roads, remember that they have been fundamental in preserving the cloud forest by preventing rampant development of this isolated region. While the reserve is the main reason for visiting the area, there are many other places to explore.

Despite the visitors, the area has a rough charm. Santa Elena is a scruffy town, trundling along in a state of organized chaos. Nearby is the Santa Elena Cloud Forest Reserve with a network of trails and The Original Canopy tour. Monteverde's Conservation League also manages the Children's Eternal Rainforest with trails that lead to views of Arenal volcano, lagoons and waterfalls.

There are tourist information offices in Monteverde and Santa Elena, but tour operators and hotels in Santa Elena can help with inquiries and by arranging tours. The driest months in the region are from January to May, with the best months for birdwatching being February, March and April. September to November are the wettest months. As this is cloud forest, remember that mist is common and rain can occur throughout the year. Walking is the simplest way of getting around the area, and is certainly feasible around Santa Elena. Buses run from Santa Elena to Monteverde.

HIGHLIGHTS

RESERVA BIOLÓGICA BOSQUE NUBOSO MONTEVERDE

Straddling the continental divide, the Monteverde Cloud Forest Reserve covers 10,500ha (25,935 acres) and is privately owned and administered by the Centro Cientifico Tropical, a non-profit research and educational association. The reserve is mainly primary cloud forest shrouded in mist and cloud, giving high humidity. In Monteverde, trade winds from the Atlantic force moist air up the Tilarán Mountains; the air cools as it rises, and then condenses to make clouds that drop

RATINGS	
Hiking	● ● ● ● ●
Natural beauty	● ● ● ● ●
Photo stops	● ● ● ● ●
Wildlife spotting	● ● ● ●

BASICS

✚ 232 F4

☎ Reserve office: 506 645 5122, for information, tours and reservations

◉ Office: daily 7–4.30; Park: daily 7–4

💷 Adult day pass for multiple entry, US$13, cannot be purchased in advance

🚌 Daily from San José's Terminal Atlántico Norte to Santa Elena; 1 bus a day from Puntarenas and Tilarán. For Fantasy and Interbus shuttle bus details ▷ 52. From Santa Elena to the reserve at 6.15 and 1, returning at 11.15 and 4

🚐 Guided tours lasting 3.5hrs, US$15, guided night tours every evening departing at 7.15pm, US$13. Tours can be reserved. Independent guides can be organized through your hotel

🏢 Bureau of Tourism of Monteverde is in Santa Elena (tel 506 645 6464, daily 8–5). Good information on activities in and around the reserve. From the bus station walk back one block to the log cabin west of the church

❓ Taxi from Santa Elena, around US$7

🚗 Coming south on the Pan-American Highway turn off at Km149, south of Río Lagarto, for about 40km (25 miles) to Santa Elena (2.5hr). A four-wheel-drive car is recommended. Going north on the Pan-American Highway, take Sardinal turn off north of Río Aranjuez, then via Guacimal to Monteverde. You can also drive from Tilarán

www.monteverdeinfo.com and www.acmcr.org are useful regional websites

● The total number of visitors allowed in the reserve at any one time is 150, so be there before 7am to make sure of getting in during high season. If you want a guide, hotels will reserve a place for the following day. Alternatively you can just turn up and see if there are spaces on any tours.

● If you intend to head from Monteverde to Fortuna, you can avoid the 8-hour bus

rain. The result is an abundance of plants and epiphyte growth with tree trunks and branches covered in dense blankets of moss and lichens, and linked by twisting vines interspersed with fallen trees and giant tree ferns. A cloud forest is an almost magical place, like the forests of fairy tales. Take away the path and imagine how quickly you could get lost. A visit to Monteverde, or any of the many other private reserves in the area, is an opportunity to see nature in grand profusion. Plants grow on every available space, insects breed, birds feed and mammals loiter and stalk. Without a trained eye nearby, you may see only insects and hear a bird take flight, but the experience is no less enjoyable. Even with a guide you'll be lucky to see mammals.

Monteverde contains more than 400 species of birds, including the resplendent quetzal, best seen in the dry months between January and May, near the start of the Nuboso trail. There are more than 100

Farming is less important to Monteverde's economy now

Self-suffcent homesteads are a Monteverde tradition

Hanging Heliconia at the Bosque Eterno de los Niños

journey via Tilarán by taking a jeep to Lake Arenal, then a boat, and a jeep for the last stretch. It takes 3 hours, costs US$25 and is more scenic.

● The best months to visit are January to May, especially February, March and April.

● Be warned that there is little chance of seeing much wildlife. As with all nature experiences, be realistic in your expectations.

● If you are driving a rental car, ensure the agreement allows you to travel to Monteverde.

● To get to Monteverde from Santa Elena, the smart choice is to get transport up the hill and walk down, enjoying the views as you go.

● Recommended equipment includes: binoculars (which are available for rent at the entrance, US$10); a good camera with 400–1,000 ASA film; insect repellent; sweater and light rainwear. Rubber boots or good walking shoes are a must for the longer walks at all times of year, but especially in the rainy season, and can be rented at the park office for US$1 or at hotels.

● A guide is a good idea if you want to see wildlife–the untrained eye misses a lot.

species of mammals, including monkeys, Baird's tapir, Costa Rica's six endangered cats (jaguar, jaguarundi, margay, ocelot, tigrillo and puma), reptiles and amphibians. The reserve is home to an estimated 2,500 species of plants and more than 6,000 species of insects. The entrance is at 1,530m (5,018ft), but the reserve's maximum altitude rises to over 1,800m (5,900ft). Mean temperature is between 16°C and 18°C (60°F and 65°F) and average annual rainfall is 3,000mm (116in). The weather changes quickly and wind and humidity often make the air feel cooler, so take a light jacket and rain gear.

The commonly used trails are in good condition and there are easy, interesting walks for those who do not want to go far, as well as trails that take about two hours, but you could easily spend all day wandering around. Trails may be restricted from time to time. There is one northwards to Arenal Volcano that is increasingly used, but not easy. Free maps of the reserve are available at the entrance, along with an excellent self-guiding Nature Trail with a guide booklet (US$2). Follow the rules and sign the register, indicating where you are going in case you get lost. Stay on the paths, leave nothing behind and take no fauna or flora out; radios and tape recorders are not allowed.

MONTEVERDE SETTLEMENT

Strung out along the bumpy road between Santa Elena and the Reserve, the settlement at Monteverde has no central focus. It was founded by American Quakers in the 1950s and started life as a group of dairy farms providing milk for a cooperative cheese factory. Quietly churning away, the La Lechería (Mon–Sat 7.30–5, Sun 7.30–12.30; free), now privately owned, produces excellent cheeses of various types, fresh milk, ice cream and milkshakes to die for. Today, Monteverde maintains an air of pastoral charm, but tourism provides more revenue for the town than dairy produce ever could.

RESERVA BOSQUE ETERNO DE LOS NIÑOS

✉ Asociación Conservacionista de Monteverde, Apartado Postal 124-5655 Monteverde, Costa Rica ☎ 506 645 5003 🕐 Daily 7.30–5.30 💵 US$5 www.acmcr.org

Adjoining the Monteverde Cloud Forest Reserve is the Children's Eternal Rainforest, established in 1988 after an initiative by Swedish school children. Currently covering 22,000ha (54,340 acres), the land was bought and maintained by the Monteverde Conservation League with children's donations from more than 44 nations around the world. Funds are used for purchasing additional land and for improving the existing reserve area. The Bajo del Tigre trail is about 3km (2 miles), taking one and a half hours. Guides can be arranged or you can go on a self-guided tour. Trips deeper into the forest go to the San Gerardo Field Station, in the western part of the reserve, where there are 7km (4.5 miles) of trails leading through primary and secondary forests and a spectacular view of Arenal Volcano. The Poco Sol Field Station is at the eastern end of the protected areas near Poco Sol Lagoon and reached on the road from San Ramón to Fortuna, with almost 10km (6 miles) of trails visiting a waterfall and providing good birdwatching. Accommodation is available at both field stations.

A papaya tree in the Reserva Bosque Eterno de los Niños

Bananas grow wild in Reserva Bosque Eterno de los Niños

A bamboo thicket at the Reserva Bosque Eterno de los Niños

Butterflies are bred at the Monteverde Butterfly Garden

RESERVA BOSQUE NUBOSO SANTA ELENA
☎ 506 645 5390 ◷ Daily 7–4 🎟 US$8 🚕 Taxi from Santa Elena US$7
www.reservasantaelena.org

Just 1km (0.6 miles) along the road from Santa Elena to Tilarán, a long, steep 5km (3-mile) track is signposted to this 310ha (766-acre) reserve. It is 83 percent primary cloud forest (the rest is secondary forest) at 1,700m (5,576ft), bordered by the Monteverde Cloud Forest Reserve and the Arenal Forest Reserve. A network of paths spreads for 12km (7.5 miles) with several lookouts where you can see and hear Arenal Volcano on a clear day. The canopy tour is recommended. You climb inside a hollow strangler fig tree, then cross between two platforms along aerial runways 30m (98ft) up, which give good views of orchids and bromeliads, then down a 30m (98ft) hanging rope at the end. There is a small information center where rubber boots can be rented and a café is open at weekends. The rangers are very friendly and enthusiastic and there are generally fewer visitors here than at Monteverde. Profits from the scheme go to five local schools.

A blue morpho butterfly at the Monteverde Butterfly Garden

HUMMINGBIRD GALLERY
☎ 506 645 5030 🕐 Daily 9.30–5 💵 US$4

Just before the entrance to Monteverde Cloud Forest Reserve is the Hummingbird Gallery, where masses of different hummingbirds can be seen darting around a glade, visiting feeding dispensers filled with sugared water. There is a slide show at Monteverde Lodge–*Sounds and Scenes of the Cloud Forests* (daily 6.15pm, US$5).

MONTEVERDE BUTTERFLY GARDEN
☎ 506 645 5512 🕐 Daily 9.30–4 💵 Adult US$9, child US$3, including 1hr tour

A dirt road opposite the Hotel Heliconia leads to the Monteverde butterfly project, a beautiful garden planted for breeding and researching butterflies, which was founded in 1991 by biologist Jim Wolf and his wife Marta Iris Salazar. The central goal of the project is environmental

Spot butterflies in the gardens at Monteverde Butterfly Garden

Stick to the paths at Monteverde Cloud Forest Reserve; the jungle is impenetrable

Let your guide handle the tarantulas of Monteverde

Ready for action: a group departs on a tour of the forest

education. Wandering through the four gardens and three greenhouses you can see hundreds of species, representing nearly half of Costa Rica's butterflies. The netted flyway allows for close encounters with the winged jewels, which fly more on sunny days (if it rains you can visit again at no extra charge). The garden raises more than 50 species and bilingual guides provide insights into the life cycle of these fascinating creatures. The best time for a visit is between 11–1.

SKY WALK AND SKY TREK
☎ 506 645 5238 🕐 Sky Walk: daily 7–4; Sky Trek: daily 7–3 💵 Sky Walk: Adult US$17, child US$11, under 6 free. Sky Trek: Adult US$44, child (8–12) US$31, under 8 free 🔳 Sky Walk: guided nature hikes at 8, 10, 1.30, US$10; Sky Trek tours: 7.30, 9.30, 10.30, 11.30, 1.30, 2, 2.30, 3 🚌 Hotel pick-ups can be arranged, US$1
www.skywalk.com

A vivid display of Heliconia *in the Bosque Eterno de los Niños*

Off the road to Tilarán, 5km (3 miles) north of Santa Elena, the highly professional Sky Walk and Sky Trek operations enable you to experience the wonders of the cloud forest canopy with added adrenaline. Canopy tours are now commonplace in Costa Rica, but Sky Walk is the ultimate. It includes over 2.5km (1.5 miles) of trails and uses six suspension bridges straddling deep canyons, to take you through the cloud forest at canopy level, the highest bridge being 42m (138ft) above the ground and the longest one being 243m (797ft). Sky Trek is an even more breathtaking experience, but not for the faint-hearted as you fly through the air on 10 ziplines strung out from giant trees. The longest cable is 427m (465 yards) long and 127m (416ft) high. On clear days the view from the highest observation tower is incredible, with panoramic views of Guanacaste, San Carlos and Puntarenas.

THE ORIGINAL CANOPY TOUR
✉ PO Box 7979-10000 ☎ 506 645 5243 🕐 Tours at 7.30, 10.30 and 2.30; free hotel pick-ups 💵 Adult US$45, child US$25
www.canopytours.com

This canopy tour, the first in the world, is in the grounds of the Monteverde Cloud Forest Lodge, 1km (0.6 miles) from Santa Elena. An intricate series of 11 tree platforms, varying between 8m (26ft) and 28m (92ft), connected by cables take you zipping and soaring through the various layers of the forest canopy, culminating with

12 rappel descents. The tour begins with a guided hike through the forest, with a talk outlining the biodiversity of the forest, before you climb up to the first platform. One of the unique experiences of the tour is a rope ladder ascent through the core of an immense strangler fig tree. The Monteverde Cloud Forest Lodge connects the Monteverde with the Santa Elena reserve and has private trails, which provide excellent birdwatching.

SELVATURA
☎ 506 645 5929 ◷ Daily 7–5 🎫 Canopy tour: Adult US$40, child US$25; Walkway: Adult US$20, child US$20 🚐 Canopy tours 8.30, 11, 1, 2.30 🚌 Hotel pick-ups included in package rates
www.selvatura.com
About 2km (1.2 miles) beyond Sky Walk, this well-rounded facility

MORE TO SEE

BAT JUNGLE
✉ 400m (440 yards) uphill from the gas station in Monteverde ☎ 506 645 6566 ◷ Daily 9.30–8 🎫 Adult US$8, child US$6
A fascinating bat exhibit that includes a flyway. Documentaries are shown, and visitors don giant ears to gain an appreciation for bats' astounding acoustic abilities.

Monteverde was founded by dairy-farming Quakers in 1951

It's not difficult to spot tiny hummingbirds at Monteverde

There are at least 2,500 species of plant in the cloud forest

also has a zipline canopy tour with 18 platforms and 15 cables, plus 3km (1.9 miles) of tree top walkways, with the highest 60m (180ft) above the ground. There is also a hummingbird garden and some 20 species of butterflies flutter around within a domed enclosure (US$10). The scintillating highlight is the Jewels of the Rainforest Bio-Art Exhibition displaying tens of thousands of insects from around the globe—part of the private collection of world-famous entomologist Dr. Richard Whitten.

BACKGROUND
Monteverde owes its formation to the pursuit of ideals. In 1951, a group of Quakers left the US to avoid the draft. Buying land in Monteverde and clearing the forests for dairy farming, the community soon realized that the forest cover was essential to preserve the soil and created a protected area of 541ha (1,336 acres). In 1972 George Powell and his wife, after a period studying the birds of the cloud forest, set out to protect more of the region, joining forces with the long-time resident Wilford Guindon to promote the creation of a reserve. Combining the Quaker reserve with a further 328ha (810 acres), the Monteverde Cloud Forest Reserve was created in 1972.

The ideals of its founders have continued as the reserve has grown. Without the backing of large environmental organizations, Monteverde moved from individual passion to global awareness through word-of-mouth recommendations and television nature documentaries. Slowly, the notion of ecotourism began to reap rewards, and the reserve spawned myriad reserves, protected areas and conservation projects across Costa Rica.

Today, there is discussion about the future of Monteverde and other reserves in the area. Some residents want to see the dreadful roads upgraded to improve access. Others want to restrict the potential damage that may be caused, believing that development has already reached unacceptable limits. Decide for yourself whether visiting Monteverde is about quality or quantity.

ECOLOGICAL SANCTUARY WILDLIFE REFUGE
☎ 506 645 5869 ◷ Daily 7–5.30 🎫 US$9 🚐 Guided tours 7–10am, 3–5pm, US$15
This private farm has four trails through forest, passing cascading waterfalls, with good chances of spotting wildlife.

ORCHID FARM
☎ 506 645 5308 ◷ Daily 8–5 🎫 US$7 This farm grows more than 400 species of orchid, including the *Guardia morada*, the national flower of Costa Rica, and the world's smallest orchid.

RANARIO
☎ 506 645 6320 ◷ Daily 9–8.30 🎫 US$9 for day pass 🚐 300m (330 yards) west of Monteverde Lodge
The Frog Pond has over 20 species of frogs and toads. Guided tours last for 45 minutes and you can return as many times as you like throughout the day.

SERPENTARIO
✉ 300m (330 yards) east of Santa Elena ☎ 506 645 6002 ◷ Daily 9–6 🎫 Adult US$7, child US$3
www.snaketour.com
More than 25 species of snakes are displayed along with their prey: chameleons, frogs etc.

THE SIGHTS

GUANACASTE

Hot, dry and much deforested, Guanacaste is nonetheless a premier tourist destination. It's cowboy country, but you're more likely to see surf boards and golf clubs than saddles and spurs. Get off the gorgeous beaches to discover bird-filled estuaries, historic houses and towns, and the mountains of the eastern border.

MAJOR SIGHTS

A woman pounding clay in a pestle at a studio in Guaitíl

The Central Plaza in Liberia gets busy in the evening

A bridge too far at Volcán Tenorio National Park

GUAITÍL

➕ 236 C5 🚌 Seven buses daily from Tamarindo at 6.45am to Santa Cruz, then to Guaitíl every few hours. Hourly from Liberia, Nicoya to Santa Cruz and from San José 🚗 Guaitíl is 12km (7.5 miles) south of Santa Cruz on the Santa Bárbara road

Guaitíl is an easy excursion from Santa Cruz. The roads that meander throughout the Nicoya Peninsula are lined with rows of pots and plates, most of which are produced in Guaitíl. The people of this small town have retained the traditional skills for making the hand-built and oven-fired red and black pottery. More than 30 years ago, Coopearte, a women's cooperative, was formed by Hortensia Briceño, and Guaitíl and its pottery gained international recognition.

The tiny linear town has studios along the road and around the soccer field. If you're interested in the manufacturing process, you may be shown the techniques and the plants used.

JUNTAS DE ABANGARES

➕ 232 E5 🚌 From Cañas to Juntas at 9am and 2pm 🚗 Juntas lies east of the Pan-American Highway
www.minatours.com

Fame flickered for this little town in the late 19th century when gold finds attracted prospectors. A century later, a few prospectors still mine for gold, but the main attraction is a mining museum at La Sierra de Abangares (tel 506 662 0310, Tue–Fri 8–5) with mining artifacts from the boom times, including the ruins, or *mazos*, of an old stamping mill, used to crush the ore. Around the mill, trails provide good opportunities for seeing some of the area's 90 species of birds. In the middle of Juntas, details of the history of mining in Costa Rica are available at the office of

Mina Tours (tel 506 662 0753), whose owner's mother, Ofelia Gamboa Solorzano, is the daughter of one of the pioneers. The road through Juntas is an alternative route—four-wheel drive advised—to Santa Elena and Monteverde for those traveling south from Guanacaste or using the Tempisque ferry.

LIBERIA

➕ 231 C3 🚌 10 a day from San José's Tracopa terminal (▷ 53) ℹ️ In the same building as Museo del Sabanero, tel 506 665 0135, Mon–Sat 9–5

Guanacaste's provincial capital, Liberia, stands at the intersection of the Pan-American Highway and Highway 21 to the Nicoya Peninsula. Since 2002, when the international airport opened, the status of Liberia has soared along with the number of visitors arriving directly from the US for instant Guanacaste gratification. Commercial interests have thrived, altering the town's colonial feel. Its traditional, white buildings that evolved to survive the blazing heat that bakes the town in the dry season, now sit alongside glitzy shopping plazas. At the end of the day, promenaders gather in the cool breeze in the central plaza. South of town, at Calle 1, Avenida 6, in a 100-year-old adobe house, is the Museo del Sabanero (Mon–Sat 8–12, 1–4, US$0.50), dedicated to the horsemen of the plains.

PARQUE NACIONAL VOLCÁN TENORIO

➕ 232 E3 ☎ 506 695 5980 🕐 Daily 8–4 💲 US$6 🚗 From San José as far as Upala, then a 15km (9-mile) journey to Bijuagua in a four-wheel-drive vehicle to the park 🚗 From San José go north on the Pan-American Highway to Cañas; 7km (4.25 miles) north of Cañas Highway 6 heads northeast 34km (21 miles) to Bijuagua

Established in 1995, Tenorio Volcano National Park is one of the country's newest national parks, protecting the watershed of Tenorio Volcano (1,916m/6,285ft) and 12,871ha (31,791 acres) of mixed forest. The town Bijuagua, which lies in the saddle between Tenorio and Miravalles volcanoes, has facilities and the park is a popular destination for hiking. A rewarding trip for the hardy, the park has some stunning natural features. Soak in natural hot springs, visit magnificent waterfalls, or see one of the park's highlights, the Río Celeste, with azure blue waters created by minerals leached from the rock. The most accessible route leads from the Bijuagua Heliconias Ecotourist Resort, which lies 3km (2 miles) out of town, along the flanks of the volcano. Other trails, for the more intrepid, lead from the crater lake through cloud forest to the summit, with views of Arenal Volcano and Lake Nicaragua.

People-watching in up-and-coming Liberia

Guanacaste is cattle-ranching country (left), but the remote region around Volcán Orosí (above) is now protected

RATINGS

Birdwatching	● ● ● ○
Cultural interest	● ● ● ○
Hiking	● ● ● ○

BASICS

➕ 230 C2
☎ 506 666 5051
🕐 Daily 8–4
💲 US$6
🚗 You will need a four-wheel-drive vehicle to get to the park. From Liberia, the Pan-American Highway heads north towards the Nicaraguan border. After 42km (26 miles) a right turn, opposite the turnoff for Cuajiniquíl, leads onto a dirt track, from where it is 17km (10.5 miles) to the Maritza Field Station
www.sinac.go.cr

TIPS

● You have to book basic dormitory accommodation at the three stations, Cacao, Maritza and Pitalla in advance with the Santa Rosa National Park administration (▷ 94).
● Call the national park office before setting out for the park as the biological stations may be closed, especially during the rainy season.
● This is one of the least developed parks in Costa Rica, so be prepared for very basic conditions. You will need to take your own food unless you can make arrangements with park authorities.

PARQUE NACIONAL GUANACASTE

The lynchpin of the Guanacaste Conservation Area, this remote national park has abundant birdlife and trails.

Close to the Nicaraguan border, at Costa Rica's northwestern fringes, Guanacaste National Park, created in 1991 and linking two older parks, protects 34,651ha (85,587 acres), in an area covering the Orosí and Cacao volcanoes. The park includes rainforest, tropical wet forest, cloud forest and tropical dry forest. There is a network of hiking trails and a wildlife inventory of more than 140 mammal species, 300 bird species, 100 amphibians, 5,000 butterflies and 10,000 insects. With fewer visitors than other National Parks, the rewards are great for those with the time and endurance to navigate this remote region.

TRAILS AND BIOLOGICAL STATIONS

Maritza Station is the most comfortable of the stations, and the closest to the Pan-American Highway. Leave the highway 10km (6 miles) north of the turning for Santa Rosa, opposite the turn for Cuajiniquíl. Trails from the station lead through gallery, dry and transitional dry-humid forest. Short trails of around two hours lead to the petroglyph site close to Cerro El Hacha, where you can see some 800 petroglyphs. You can walk to the summit of Cacao, a long day's walk. Higher up the slopes at 1,100m (3,608ft) above sea level is Cacao Station. Temperatures here are lower, rainfall higher and this part of the park has areas of transitional dry-humid forest and cloud forest. Access is from the Pan-American Highway 23km (14 miles) north of Liberia at Potrerillos. If you want to trek between the park's stations, decide whether you want to start or end in relative comfort: Cacao Station is far more basic than Maritza and doesn't have electricity. A four-hour hike goes through cloud forest to the top of the volcano; check at the station for permission before setting out. Pitilla Station may be physically close to Cacao, but access is 28km (17 miles) east along Highway 4 from the junction with the Pan-American Highway, then heading south at Santa Cecilia along 9km (5.5 miles) of dirt road. It is one of the best spots for birdwatching, but be prepared for basic conditions at the lodge.

Don't miss See Lake Nicaragua from the top of Volcán Orosí.

White Ibis flying over the marshes of Palo Verde National Park (above). You can also see geological formations at the park (right)

PARQUE NACIONAL PALO VERDE

See thousands of birds wading through this watery wonderland, and deciduous forest at the Lomas Barbudal reserve.

At the northernmost limits of the Gulf of Nicoya, the floodplains of the Tempisque River are protected by Palo Verde National Park, covering 18,651ha (46,068 acres). Lodges and haciendas are scattered along the Pan-American Highway and provide good bases for exploring the park. A journey this far is rewarded by excellent birdwatching. The road leaves the Pan-American Highway at Bagaces, from where a four-wheel-drive vehicle drives the 28km (17.5 miles) to the Palo Verde Station. At the northern limits of Palo Verde National Park, Lomas Barbudal Biological Reserve protects precious tree species. The four-wheel-drive track for Lomas Barbudal is 10km (6 miles) north of Bagaces, along the Pan-American Highway, close to Pijije. The reserve's office is 6km (3.75 miles) down this road, which eventually joins the road to Palo Verde National Park.

FLORA AND FAUNA

The park's 12 habitats, including marshes, lagoons, mangroves and forests, are home to the largest concentration of waterfowl and wading birds in Central America—275 resident and migrating species, and it is the country's only nesting site of the jabirú stork. Many of the bird species are found on the Isla de los Pájaros. Mammals are also abundant and 150 species of tree have been recorded. The annual raptor migration in October and November is a spectacular phenomenon.

Several trails in the park lead from the Palo Verde Biological Station, where accommodation is available. Some 6km (3.7 miles) along the Pan-American Highway, near San Joaquín, Hacienda Solimar (tel 506 669 0281) is a ranch recommended for birdwatchers.

RESERVA BIOLÓGICA LOMAS BARBUDAL

An important reserve for the protection of rare tree species, Lomas Barbudal includes mahogany, rosewood and the cortez tree, which blooms riotously a few days after a rain shower in the dry season. With seven habitats, Lomas Barbudal is home to 130 bird species including the scarlet macaw. The reserve's savannas and dry forest support cacti and bromeliads and the insect life is unusually rich.

RATINGS	
Birdwatching	●●●●●
Ecological diversity	●●●●
Photo stops (wildlife)	●●●●

BASICS

✚ 231 D4
☎ Office in Bagaces: 506 671 1290
◉ Reserve office: daily 8–4
🌿 Palo Verde: US$6; Reserva Lomas Barbudal: donation requested
❓ Accommodation is available at Palo Verde Station, tel 506 661 4717
www.ots.ac.cr

TIPS

● The area receives the largest concentration of waterfowl and wading birds between September and March, with a distinct dry season between December and March.
● The Lomas Barbudal reserve is at its most breathtaking in March when the cortez trees are ablaze with yellow flowers.
● In the dry season wildlife concentrate near the depleted water supplies. One of the best ways to spot mammals is to wait quietly near a water hole.
● Instead of driving to the park from Bagaces, rent a boat from the town of Puerto Humo and journey upriver passing Isla de los Pájaros. Upstream from the park, crocodiles gather among the encroaching vegetation.

Parque Nacional Santa Rosa

Home to La Casona, a symbol of Costa Rica's national pride, this park has open dry tropical forest where wildlife is relatively easy to see. At Playa Nancite you can watch sea turtles come ashore to nest.

Dry tropical forest dominates Santa Rosa National Park

Sunset at Playa Nacinte (above). A black iguana (top)

Surf's up at Playa Naranjo in the south of the park

BASICS

✚ 230 B2

☎ Park administration: 506 666 5051

🕐 Open 24 hrs, but the entrance may be barred to traffic before 8am

💵 US$6

🚌 Any bus between Liberia and La Cruz will pass the entrance. For the Murciélago sector, buses leave Liberia for Cuajiniquil at 5.30am and 3.30pm, returning at 7am and 4.30pm

🚗 Follow the Pan-American Highway north of Liberia for 32km (20 miles), then turn west at the signpost. Access to the Murciélago sector is 10km (6 miles) north of the main entrance, via the road west towards Cuajiniquil

🏛 The park entrance sells maps, bird lists, a small brochure and museum guide

SEEING PARQUE NACIONAL SANTA ROSA

Tucked in the northwestern corner of Costa Rica, 48km (29 miles) south of the Nicaraguan border, Santa Rosa National Park holds a special place in the hearts of local and international visitors for its historical and natural importance. The national park has grown to encompass the 38,673ha (95,522 acres) of the entire Santa Elena Peninsula, and now protects the largest remaining area of dry tropical forest in Central America. South along the coastline, Playa Naranjo is one of Costa Rica's most beautiful beaches, and one of the hardest to reach. The historical significance of the region is an essential part of the national identity. Some 7km (4.5 miles) from the entrance of the park is the Casona de Santa Rosa, which resonates with every Costa Rican as the site of the country's struggle in 1856 against William Walker's attempts to take over and unite Central America. Tragically, La Casona was almost completely destroyed by fire in May 2001, but has since been rebuilt as an exact replica. While it is possible to reach Santa Rosa National Park by bus, the reforestation zone of Murciélago is more difficult to access, and a four-wheel-drive vehicle is essential for navigating the region. Visitors can camp at the administrative entrance to the park from where a number of short trails lead out and a detailed trail map is available. Within the Murciélago is Playa Blanca, a white sand beach that you can visit in the dry season in a four-wheel-drive vehicle. At other times of the year you will need permission from park authorities. Access to the beautiful and deserted turtle-nesting beach of Playa Nancite is restricted to biologists only owing to the importance of the seasonal *arribadas* (arrivals).

HIGHLIGHTS

FLORA AND FAUNA

The immediate appeal of Santa Rosa National Park is the abundant and relatively easy-to-see wildlife. During the dry season, from November to May, the mainly deciduous trees shed their leaves and the animals depend on shrinking water holes until they dry up

La Casona (above) and inside the museum before the fire (inset)

completely. The open dry tropical forest makes it easier to spot the white-tailed deer descending from the park's upper reaches, and the dozing howler monkeys found within the park. Many unique species of tree can be seen including the pochote—called the naked Indian—and the region's namesake, the guanacaste. There are estimated to be some 115 species of mammal in the park, including white-tail deer, coatis, and spider and white-faced monkeys. In coastal regions, mangrove swamp is the predominant vegetation. Between August and December on Playa Nancite, the phenomenon of the *arribada* involves thousands of olive ridley turtles arriving on the beach. To the north, the Murciélago sector, reached through Cuajiniquíl, protects over 70 species of bat found in this part of the park.

LA CASONA

The Santa Rosa Hacienda—La Casona—has become an essential visit for every Tico. Records show the property was created in 1663, but the strategic significance of the region was bought to the fore by the prying eyes of American filibuster William Walker (▷ 39). In the 1850s, Walker saw the hacienda as an essential foothold for his imperialist ideals. An advocate of slavery, he believed the independent aspirations of Central America had strayed too far from the interests of its northern neighbor. Having walked into Nicaragua and gained the presidency, Walker's attention turned to Costa Rica, next step to the south. His attempts to conquer Costa Rica were started at, and floundered at, La Casona. The Costa Ricans, under the leadership of José María Cañas, defeated Walker's band of filibusters on the afternoon of 20 March 1856. The strategic significance of the area was reinforced again in 1919 when troops marched from Nicaragua to overthrow President Federico Tinoco, and again in 1955 during the presidency of José Figueres Ferrer "Don Pepe." On both occasions the invading troops were defeated.

History made this unassuming hacienda building important, but that importance led to its destruction. The arson attack of May 2001, by a couple of vengeful hunters angry that hunting was banned in the park, completely destroyed the collection of military paraphernalia and

TIPS

● Isla Desnuda provides the best opportunities for wildlife spotting very early in the morning or late afternoon. Despite the low-level light, it should also provide the best opportunities for photography.
● Entrance to Playa Nancite is restricted to permit holders. Apply to the park authorities for a permit at least 20 days before your intended visit, but most permits are taken by researchers during the mass turtle nestings.
● The park has several *miradores* (look-out points) that provide wonderful panoramas revealing the region's vast frontier landscape and sheer diversity. The best views are from Mirador Tierras Emergidas and Mirador Yalle Naranjo, located en route from the administration center to Playa Naranjo and the coast.
● Behind La Casona, there are good views across the surrounding area.
● The small beach of Playa Blanca, with its pristine white sand, is one of the most isolated and beautiful beaches in Costa Rica and is also one of the safest bathing areas in the region.

Sun, sea and sand: Playa Naranjo (above).
An olive ridley turtle returning to the ocean after laying her eggs (inset)

MORE TO SEE

BAHÍA DE SALINAS

From the Murciélago sector of the park, a dirt road continues north eventually reaching one of the quietest corners in the country, Salinas Bay (a four-wheel-drive vehicle is essential, even in the dry season). Locals claim that the beaches of Jobo and Rajada are the best in the country.

BAHÍA JUNQUILLAL WILDLIFE REFUGE

This refuge is also part of the Santa Rosa National Park. It's a popular spot with local families. There is a peaceful, pleasant beach with facilities for camping.

AIRSTRIP

Close to Cuajiniquíl is the airstrip built by Oliver North during the 1980s to supply the Nicaraguan Contras. It was built on a property formerly owned by the Nicaraguan leader Somosa before it was purchased for the national park.

exhibits recording the lifestyle and events that took place at La Casona. The building was reconstructed using money raised through private donations from Ticos outraged at such a sacrilegious act. Restoring La Casona to its former glory was an impossible dream, but the addition of original features, including late 19th-century roof tiles salvaged from the flames, have added a historical aura to an otherwise sterile replica.

TREKS, TRAILS AND BEACHES

Behind La Casona, the short (1km/0.6-mile) Indio Desnudo (Naked Indian) nature trail, with annotated signposts, takes a loop through fine stands of dry tropical forest past the red peeling bark of the gumbo limbo tree. Sendero Los Patos, which begins 5km (3 miles) beyond the National Park administration center, provides good opportunities for wildlife spotting. The Tierras Emergidas trail runs parallel to the entrance road. The longest feasible one-day trek is to Mirador Valle Naranjo, some 6km (4 miles) from the administration buildings. Longer treks to Playa Naranjo and Playa Nancite (access to Playa Nancite is restricted, see below) require an overnight stay and should be booked with the administration offices. (There is a four-wheel-drive track leading to both beaches, but do not rely on being able to use it.) The trek descends gently over 12km (7.5 miles), moving through dry tropical forest and a multitude of butterflies. By the time you've reached the lower altitudes, your eye will be well trained to spotting the iguanas, crabs and monkeys that are very much in evidence. With luck, you may even see green macaws, white-lipped peccaries, tapir and possibly pumas, which are reported to be increasing in number in the park. A left fork leads to Playa Naranjo, which has more trails than Playa Nancite. Towards the southern end, Sendero Carbonal leads to the brackish Limbo Lagoon where you may find the American crocodile. Playa Naranjo itself is awesome. Stretching around the bay, it is a popular surfing spot. In the bay is the surfing high spot of Witches' Rock—one of the oldest geological formations in Costa Rica, dated at 680 million years old.

PLAYA NANCITE

Playa Nancite is treasured as the nesting site of three species of sea turtle, the largest at almost 2m (6.5ft) in length being the leatherback and the second largest the green turtle. The olive ridley may be smaller, but makes up for it in sheer numbers, arriving in thousands in an incredible natural phenomenon. At night from August to December, thousands of olive ridleys gather in the offshore waters, enduring a mating cycle that lasts up to nine hours. After mating, the female turtles arrive in thousands over a three- to seven-night period and each deposits between 90 and 120 eggs in deep nests where they incubate in the sand for 50 days. After hatching, the young turtles struggle to the surface, then cross the beach to the treacherous coastal surf. All manner of terrestrial and marine predators feast on the young during this dangerous trek. The vast number of eggs produced in one small space gives each individual a greater chance of survival. Estimates suggest that at the peak of the *arribadas* (arrivals) as many as 75,000 turtles

Deciduous dry forest (above)

THE SIGHTS

Limbo Lagoon in Santa Rosa is a crocodile habitat

You may spot capuchin monkeys playing in the trees

Despite their appearance, black iguanas are largely herbivorous

may nest on the beach, before migrating as far north as Mexico and south to Peru. They return every two or three years. Researchers at the Santa Rosa Investigation Center have been studying the phenomenon since it was first discovered in 1972. In recent years, figures suggest the numbers of olive ridleys arriving at Nancite are declining—a disappointingly familiar tale—the causes of which remain unknown.

BACKGROUND

As early as 1663, the land that now forms the Santa Rosa National Park was treasured for cattle raising with the founding of a ranch in the area. The inauguration of the National Park in 1971 saw a shift away from ranching to conservation for the coastal region which was complemented by the creation of the Guanacaste and Rincón de la Vieja national parks. The creation of the Rincón Cacao Biological Corridor added the final piece of a migratory corridor that incorporates nine of the 12 ecosystems found in Costa Rica, leading from the Pacific to the volcanic peak at Rincón de la Vieja, which rises to 1,916m (6,284ft).

In the world of conservation, the Area de Conservación Guanacaste (ACG—Guanacaste Conservation Area) is a beacon of hope and in 1999 the Santa Rosa National Park was declared a UNESCO Natural World Heritage Site. Official estimates say the region protects some 235,000 species—more than exist in the entire US. Proving that conservation is an ongoing process, work continues to protect more of the area and add to the migratory corridor.

The Monumento a los Heroes, near La Casona, is a concrete arch dedicated to the victims of Santa Rosa's battles

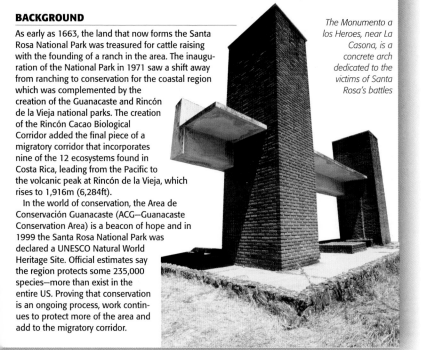

Hiking trails cross rivers to thermal pools and lagoons in Rincón de la Vieja National Park. Inset, there is a huge variety of plant life

RATINGS	
Hiking	●●●●
Photo stops (landscape)	●●●
Wildlife diversity	●●●●

BASICS

✚ 231 D2

☎ 506 666 0630/661 8139

💵 US$6, an extra US$3 toll for the access road to the Las Pailas entrance

🚗 There are two routes into the park: the southern route, which has less traffic, goes from Puente La Victoria on the western side of Liberia and leads, in about 25km (15.5 miles), to the Santa María sector, closest to the hot springs. The northern route turns east off the Pan-American Highway 5km (3 miles) northwest of Liberia to Curubandé. Beyond Curubandé, you reach Posada El Encuentro, cross the private property of Hacienda Lodge Guachipelín (US$3 for road maintenance), and beyond Rincón de la Vieja Mountain Lodge

❓ Taxi from Liberia US$30–40. Hotels in Liberia will book a taxi for US$15 per person, minimum 6 people; depart at 7am, 1 hour to entrance, return at 5pm

TIPS

● At the summit, the Laguna Jilgueros is a good site for spotting wildlife, including tapirs.
● Take insect repellent; the water provides a breeding ground for mosquitoes.
● Do not drink water from the streams; volcanic springs contain high levels of chemicals.

PARQUE NACIONAL RINCÓN DE LA VIEJA

Steaming geysers, blue lagoons and bubbling mud emphasize the volcanic nature of this park, where wildlife thrives.

More than 600,000-years-old, Rincón de la Vieja Volcano was formed by the eruption of several volcanic cones that eventually merged to become one, straddling the continental divide. The name means Old Lady's Corner; according to Guatuso legend an old witch living on Rincón de la Vieja sends smoke skyward whenever she is annoyed. It is also believed that the park once served as a natural lighthouse for sailors off the Pacific coast. The last major eruptions occurred from 1966 to 1970, although there were minor eruptions in 1999, when it belched out ash clouds as far west as Santa Rosa National Park.

HIGHLIGHTS

Located in Guanacaste's cordillera, 27km (17 miles) northwest of Liberia, Rincón de la Vieja National Park protects 14,161ha (34,978 acres) of territory, ideal for hiking and horseback riding. The park lies astride the cordillera creating the conditions for a wide variety of species. Steaming mud pools, hot springs, steam vents and fumaroles have earned the park the nickname "Little Yellowstone." The main attractions lie to the south side of the Santa María crater, but exploring the park fully takes three days. There are hikes to the summit with fine views (on clear days) across the lowlands. Most places of interest are reached from either the Las Pailas or Santa María Hacienda rangers' stations, which are linked by a path. The massif, rising to a height of 1,916m (6,284ft) at Santa María Volcano, is visible from Liberia, and the lower summit of volcano Rincón de la Vieja has a lagoon at the southern end, which can be reached on a two-day trek. There are four ecosystems and 250 species of birds. Howler monkeys, armadillos and coatis are among the mammals. Ticks and other biting insects also abound. A number of trails lead from Las Pailas and Santa María Hacienda rangers' stations: the Enchanted Forest and Hidden Falls trails lead to thermal pools, 3km (2 miles) from Santa María entrance. A 30-minute hike from the park office, there is a beautiful Prussian-blue lagoon: the intense hue is a result of the mineral properties of the stones lying beneath the water.

Sun-seekers, surfers and leatherback turtles all love Playa Grande, one of Costa Rica's best beaches

PLAYA GRANDE

Playa Grande and Parque Nacional Marino las Baulas de Guanacaste are important nesting sites for turtles.

Beautiful Playa Grande's appeal is clear. Stretching like a golden carpet into the distance, the beach is as popular with surfers as it is with leatherback turtles. Playa Grande is considered to be one of the best surf spots in the country; the beach forms the most western point of the Nicoya Peninsula and receives swells from the north, south and west. Along the coast of a peninsula created by Tamarindo's estuary, 485ha (1,198 acres) of beach and mangrove swamps are protected in the Parque Nacional Marino las Baulas de Guanacaste with an additional 22,000ha (54,340 acres) covering the marine reserve.

PARQUE NACIONAL MARINO LAS BAULAS DE GUANACASTE

Away from the beach, the estuarine waters of the national park protect mangrove swamps, where all six Costa Rican mangrove species are found. From a drifting boat you can see a great deal of wildlife including caiman, crocodiles and roseate spoonbills. Created to protect the nesting habitat of the leatherback turtle, Marino las Baulas de Guanacaste National Park has successfully reduced the poaching of turtle eggs from the beaches of Playa Grande. But while the local solution may be working, the broader global picture does not bode well. There has been a dramatic drop in the numbers of leatherbacks in the park (▷ 26). In 1988, the annual *arribadas* saw 1,365 females coming on shore to lay their eggs; by 2003, this figure had fallen to 155 before rebounding in 2005, when more than 400 arrived. Growing to a massive 2m (6.5ft) in length and weighing as much as half a ton, mature adults arrive at the beach between October and March, where they haul themselves up the beach to deposit between 80 and 100 eggs the size of table-tennis balls before returning to the ocean, exhausted. Turtle-watching tours are usually arranged from, and begin in, Tamarindo, a short boat trip across the mouth of the estuary. If you have time, a visit to El Mundo de la Tortuga (tel 506 653 0471, open in the nesting season; US$6) on the main road close to the beach, will provide answers to questions about the turtles' world. The national park office, at the town's entrance, runs trips to the beach in the nesting season.

RATINGS

Peace and tranquility	●●●●
Wildlife spotting	●●●●
Beach life	●●●●●

BASICS

✚ 230 A4
☎ Park office: 506 653 0470
💲 US$6
🚌 Buses from Tamarindo to San José stop at Huacas, from where it is 9km (5.5 miles) to Playa Grande
🚗 Playa Grande is 1 hour by car from Liberia. From the junction at Huacas the main road leads straight ahead to Matapalo and after 9km (5.5 miles) to Playa Grande.
❓ Taxi from Huacas costs around US$8

TIPS

● At low tide, it is a beautiful walk (30 minutes approximately) along Tamarindo beach to Playa Grande. At high tide, river taxis will take you across the estuary (US$1), or, like the surfers, you can swim across. There are beach clubs and bars at the southern end of the beach.
● Take care when swimming as the current can be strong.

Costa Rican families relax at Playas del Coco

Tamarindo is a popular base in Gaunacaste, with fishing, boating, diving and surfing just some of the watersports on offer

PLAYA TAMARINDO

🟩 230 A4 ℹ️ On the main road, next door to Tamarindo supermarket, 200m (220 yards) from La Rotunda, tel 506 653 0981, daily 8–6 🚌 Shuttle bus services (▷ 52) with Fantasy Bus Grayline and Interbus between Tamarindo and San José (US$29), Jacó, Sámara. www.tamarindo.net

Some five hours drive from San José, and just 90 minutes from the Daniel Oduber Quirós airport in Liberia, Tamarindo has grown from a small village to an extremely popular sun and surf destination. Sunsets draw out all sections of Tamarindo society at dusk to watch the sinking sun. Either side of the magic moment, Tamarindo is a flurry of activity. While the town is driven by surfing, an increasingly upscale blend of hotels, bars and restaurants makes it a good beach stop.

The beach is attractive, with a craggy coastline, fringed with tamarind trees. Beach hikes lead south from Tamarindo to Playa Langosta then south to Playa Avellanas and Playa Negra. If you are lucky, you may see monkeys. To the north, a 3km (2-mile) walk takes you to Playa Grande, a leatherback nesting site (▷ 99). Aquatic activities are many and varied, but watch for strong tides in places. Tamarindo's three surf breaks make it a good place for beginners. Snorkeling, kayaking, sailing and fishing can also be arranged. You can easily walk around Tamarindo, but mountain bikes and scooters are available for rent from the main street, running parallel to the beach.

PLAYAS DEL COCO

🟩 230 B3 🚌 Daily buses from San José Tracopa terminal via Liberia 🚗 Leave the Pan-American Highway at Liberia, where a left turn on Highway 21, passing Daniel Oduber Quirós airport, leads west for 35km (22 miles) to Playas del Coco

The frigatebird, also known as the pirate of the skies

One of Guanacaste's northernmost beaches, Playas del Coco is a lively beach community, with a rash of hotels to suit all budgets. Restaurants range from humble spots to temples of gastronomy. Unlike Tamarindo to the south, a more sedate vibe prevails, as Playas del Coco is a popular destination for Costa Ricans on the weekends. Coco is one of the country's most popular dive spots, with operators providing courses and trips to more than 30 dive sites within a 20-minute boat ride from town (▷ 146–147). The town is also a departure point for trips out to Witches' Rock (▷ 134), and is a good base for sport fishing. For more peace and solitude, head 3km (2 miles) southwest of Coco to Playa Ocotal where rocky headlands shelter tiny coves that have been developed as dive sites and provide excellent snorkeling. Often considered the poor relation of Tamarindo, Playas del Coco's profile will change if investors are granted permission to build a marina here as planned.

REFUGIO DE FAUNA SILVESTRE ISLA BOLAÑOS

🟩 230 B1 ☎️ ACG: 506 666 5051 🌐 During the nesting season, Jan–Mar, no visits are permitted. Contact Area de Conservación Guanacaste, tel 506 666 5051 or the National Park service in San

José, tel 506 283 8004, for access during the rest of the year 🎫 US$6 www.sinac.go.cr

Close to Nicaragua's border, in Salinas Bay, Isla Bolaños Wildlife Refuge is a small island reserve protecting 25ha (62 acres) of stunted forest. Protected status is afforded to this barren land because it is one of Costa Rica's few nesting sites of the brown pelican, and the only known nesting site of the American oystercatcher. You may also see graceful frigatebirds. Access is limited during the nesting season, but you can walk around the island at low tide. Boat trips can be organized from Puerto Soley.

REFUGIO NACIONAL SILVESTRE PEÑAS BLANCAS

🟩 232 F5 ☎️ Fundación de Parques Nacionales: 506 257 2239. Area de Conservación Pacífico Central (ACO-PAC): 506 416 7068 🕐 Daily 8–4 🎫 US$6 🚗 Leave the Pan-American Highway east of Esparza at Macacona, and head north to Peñas Blancas. There is a trail to the refuge from Peñas Blancas, but take a topographical map

Peñas Blancas National Wildlife Refuge is one of the least visited protected areas of Costa Rica. The reserve extends to 2,400ha (5,928 acres) and is distinctive for its rugged volcanic terrain and white rock deposits of diatomite, composed of skeletal remains of planktonic algae. Covering altitudes from 600m (1,968ft) to 1,200m (3,936ft), the refuge includes tropical dry, semideciduous and pre-montane forest. The region was once logged, but visitors can still enjoy the birds and butterflies, and may see peccaries or deer. There are no services in the park, but wilderness camping is allowed. Getting to the refuge is difficult without private transport.

CENTRAL PACIFIC AND NICOYA

This region reaches from the arid climate of the north-west to the humid jungle-clad hills of the south. It is home to the country's most popular national park, Manuel Antonio, lively surfer towns, rivers teeming with crocodiles and spectacular beaches.

MAJOR SIGHTS

Don't trip over buttressed roots at Hacienda Barú

Dominical is renowned for its surfing beaches

You can ride horseback along Jacó's long beach

Life in the slow lane: a three-toed sloth at Hacienda Barú

DOMINICAL

🕂 239 K9 🚌 Hourly buses from San José to San Isidro de El General from Calle 16, Avenida 1–3. From San Isidro several daily buses go to Dominical 🚗 It is a 3.5hr drive from San José. Go south on the Pan-American Highway as far as San Isidro de El General, where a right turn leads to Dominical www.dominical.biz

A 44km (26-mile) drive south from Quepos along the *costanera sur* (coast road) leads to Dominical, a small town at the mouth of the Río Barú. Dominical owes its success to the surf that pounds the coastline. If you want to surf, or learn how, it's a great spot. Locals can offer advice on places to go. Most hotels and restaurants lie along the road from Quepos or line the beach. Apart from surfing, there are tours and trips to Hacienda Barú, plus hiking and horseback riding in the forested hills of Escaleras. A turnoff 10km (6 miles) along the road to San Isidro, leads to a couple of waterfalls, the largest being Nauyaca Waterfalls, 50m (164ft) high (tel 506 787 8013, tours 8 and 2, US$40).

HACIENDA BARÚ

🕂 239 K9 ☎ 506 787 0003 🚌 The Quepos–Dominical bus passes the hacienda 🕐 Daily 🥾 Guided walks start at US$20 per person, rising to US$60 for a night in the jungle 🍽 Open-air restaurant 🚗 Hacienda Barú is 2km (1.25 miles) north of Dominical on the Manuel Antonio road www.haciendabaru.com

Hacienda Barú is an eco-friendly adventure park set in a privately owned National Wildlife Refuge. The owner, Jack Ewing, and his wife arrived in 1972 at a time when Costa Rican conservation was in its infancy. By the end of the 1980s, the cattleman-turned-conservationist had bought and protected the diverse property of 19.2ha (47.4 acres), where 310 bird species have been recorded.

Interpretive pamphlets allow you to wander the trails alone as slowly as you like. Guides are available if you prefer. Trails lead through forest, to an observation tower where you may see sloths, monkeys and peccaries.

Activities include tree climbing, and a night spent in the jungle. The beach is used by nesting olive ridley turtles and the rare hawksbill turtles that arrive from July through to October. Basic accommodation is available.

ISLA TORTUGA

🕂 237 E7 ⛴ Boat excursions from Montezuma; Calypso Cruises offers tours daily from Puntarenas www.calypsocruises.com

Isla Tortuga, 3km (2 miles) southeast of Curú (▷ 105), is a rugged, forested island fringed by a gorgeous white sand beach melting into jade waters good for snorkeling. The owners welcome day-visitors arriving on boats. Kayaks and aqua-bikes are available, sand volleyball is popular, and a loop trail that leads into the forested hills offers lovely views

over the Gulf of Nicoya. Many visitors are content to laze in a hammock beneath plams. The journey to the island is a treat in itself, passing between the Islas Negritos wildlife refuge—twin islands that protect an important nesting site for frigatebirds, brown boobies, and other seabirds. Calypso Cruises (tel 506 256 2727, US$99 including transfers from San José) has trips aboard the sleek *Manta Ray* catamaran.

JACÓ

🕂 238 G7 🚌 Several daily from San José Coca-Cola Terminal 🚗 Jacó is west of the Pacific *costanera* parallel to the beach, 117km (73 miles) from San José

Jacó, a classic stroll-and-discover beachside town, is a popular place as the closest beach to San José, a three-hour drive away. Costa Rica's original surf capital has no shortage of activities.

While Jacó is hardly paradise, the beach is 3km (2 miles) in length, with the busy main street, lined with bars, shops and businesses, running parallel.

Bahía Herradura, used in the 1992 movie *1492: Conquest of Paradise,* is the next beach north of Jacó. The climate for beach lovers is ideal from December to April when breezes keep temperatures in the mid 20s°C (around 77°F). The surf is best from May to November. Swimmers should take care because dangerous currents cause deaths each year.

If you are looking for a peaceful enclave, 5km (3 miles) to the south of Jacó is Playa Hermosa, a low-key surfing community, with mid- and budget-range accommodation.

In recent years, Jacó's image has been tarnished by a visible sex industry and petty crime. Local activities include zipline, horseback rides and kayak trips, plus the Pacific Rainforest Aerial Tram (tel 506 257 5961).

In need of renovation: the church of San Blas in Nicoya

Expatriates who have bought holiday homes in the Nosara area have joined together to limit further development

MALPAÍS

237 D7 Daily bus service from Cóbano to Malpaís From Paquera follow road to Cóbano, from where a road leads west for 11km (6.7 miles) to Carmen then south for Malpaís
www.nicoyapeninsula.com

At the southern tip of the Nicoya Peninsula, Malpaís is a small village strung out across a 3km (2-mile) road which abuts Cabo Blanco Nature Reserve to the south (▷ 108). As wild and remote as its name suggests, Malpaís (meaning "bad land") is famed as one of the best surfing destinations in Costa Rica. The area's appeal extends beyond its powerful surf breaks. Long white sands, creeks and natural pools stretch along the rugged coast. Fringed with forest, the beach abounds with howler monkeys and birdlife. To the north, Malpaís joins with Santa Teresa, a tiny former fishing village that has seen rapid development. Stylish lodges offer yoga, while rustic cabins satisfy the surfer community. Activities range from sportfishing to horseback riding, and even ultralight flying.

MONTEZUMA

237 E7 Regular buses from San José to Puntarenas. Then from Paquera to Montezuma (1hr 15min) Launches from Puntarenas to Paquera (1hr 15min) Road paved from Paquera to Montezuma, passing through Cóbano. During the rainy season a 4WD vehicle is recommended

A testing journey to the southern tip of the Nicoya Peninsula, four hours from Puntarenas, takes you to Montezuma. Once a quiet sleepy hamlet, Montezuma is a small village which made its way onto the tourist circuit by virtue of its laid-back alternative lifestyle. It is no longer a secret hideaway and little evidence of the Tico way of life remains. At busy periods, hotels are full every day, so check in early. Although it gets crowded, there are beautiful walks along wonderful beaches, rounded off by rocky points, great for exploring tidal pools.

Some 20 minutes on foot up the Montezuma River is a beautiful waterfall with a swimming hole. Intrepid walkers can continue up to more waterfalls, but accidents and deaths have been reported. Tour operators offer a range of tours including snorkeling at Isla Tortuga (US$40), horseback-riding tours (US$25), and mountain bike rental (US$5 per day). A popular trip is the boat taxi to Jacó (US$30), which goes to the Pacific coast in one hour. Farther afield, Cabo Blanco Nature Reserve is an enjoyable day-trip.

NICOYA

236 C5 Regular daily buses from San José. Hourly between Liberia and Santa Cruz Area de Conservación Tempisque (ACT) office on the north side of the square can help with visits to nearby Barra Honda National Park

Nicoya may be the provincial capital but it is really just a pleasant market town distinguished by possessing the country's second oldest church, the adobe Iglesia de San Blas. Although the pulpit dates back to the 16th century, the building was consecrated in 1644; it contains a museum of pre-Columbian objects. Before the Spanish conquest, Nicoya was the heart of the Chorotega community and takes its name from the local Indian chief. It is an important transport hub, with links to the beach communities of Sámara and Nosara to the south, the Tempisque ferry to the east, and Playa Naranjo on the tip of the peninsula.
Don't miss The Fiesta de la Yegüita, on 12 December, has parades, fireworks and bullfights.

NOSARA

236 B6 Daily direct bus from San José at 6am A good paved road leads from Sámara to Nicoya
www.nosara.com

THE SIGHTS

Nosara, 26km (16 miles) north of Sámara, is a small village with little to see or do, which makes it ideal if you like lazing on beaches. Most people come for the three unspoiled beaches nearby or to see the mass nestings of the olive ridley turtles at Ostional (▷ 108). Playa Nosara is to the north of the village across the Nosara River. Playa Pelada, the prettiest beach, south of the river, is a popular spot for surfers and has a bat cave. Playa Guiones is an expanse of white sand backed by dunes and forest. Nosara village is a long, hot walk 5km (3 miles) north of Playa Guiones. Much of the property backing Pelada and Guiones beaches is owned by expatriates, and the hills above Nosara are dotted with the homes of the rich and famous. Activities include hiking in the privately owned Reserve Biológica Nosara (tel 506 682 0035). Horseback-riding tours, fishing and boat trips into the mangrove swamps of the Nosara River can be arranged.

Exploring the Nicoya peninsula by mountain bike

Don't go caving alone in Barra Honda National Park

PARQUE NACIONAL BARRA HONDA

✚ 237 D5 ☎ 506 659 1551 🕐 Daily 8–4 💷 Entrance: US$6; cave descents: US$14 including guide and equipment 🚌 Daily from Nicoya to Quebrada Honda (first bus at 10.30am, last bus returns at 4.30pm, giving you only 2hr in park); then an hour's walk to Santa Ana and the park offices from bus drop-off point
www.sinaccr.net

To the west of Nicoya, a limestone outcrop contains Costa Rica's largest cave system and forms the heart of Barra Honda National Park. A network of 42 caves has been discovered, but only 19 have been explored. Because access is difficult, the caves are in excellent condition. A guide is compulsory to visit the caves, accessed by a fixed ladder. Caving is dangerous in the rainy season (May to November), and the dry season is hot; ensure that you have enough water.

PARQUE NACIONAL CARARA

✚ 238 G7 ☎ 506 200 5023 🕐 Daily 7–4 💷 US$8 🚌 Regular buses from San José or Puntarenas to Jacó go over the Río Tárcoles bridge and past the park entrance 🚗 Fom San José, head west on the Orotina Highway to Río Tárcoles bridge; 3km (1.8 miles) past the bridge is the rangers' station

Just 90km (56 miles) from San José, Carara National Park has the most accessible forest in the country and is a popular protected area. There are self-guiding trails for you to see some of its 750 plant species plus perhaps scarlet macaws, monkeys and poison-arrow frogs. Next to the park is La Catarata (tel 506 661 8283, Dec–Apr 8–3, US$10), a private reserve with an impressive waterfall with natural pools for bathing. It's a steady hike but worth the effort.

It is extremely rare for hammerhead sharks to attack humans

PARQUE NACIONAL ISLA DEL COCO

One of the largest uninhabited islands in the world, this remote UNESCO World Heritage Site is a diving paradise.

BASICS	RATINGS				
✚ 236 inset ☎ 506 258 7350	Marine life	●	●	●	● ●
🕐 Coco is an uninhabited island.	Wilderness	●	●	●	●
Most people stay offshore on board	Sports and activities	●	●	●	● ●

the dive vessel, *Okeanos Aggressor* (www.aggressor.com) as part of an all-inclusive package. Passengers are shuttled to the island to enjoy spectacular birdwatching (▷ 130–131)

TIPS
● A permit is required to visit the island.
● Diving is only recommended for very advanced divers due to strong currents.

Over 550km (330 miles) southwest of Costa Rica, the volcanic Isla del Coco rises from the sea floor at the western tip of the Coco Tectonic Plate. With an area of just 23sq km (9sq miles), the island rises steeply to the highest point of 634m (2,080ft) at Cerro Yglesias. The coast is lined with steep cliffs and the rugged terrain creates numerous rivers; some of the resulting waterfalls plunge into the ocean. Only the bays of Wafer and Chatham make the island accessible. Temperatures of 30°C (86°F) and an annual rainfall of 7,000mm (276in) guarantees cloud cover and verdant rainforest. The island's isolation means that several endemic species exist. Of the 87 bird species, three—the Coco Island flycatcher, cuckoo and finch—are only found here. Green, hawksbill and olive ridley turtles visit the bays. Offshore, the protected waters are rich with coastal reefs. Over 300 species of fish are found here, but the real interest lies in the hammerhead sharks that school in their hundreds, and the abundance of white-tipped sharks, whale sharks and manta rays.

The island showed no signs of habitation prior to the arrival of the Spanish. Poorly marked on navigational maps, only experienced sailors could find it. Legend claims that the pirates Benito Bonito, William Davies and Captain Thompson buried treasure here between the late 1600s and 1821, including the Lima Booty which is supposed to include a life-size statue of the Virgin Mary and Child in solid gold. Since then, over 300 expeditions have searched for the elusive sunken treasure. The island was a prison between 1872 and 1874. An exploratory trip in 1898 to reopen the penitentiary became a scientific expedition that realized the area's natural importance. Marine life is the main draw and most visitors are serious divers, arriving on live-aboard boats (▷ 131).

Puntarenas was once Costa Rica's main dock and a commercial fishing port, but the town has hit hard times

One of the mysterious Diquis spheres by the Quepos roadside

PARQUE NACIONAL MARINO BALLENA

⊞ 239 K9 ☎ 506 786 7161 ⊙ Park office in Playa Ballena: 8–4 (erratic) 🕭 US$6, but this is rarely collected 🚌 Buses to Uvita from San José Coca-Cola terminal 🚗 Take the *costanera* southeast from Dominical for 17km (10.5 miles) to Uvita, the main access point for the park www.marinoballena.org

On the Pacific coast, between Punta Uvita and Punta Piñuela, the Ballena (Whale) Marine National Park is one of the least-developed national parks. The main attractions are underwater: coral reefs and abundant marine life that includes dolphins and, occasionally, humpback whales. Offshore, Las Tres Hermanas and Isla Ballena mark the southern boundary of the park, providing nesting sites for frigatebirds, white ibis and brown pelicans.

Although there are three rangers' stations, rarely staffed, and signposts line Highway 34, the *costanera*, facilities in the park are nonexistent. However, a turtle nesting project at Bahía is administered by the local community and visitors are welcome. Boat trips to the islands can be arranged from Bahía, and diving is starting up.

Next to the Marino Ballena National Park, south of Uvita, is Rancho La Merced, a wildlife refuge with 500ha (1,235 acres) of rainforest and mangroves. The area can be explored, ideally on horseback, with trips to waterfalls, the beach, the mangroves or around the ranch.

PUNTARENAS

⊞ 237 F6 🚌 Regular buses from San José Terminal Puntarenas ⛴ Vehicle and passenger ferries to Paquera on the south side of the peninsula ℹ Casa de la Cultura, Calle 3, Avenida 1, tel 506 661 5036, 8–6

West of San José, the gritty provincial capital of Puntarenas is the main transport link on the Pacific coast. The northern side of this thin coastal sand spit is a bustling array of scruffy fishing and ferry docks. The southern side, six blocks away, is made up of the Paseo de los Turístas, a promenade and beach dotted with bars, cafés, restaurants and hotels. Neither aspect is particularly successful; both fishing and beaches are distinctly average. The Museum of Marine History (Avenida Central, Calle 3–5; Tue–Fri 9.45–noon, daily 1–5.15; free) in the Cultural Center is by the tourist office.

QUEPOS

⊞ 239 H8 🚌 From the Coca Cola terminal in San José 🚗 Highway 34, the *costanera*, passes Quepos a couple of kilometers (a mile or so) to the east; look for the signs

On the Pacific coast, 145km (90 miles) from San José, Quepos bears a legacy, in name at least, from the Quepo Indians who inhabited the region at the time of the Spanish conquest in 1519. As the main access point for Manuel Antonio National Park, which lies 7km (4 miles) over the rocky Punta Quepos peninsula, this unassuming

Pelicans wait for scraps from boats in Puntarenas

town pulsates with the crowds that converge in search of the palm-fringed beaches and wildlife encounters of the National Park (▷ 106–107).

Quepos has successfully moved beyond a dependency on banana exports, the raison d'être behind the now largely empty port development. The United Fruit Company began large-scale production in the 1930s, but plantations in the region were overwhelmed by disease in the 1950s and, economically, Quepos was crippled. The oil-producing African palm has replaced banana agriculture in the region (palm oil is used in the production of margarine and soap).

The lively bars and restaurants buzz and hum, but hanging silently in the background, the atmosphere of an old port town remains. A marina completed in 2007 has enhanced Quepos's reputation as a sportfishing hub.

REFUGIO NACIONAL DE VIDA SILVESTRE CURÚ

⊞ 237 E7 ☎ 506 641 0100 ⊙ Daily 7–3 🕭 US$8 🚌 Buses from Montezuma (leaving from Hotel Montezuma at 8am) to Paquera pass the park entrance

Between Bahía Ballena and Paquera, Curú National Wildlife Refuge vies for the title of smallest protected area in the country with a mere 70ha (173 acres). Rising from three beaches, good for swimming and snorkeling, there are five ecosystems, including mangroves. Mammals are equally diverse with deer, pacas, racoons and monkeys. The privately owned refuge is a good place to spot marine turtles nesting, in season. The Montezuma–Paquera bus can drop you at the locked gate. Make advance reservations for basic accommodation.

Parque Nacional Manuel Antonio

Manuel Antonio is a crowd-pulling area of outstanding natural beauty with short hiking trails, magnificent vistas, monkeys and rich birdlife. And the golden beaches are just as special.

Horse power: a sunset ride along Manuel Antonio's beach

Tropical forest and squirrel monkeys (top) in Manuel Antonio

The horseshoe bay of Playa Blanca

RATINGS	
Accessibility	●●●●●
Natural beauty	●●●●
Wildlife	●●●●

BASICS

✚ 239 J8

☎ 506 777 0654

🕐 Tue–Sun 7–4

💵 US$7

🚌 For San José to Quepos, ▷ 105. From Quepos main terminal to the road at Manuel Antonio, every 30 min

🅿 Arrive early to get a parking space. You can have your car watched for US$2.50 per day (car theft is not unusual; lock valuables in the trunk)

📷 Accredited wildlife guides can be arranged at the entrance to the park, or you can make arrangements at your hotel, US$20 per person

❓ Taxi from Quepos costs US$3

Iguanas are a common sight in Manuel Antonio

SEEING PARQUE NACIONAL MANUEL ANTONIO

Around 150km (90 miles) southwest of the capital (four hours by car) Manuel Antonio National Park is a genuine tropical wilderness and acclaimed as one of the most scenic landscapes of Costa Rica. Whether you are a lover of golden beaches and crystalline waters, or like to wander through tropical forests teeming with wildlife, there is something in this park for you. From the southeastern corner of Quepos (▷ 105), a road winds up and over the peninsula of Punta Quepos, passing the smart hotels, restaurants, bars and boutiques that flourish along this rocky outcrop, and have earned the area the title of Costa Riviera. The park's entrance is by the bridge over the Quebrada Camaronera tidal estuary; parking charges apply. As you enter the park, pick up a map and information on the trails, beaches and flora and fauna. Guides can be hired. Activities range from kayaking to surfing to dolphin watching and scuba diving.

HIGHLIGHTS

FLORA AND FAUNA

Manuel Antonio National Park is one of the smallest in the country. But its flora and fauna is impressive with an inventory of 109 species of mammal and 184 species of bird. High annual rainfall makes this a humid forest. The diversity is complemented by mangroves. Offshore, a dozen islands provide nesting sites for seabirds; the waters are rich with marine life, and biologists have identified 78 fish species. Punta Catedral, once an island, is now connected to the mainland by a sandbar. A trail, with viewing points, climbs over the headland. The former island is home to primary and secondary forest and an early morning walk will find you face to face with surprisingly timid wildlife including pacas, agoutis and iguanas. With a guide you'll see a lot more. Longer trails head east along the coastline passing the tree-fringed beaches of Manuel Antonio, heading out to Playa Escondido and on to Punta Serrucho and Playa Playitas. The trails are the best place to see monkeys, including white-faced capuchins and the rare squirrel monkey. But it is equally enjoyable to stroll just beyond the park entrance to one of the five sandy beaches, with gentle gradients good for swimming.

BACKGROUND

The threat to Manuel Antonio's natural wealth began with the arrival of the Spanish. After the indigenous peoples had been sold or wiped out by illness, land was cleared for farming. Much of the region was used for banana plantations, but the stunning vistas of the peninsula attracted foreign buyers. With locals denied access, state authorities became aware of plans to clear the land for agriculture. In haste, Manuel Antonio was declared a national park in 1972. Since then development has been limited to the access road to the west of the park. There is no denying that a booming tourism industry—150,000 people visit Manuel Antonio each year—and a national park do not sit easily together, but the extent of the damage depends on your perspective. The environmental impact is clear to see. Monkeys rather depressingly scavenge for food. Litter, pollution, sewage and petty crime are serious issues, and with up to 600 visitors each day, wildlife flees to quieter areas. For the time being at least development is limited but the future could be very different.

An aerial view of Manuel Antonio showing Cathedral Point

TIPS

● The best time to visit the park is early; aim to be at the park entrance by 7am to increase your chances of viewing wildlife.
● When hiking the trails, be aware of snakes that can easily be mistaken for jungle vines.
● Some of Manuel Antonio's beaches are lined by the poisonous manzanillo tree.
● Walking to the park from Quepos is not advised. Searing heat, steep inclines, serpentine twists and hazardous traffic make for a challenging and potentially dangerous hike.
● When returning from the park, the standard bus fare to Quepos is 200 colones per person.

MORE TO SEE
RAINMAKER CONSERVATION PROJECT

A short trip northeast of the park, a network of cable bridges between trees link platforms that afford a unique bird's eye view of the forest canopy (▷ 152).

Manuel Antonio

Quebrada Camaronera

Naranjo

Parque Nacional Manuel Antonio

Playa Espadilla

Entrada

Laguna Negra

Playa Espadilla Sur

Playa Puerto Escondido

Punto de Vista

Colonia de Tortuga

Playa Manuel Antonio

Punta Catedral

Isla Olocuita

0   1 km
0   1 mile

Punta Serrucho

Playa Playita

Pacific paddling: Try surf kayaking at Playa Sámara. The beach is relatively undeveloped but you can rent kayaks and other equipment

Stay dry at Playa Sámara and go for a horseback ride

REFUGIO NACIONAL DE VIDA SILVESTRE OSTIONAL

🔲 236 B6 🕓 Daily 8–4 💲 US$8; a guide (US$7) is compulsory during nesting season 🚌 Daily from San José at 5am to Santa Cruz and Liberia 🚐 Trips to the nesting grounds are arranged through hotels in Nosara and Sámara 🚗 Ostional is a 30-min drive north of Nosara. Visit the Ranger Station for details. Four-wheel-drive vehicle needed in rainy season

A short drive north of Nosara is Playa Ostional, a wide beach protected for the natural spectacle of the *arribada*, when tens of thousands of *lora* (olive ridley turtles) arrive to nest. Along with Playa Nancite to the north, Ostional is one of the world's most important nesting sites for the turtles. The *arribadas* occur between July and November with the largest numbers arriving between August and October, at the end of the lunar cycle. But you can normally see some turtle activity

at any time of the season. The beach is occasionally used by leatherback and green turtles. Locals are permitted to harvest turtle eggs under a program that incorporates conservation goals with the community's needs.

The beach is part of Ostional National Wildlife Refuge, protecting 352ha (869 acres) of land, including Nosara beach and a marine zone. The reserve's forest supports groups of howler and capuchin monkeys. On the north bank of the Río Nosara, mangroves, good to explore by kayak, are home to 100 bird species.

RESERVA NATURAL CABO BLANCO

🔲 237 D7 ☎ 506 642 0093 🕓 Wed–Sun 8–4 💲 US$8 🚌 Buses depart Montezuma at 8.15, 10.15, 2.15 and 4.15. A private shuttle service leaves Montezuma at 8am and 9am and picks you up outside the park at 3pm or 4pm, US$3 ⛴ Local boatmen can arrange transport farther up the peninsula or to the mainland. It's best to try and get a group to spread the cost ❓ A taxi will cost around US$10 per person

Neatly covering the southwestern tip of the Nicoya Peninsula, Cabo Blanco Nature Reserve is a precious reserve, both ideologically and biologically. Created in 1963, it is the oldest protected area in the country apart from the frontier corridor to the north with Nicaragua. The reserve is the legacy of Nicolás Wessberg and his wife, Karen Mogensen, who set out to preserve the stands of moist forest as development gradually denuded the surrounding area. The 1,800ha (4,448 acres) of the reserve were finally donated to the National Parks program in 1994, when Doña Karen bequeathed the land to the state.

Today, the reserve is easily visited on short trips from nearby Montezuma. It is composed of

tracts of evergreen and deciduous species in a beautiful moist forest that fringes the beaches and rocky headlands. With roughly 2,300mm (90in) of rain a year, this is one of the wettest spots on the peninsula. A couple of trails lead through the park, which for its size has a good variety of wildlife, including porcupines, armadillos and three species of monkey. The reserve is also an important site for seabirds including brown pelicans, frigatebirds and the largest nesting colony of brown boobies. Just beyond Cabo Blanco is beautiful Playa Balsitas, with lots of pelicans and howler monkeys; however, this area of the reserve is closed, although there are plans to open a trail from Malpaís.

SÁMARA

🔲 236 C6 🚌 Direct bus from San José Tracopa terminal. Daily from Nosara www.samarabeach.com

Around five hours' drive from San José, Sámara is a smallish village, set in a horseshoe bay, lined with thick jungly vegetation. Although relatively small, the beach is peaceful and excellent for bathing, with a rugged quality that development has thankfully not diluted. With several good international restaurants, internet facilities, a language school and a surf school, the village has a relaxed pace, where the gentle trickle of residents from around the world blends well with the ticking over of everyday life. The place offers a good excuse to get away for a few days and relax by the sea. For the more energetic, there are activities and excursions that can be arranged, with a clutch of tour operators offering watersports and horseback-riding tours in the area. Surfing is a local staple.

Olive ridley turtles nest at Ostional all year round

SOUTHERN REGION

Encompassing the country's highest mountains as well as its most biologically diverse national park, Corcovado, the Southern Region is the wildest and most remote area of Costa Rica. There are marvelous botanical gardens, countless wildlife-watching opportunities and, for surfers, several world-class breaks.

MAJOR SIGHTS

Spinner dolphins escort a boat from Delfín Amor in Drake Bay

Boruca Indians sell their handicrafts to visitors

Stilt houses in the duty-free port of Golfito

BAHÍA DRAKE

✚ 242 L11 🚌 Daily buses from San José Tracopa terminal to Palmar Norte. Overland connections to Sierpe then boat to Drake ℹ️ Corcovado Expeditions office in Aguijitas, tel 506 833 2384 🚗 Leave Pan-American Highway at Chacarita and follow road to Rincón. A right fork leads to Aguijitas. The road, only passable in dry season, demands a four-wheel-drive vehicle

A crescent-shaped bay on the north end of the Osa Peninsula, Drake (pronounced Dra-kay) Bay is named after Sir Francis Drake, the English buccaneer who, in March 1579, beached his ship on Playa Colorada in the bay in order to repair it. Drake is good for swimming, but the beach is pebbly and attracts lots of hotel boats. The main attraction is diving off Isla del Caño (▷ 117), and nearby Corcovado National Park (▷ 112–115). If you want to learn to dive, PADI dive centers offer courses to beginners. Diving in the area is mainly to view fish rather than coral but divers may spot white-tipped sharks and rays. Several hotels also arrange sportfishing. Researchers at the Delfín Amor Eco Lodge (▷ 205) have recorded 25 species of dolphins and whales in Drake Bay, including humpback whales and bottlenose dolphins as well as sea turtles. The lodge runs dolphin- and whale-watching tours; the best time is mid-November to end April. Day-trips to Isla del Caño, Corcovado and the mangroves of the Sierpe-Térraba estuary are offered by Corcovado Expeditions.

BORUCA

✚ 242 M10 🚌 From San José to Buenos Aires at 5am, 7am and 8.30am. From Buenos Aires 2 buses daily to Boruca 🛍️ Galería Namú (▷ 138) runs ecotours to the area, US$45 per person per day 🚗 Take Pan-American Highway

as far as the signs for Buenos Aires. Turn left and continue to Brujo, crossing bridge over the Térraba River, then turn right onto an uphill road which is signposted Boruca, from where it is a 40-min drive ❓ Taxi from Buenos Aires US$40

Nestling in the Río Térraba valley, two hours south of San Isidro de El General, the small community of Boruca is the focal point of the Boruca Indians, a tribe numbering less than 3,000 people. For much of the year, the village of 200 people is almost lifeless. But the rather unprepossessing homes scattered around an unkempt church belie a rich cultural heritage that has been eroding steadily since the arrival of the Jesuits in 1649. Today a cultural museum, sitting in the shadow of the church, is a sad reflection of the value placed on indigenous people in the country. But each year on the last day of December and the first two days of January the hardships of agricultural life are discarded in the celebrations of *La Danza de los Diabolitos*, the Dance of the Devils (▷ 28). If you can time your visit to coincide with the festival, visitors are welcomed.

GOLFITO

✚ 243 N11 🚌 Daily bus service from the Tracopa terminal in San José; regular service from Ciudad Neily 🚤 From Puerto Jiménez 🚗 Highway 14 leaves Pan-American Highway at Río Claro, 15km (9 miles) north of Ciudad Neily

The regional hub of Golfito is important as much for its tax-free trade status as for its positioning as the stepping off point for Playa Zancudo and Pavones to the south. It flourished when the United Fruit Company set up in the port in the 1930s. Bust

Walking on water: a Jesus Christ lizard at Caño Island

followed boom when the company pulled out in 1985. Arriving from the south, you'll pass a few of the better hotels in the town. To the north is the administrative heart of Golfito and the *depósito libre*—the tax-free zone where items are sold at about 60 percent of prices in the capital. It is the source of the town's relative affluence. Across the bay, or around the north shore, is Playa de Cacao, Golfito's closest beach. Today Golfito is a sportfishing hub, and a new marina promises future fortune.

JARDÍN BOTÁNICO WILSON

✚ 243 N11 ☎ 506 773 4004 🕐 Daily 8–4 💰 US$6 🍽️ A full-day guided tour costs US$24, half-day US$15 🚗 From Golfito, take Pan-American Highway south towards the Panamanian border; on reaching Ciudad Neily, head north www.ots.ac.cr

The Wilson Botanical Gardens, 6km (3.5 miles) south from San Vito, are one of the world's premier collections of tropical plants, open for day visits and overnight stays. The Wilson Gardens are part of the Las Cruces Biological Station, owned and operated by the Organization for Tropical Studies. As with La Selva and Palo Verde, the station is a focus for biologists, students, birdwatchers and naturalists, keen to take advantage of the phenomenal diversity of the region. The gardens have a network of trails and

Flowering inferno: exotic plants at Wilson Botanical Gardens

paths through the 10ha (24 acres) that take from 20 minutes to two and a half hours to walk, and self-guiding leaflets provide information allowing you to wander through the gardens at your own pace. Alternatively, go with a guide who will point out some of the 700 species of palms found in the garden; there are a total of 1,000 in the neotropics. Resident bird species total 331. For the complete experience, accommodation in airy cabins is available.

PALMAR NORTE AND PALMAR SUR

✚ 242 L10 🚌 Several daily express buses go to and from San José. Regular buses go to San Isidro de El General. Several daily buses to Sierpe, the first at 7am for the boat from Sierpe to Drake

At a major intersection on the Pan-American Highway, 120km (74 miles) south of San Isidro de El General, Palmar Norte is of particular interest to people fascinated by big trucks. The town, an important transport hub, is one big truck stop. Roads lead southeast to Golfito and the Panama border, south to Sierpe, northwest to follow the Pacific coast and inland to San José.

The most interesting features of the area are the mysterious, spherical stone carvings, *esferas piedras*, left by the Diquis culture. The region is littered with these curious objects that are most easily seen outside the Instituto Agropecuario in Palmar Norte or in Palmar Sur's main square, which lies on the opposite bank of the Térraba River, a couple of kilometers (a mile) to the south. As with much of Costa Rican archaeology, the construction and purpose of the stones, believed to be around 2,000 years old, is still open to debate. The largest stone carving in the region, at 1.7m (5.6ft) across, is thought to weigh 9 tons.

Head into the clouds: the little-visited La Amistad park

PARQUE INTERNACIONAL LA AMISTAD

The largest park in the country and with incredible natural diversity, La Amistad reaches beyond national boundaries.

BASICS
✚ 240 M8 ☎ 506 730 0846 in Buenos Aires 🕐 Daily 8–4 (call ahead to check station is manned) 💵 US$5 🚌 4 daily from San José Tracopa terminal to San Vito. Get off at Las Tablas, then jeep-taxi to Carmen. From Carmen it is a 4km (2.5-mile) hike to Altamira, then a 1.5km (1-mile) walk to the entrance

RATINGS	
Hiking and trekking	●●●○
Wilderness	●●●○
Wildlife	●●●●

TIP
● Serious trekkers can contact the Asociación Talamanqueña de Ecoturismo y Conservación (ATEC, ▷ 155) about a 10-day trans-Talamanca hike.

As the largest protected area in Costa Rica, La Amistad protects the Talamanca mountain range of south-central Costa Rica, covering an expanse of 199,147ha (491,893 acres), and extending south into Panama. La Amistad demonstrates how Costa Rica lies at the convergence of North and South American flora and fauna. Its inventory of species is unparalleled. Secluded, difficult to reach and lacking in services, the park is the preserve of the intrepid and time-rich. There are three rangers' stations at Tres Colinas, Estación Pittier and Altamira. On the Pacific side, your best access point is at the Monte Amou Lodge.

La Amistad National Park is the cornerstone of the International Amistad Biosphere Reserve, created by the United Nations in 1982. The reserve includes Tapantí-Macizo de la Muerte National Park (just south of Cartago), Chirripó National Park, four Indian reserves and several other protected areas. When Panama created the adjoining La Amistad National Park in 1990, the entire Talamanca mountain range became a World Heritage Site.

The Talamancas are the highest non-volcanic mountain range in Central America, created by uplift of the earth surface which was subsequently eroded by glacial activity and heavy rainfall. That rainfall—up to 6,000mm (236in) a year in places—has created steep-sided slopes that have kept humans out of some areas of the park. Temperatures range from 25°C (77° F) down to -9°C (16° F). Eight of the twelve ecosystems found in Costa Rica are present, including lowland tropical rainforest, cloud forest and *páramo*. Altitude peaks at 3,820m (12,530ft) at Cerro Chirripó. Over 9,000 species of flowering plants are found here, as well as Costa Rica's six species of cat, the quetzal and the harpy eagle.

Parque Nacional Corcovado

The most magnificent jewel in Costa Rica's green crown, this paradise for wildlife watchers gives visitors the rare chance to take long-distance treks through lowland rainforest and across flawless beaches.

If you get lost in Corcovado, follow a river downstream

Look but don't touch: a tiny poison-arrow frog in the forest

Cooling off in the San Pedrillo River in Corcovado

RATINGS

Adventure and challenge	● ● ● ● ○
Hiking	● ● ● ● ○
Wildlife	● ● ● ● ●
Photo stops	● ● ● ● ○

BASICS

✚ 242 L12

☎ 506 735 5580. To reserve accommodation (essential), contact MINAE, Puerto Jiménez on this number

💵 US$8 per day, or US$17 for a 5-day pass, paid at one of the rangers' stations

🚌 1 daily bus from San José Terminal Atlántico Norte to Puerto Jiménez.

🚢 Costa Rica Expeditions (▷ 178) organize the Corcovado Rainforest Odyssey, a 3-day, 2-night trip, which includes air transportation and accommodation at the Corcovado Lodge, all meals, a bilingual naturalist guide and canopy tour, US$483.65. Check the website for last-minute discounted special offers, www.costaricaexpeditions.com

🚗 Leave the Pan-American Highway at Chacarita and take a good road that follows the southern shore of the peninsula to Rincón; 14km (8.5 miles) beyond Rincón is La Palma, from where the road heads west to the Los Patos station

SEEING PARQE NACIONAL CORCOVADO

In the southwest corner of Costa Rica, the park protects one third of the Osa Peninsula (42,469ha/104,898 acres). Three rangers' stations provide access to the park. San Pedrillo, to the north, is reached through Drake from where you need to charter a boat or walk round the headland. Los Patos in the middle of the peninsula is reached from La Palma, served by buses coming from the Pan-American Highway to Puerto Jiménez. The final option is through La Leona to the south, reached from Carate, which has road access from Puerto Jiménez, 43km (27 miles) away. You can visit the park using any combination of entrances and exits.

The closest point approaching the park from the south is Carate, an excellent base for short trips to the park. It has good links with Puerto Jiménez to the east. From the capital, most people using public transportation choose to access the park from Puerto Jiménez, on one of the direct bus services. You can get off the bus at La Palma, 24km (15 miles) north of Puerto Jiménez, from where a 12km (8-mile) road leads to the park entrance. If you choose the route from Carate to La Leona be prepared for a hot, exposed beach hike. A new station at El Tigre, at the eastern entrance to the park, offers a series of short trails. Budget permitting, you can get an air taxi from Puerto Jiménez to Carate, San Pedrillo and even La Sirena for as little as US$99 per person with five people. Trails range from short tracks that take just a couple of hours to marathon challenges involving two-day hikes along beaches and through dense humid tropical forests where you have to negotiate swamps and rivers and camp overnight in the jungle. Basic accommodation is available at the rangers' stations San Pedrillo, Los Patos, La Leona and, the most commonly used, La Sirena. Bring a sleeping bag and mosquito net. You can camp for US$2 a night and meals are available.

HIGHLIGHTS

FLORA AND FAUNA

After Monteverde and Arenal, Corcovado National Park is probably the most recorded part of Costa Rica. National Geographic, Discovery

Río Agujas flows towards Golfo Dulce (above). A palm leaf (top)

I spy: a birdwatcher at Lapa Rios lodge on the Osa Peninsula

Remarkable reptile: a Jesus Christ lizard at Corcovado

Channel, the BBC and countless naturalists have described its delights, and with good reason. Often heralded as Costa Rica's Amazon, it contains the greatest expanses of primary forest on the Pacific and is true to the popular image of a rainforest: diverse species, soaring trees, magnificent buttresses and creeping vines. As ever, it's the combination of temperatures in the high 20°sC (around 82°F) and rainfall as high as 5,500mm (215in) that has endowed the park with eight different ecosystems. Cloud forest on some of the higher summits gives way to montane forest, which covers over half the park. There is swamp forest around Corcovado lagoon, mangrove forests along the river estuaries, herbaceous swamps and pristine coastline as well as more than 13 vegetation types, with over 500 species of tree.

Wildlife is equally diverse. Corcovado is home to the largest population of scarlet macaws in Central America. All six big cats in Costa Rica are found in the park, and the beach at Llorona to the north is used as a nesting site by four species of turtles. The staggering inventory extends to 140 species of mammals, more than 10 percent of the mammal species in the entire Americas, 367 species of birds, including the endangered harpy eagle, reptiles, 40 freshwater fish and 177 species of amphibians, such as the red-eyed tree frog and the poison-arrow frog. Monkeys abound: Corcovado and Manuel Antonio (▷ 106–107) national parks are the only two areas in Costa Rica where you will find the squirrel monkey. When it comes to wildlife spotting, your expectations should be realistic; you'll need a guide, patience and a good deal of luck to tick significant numbers off your list.

LA SIRENA

The area around the La Sirena rangers' station is the best place for viewing wildlife, where treks through wild, virgin landscapes last from 30 minutes to a few hours. You can explore inland paths and the Corcovado lagoon. It's definitely worth staying overnight at La Sirena.

It's about 18km (11 miles), and a six-hour hike, from Carate to Sirena, a coastal trail, which you can make in one day as long as the tides don't work against you; check with the wardens to ensure that you can get through. About 40 minutes beyond Carate is La Leona station. From La Leona to the end of Playa Madrigal is another two and a half hours of walking, over a partly sandy beach with some rock pools

---

TIPS

● If short of time or money, the simplest way to the park is to take the pick-up truck from outside Carolina's in Puerto Jiménez to Carate, from where you can go on short treks in the south of the park.

● Entering the park through Carate and exiting through La Palma, or vice versa, is the simplest and cheapest option.

● Always sign the rangers' book before you set off on a hike, regardless of length or difficulty. If you do not return, they will come to look for you.

● Many of the river trails along the beach will be impassable at high tide, and visitors have often been stranded. Consult the rangers before you set off and be sure to obtain a tide chart from the park information office.

● Setting off early on hikes is recommended, but leave after dawn to minimize chance encounters with snakes.

● Accommodation must be booked through the MINAE office in Puerto Jiménez.

● If making an independent trek, bring topographical maps from the Instituto Geográfico Nacional in San José.

and shipwrecks. At points the trail rises steeply into the forest and you are surrounded by mangroves, almonds and coconut palms. Look out for scarlet macaws feeding on the almond trees that skirt the beach. A couple of rivers break the beachline. The first, Río Madrigal, is about 15 minutes' walk beyond La Leona. Clear, cool and deep enough for swimming, it's a refreshing stop and a good place to spot wildlife.

From La Sirena there are opportunities for shorter hikes. The one-hour Guanacaste trail, named after the number of Guanacaste trees found along it, begins half a kilometer (quarter of a mile) from La Sirena rangers' station. It starts through dense primary forest that gives way to sparser secondary forest. The trail can be muddy and hazardous in places and several rivers need to be crossed. The Esuvellas trail is slightly longer and can be accessed from behind the rangers' station. Shaded by canopy, the trails are level and relatively easy, with

A waterfall in tropical Corcovado National Park

San Pedrillo beach: coastal trails can be hot and exposed

just a couple of rivers to negotiate. From La Sirena you can walk north along the coast to Llorona, continuing north on a forest trail and then along the beach to the station at San Pedrillo. You can stay here and eat with the rangers if you've made a reservation.

Buttressed roots support giant ceibo trees in the rainforest

LOS PATOS

From Sirena you can hike inland on a trail to Los Patos (20km/12 miles), that will take between six and nine hours, passing several rivers full of reptiles. This is only recommended for very experienced hikers, with searing heat, high humidity and no breeze. However, the rewards are great, providing some of the best opportunities to see elusive mammals. The rangers' station at Los Patos has a balcony, which is a great observation point for birds. From Los Patos you can carry on to the park border, before criss-crossing the Río Rincón to La Palma, a settlement on the opposite side of the peninsula (13km/8 miles), a further six-hour hike. From La Palma there is transport to Puerto Jiménez.

SAN PEDRILLO TO LA LEONA

Close to Drake Bay, San Pedrillo is the most northern of the three rangers' stations. From the east side of the rangers' station, a one and a half-hour trail ascends to the northern parameters of the National Park. Before the plateau, there is a look-out point from which you may see dolphin and whales. From the boundaries of the park, you can hike to Playa San Josecito or return towards the rangers' station and hike to the San Pedrillo River (one hour). This is a steep descent and can be dangerous in the rainy season. Crossing the San Pedrillo River will bring you to a magnificent waterfall (swimming is not advised). Crossing the river from the left side will bring you back to San Pedrillo.

Walking the coastal path from San Pedrillo to La Leona takes three days, without allowing for time spent exploring trails around Sirena. The Sirena River is the park's deepest river, but not for the nervous. Crocodiles can be seen reposing on the banks and sharks feed at the river mouth at high tide (only cross at low tide). There is myriad birdlife along the riverbanks and beautiful waterfalls at Playa Llorona.

Bridge over muddy water: river crossings in Corcovado demand an adventurous spirit

BACKGROUND

Corcovado was granted National Park status in 1975 and now protects the largest area of tropical rainforest in the country. Some 30sq km (11sq miles) were deforested before it became a national park; the area's timber was more valuable than its gold.

Gold mining in the park was started by the indigenous populations in the 8th century. The Costa Rican gold rush of the 1930s ushered in a renewed period of mining and the 1970s saw the introduction of damaging techniques, causing the contamination of the southern third of Corcovado. In 1979, an economic slump saw banana prices plummet. But the price of gold rocketed and many men relocated to Corcovado. By the mid 1980s there were 3,000 illegal miners in the park. A technique known as placer mining has since proved responsible for 80 percent of the park's landslides. Soil sediment and the leaching of mercury, compounded the problem. And the human presence in the forest led to hunting and poaching. Following reports by the World Wildlife Fund, the park was cleared of gold prospectors in 1985.

Corcovado is now a gold mine of ecotourism

Beached: driftwood is washed up by the tide on Playa Zancudo. The town is popular with expatriates and offers basic amenities

Coconut palms line the world-class surfing beach of Pavones

PARQUE INTER-NACIONAL LA AMISTAD

See page 111.

PARQUE NACIONAL CHIRRIPÓ

See pages 118–120.

PARQUE NACIONAL CORCOVADO

See pages 112–115.

PARQUE NACIONAL PIEDRAS BLANCAS

🏢 243 M11 ☎ 506 775 0901 🅾 Daily 8–4 💵 US$4 🚌 2 buses daily from San Jose Terminal Alfaro to Golfito. Get off at Villa Briceño, 45km (28 miles) before Golfito. If staying at Esquinas Rainforest Lodge, arrange for them to pick you up 🚗 From Briceño on the Pan-American Highway a rough road leads to Esquinas Rainforest Lodge and Piedras Blancas

Primordial and challenging, this relatively unexplored park pulses with wildlife, ranging from sloths, coatis, peccaries, caimans and turtles to red-eyed leaf frogs, iguanas and ocelots. The park's real attraction is the opportunity to experience the jungle without sharing it with hundreds of other visitors. Smart lodges organize guided hikes on the network of trails and the park also runs the Esquinas Rainforest Lodge (▷ 206). The land was initially purchased by the Austrian government to preserve the rainforest from loggers. By 2004, 15,000, mostly Austrian, individuals had donated US$2million.

PAVONES

🏢 240 L9 🚌 2 buses daily from Golfito to Pavones. For transport from San José to Golfito ▷ 110 🚤 A water taxi from Golfito (US$5 per person) is the best way to reach Pavones; contact the ABOCAP (Asociación de Boteros, tel 506 775 0712) 🚗 Just outside Golfito, take the turnoff at El Rodeo and then the car ferry to Pavones

Formerly a sleepy little village, Pavones, a three-hour journey south of Golfito, has become a world-class surfing destination, with surfers arriving in droves to ride the country's longest left hander which, if the swell is right, can allow for an awesome three-to four-minute ride. April to September is the best time for surfing. Regardless of the time of year, surf culture prevails, testified by the mellow vibe, basic accommodation, and the sun-tanned and sculpted torsos on show. While surfing is the main activity in the area, fishing, horseback riding, kayaking trips, hiking to waterfalls in the area, snorkeling and sunset tours can easily be arranged. Pavones's two rocky black-sand beaches, Río Claro and Pavones, stretch south at the mouth of the Golfo Dulce to Punta Banco with the remote tropical retreat of Tiskita Jungle Lodge (▷ 206). If you want a quiet beach, Zancudo (below), is a better choice than Pavones.

PLAYA ZANCUDO

🏢 243 N12 🚌 1 bus a day from Golfito at 2pm 🚤 The best way to town is by water taxi. Contact Zancudo Boat Tours, tel 506 776 0012, US$12.50 per person, minimum US$30. Or visit Land Sea Tours' office in Golfito (tel 506 775 1614), which will arrange transport from town 🚗 Drive to Zancudo from Paso Canoas, or by cutting through on the Golfito–Río Claro road 10km (6 miles) from the Pan-American Highway, turning right at Bar El Rodeo and catching the ferry across the Río Coto Colorado. Either way be prepared to get lost as signposts are poorly marked

Leaving the bay of Golfito and heading south, you cross the mangrove estuary of the Río Coto Colorado and eventually arrive in Zancudo, with not only a fine miles-long beach but excellent sportfishing facilities too. Arriving at dusk, you are greeted by the beams of the setting sun shining through the coconut palms. For beach lovers, Zancudo has a captivating charm that has attracted American and European expatriates who have created a balance of laid-back comforts while avoiding any complicated trappings. In contrast to Pavones, the beach provides good bathing conditions and at dusk the town gathers to enjoy the mesmerizing sunset. Fishing fans will find a top-notch fishing lodge, which organizes trips to deep waters that offer world-record-size fish.

PUERTO JIMÉNEZ

🏢 243 M12 ⛴ Ferries cross the Gulf of Dulce to Golfito three times daily ℹ Ask at Restaurant Caroline's on the main street, and visit Escondido Trex (tel 506 735 5210, www.escondidotrex.com). They offer tours on the Osa Peninsula and around the Dulce Gulf 🚗 The 79km (49-mile) road from the Pan-American Highway to Rincón is badly eroded, from Rincón a potholed dirt road heads south for 35km (21 miles) to Puerto Jiménez

The main point of entry for Corcovado National Park, Puerto Jiménez is the most significant town on the Osa Peninsula. Once the gold-mining hub of the area with a single, dusty main street, Puerto Jiménez retains the feel of a lawless frontier town. Today, Puerto Jiménez is a popular destination with a laid-

A Puerto Jiménez local

Sunset at Puerto Jiménez, gateway to Corcovado

Harvesting coffee beans in Durika Biological Reserve

San Isidro's concrete cathedral has divided opinion

Beach scene at Puerto Jimenez

back lifestyle, reasonable beaches and the beautiful national park not far away. One attraction of Puerto Jiménez, five blocks square, is its relative freedom from road traffic. There are budget accommodations, a smart sportfishing lodge, good walks to the jungle and beaches only a couple of blocks from the main street. But you don't even have to go that far to see wildlife: scarlet macaws roost in trees around the football pitch. If your accommodation is out of town, make arrangements to be picked up from the airstrip, dock or bus station. Regular pick-ups make the trip to Carate from Puerto Jiménez, from where you can go to Corcovado.

RESERVA BIOLÓGICA DURIKA

🏕 240 M9 • Apd Postal 9-8100 ☎ 506 730 0657 💲 US$35 per person 🚌 Several daily buses from San José to Ciudad Neily and Paso Canoas pass through Buenos Aires 🚌 Reserve is 17km (10.5 miles) east of Buenos Aires, off the Pan-American Highway, reached by four-wheel-drive vehicle via a challenging mountain drive www.durika.org

Lying 17km (10.5 miles) east of Buenos Aires, the private Durika Biological Reserve spreads over 800ha (1,976 acres) in the Talamanca Mountains. The community aims to encourage re-forestation and conservation of the region and ecotourism plays a part in that process. Good trails through the area and to nearby Cerro Durika (3,280m/ 10,758ft) give an insight into this rarely visited part of Costa Rica. Accommodation is available in five rustic cabins. All sorts of healthy pursuits for mind and body are available, including yoga, kung-fu and short hikes to *campesino* (peasant farmer) and Indian communities and longer hikes to the mountain peaks. The steep, winding access road is one of the most daunting drives in the country. A jeep-taxi from Buenos Aires is recommended.

RESERVA BIOLÓGICA ISLA DEL CAÑO

🏕 242 K11 ☎ 506 735 5717 💲 US$6 🚢 The only way to visit the island is as part of a tour. Most people take an all-inclusive tour from Corcovado, around US$70 per person 🛈 The office for the Osa Peninsula Conservation Area is in Puerto Jiménez (daily 8–1, 2–5)

Some 20km (12 miles) west of the Osa Peninsula, Caño Island Biological Reserve has a striking coastline formed by jagged cliffs, white sandy beaches and coral reefs. It is a popular day trip from Sierpe and Drake Bay. The island's main interest, on land at least, is archaeological. Remains indicate that the island was used as a pre-Columbian cemetery. The stone spheres found in the mainland's Diquis Valley are present here, adding to the mystery of how and why these stone spheres were made.

The island attracts divers and snorkelers. The 2,700ha (6,669-acre) marine reserve protects

coral reefs, parrotfish, olive ridley turtles and the giant conch. Excellent dive sites include "The Depth of the Devil," with reef sharks, barracuda and rock pinnacles thrusting from the deep.

SAN ISIDRO DE EL GENERAL

🏕 239 K8 🚌 Hourly from San José, Calle Central, Avenida 22–24 🛈 CIPROTUR, the Centro de Información y Promoción Turística del Pacífico Sur, Calle 4, Avenida 1–3, tel 506 771 6096; a regional tourist board www.ecotourism.co.cr

The largest town south of San José, San Isidro de El General, shortened to San Isidro, rests at the base of a broad fertile valley created by several rivers. Completion of the Pan-American Highway in the 1950s has seen the town grow as a transport hub for journeys north, south and east. Its main areas of interest are in a seven-block square, all within walking distance. The town is the main departure point for ascents of Cerro Chirripó, and descents of the Río General white-water rapids.

San Isidro is best known to Ticos for one significant event: José Figueres Ferrer (▷ 39) used it as a foothold from which to launch the civil war of 1948. The conflict gave birth to the modern political era in Costa Rica and led to the abolition of the nation's army.

In the mid-1950s, the cathedral of San Isidro Labrador, patron saint of the town, was consecrated. For some, the concrete church is a bold statement, for others nothing short of sacrilegious. Inside, it is bright and breezy with a fresh approach to religious iconography. The old marketplace, now the Complejo Cultural, at Calle 2, Avenida 1-0, contains the Museo Regional del Sur (Mon–Fri 8–12, 1.30–4.30).

THE SIGHTS

Parque Nacional Chirripó

Costa Rica's second largest national park (50,150ha/123,870 acres) embodies the adventure and biodiversity of the country. The park's main attraction lies in the challenge of conquering Cerro Chirripó, the country's highest peak, at 3,820m (12,497ft).

Don't forget a sunhat: Hikers set off for Cerro Chirripó

The Poor Man's Umbrella plant. Chirripó National Park (top)

The modest main street of San Gerardo de Rivas

RATINGS	
Hiking	● ● ● ●
Wilderness	● ● ● ●
Accessibility	● ●
Photo stops	● ● ● ●

BASICS

✚ 240 L8

☎ 506 742 5083

◉ US$15, two days, then US$10 for each additional day. Each night at the refuge costs a further US$10

🚌 Local buses from San Isidro de El General, ▷ 117, to San Gerardo de Rivas and Parque Nacional Chirripó at 5am and 2pm, returning at 7am and 4pm. They leave from the bus terminal, south of the main plaza. Regular buses ply all routes with terminals on or close to the highway

🚗 Around US$500 for a 3-day organized round trip. Contact the regional specialists Costa Rica Trekking Adventures, who will organize your trip, tel 506 771 4582

www.chirripo.com

SEEING PARQUE NACIONAL CHIRRIPÓ

With neighboring La Amistad International Park, Chirripó protects the Talamanca Mountains from south of Cartago down to the border with Panama. The ecological wealth of the park is due to the diversity of landscape that ranges from pastures at 1,000m (3,280ft) around San Gerardo de Rivas to the barren scenery at the peak of Cerro Chirripó. The park's main access point is San Gerardo de Rivas, which has good transport links to San Isidro (20km/12 miles northeast), and where there is a rangers' station (daily 6.30am–4.30pm). Inside the park there are *refugios* (huts) at Llano Bonito (open sided, insect ridden), halfway to the summit and another basic refuge about 3km (2 miles) farther uphill. The Centro Ambientalista lodge, 5km (3 miles) from the summit, has bunk beds and cooked meals (by pre-arrangement); reservations are strongly advised via the ranger station.

Temperatures vary immensely; the driest period is between mid-December and mid-April, when most people visit the park. During Semana Santa, the park gets very crowded and on weekends the *refugios* often fill up quickly. At night, temperatures drop, at their lowest, to -9°C (16°F) and with thick fogs and windspeeds in excess of 80kph (50mph), conditions can be bitter. Warm clothing is essential, as is rain gear from May to the end of December. It is possible to walk a circuit of the park, but you will need a guide and good topographical maps. You can rent porters to carry your equipment to the hut (US$30 per day, tel 506 742 5073). Most of the local lodges are able to assist with arrangements. If all you want to do is climb the peak and let someone else do the organization, most tour operators in San José will arrange it.

HIGHLIGHTS

FLORA AND FAUNA

The ecological richness of Chirripó is difficult to imagine. In a world of subtle tropical variations, the presence of classic glacial formations like U-shaped valleys, moraine deposits and glacial lakes appear out of place. From around 3,000m (9,840ft), the barren *páramo* landscape is of stunted forest, mosses, alpine grasses and savanna covering a

broad open plateau. The oak landscape just below the summit area is recovering from a fire in 1992. Around the summit, trails lead to the rocky outcrop of Cerro Crestones, the Valles de los Conejos (Valley of the Rabbits) and the Sabana de los Leones (Lions' Savanna).

At lower altitudes, and warmer temperatures, meadows give way to cloud forest (more than half of the park's total area) with an incredible diversity of flora and fauna, in particular the birds, of which there are over 400 species including the resplendent quetzal. The park contains 263 species of amphibians and reptiles and is home to the largest tapir population in the country, as well as significant numbers of puma, jaguar, coatis, monkeys and other species of mammals.

Las Morenas lakes seen from Cerro Chirripó's summit

CLIMBING CERRO CHIRRIPÓ GRANDE

For those in search of a good long trek, a two-day trip in Chirripó National Park is the answer. As far as walks go, it's a pretty tough number, but the trail is well marked and there's little chance of getting lost. While technically and navigationally the ascent of Cerro Chirripó Grande is straightforward, with a reasonable level of fitness required, conditions can be brutal with cold temperatures and muddy terrain.

The trail skirts through evergreen forest, floats among cloud forest cloaked in swirling mists and eventually leads onto the barren *páramo* savannas. Along its length, the fauna changes constantly and the views from the top to the Atlantic, the Pacific and down the spine of the Talamanca range are spectacular, especially at sunrise.

Climbing steadily from a starting altitude of 1,400m (4,600ft), the 18km (11-mile) ascent takes eight to ten hours (conservative estimate) to the Centro Ambientalista el Paramoa *refugio* at 3,400m (11,155ft) above sea level, where there is basic accommodation, equipped with running water, toilets and a cold shower. Leaving by 6am will get you past the steep open plains under the shade of the tree canopy, therefore avoiding the merciless sun. From the refuge, it's a couple of hours, mostly on the flat, to ascend the last 400m (1,300ft) of the hike. Organizing the two- or three-day trip is straightforward. The refuge has 15 dormitory rooms, with four beds in each, and a kitchen for preparing food. Basic accommodation at the refuge is reserved through MINAE (the Ministerio del Ambiente y Energia), which has offices in San Isidro (tel 506 771 3155) and San Gerardo de Rivas (tel 506 742 5083).

TIPS

● Supplies in San Gerardo de Rivas are limited. If you are hiking, buy in San Isidro before arriving in the area.

● With often freezing conditions, a stove for cooking and making hot drinks is essential.

● Don't underestimate the severity of the climate and remember that sunscreen is essential this close to the equator.

● The refuge can get very full, particularly in the dry season from January to April, and on weekends, so book in advance if possible. Sleeping bags and small gas stoves are available for rent for a small fee.

● Topographical maps, necessary for long-distance hikes in the park, are available from the Instituto Geográfico Nacional or Lehmann's bookstore in San José.

● Basic maps of the park can be bought from the MINAE office (Ministerio del Ambiente y Energia) for US$0.80.

Day 1: Start the trek early, around 6am or earlier if possible, and aim to get to the lodge in one day. It is a long, sometimes slippery, uphill trek with barely any level ground, let alone downhill sections, to break the monotony. While the scenery compensates, you don't want to be struggling toward the top with nightfall approaching. Water is available at the very basic, open-air Llano Bonito refuge at 2,500m (8,200ft) reached after about three hours. It is possible to stay at Llano Bonito but the conditions vary and are not reliably clean.

Day 2: Another early start, leaving the lodge around 3.30am, the trek goes along a mainly level trail to the final summit push, a rock scramble of approximately 200m (650ft or so), to the peak for sunrise. Desolate and harsh, this lunar landscape is only 10 degrees from the equator. If short of time, you can head downhill and catch the

Views of remote Chirripó National Park (above and top) — *The landscape changes from lush forest to barren highlands* — *The interior of jungle lodge Hotel Chirripó Pacífico*

MORE TO SEE
THERMAL SPRINGS

Close to San Gerardo de Rivas these hot springs are rather handy for weary legs after the stiff climb. From the rangers' station turn left towards Herradura and follow the signposts. Admission for the day is US$2.

CERRO CRESTONES

If you have time, rather than taking the straightforward descent from Chirripó (the most popular route), you could take things more slowly and enjoy the simple trek to the outcrops of Cerro Crestones.

4pm bus to San Isidro. Other trails in the area are easily navigated, although you may feel more comfortable with maps or a guide.

BACKGROUND

On 19 August 1975, Chirripó National Park was officially established. The park was expanded in 1982 and was designated a UNESCO Biosphere Reserve before being granted World Heritage Site status in 1983. Chirripó, meaning "land of eternal waters," evolved through volcanic and tectonic activity. A series of glacial lakes, rock bed striations and curved moraines provide evidence of Chirripó's history. Geologists believe that 25,000 years ago, during the last ice age, the area was covered with glacial ice. The last glaciers disappeared 10,000 years ago. Before the arrival of the Spanish, the *páramo* highlands were considered to be sacred by the area's indigenous population, a reverence that precluded exploration. In 1904, Agustín Blessing, a Talamancan priest and missionary, became the first man to conquer Cerro Chirripó.

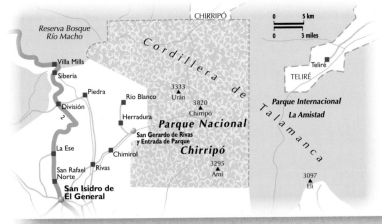

THE CARIBBEAN LOWLANDS

Until recently, the Caribbean coastal plain was geographically and culturally isolated and it can feel like another country. Increasing numbers of visitors arrive at the lodges for fishing, watersports and trekking. But the highlight is watching turtles and other wildlife at Tortuguero and Barra del Colorado parks.

MAJOR SIGHTS

Parque Nacional Tortuguero

It's a waterborne adventure to reach this wildlife-filled rainforest paradise, but Tortuguero is one of Costa Rica's treasures. The sea turtles grab the headlines, but look for frogs, jaguars and Jesus Christ lizards too.

A green turtle equipped with CCC satellite communications

Motor boats (above) can disrupt animals, unlike canoes (top)

In one of the world's wettest places you won't be dry for long

RATINGS

Good for kids	●●●○
Photo stops (landscape)	●●●●●
Wildlife spotting	●●●●●

BASICS

✚ 235 L4

☎ 506 709 8086

🎟 US$7 for 1 day. A 3-day pass is US$10, which is paid to the headquarters at the southern end of the town before beginning any trip through the waterways. Guides cost US$5 per member of the group

🚤 Transport by boat to Tortuguero is easily arranged. The simplest option is from Moín, a few kilometers (a couple of miles) north of Limón from where you hire a private boat heading up the coastal canal; a water-taxi also departs Moín at 3pm, tel 506 799 1167; US$25). It is also possible to catch a boat from GEEST Casa Verde, a short bus ride from Cariari. Or you can charter a vessel from Puerto Viejo de Sarapiquí, the most expensive option. Most all-inclusive packages leave from Caño Blanco Marina close to Matina. If you need to charter a vessel there are several options. Willie Rankin (tel 506 795 2556) travels from Moín to Tortuguero

📷 Nighttime trips along the beach are coordinated through the lodges or the information kiosk in town

SEEING PARQUE NACIONAL TORTUGUERO

Tortuguero National Park, 84km (52 miles) north of Puerto Limón, is the most important nesting site for leatherback and green turtles in the Western Hemisphere. The park's 29,068ha (71,798 acres) is made up of a network of waterways that meander through the vast alluvial plain created by rivers flowing off the Central Highlands' eastern slopes. By the time the rivers reach the coast they have slowed almost to a standstill and with high rainfall, the dense forest is often flooded. The flat landscape is bursting with plant life crowding up to the edge of waterways, only occasional gaps providing a glimpse of the world within.

While listening for nesting turtles on beaches after dark is the major attraction, trips inland along the natural rivers and man-made channels are a year-round pleasure. The usual way to see the forest is from a small launch passing along narrow creeks. Turtle tours are arranged through your lodge or tour operators in Tortuguero. Most people visit Tortuguero as part of a package tour from San José. Flights from San José with Sansa and Nature Air land at the airstrip, 4km (2.5 miles) north of town.

Tortuguero village is the hub of the area. Flowing north from the village is the Laguna de Tortuguero which leads for 5km (3 miles) to the Caribbean. Lodges have spread along either side of the waterway, and on the canal running parallel inland to the west. You can also find rustic accommodation in the village and organize a guide independently. La Pulpería (tel 506 709 8095) has information about tours and boat rental. The ranger station at the south end of the village has information about the turtles and the area. You need to register here for turtle tours if you are not part of a lodge package.

HIGHLIGHTS

TURTLE WATCHING

The main reason for visiting Tortuguero is to see nesting turtles. The Caribbean beaches of the National Park protect the nesting sites of the green turtle and also, in smaller numbers, the huge leatherback, hawksbill and loggerhead turtles. To see one of these magnificent

creatures emerge from the ocean surf, haul itself up the beach and dig a nest is an unforgettable experience. And to witness the tiny hatchlings emerge from their sandy burrow before heading frantically for the ocean, like wind-up mechanical toys, is similarly memorable.

Tours to see nesting turtles take place at night. Strict rules govern the tours which are led by authorized guides. You must be accompanied and flashlights, cameras, video cameras and smoking are prohibited. Tours last for two hours; some may find trudging blindly along the beach and struggling through undergrowth difficult. You are advised to wear dark clothes and closed shoes. These restrictions are designed to limit disturbance to turtles; being quiet is also requested.

As with many activities in Costa Rica, getting the timing right to see this natural phenomenon is essential. The green turtles lay their eggs at night between June and October, with the hatchlings emerging from the depths of their sandy nests until November at the latest. Leatherbacks can be seen between March and June.

WILDLIFE

Tortuguero is one of the country's most diverse national parks and home to over half the bird and reptile species in the country. There are more than 300 bird species in Tortuguero. The looping flight of the keel-billed toucan crossing the open waterways is a common sight and you may be lucky and see an endangered green macaw. Wildlife viewing in the area is spectacular and best seen from a boat. Mammals are numerous with howler monkeys and sloths commonly spotted, while hidden within the undergrowth the tracks of jaguar, ocelot and tapir go unseen by most as do endangered manatees that graze in the watery channels. The fishing bulldog bat, a large bat with a 60cm (23in) wingspan hunts on the waters of the canals. Reptiles and amphibians are on the scene in large numbers: you may see crocodiles and tiny poison-dart frogs.

TOURING THE WATERWAYS

From Tortuguero Lagoon a network of smaller channels is accessible by launch. If you travel in silence and with a good guide, you are certain to see much wildlife. Most tours leave early in the morning when birdlife is most in evidence and the chance of seeing mammals is

TIPS

● With an average temperature of 26°C (79°F) and rainfall between 4,500mm and 6,000mm (176in and 236in) a year, Tortuguero is one of the wettest spots in the country. While rainfall is slightly less in February and March there is a high chance of rainfall throughout the year.

● According to the information center, July to October is the best time to see green turtles nesting. The leatherback or *baula* nests between March and June.

● Keep an eye on the tagged turtles at www.cccturtle.org

Locals often travel by boat (top). Tortuguero's church (above)

Riverside plants at Caño Palma biological station in Tortuguero

Stealthy kayakers go wildlife spotting in Tortuguero

MORE TO SEE

CERRO TORTUGUERO

At the mouth of Tortuguero Lagoon, Cerro Tortuguero rises to 119m (390ft). While the height is nothing in an area that is overwhelmingly flat, the views from the top are spectacular. Walks up the hill can be arranged through lodges and local guides.

LOMAS DE SIERPE

Rarely visited, these hills rise to 335m (1,100ft) and lie to the west of Tortuguero. They make a good day-trip for those wanting a more challenging trek.

PARISMINA

Perched at the mouth of the Río Parismina, the small riverside hamlet of Parismina is one of the best places in the world to fish for tarpon and snook. Several dedicated fishing lodges cater to anglers.

also higher. Tours with lodges are normally included in the price. If you organize your own tour you have a slightly greater variety to choose from; the secret to a good tour is being quiet. On a self-organized tour you can take a guide who uses paddle power. Most boats use motor engines to get to the quieter channels. On entering the park they are legally required to switch to electric engines to reduce noise and wave-wash damage to the banks. Keen to maximize the time clients spend wildlife viewing, many guides stay in the channels as long as they can. In order to make up time when they return to the main river, they may increase speeds so that waves crash against the banks. Never encourage your guide to go fast.

BACKGROUND

The land between Limón and the Río San Juan on the border of Nicaragua is tantamount to an offshore island. It can only be reached by air or river travel through the inland waterways and canals surrounding Tortuguero or Barra del Colorado. It is the largest area of tropical wet forest in Costa Rica. During the 1940s, logging companies exploited the area for timber and the coastal canals of the northern Caribbean were built in the mid-1960s to connect the river-dwelling indigenous communities and to provide a more efficient means of transporting lumber to Limón. However, this is still one of the least accessible parts of the country.

Tortuguero village was first populated in the time of pirates when turtles provided a supply of meat for the mariners. The turtle harvest continued until research by Archie Carr, a prominent figure in the Costa Rican conservation movement, in the 1950s suggested that the green turtle was probably heading for extinction; virtually every nesting female turtle in Tortuguero was caught and exported for turtle soup. And indeed, Tortuguero, which means "turtle seller," still makes a living from its turtles.

The research continued with the creation of the Caribbean Conservation Corps (tel 506 224 9215). Carr's work and energy were crucial in the creation of Tortuguero National Park. Today the Corporation has an exhibition to the north of town (tel 506 709 8091, daily 10–12, 2–5.30) and continues tagging work with the turtles monitored by satellite. Nonetheless, the conservation ethic remains weak among the local populaton—report anyone digging up turtle nests.

Caribbean charm: palm-backed Playa Negra near Cahuita

The Salsa Brava wave peaks from December to February

PARQUE NACIONAL CAHUITA

Cahuita National Park has some of Costa Rica's best coral reefs. Its beaches capture the Caribbean's essence.

BASICS	RATINGS			
✚ 241 P7 ☎ 506 755 0302 ⏰ Daily 8–4 💵 US$6 🚌 Several daily from San José Terminal Gran Caribe 🚗 Cahuita is down an unassuming road off Highway 36, 10km (6 miles) south of the petrol station at Penshurst. From San José head east along the Guápiles road to Puerto Limón and turn south	Accessibility	● ● ● ○		
	Wildlife	● ● ● ●		
	Natural beauty	● ● ● ●		

TIPS
● Valuables go missing if left unattended on beaches.
● The best time for snorkeling is mid-February to April.

The Afro-Caribbean village of Cahuita, 43km (26 miles) south of Puerto Limón, epitomizes the south Caribbean: laid-back but with enough energy to keep things ticking along. The beaches stretching from the southern limits of the town are perfect, shaded by coconut palms reaching out to the ocean. These golden sands mark the northernmost point of Parque Nacional Cahuita.

Two rangers' stations give access to the park. At the southern end of Cahuita town, Kelly's Creek station works on a voluntary donation system. The Puerto Vargas station at the southern end of the park charges a US$6 entrance fee. Cahuita National Park was created in 1970 to protect the coral reef that lies off Punta Cahuita. The best example of coral in the country, the reef can be reached on a tour, or snorkelers can swim out to see the brain coral and leafy sea fans in the glassy water. The reef has suffered from the earthquake of 1991 and from the chemical run-off from plantations and increased sediment caused by deforestation.

A path follows the coastline around Punta Cahuita moving through the coconut palms and entering the mixed forest, where you have a good chance of seeing howler monkeys, coatis, racoons, snakes, butterflies and perhaps even scarlet macaws. Areas of swamp are good places to see green ibis, yellow-crowned night herons and northern boat-billed herons.

You can stroll through a small portion of the park by entering from Cahuita. Walking through, a comfortable day's hike of 7km (4 miles), you eventually arrive at Puerto Vargas and the junction with Highway 36 from where you can catch a bus back to Cahuita. Alternatively, take an early morning bus south to Puerto Vargas and walk back, heading north, to Cahuita.

PUERTO LIMÓN

✚ 235 N6 🚌 Frequent buses from the Gran Terminal del Caribe in San José 🚗 From San José head east on Highway 32 to Limón

Arriving in Puerto Limón, you can feel the difference in atmosphere and it isn't the high humidity. Columbus dropped anchor on Isla Uvita off the coast and waves of workers arrived from China and the Caribbean, creating a unique cultural diversity. Usually visited only in passing, the best time to be in Limón is Carnaval (▷ 156). A cruise terminal draws cruise ships, but in-town attractions are few and most passengers sign up for excursions further afield. There is a 24-hour police booth on the main square.

PUERTO VIEJO DE TALAMANCA

✚ 241 P7 🚌 Daily from San José Terminal Gran Caribe ℹ Asociación Talamanqueña de Ecoturismo y Conservación (ATEC), on main street, 200m (220 yards) from the beach, Old Harbor, tel 506 750 0191, Mon–Sat 8am–9pm, Sun 10–6 🚗 From Puerto Limón, take Highway 36 south and follow the signs for Cahuita and Puerto Viejo

Puerto Viejo, 17km (10 miles) south of Cahuita, with its good beaches, excellent surfing and vibrancy, has become the main party town of the Caribbean coast. Surfers seek out the glorious Salsa Brava wave. To the east the enjoyable golden beaches of Playa Cocles, Playa Chiquita, Punta Uva and Manzanillo offer a quiet retreat along a road lined with hotels and restaurants. Away from the beach, you can explore botanical gardens or visit the KeKöLdi indigenous reserve.

With the arrival of expatriates, setting up homes in backwaters, the Afro-Caribbean make-up of the town is being slowly diluted.

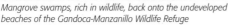

Mangrove swamps, rich in wildlife, back onto the undeveloped beaches of the Gandoca-Manzanillo Wildlife Refuge

Cancelled service: the derelict railroad across the lowlands

THE SIGHTS

REFUGIO NACIONAL DE VIDA SILVESTRE BARRA DEL COLORADO

✚ 234 K3 ☎ 506 711 1201 🕐 Daily 8–4 💷 US$6 for 1 day, US$10 for 3 days 🚤 Boats can be arranged from Tortuguero, taking 1.5hr. Costs vary from US$30, if arranged by your lodge, to US$100. Ask around. It is possible to sail from Puerto Viejo de Sarapiquí

Tucked up in the northeastern corner of the country, Barra del Colorado is reached by a couple of daily flights or a boat journey of several hours. One of the most cut-off parts of the country, the sleepy backwater is divided into Barra del Sur, which has the airstrip and lodges, and Barra del Norte, which is on Isla Calero, the largest island in Costa Rica. In addition to tourism, locals fish for spiny lobster. Two major attractions draw visitors: excellent sportfishing for snook and tarpon (best from September to April) and the Wildlife Reserve.

National Wildlife Refuge Silvestre Barra del Colorado is one of the country's largest protected areas, covering the border with Nicaragua along the Río San Juan. A torrential 6,000mm (234in) of rain a year and temperatures averaging 26°C (79°F) create conditions similar to those in Tortuguero. Established in the mid-1980s, its potential for ecotourism remains untapped. If you have the time and the money—Barra is more expensive than Tortuguero—exploring the waterways is an amazing experience. Accommodation is available at lodges throughout the area.

REFUGIO NACIONAL DE VIDA SILVESTRE GANDOCA-MANZANILLO

✚ 241 Q7 ☎ 506 754 1103 or 506 759 0600 🕐 Daily 8–4 💷 US$6 🚌 Bus from San José to Puerto Viejo (▷ 53), then local bus to Manzanillo 🚐 Trips to the land sections of

Gandoca-Manzanillo can be organized through ATEC (see Puerto Viejo de Talamanca ▷ 125) 🚗 Drive east from Puerto Viejo for 12km (7 miles) along the road to Manzanillo. You can also walk all the way, along the beach

At the southeastern corner of Costa Rica, Gandoca-Manzanillo National Wildlife Refuge protects some of the country's most pristine wetlands. A combination of geographical, historical and cultural factors have limited human impact on the tropical forest and the inland and coastal waters have been left largely unscathed.

The land portion of the refuge protects creeks, lagoons and the only natural population of mangrove oysters on the Central American Caribbean. The inland waterways are home to manatee, crocodiles and caiman, while the forests provide a refuge for tapir, jaguar and monkeys. Over 300 bird species have been recorded.

The coastal waters are equally diverse. White sandy beaches to the south of Punta Mona are used by leatherback, loggerhead, green and hawksbill turtles. Below the surface, the 4,436 ha (10,957 acres) of marine reserve protects large areas of coral.

Fish species in the reserve number over 500 and mammals are topped off with three species of dolphins—the bottlenose, Atlantic spotted and the little-known tucuxi. Local organizations work to ensure that tourism and nature interact with minimum impact (for volunteer opportunities ▷ 156). Exploring the coast is straightforward, but a guide is recommended if you go inland.

RESERVA BIOLÓGICA HITOY CERERE

✚ 241 N7 ☎ 506 758 3170 🕐 Daily 8–4 💷 US$6 🚌 Buses from Puerto Limón for the Estrella Valley pass 15km (9 miles) short of the rangers' station 🚐 The easiest way to visit the reserve

is on a tour from Cahuita or Puerto Viejo with ATEC (▷ 155) 🚗 From Penshurst, a road heads inland climbing the Estrella Valley to Hitoy Cerere Biological Reserve. It's a tough drive and needs a four-wheel-drive vehicle

Biologists speculate that Hitoy Cerere Biological Reserve may provide some of the greatest diversity in Costa Rica. This has created interest in the park as a source for natural remedies. Some 60km (37 miles) south of Puerto Limón, the reserve extends to 9,950ha (24,577 acres) and offers some tough day-hikes.

Rainfall in the park is a steady 3,500mm (138in) a year, with temperatures in the high 20s°C (low 80s°F). Three trails lead from the rangers' station through the lush forest rich with epiphytes and many streams, rivers and waterfalls. Wildlife is profuse with sloths, howler and white-faced monkeys to be seen, while on the ground you may see otters, peccaries, even jaguars and tapir. More than 100 species of bird have been spotted in the park.

SIQUIRRES

✚ 235 L5 🚗 On Highway 32, 58km (35 miles) west of Puerto Limón

Siquirres, 25km (15 miles) after Guácimo, is another banana town and the largest settlement along this section of Highway 32. Few people stop here, but you can tour La Esperanza banana plantation (tel 506 768 8683). Also nearby is Parque Nacional Barbilla with 11,944ha (29,502 acres) of tropical forest. Created in 1982, the park still has no facilities.

Siquirres is the closest access town for reaching Tortuguero by car. Head north through Carmen and Maryland for 37km (22 miles) to Caño Blanco marina where you can safely park your vehicle while in Tortuguero.

This chapter gives information on things to do in Costa Rica, other than sightseeing. Costa Rica's best shops, arts venues, nightlife, activities and events are listed region by region.

What to Do

SHOPPING

Shopping is rarely the main reason for visiting Costa Rica. But if you're on an organized tour there will always be a souvenir-buying stop and there is certainly no shortage of things to buy, from small collectibles to genuinely well-made wooden furniture. Bargaining is not the rule, but you may find occasional opportunities for negotiation. Ambling around general produce markets provides a kaleidoscopic immersion into Costa Rican life, with souvenirs sold alongside selections of fruit and vegetables, meat, poultry and fish. But if you're just looking for a fruit snack you'll find a fruit stand on almost every street corner.

ARTS AND CRAFTS

With row upon row of carefully decorated gifts sitting in neat lines it's easy to think Costa Rica's shops are only full of

Traditional earthenware plates from Guaitíl

mass-produced items. Look a little closer and you'll see the quirky touch and character of the hand-painted souvenirs.

The main place to buy gifts—for some, the only place—is Sarchí in the Central Highlands. The town has become the artisan capital of the country, churning out vividly hand-decorated *carretas* (oxcarts). Time has seen the carts evolve and shrink to become garden ornaments, drinks cabinets and jewellery boxes. Don't worry about getting them home—they can be flat-packed and shipped if required, as can the sturdy wood and leather rocking chairs. You can relax even

further lying in a hammock. But if you can't get to the one-stop shop that is Sarchí, don't worry. You can buy gifts in most towns: wooden carvings are popular, with decorative and functional pieces including bowls and trays, as well as figures and animals.

Jewelry sees semiprecious jade set in gold and silver, and jade, copper and bronze are used to create pre-Columbian replicas. Indigenous pieces are available in a few select places, including the deep red ceramics of the Chorotegas in Guaitíl, the masks and woven goods of the Boruca, or the *jícara* (or carved gourds) of the Guaymi and Bribrí in the far south. Fill any spare space in your bag with freshly roasted coffee, liqueurs or stationery made from banana leaves.

Don't buy any archaeological artifacts or items made from endangered species including turtles, animal skins and coral.

MUSIC

Music makes a memorable gift. The Costa Rica Pura Vida collection, sold in market squares and record shops, is a broad-based selection of folk sounds. Less manic on the marimbas is the ambient jazz feel of Editus who, with Panamanian Rubén Blades, won a Grammy for their album *Tiempos*. Also look out for Costa Rica's very own boy band—the Brillanticos.

TEXTILES

Textiles provide plenty of options beyond the simple T-shirt, with mats, table cloths and napkins evoking memories of Costa Rica when you're having a meal back home several months later. Although they're from Panama, vivid *molas* (bright appliqués) are available in parts of the south.

Contemporary, traditional and religious art hangs on the walls of galleries dotted around San José and Escazú. Ceramic creations are no more distinctive than in the bright pieces by Cecilia Figueres.

Get in the swing of things with a hammock

PHOTOGRAPHY

Capturing wild animals on film requires patience, a good SLR camera, a zoom lens and a tripod to keep things steady. For the amateur, a good quality point-and-shoot camera will capture the moment quickly. Film should be fast (400 ASA) for the poor lighting. Although Kodak and Fuji (good for slides) have opened up air-conditioned stores all around the country, take all the photography supplies you need to avoid getting stuck with something you are not familiar or comfortable with, especially if you use a digital camera: memory cards and batteries may not be easily found.

ENTERTAINMENT 🎵

A vibrant dance and theater scene exists in Costa Rica and you'll find everything from opera and ballet productions at the sublime Teatro Nacional to innovative creations like *The Full Monty*.

Almost all productions will be in Spanish with the exception of those produced by the Little Theatre Group (tel 506 355 1623 for details or look in listings). Theaters often have workshops, especially for children. Orchestral works, jazz, concerts and dance are common. Seasons for the Teatro

Meet other visitors in bars such as this one in Playas del Coco

Nacional, Teatro Melico Salazar and others start in March.

Modern cinemas show the latest releases and a couple of art movie theaters reminisce on past glories. Films are in English with Spanish subtitles, which can be useful if you're trying to improve your language skills. Most theaters have comfortable seating and air-conditioning. *Viva* in *La Nación* on Thursday will tell you what is showing. Prices vary from US$3 to US$5, often with cheaper tickets before 4pm. Saturday and Sunday afternoon showings are very popular with families and young couples, especially during the rainy season.

Live music is very popular and a cover charge of around US$4 is typical. Music may be a head-thumping rock act, a Tico Brillcream boy band such as the Brillianticos, or something a little more suave. In some bars the tendency is to just turn up and see what happens. Clubs, too, are busy and cover music from techno and garage, to reggae, jazz and salsa. Entrance fees are normally between US$3 and US$7.

TICKETS

Theater tickets can be bought in advance from the ticket offices (Mon–Sat 10–1, 2–5). Ticket prices range from as little as US$2 for a minor show at the Teatro Melico Salazar to around US$12 to US$15 at the Teatro Nacional. High-profile international performances can vary in price from US$30 to US$70 and usually sell out very quickly, so it is advisable to buy tickets as early as possible. There are discounts available for students at most performances and it is always worth looking in the press listings for two-for-one specials, often on Wednesday. When it comes to live music, Costa Rican groups generally have a very low profile outside the country and only when it comes to visiting international bands is there a feeding frenzy for tickets.

RESOURCES

La Nación

On Thursdays, the *Viva* section of the national newspaper *La Nación* has comprehensive listings of nightlife venues, theaters, bars and cinema schedules.

The Tico Times

The weekly English-language newspaper often has reviews and lists of forthcoming events.

NIGHTLIFE 🍸

It is not surprising that the capital city San José should have varied nightlife, but from Guanacaste's surf spots to the chilled-out enclaves of the Caribbean, you can find all sorts of nocturnal fun.

There are plenty of simple bars where you can hunker down with a beer and a few *bocas* (snacks), and a plethora of tourist magnets including the ubiquitous American-style sports bars serving Tex Mex alcohol-mopping fodder with a wide-screen TV backdrop. With laid-back jazz bars, sizzling Latin salsa clubs, rustic beach shacks and dingy hole-in-the-wall bar-café-sodas, all tastes are catered to. In the capital, Joséfinos are generally well dressed and usually look smart when hitting the town. In addition to the myriad bars, the greatest concentration of clubs is in El Pueblo.

Smart jeans will get you in to most clubs, but locals will be dressed to impress. Along the coast, surfer culture prevails and nightlife is generally more laissez-faire with the friendly social scene pivoting around low-key beach bars.

There are a few gay-friendly dance clubs playing a mix of techno and Latin themes and many gentlemen's clubs in the city. Given the number of casinos around San José it seems that gambling is a national sport. Better odds are available at the smart hotels, although the odds are reported to be lower than in North American casinos: the most popular casinos are at the Hotel Costa Rica Morazán, Hotel Gran Costa Rica and the top floor of the Hotel Aurora. Out of town the Meliá Confort Corobicí near Parque Sábana and the Best Western Irazú, Hotel Herradura and the Meliá Cariari have popular casinos.

SPORTS AND ACTIVITIES

When you're bored with relaxing in a beachside hammock, you can take advantage of the enormous range of activities offered by tour operators in Costa Rica, who make the most of the country's natural diversity. Thrill seekers can go white-water rafting, learn to surf or take mountain bike tours through the jungle, while those with more sedate tastes can try birdwatching or sunset rides on horseback.

WHAT TO DO

BIRDWATCHING

Low key it may be, but sooner or later, every visitor to Costa Rica will get involved in, maybe even hooked on, wildlife watching. Birdlife is vibrant for the generalist and hypnotic for the specialist. With more species of birds than the

Birdwatching is highly rewarding in Costa Rica

whole of North America or Europe—875 at the last count—Costa Rica is undoubtedly a birdwatcher's paradise. Thousands of birders visit Costa Rica every year, either on their own or as part of a small group birdwatching tour, to see some of the most magnificent birds in the Neotropics; the resplendent quetzal, three-wattled bellbird, bare-necked umbrella bird, violaceous trogon, scarlet macaw, chestnut-bellied heron, turquoise cotinga, sunbittern and hundreds more species.

Birdwatching is good all year round. Of course, rainforests need rain, but you'll seldom miss a day of birdwatching

because of the weather. Most places have the highest rainfall between September and November, while Costa Rica's tourist high season is from December to April. If you've already seen many of the North American migrants, you'll be happy to visit Costa Rica later in the year to see the resident bird species. Birds are often easier to spot during the breeding season. Nesting reaches its peak from April to June according to locality and continues on a diminishing scale until August or September.

If you want to experience the raptor migrations between North and South America, then plan your birdwatching trip during March and April or September and October. La Selva Biological Station and Selva Verde Lodge along the route of the Río Sarapiquí, the Siquirres–Guácimo area along the route of the Reventazón, Pacuare and Parismina rivers and several spots along the southern Caribbean are good places to see migrations.

The resplendent quetzal is considered by many to be the most beautiful bird in the world. While Monteverde is famous for quetzals, you can easily see them less than two hours from San José in the Cerro de la Muerte highlands (guided walks can be arranged at Finca Eddie Serrano Mirador de Quetzales, ▷ 153).

Two of the best known birding spots are La Selva Biological Station, south of Puerto Viejo de Sarapiquí which runs

birdwatching courses—and the world famous Monteverde Cloud Forest.

Once out of the towns and cities of the Central Valley you'll find a tremendous diversity of habitats from the lush cloud forests of Monteverde, to the dry deciduous forests of Guanacaste, to the rainforests of the Caribbean lowlands and even the subalpine *páramo* in the Cerro de la Muerte highlands. During recent years many new private reserves with comfortable lodges have opened up throughout the country, some bordering

The keel-billed toucan stands out in a crowd

national parks. A typical birdwatching trip might include Villa Lapas (bordering Parque Nacional Carara), Tiskita Lodge in the south Pacific coast (near Punta Banco), Monteverde Cloud Forest, Tortuguero National Park on the Caribbean coast, and a visit to La Selva Biological Station. When planning a birdwatching trip, contact a specialist. While Costa Rica looks small on a map, it's very mountainous and what seems like a short journey might take several hours to drive. Always allow yourself at least three nights at each place to give you two full days to see the birds. The Birding Club of Costa Rica has

monthly outings that you can join with a temporary membership (fee US$10); get details and a complete and up-to-date Costa Rica bird list by emailing costaricabirding@hotmail.com. More general tours can be arranged through tour operators in San José. From the United States you can organize tours with Cheeseman's Ecology Safari Tours, Field Guides or Wings.

Resources
A Guide To The Birds Of Costa Rica (by Gary Stiles and Alexander Skutch, published by Cornell University Press). Serious birders will need this bible.

See the rainforest canopy on an aerial tram or canopy tour

La Selva is part of the Organisation for Tropical Studies (www.ots.ac.cr). See www.cloudforestalive.org for live views of the quetzal nesting or for more information on Monteverde.

Birdwatch Costa Rica, Apdo 7911, 1000 San José, Costa Rica, tel 506 228 4768; www.birdwatchcostarica.com.

Field Guides, 9433 Bee Cave Road, Building 1, Suite 150, Austin, TX 78733, tel 800/728-4953 or tel 512/263-7295; www.fieldguides.com.

Wings, 1643 N.Alvernon, Suite 105, Tucson, AZ 85712, tel 888/293-6443 or 520/320-9868; www.wingsbirds.com.

Cheeseman's Ecology Safari Tours, 20800 Kittredge Road, Saratoga, CA 95070, tel 800/527-5330 in the US or 408/867-1371; www.cheesemans.com.

BUNGEE JUMPING
Probably the biggest buzz in Costa Rica, Tropical Bungee will attach you to a big elastic band outside an inflatable raft and let you freefall to the Río Colorado some 80m (262ft) below. Since they started in 1991, Tropical Bungee have had over 10,000 jumps to their name. They are based on the Pan-American Highway close to Grecia, tel 506 248 2212; www.bungee.co.cr.

CANOPY TOURS
The rainforest canopy is where most of the wildlife action takes places and there are now a multitude of ways of getting you up there. The calmest is probably exploring on a suspension bridge, strung out along the trees where you are free to walk at leisure, or with a guide, in complete silence if you wish. The main suspension tours are in Santa Elena, close to Puerto Viejo de Sarapiquí, and Rainmaker near to Quepos.

An equally calm way through the canopy is on an aerial tour, using adapted ski lifts to carry you. The most well known (and expensive) is on the eastern fringes of Braulio Carrillo National Park, with a similar operation near Jacó.

The best way to get an adrenaline rush is the zipline, which whizzes you down high-tension steel cables strung out between giant forest trees. You won't see much as you fly through the air, but it is good fun and you do get close to the forest canopy. It's a popular option and spreading like wildfire. But be wary, there have been several fatal accidents on ziplines in Costa Rica. If you do not receive sufficient reassurance of the safety of the equipment, don't do the ride. The advent of licensing should ensure that every operator has properly considered safety.

Finally there is the good old-fashioned option of climbing a tree. A couple of places, in particular Hacienda Barú (▷ 102), let you use tree climbing grappling and ropes. Prices vary greatly, starting at US$8, rising to around US$75.

DIVING
Costa Rica suffers on the diving front primarily because of occasional poor visibility in the 9–15m (30–50ft) range in the wet season. Go when there is less rain and you can enjoy the warm waters.

Giant manta rays glide through Costa Rica's waters

The northern Pacific coast around Playas del Coco is a local diving hotspot with trips out to nearby islands. Farther south, Drake, on the northern coast of the peninsula, is a popular base to visit Isla del Caño where you're almost guaranteed sightings of sharks and rays. On the Caribbean side, the dive action is in the coral waters off the coast of Cahuita National Park and farther south around Gandoca-Manzanillo National Wildlife Refuge. Each region has specialist dive shops that can arrange diving—although it might be a good idea to make advance reservations at Drake if you're planning to visit. The

best diving happens far away in the clear waters around the Cocos Islands, 500km (310 miles) southwest of Costa Rica in the Pacific. Undisturbed corals and hammerhead and white-tipped sharks await visitors on the live-aboard dive boats sailing from Puntarenas.

The cost of diving starts at around US$35 for a beach dive on the south Caribbean, rising to around US$80 for a two-tank dive. A PADI Open Water Course out of Playas del Coco is about US$375. Diving trips out to the Cocos Islands on live-aboard boats start at around US$2,895 for a nine-day trip, with six full days diving and equipment rental.

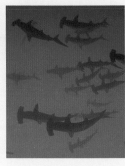

Hordes of hammerheads feed at Cocos Island

GOLF

In Costa Rica the Pacific Coast has seen a spate of 18-hole championship links courses come to fruition, including Los Sueños Marriott in the Central Pacific. Farther north close to Tamarindo and Playa Conchal are the Garra de León and Royal Pacific courses, or just south of Tamarindo is Hacienda Pinilla. In the Central Highlands you'll find the opportunity to swing your clubs at the Melía Cariari outside San José or a short distance west of Santa Ana at the Valle del Sol. Green fees tend to range from US$45 to US$140 at the country clubs, but operators may offer deals.

HOT AIR BALLOONING

Several hot air balloon operators have taken off in Costa Rica (▷ 143), with trips over the Central Highlands and the Lake Arenal area proving the most popular.

MOUNTAIN BIKING

As befits the host of the world's toughest mountain bike race (La Ruta de los Conquistadores, ▷ 29), pedal power has made a big impression in parts of Costa Rica, with operators renting bicycles by the hour, the day or the week. You can strike out on your own and just see where your instincts take you, but if you're really into the idea of mountain biking joining a tour is the best way to get to some of the off-road trails.

Possibilities vary greatly. According to Brenda Kelly at Coast to Coast, Guanacaste is ideal for hugging the coastline, getting fantastic views and a challenging ride. Several two-day trips out of San José give you the chance to get seriously muddy, ending up in places like Manuel Antonio, or mixing the biking with paddling down white water. The ultimate adventure is a coast to coast ride that takes 14 days, lots of muscle and determination—there are some serious uphill sections—but it's ultimately rewarded with views from the continental divide and down the Orosí Valley. Coast-to-Coast Adventures (tel 506 280 8054, www.ctocadventures.com) can provide bespoke bicycling tours or you can fit in with their busy schedule. They provide all the gear, including bike, water bottle and helmet. Mountain bike rental from a general rental company works out at around US$5 an hour. A four-day trip with Coast to Coast is US$550 all inclusive. For serious adventure sports fans, Coast to Coast offer several trips that combine bicycling, hiking and rafting.

RAFTING

Rafting in Costa Rica takes you through some of the most spectacular scenery in the country. One moment you're drifting through valleys that merge the highlights of the Hanging Gardens of Babylon with the Garden of Eden, the next you're being forced head-first through a wall of water. It isn't everyone's idea of fun, but it is certainly exciting.

White-water rafting needs mountains (or at least hills) and water. "Costa Rica has an abundance of water," according to Michael Mayfield and Rafael Gallo in *The Rivers of Costa Rica: A canoeing, kayaking and rafting guide*. It is this

Be prepared for adventure on a bicycle ride in Costa Rica

surfeit of water that fills the channels of the Reventazón, Pacuare and Sarapiquí rivers on the Caribbean slope, and the General and Corobicí on the Pacific, creating a fantastic array of aquadventure.

White-water rafting in Costa Rica started in the 1980s. From early pioneer days of struggling with equipment to remote put-ins, the most popular rivers and routes are now well established with fairly easy access.

Most trips in Costa Rica start from San José and head out to the chosen river. All-inclusive trips remove the need to think about food and refreshment. You will need a change of clothes for the night if you are

on a two- or three-day trip, and some dry clothes for the end of the trip.

As with all adventure sports, safety is paramount—fatal accidents have occurred in Costa Rica. Good commercial outfits like Costa Rica Expeditions or Rios Tropicales will assess your experience and suitability before taking your reservation. You receive a complete safety briefing before beginning rafting and if you're not up to standard you will be asked to leave. Likewise, if you are not satisfied with the level of safety, seek reassurance and if still not satisfied, ask to leave.

You don't have to be an adrenaline junky for white-

Hold tight! White-water rafting on the Pacuare River

water rafting, or even be incredibly fit. Rafting assesses rivers in terms of difficulty. A simple trip or float down parts of the Corobicí or Sarapiquí is a Class I or II; gentle and relaxing, it's a great way to see wildlife. Class III marks the beginning of white-water rafting, with Classes IV and above requiring previous experience. The most popular Class III and IV rivers are sections of the Pacuare and Reventazón, near Turrialba, the Sarapiquí and General. Class V requires experience and expert knowledge.

You can raft all year although conditions vary. If you want to go down a particular river it is worth planning in advance

with a specialist tour operator. Costs vary considerably depending on the number of days, with a one-day trip starting at around US$75, a couple of days costing US$250 and three days US$300, including all meals and transport to and from San José.

SOCCER

The national sport in Costa Rica is soccer and it's a great experience to join the migrating fans to a Sunday morning match. The quality may not be fantastic, but soccer lovers know that the game is more about loyalty. And in Costa Rica of that there is no doubt. The 12 teams of the national league play on Sunday mornings, and sometimes on Wednesday, and tickets are rarely sold out. The two dominant sides are Saprissa, who play in Tibas north of San José, and La Liga in Alajuela. By all accounts the country went mad in 1990 when the national squad qualified for the World Cup, and every time Paulo Wanchope touched the ball for the UK's Manchester City team, Costa Rican newspapers plastered the sports pages with reports.

SPORTFISHING

Fishing just doesn't get any better than you will find in Costa Rica, with tarpon and snook on the Caribbean; marlin, sailfish, dorado, tuna and other species on the Pacific and trout, rainbow bass (*guapote*), bobo, machaca and more in inland lakes and rivers. According to Jerry Ruhlow—who has been living, fishing and writing about it in Costa Rica since 1983—it is essential to plan ahead. Peak fishing varies with the time of year and beach accommodations and the top boats are often hard to find when fishing is at its best, so make reservations in advance. The best seasons in the different parts of Costa Rica

vary from year to year, depending on weather, water temperatures and other factors.

On the southernmost Pacific coast, in the Golfito, Puerto Jiménez and Drake Bay region, marlin action is best from August to December. There are sailfish year round, but the peak is from late November to March. It may slow from April into June, then pick up again in July. If non-stop action is your preference and you don't have to hang a billfish to be happy, the Golfito region is your best bet. More than 40 International Game Fish Association (IGFA) certified world records have been established here and the

Hauling in a swordfish off the Pacific coast

species you can expect to catch at almost any time of year include tuna (sometimes to 180kg/400lb), wahoo, amberjack, jack crevalle, grouper, cubera, barracuda, big roosterfish, corbina and snook.

The next major fishing area, heading north, is Quepos where December to end of April is the best season for billfish, although some marlin and sailfish are taken year round. Dorado and small tuna are nearly always plentiful, and they often get giant yellowfin tuna too.

Mid-December to April are the best months for boats based in Playa Carrillo and the Sámara region as the main

body of fish continue moving north. They often get there earlier and stay longer, depending on water temperature and other factors. Dorado and tuna are also plentiful in these months.

A northerly wind blows from December into May in the northernmost region, but once the calm has returned the fishing is little short of sensational from late May or June into early September, with marlin peaking in August and September. There are two major tournaments in March and July—a few years ago one of those tournaments posted a record 1,696 billfish in a four-day competition out of

Fish for tarpon and snook off the palm-fringed Caribbean coast

Flamingo Marina. Charter boats operate out of Tamarindo, Flamingo, Portrero, Ocotal and Playas de Coco. There's always plenty of dorado and tuna in the area, and anglers working the nearby Catalina and Murcielago (Bat) Islands also score wahoo, amberjack, cubera and roosters.

On the northern Caribbean coast, tarpon and snook are around most of the year, with slumps from May to mid-July when the rains are at their heaviest. Peak season is from about September through April, although late July during the *veranillo* (little summer), when rains usually stop for

two or three weeks, is also excellent most years. Rainbow bass and other freshwater species can be caught here year round in the rivers and lagoons. Most consistent fishing is out of the lodges near the mouth of the Río Colorado, but some are also caught at Tortuguero and Parismina. The northern Caribbean coast does not offer much in the way of sportfishing.

For inland waters, Lake Arenal offers year-round fishing, but the quality will vary depending on wind and water level. It is a beautiful 35km-long (22 mile) lake about three hours' drive from San José. Guides are available locally with fully equipped boats complete with tackle. Rainbow bass are the species most anglers go for. A beautiful fish in shades of pink, green and blue, with a vicious set of teeth, they are found only in Costa Rica and a few inland waters of southern Nicaragua. The IGFA record is 5.7kg (12.5 lb), taken here. Rainbow bass, bobo, machaca, tepemechin and other tropical species are also found in rivers throughout the country, along with rainbow trout in some high mountain rivers.

Caño Negro Lagoon is a huge inland waterway that offers all of the above, plus tarpon and snook. Some waters are seasonal, and regulations often change from year to year, so check in advance.

SURFING

Costa Rica offers the surfer world-class waves in beautiful surroundings with air and water temperatures averaging in the high 20°sC (82°F). Most breaks work better at the end of the wet season, supposedly when the rivers have had time to form the sand bars properly. The tidal range for the Pacific coast is quite large, being up to 3.5m (12ft) and this can affect the size of the waves. If surfing

on the Pacific coast, you'll need a tide chart—freely available in most surf centers or printed in the free regional magazines. On the Caribbean coast the variation is not a problem, with daily fluctuations of around 0.5m (1.5ft).

A four-wheel-drive vehicle is a necessity if traveling along much of the Costa Rican coast as many waves are only accessible along dirt tracks and these can be inaccessible during the wet season. Check at a local surf shop before leaving. Also a number of breaks are only accessible by boat. You may need to check how to access these waves before leaving and being disappointed.

Surfing Playa Junquillal, south of Playa Negra

One of the towns most associated with surfing in Costa Rica is Tamarindo. Located 450km (280 miles) northwest of San José, Tamarindo is an excellent place from which to access the quality breaks that lie along the north Pacific coast. Best surfing conditions are from December to June. Tamarindo itself has lots of good hotels and three good breaks; El Estero, a long right-hander; Pico Pequeño; and Langosta, a strong point wave. Just north of Tamarindo lies Potrero Grande. Known as Ollie's Point (supposedly after Oliver North who had a secret base nearby), Potrero Grande is a fast right-hander breaking

SURF SITES IN COSTA RICA

1 Potrero Grande	16 Playa Jacó		
2 Playa Naranjo	17 Roca Loca		
(Roca de la Bruja)	18 Playa Hermosa		
3 Playa Grande	19 Playa Esterillos Oeste		
4 Playa Tamarindo	20 Playa Esterillos Este	28 Pavones	
5 Langosta	21 Playa El Rey	29 Punta Burica	
6 Avellanas	22 Boca Damas	30 Manzanillo	
7 Playa Negra	23 Quepos	31 Puerto Viejo	
8 Nosara	24 Playa Espadilla	32 Playa Negra, Cahuita	
9 Playa Coyote	25 Playa Dominical	33 Westfalia	
10 Malpaís	26 Bahía Drake	34 Isla Uvita	
11 Cabuya	27 Matapalo	35 Playa Bonita	
12 Boca Barranca			
13 Puerto Caldera			
14 Playa Tivives & Valor			
15 Playa Escondida			

over a reef. A southerly swell can give a wave of up to 2m (7ft). Access is by boat. Playa Grande is the most westerly point of Costa Rica and as a result can get swells from north, south and west.

To the far north is Santa Rosa National Park and Playa Naranjo, home of Peña Bruja, mistakenly translated in the 1980s as "Witches Rock." The name has now stuck and the beach provides a high-quality and picturesque beach break. Access is by four-wheel drive during dry season (boat during the wet) and camping is available at the rangers' station.

South from Tamarindo around the coastline of the Nicoya Peninsula lie Avellanas, Playa Negra, Callejones and Junquillal. Playa Negra is 10 minutes south of Avellanas and a popular spot. This solid right-hand wave can be busy and dangerously shallow at low tide. Farther south lies Callejones which can be much less crowded than Playa Negra.

Toward the end of the peninsula and the Cabo Blanco

Reserve are a number of beautiful and uncrowded beach breaks, including Nosara, Sámara and Punta Guiones. After this spot, the waves become more of a challenge to get to, with many only accessible by four-wheel drive.

Boca Barranca, just north of Jacó, has a long left-hander that breaks over a sand bottom and into the river mouth. The best time to surf here is early in the morning and on a good day it can hold up to 3m (10ft). The river is supposedly free of crocodiles but it's worth keeping a wary eye out.

Playa Escondida lies at the mouth of the Gulf of Nicoya and is accessible only by boat. A number of quality breaks can be found close to Jacó. Roca Loca is five minutes' walk south of Jacó and is accessible only by climbing down the cliffs—but has a good quality wave that is not for the fainthearted. Ten minutes south of Jacó lies Playa Hermosa, a high-quality break that can be crowded.

On the journey south towards Quepos is Esterillos,

some 40 minutes' drive from Jacó. It is a quiet, uncrowded beach break with entertainment provided by the nearby town. Between Esterillos and Quepos lies the town of Parrita, offering both reef and beach breaks, and Playa El Rey, which is accessed via a palm tree plantation. Just north of Quepos lies Boca Damas. Next to the mouth of the Río Damas, this spot can hold a sizeable swell. Quepos itself offers lively nightlife and a beach break with strong lefts.

Farther south again is the town of Dominical. This surf town is basic, but offers some of the best beach breaks in Costa Rica. It also has a left and right reef break and the area is often frequented by pods of dolphins.

The South Pacific coastline is dominated by the Osa Peninsula. At the north end close to the mainland is Bahía Drake. Only accessible by boat, Drake is a beautiful spot for surfing. At the southern tip of the Peninsula is Matapalo, which can be reached by car

from Puerto Jiménez or by boat from Pavones, just across the mouth of the Golfo Dulce. The best waves are a 20-minute walk through jungle teeming with native fauna. The three spots worth checking out in the area are Back Wash; Pan Dulce, a small white sand bay with a hollow right-hander; and powerful Matapalo.

Across the Gulf lies Pavones, the longest ride in Costa Rica. On a large swell the left-hander can give a ride for 800m (0.5 mile) as the different sections connect. Pavones is a 5-hour drive from south of Dominical, or a short boat taxi from Golfito, but its quality can lead to a crowded line up.

Hikers arrive at the San Pedrillo River on Osa Peninsula

Towards the border with Panama lies Punta Banco, 3km (2 miles) south of Pavones. It's a good place to check if the waves at Pavones are too crowded. Punta Burica is the last beach on the Costa Rican Pacific coast before Panama, which shares this headland with Costa Rica. This beach is only accessible by boat.

Storms in the Caribbean Sea produce swells which break on the coral reefs close to Costa Rica's coast. The best waves are found from November to March. The coastline is shorter than the Pacific coast, with most of the breaks to the south of Limón. The three quality breaks in Limón are

Playa Bonita, breaking over a coral reef which can be a challenging drop; Portete, which is a hollow right-hander breaking over coral; and Isla Uvita, only accessible by a dawn boat out of Limón, with a wave that breaks in three sections over a shallow coral reef. On a good day this can produce a wave of up to 3m (10ft).

South from Limón towards the Panamanian border lies Cahuita, a beautiful National Park with great beaches and waves. Farther south still is Puerto Viejo. Known as "Salsa Brava," Puerto Viejo is an extremely powerful wave breaking over coral—you may need to pack a spare board for this one. Ten minutes farther down the coast is the fun beach break of Playa Cocles, which can have strong currents, and Manzanillo, which has uncrowded waves.

If your appetite for waves has been whetted, you can rent surf boards and arrange for tuition at most of the major surf spots, such as Dominical (▷ 102).

TREKKING AND HIKING
Short treks ranging from 20 minutes through to multi-day trips can be found throughout the country, but with so many competing activities, hiking and trekking often take a bit of a back seat. But as well as short guided walks lasting a few hours there are some very good hiking opportunities: just examine a topographical map.

The most popular hike has to be up Cerro Chirripó, the country's highest peak at 3,820m (12,530ft). The shortest route is a steady trudge up and down, but there are many variations on that theme that add to the two- or three-day hike. Second on the list is hiking through the tropical wet forest of Corcovado National Park on the Osa Peninsula: hot, sweaty, hard work and very rewarding. Less common walks head from

the cloud forests of Monteverde down the Caribbean slope to Arenal, and farther north trails lead through the national parks of Rincón de la Vieja and Tenorio. The ultimate trek is a crossing of the continental divide following ancient indigenous trails from Puerto Viejo de Talamanca heading west to the Pacific. Several tough days, carrying all your own gear, through an altitude gain of over 3,000m (9800ft)—scenic, arduous and hopefully satisfying.

WINDSURFING
Westerly trade winds blow across northern Costa Rica between December and April.

Go high-speed windsurfing on man-made Lake Arenal

Reluctantly the air is pushed up and over obstacles eventually being forced through the corridor that is Lake Arenal. The most reliable winds in the northern hemisphere provide the western end of the lake, and Bahía Salinas on the Pacific to the north, with world-class windsurfing destinations.

Opportunities for novices and experts exist. Beginner courses are provided by a couple of lodges in the area, with boards, wetsuits and even money-back guarantees provided. For the experts, if you fancy a change you can try out the latest watersport developments including kite-surfing.

FOR CHILDREN ⊗

For both tots and teens, Costa Rica teems with life, bombarding the senses on all sides with shades of green and cacophonous noise.

In general, organized activities are not as necessary as in other Latin American countries. In San José, theaters, including the Eugene O'Neil Cultural Center, organize special workshops for children, and the Teatro Melico Salazar often has performances which may be suitable for children. Children will generally pay

Costa Rican society is very family friendly

reduced rates for tickets. Along the coast, especially in family-friendly resorts like Tamarindo, children are welcomed in restaurants and travel with children can often bring you into closer contact with local families and usually presents no problems—in fact the path is often smoother for family groups. Shopping for arts and crafts can also be an enjoyable pastime for children, with places like Sarchí providing plenty of objects to stir a child's curiosity and cafés for respite. A lot of time can be spent waiting for buses, so remember to pack toys. Also, take children's reading material with you as it is difficult, and expensive, to buy.

FESTIVALS AND EVENTS

Public holidays are normally a cause for celebration and Costa Rica is no different.

Large festivals tend to go big on processions, costumes and marching bands, but find a small town and you'll find bull-friendly bull fighting (where the lucky beast leaves the ring exhausted but alive), horse-racing, and a chance to rub shoulders with the towns-folk at any minor gathering. The main holiday periods of the year are Christmas, New Year, and Easter, when much of San José decamps to the beaches. Reserve in advance.

On national holidays, banks, government offices and stores close down. National holidays are listed here; regional and local festivals are listed in the relevant chapter.

CALENDAR

Some festivals and holidays take place across the country:

1 January New Year's Day.

March (second Sunday) National Oxcart Day with music and vibrant processions in Escazú.

March–April Maundy Thursday and Good Friday, Easter Week.

11 April Juan Santamaría Day, celebrating the victorious Battle of Rivas against William Walker in 1856.

1 May Labor Day, which heralds the President's State of the Nation address, cricket matches and a day off.

25 July Annexation of Guanacaste, celebrating Guanacaste's decision to stay with Costa Rica rather than join Nicaragua in 1824.

2 August Virgin Mary, Queen of Angels, Patron of Costa

Rica celebrated with pilgrimages to Cartago's Basilica.

15 August Day of the Virgin marks Mary's Assumption to Heaven and also Mother's Day in Costa Rica.

15 September Independence Day with parades and marching bands through the streets of San José.

12 October Spanish discovery of the New World celebrated with particular energy in Limón and the Caribbean.

You will hear local music at fiestas and festivals

2 November All Soul's Day or the Day of the Dead, showing respect to those who have died.

25 December Christmas celebrations build before and continue in the week after, particularly in San José, but also at a smaller scale throughout much of the country.

31 December, 1 and 2 January *La Danza de los Diabolitos* is a lively festival with traditional masks, costumes, music and country dancing in the Indian village of Boruca.

SAN JOSÉ

KEY TO SYMBOLS

⊕ Shopping
🎭 Entertainment
🍷 Nightlife
🏅 Sports
⭐ Activities
♥ Health and Beauty
🎈 For Children

WHAT TO DO

⊕ SHOPPING

BOUTIQUE ANNEMARIE
Hotel Don Carlos, Calle 9, Avenida 7–9
Tel 506 221 6707
In the main lobby of the Hotel Don Carlos, this souvenir and gift shop has one of the largest selections in Costa Rica with thousands of handcrafted items and pieces of art on display.
🕐 Daily 9.30–7.30

LA CASONA
Avenida Central, Calle Central–1
This dark, labyrinthine market of *artesanía* shops has lots of interesting stalls to sift through, selling everything from exotic wooden salad bowls, jewelry boxes and sculptures to Café Britt coffee, Guatemalan imported textiles and folkloric paintings. Prices vary greatly from stall to stall, and bargaining is expected. Sunday morning match days are a good time to wander unhassled, with most stallholders glued to fuzzy TV sets.
🕐 Mon–Sat 9.30–6.30, Sun 9.30–5

CENTRO COMMERCIAL EL PUEBLO
Barrio Tournón
Tel 506 221 9434
The Centro shopping and nightlife complex is a great place for exploring, window shopping, taking a meal and then dipping into a few bars before hitting a disco. At certain times the lines of cars unloading exquisitely dressed Ticas accompanied by young suitors makes the whole place feel like a film premiere. Art galleries, shops, travel agencies, fast-food chains, bars and restaurants cater to every taste. The Centro is just beyond comfortable walking distance from downtown San José, but for the fit and energetic, from Plaza de la Cultura, head straight up Calle 3 to Avenida 13 (6 long blocks), turn right at El Moro castle, after 100m (110 yards) the road bends left, crossing the river. From here, it's a 10-minute walk to El Pueblo. In the evening a taxi is strongly recommended, US$3.
🕐 Daily 11am–5am

A painting by Leonel González at Galería 11–12

EL CABALLO BLANCO
Moravia
Tel 507 235 6797
Some 8km (5 miles) east of San José, Moravia is a popular spot for souvenir hunters and is often included in day-trips from the capital. The White Horse is a well-established store that stocks good-quality leather goods as well as other items.

GALERÍA 11–12
Plaza Itskatzú, Escazú
Tel 506 288 1975
www.galeria11-12.com
Anyone who is interested in collecting Costa Rican art should head to the bohemian district of Escazú where the works of Rolando Garitan and Fernando Carballo, two of the country's most renowned contemporary artists, are exhibited at Galería 11–12. The gallery has its roots in the Monday workshop, which was set up in the early 1980s as a meeting place for San José's poets, writers and painters. While the main gallery is geared towards collectors of contemporary art, there are also spaces dedicated to Costa Rica's master painters. Prices range from a few hundred dollars for small pieces to tens of thousands for works by leading artists.
🕐 Mon–Sat 9–7, Sun by appointment

GALERÍA NAMÚ
Avenida 7, Calle 5–7
Tel 506 256 3412
www.galerianamu.com
Opposite the Alianza Francesa building, Galería Namú is the best one-stop shop for home-grown art. Indigenous art and crafts would be the traditional phrase, but Namú has blended conventional themes of rugs, throws, textiles and mask carvings, with many more contemporary developments. The result is some inspired work. Any piece bought comes with an information sheet. If San José is at the start and end of your trip, pop in on the first day, think about what you want to buy while you travel, and then visit again to purchase it just before you leave. If you're just passing, take your credit card and give yourself more than a half hour. Namú also arranges tours to indigenous villages.
🕐 Mon–Sat 9–6.30, Sun by appointment only
💵 From US$10

LIBRERÍA LEHMANN

Avenida Central, Calle 3
Tel 506 223 1212

On the main Avenida Central, this large well-laid-out bookstore with an academic slant stocks a limited range of Costa Rican wildlife and nature books. For Spanish speakers, there is a good range of contemporary Latin American fiction and just a couple of shelves dedicated to English literature: Shakespeare, Emily Dickinson and Oscar Wilde, with the odd John Grisham or Catherine Cookson. Telescopes, globes, CDs, stationery supplies and maps are also sold.

🕐 Mon–Fri 8–6.30, Sat 9–5

MERCADO DE ARTESANÍAS LAS GARZAS

Calle de las Artesanías
Moravia
Tel 506 236 0037

This is the largest one-stop shop in Moravia for local crafts, with countless stalls to tempt with all sorts of products from oxcarts to wooden salad bowls to folk art and a few less predictable offerings. Upbeat banter and tenacious bartering is the norm; you should expect to pay around 15–20 percent less than the marked price, with further discounts for paying in cash.

🕐 Mon–Sat 9–6, Sun 10–4

MERCADO CENTRAL

Avenida Central, Calle 6–8

The heart and soul of the city, filled with life, noise and general chaos, the central market is not to be missed. Behind all the daily commerce and greetings, you'll find a few typical items for sale such as leather and wooden goods, many without the price increases found in stores catering to tourists. You may have to look around, but you should find a memorable souvenir.

🕐 Mon–Sat 6am–8pm

7TH STREET BOOKS

Calle 7, Avenida Central–1
Tel 506 256 8251

This friendly bookstore is run by Canadians Marc Roegiers and John McCuen. Just off the Avenida Central, one block east of Plaza de la Cultura, it has a good selection of English-language books, including translations of Latin-American heavyweights like Jorge Luis Borges and Gabriel García Márquez to contemporary fiction, including Nick Hornby and Anne Tyler. Costa Rica wildlife guides are also sold and an on-site café tempts settling in with a cappuccino.

🕐 Daily 9–6

Bargain hunting at San José's Mercado Central

🎭 ENTERTAINMENT

TEATRO EUGENE O' NEILL

North American Cultural Center
Avenida Central, Calle 37
Los Yoses
Tel 506 207 7554
www.cccncr.com

This dynamic theatrical wing of the non-profit North American Cultural Center has a varied program ranging from classic productions to contemporary dance to children's plays and pop concerts. With close links to the University, it draws on the talents of San José's rising artistes. In addition to hosting its own productions, performances from the National Dance company and other national organizations can also be appreciated. Los Yoses is beyond comfortable walking distance from downtown, but just a five-minute taxi ride from Plaza de la Cultura. Prices are dependent on the type of performance; call or check the website for information (in Spanish).

TEATRO MELICO SALAZAR

Avenida 2, Calle Central–2
Tel 506 233 5424
www.teatromelicosalazar.co.cr

Performances and shows at the elegant Melico have a broader appeal than those at the National Theater and range from pop and jazz concerts to ballet and orchestral works.

🕐 Ticket office: Mon–Sat 10–12, 1–5
💵 From US$2–7, up to US$70 for international performances

TEATRO NACIONAL

Plaza de la Cultura
Tel 506 221 9417
www.teatronacional.go.cr

A Saturday night visit to the theater is a popular pastime for wealthy Joséfinos. Check the website for the monthly schedule, or stop by for a tour and a coffee in the lovely café.

🕐 Ticket office: Mon–Sat 10–1, 2–5
💵 Depending on performance: US$15–30; discounts for students and seniors. Visit to theater: US$3

🌙 NIGHTLIFE

BONGOS BAR

Entrance to El Pueblo
Barrio Tournón
Tel 506 222 5746

This bar has a tropical rainforest theme and is normally the first stop on an El Pueblo bar hop. Happy hour is daily from 6pm–8pm and a good time to mix and mingle with yuppie 30-plus single Joséfinos. The music runs the gamut of classic rock, sultry Latin dance and '80s fun and frolics. At the weekend the vibe is more youthful. Saturday is Saturday Safari and ladies get in free until 10pm.

CHELLE'S
Calle 9, Avenida Central
Tel 506 221 1369
Heading east along Avenida Central, the bright lighting and unwholesome exterior makes Chelle's stand out. The other dependable factor is the wonderful selection of drinkers that roll up, more concerned with getting a drink than fussing over furnishings. Sticking to a red vinyl seat with a warm beer and a salty *bocas*, or a thick smoothie and a cheap lunch was never more fun.
🕐 Open 24 hours

EL CARTEL DE LA BOCA DEL MONTE
Avenida 1, Calle 21 and 23
Close to Cine Magaly
Tel 506 221 0327
www.cuarteldelaboca.co.cr
The unprepossessing exterior of this cavernous bar hides one of San José's best nights out, a 15-minute walk from the National Museum. With scattered beer barrels, sticky tiled floor, alcoves and a gate reminiscent of a subway station, it's pleasingly less polished than the nightspots of El Pueblo and is an institution amongs San José's barflys. The cocktail list stretches to more than 100, ranging from traditional margaritas to frozen banana daiquiris and anything else that takes the bartender's mood. A beer will set you back 800 colones. Every Monday, Wednesday and Friday there is live music and often on the weekend there are improvised performances, from rock to salsa to reggae.
🕐 Mon–Fri 11.30am–2pm, 6pm–2am, Sat, Sun 4pm–2am
🎵 US$4 live music cover charge (Mon)

INFINITO
El Pueblo
Barrio Tournon
Tel 506 223 2195
Of the nocturnal offerings at El Pueblo, glitzy Infinito gets a slightly older crowd and packs in three dance floors playing

FESTIVALS

EL TOPE
December 26
As working Joséfinos receive their *aguinaldo* (Christmas bonus) the festive season gets into full swing. El Tope is an annual horse parade which begins at noon on December 26 and travels along San José's principal avenues. Many Ticos come from outside the capital to show off their specially trained horses. In the evening, the Festival de la Luz takes place with a flotilla of vibrant floats and general revelry ensues beneath a firework display. A carnival starts next day at about 5pm with bull-running (public participation) at El Zapote south of the city.

LABOR DAY
May 1
Marches, parades and the president's state of the nation address take place Labor Day.

CULTURES DAY
October 12
Indigenous peoples march to protest the Spanish conquest.

INTERNATIONAL ARTS FESTIVAL
March
Art events held across the city.

different styles so you can move from rock to reggae before heading home. The eclectic decor with lots of red leather and wood panelling adds to the sultry vibe.
🕐 Mon–Wed 6pm–5am, Thu–Sun 6pm–6am
🎵 US$3

JAZZ CAFÉ
Avenida Central, next to Banco Popular
San Pedro
Tel 506 253 8933
Out in San Pedro, a US$2 taxi ride from Plaza de la Cultura, this sleek jazz venue offers the best live music in the city with

a convivial laid-back feel. Renowned as a launch pad for rising local talent, as well as a top venue for visiting jazz stars, who have included Chucho Valdés, it is a must for jazz devotees. The interior is stylish, the lighting atmospheric and good food and cocktails ensure a relaxed evening's entertainment. There is music almost every night.
🕐 Mon–Sat 2pm–1am
🎵 Varies according to artist

OLIO
Calle 33, Avenidas 3 and 5
Barrio California
Tel 506 281 0541
A classy favorite of a mature bohemian crowd, this hip, brick-walled tapas bar with stained-glass lamps oozes warmth. Singles favor the main room and bar, while couples snuggle into romantic nooks. A large wine list includes South American vintages.
🕐 Mon–Fri 11.30am–1am, Sat 4pm–12

LA PLAZA
Opposite El Pueblo Shopping Center
Tel 506 257 1077
A short hop from the bars of El Pueblo, the sleek La Plaza is one of San José's most popular dance spots among the young party crowd. It has an airy colonial design and open-plan interior, while the music ranges from Latin salsa to trance, hip hop, electronica and rock.
🕐 Wed–Sat until 4am
🎵 Admission US$3

THE SHAKESPEARE BAR
Avenida 2, Calle 28, 26–28
Tel 506 258 6787
Inside the Sala Garbo cinema, the Shakespeare Bar is a popular port of call for Joséfinos en route to a movie, dinner or a show at the Laurence Olivier Theater nearby. If you feel like lingering, you can join the aspiring pianists, enjoy a game of darts or chill out to the occasional live music.
🕐 Daily 5–12

WHAT TO DO

CENTRAL HIGHLANDS

ALAJUELA

⚽ LIGA DEPORTIVA ALAJUELENSE

Calle 9, 4 blocks north and 6 blocks east of Plaza Central, Alajuela
Tel 506 443 1617
www.ldacr.org

Alajuela's soccer team, Liga Deportiva Alajuelense, is one of Costa Rica's best. Games are usually held at 11am on Sundays, but check locally, or watch for fans heading to the stadium in Alajuela's northeast. Tickets can be bought at the stadium on match days.
💷 US$6.50–14

★ FLOR DE MAYO

Río Segundo de Alajuela
Tel 506 441 2658
www.hatchedtoflyfree.org

For nature lovers, a visit to this macaw breeding facility in the private estate of Richard and Margot Frisius is a joyous experience. Visitors can witness hatchlings being raised in incubators and juvenile birds testing their wings in large flyways in preparation for release.
By appointment only
US£20 donation

♡ PURAVIDA SPA

Apto 1112
Alajuela
Tel 506 392 8079
www.puravidaspa.com

Surrounded by coffee plantations, the American-owned Good Life Center for Yoga Meditation and Renewal offers five- and seven-day packages that include yoga, meditation, aerobics, spa treatments, hikes and volcano and rafting trips.

Accommodation ranges from tents to luxury villas.
💷 US$1,070–1,875

♡ SPA VILLAGE AT XANDARI

Tel 506 443 2020
www.xandari.com

On a coffee *finca* (ranch) north of Alajuela, this luxurious spa provides pampering with a view. Treatments in open-air palm-roofed pavilions include massage, homeopathic remedies, reflexology, mud wraps and facials.
💷 Massages from US$75

Seeing the backcountry with Motorcycles Costa Rica

✪ WATER LAND

Just off the airport highway on the road to San Antonio de Belén
Tel 506 293 2891
www.waterlandcr.com

Water Land is a good aquatic theme park with water slides, a wave machine and underwater caves, and miniature golf and picnic areas in gardens.
🕐 Tue–Fri 9–5, Sat–Sun members only
🎫 Adult US$10, child US$5

ATENAS

★ MOTORCYCLES COSTA RICA

Atenas
Tel 506 446 5015
www.motoscostarica.com

Some 25km (15 miles) from Alajuela, Atenas, the small town famous for its delightful climate, is the base for this friendly operation that organizes motorcycle tours of the Central Highlands, Arenal and the beaches of Guanacaste. For greater freedom, Suzuki sport bikes are available to rent.
💷 From US$1,695 including guides, accommodation, meals, drinks and bike rental. Suzuki motorbike US$50–85 per day (3-day minimum) or by the week for less

ESCAZÚ

🛍 BARRY BIESANZ

Tel 506 289 4337
www.biesanz.com

Barry Biesanz is one of the country's top craftspeople (▷ 31). His distinctive carvings use a mix of dark and light woods. The boxes—humidors, jewelry boxes or what Barry calls for "small things"—are exquisite.
🕐 Mon–Fri 8–5, Sat, Sun by appointment only
💷 From US$5

🛍 MULTIPLAZA

North of Escazú on Highway 27
Tel 506 201 6025
www.multiplazamall.com

The largest shopping mall in Costa Rica, a 15-minute bus ride from the capital, is where you will find familiar American brands. Librería Internacional has a good selection of English-language fiction and Costa Rica wildlife and cultural guides, and E-Music stocks international music.
🕐 Daily 10–9, Sun 10–8

GRECIA

★ TROPICAL BUNGEE

Grecia
Tel 506 248 2212
www.tropicalbungee.com

For adrenaline junkies, exhilarating jumps from a bridge down to the Río Colorado 80m (262ft) below are available on

day-trips from San José. With over 20,000 jumps to their name, this company has a 100 percent safety record.

🪂 One jump: US$65

⊗ WORLD OF SNAKES
1.5km (1 mile) from Grecia, heading towards Alajuela
Tel 506 494 3700
www.theworldofsnakes.com
This open-air serpentarium exhibits more than 150 snakes representing half of the country's serpent species. World of Snakes also has a research and conservation program. Multilingual tours with knowledgeable guides last 45 minutes.

🕐 Mon–Thu 8–5
🎟 Adult US$11, child US$6

LA GUÁCIMA

⊗ RANCHO SAN MIGUEL
3km north of La Guácima
Tel 506 438 0849
This stud farm raises Andalusian horses and offers riding lessons. The highlight, however, is the once-weekly dressage show in the tradition of the world-famous Lipizzaner Stallions. It's a magnificent spectacle as the horses perform pirouettes, leaps and other maneuvers to Spanish classical music.

🕐 Sat 8pm
🎟 US$26

HEREDIA

⊕ CENTRAL MARKET
Calle 2–4, Avenida 6
Heredia
This vibrant market is a compact version of the Mercado Central in San José. Earthy sights, smells and tastes make for an absorbing foray into provincial Heredia. Stalls are crammed with fruit and vegetables, herbal remedies, flowers and inexpensive crafts.

🕐 Mon–Sat 6–6

⊗ BULEVAR BAR
Avenida Central, Calle 5–7
Heredia
Tel 506 237 1832
The University ensures buoyant

nightlife in quiet Heredia. A block from the University, Bulevar is one of the happening places with a good mix of students, tourists and young professionals. Food is available and there is live music on Tuesday and Saturday.

🕐 11am–1am
🍺 Beers US$1.50, cocktails US$2.50

⊗ LA CHOZA
Avenida Central, Calle 7–9
100m (110 yards) west of the main university entrance Heredia
Tel 506 237 1553
La Choza is another unpretentious, lively bar that packs a university crowd in every night. The split-level bar has an

Relax at one of Costa Rica's new crop of spas and health resorts

upstairs balcony and TV screens competing with a mix of Latin pop, rock and salsa. There is karaoke every Thursday at 9pm and marauding mariachis occasionally on Wednesdays.

🕐 Mon–Fri 4–1, Sat, Sun 3–1, Sunday football match day 11am–1am

⊗ CASTILLO COUNTRY CLUB
On road to Monte de la Cruz
Heredia
Tel 506 267 7111
www.castillocountryclub.com
East of Heredia, on the lower slopes of the Barva volcano, Castillo Country Club offers swimming, sauna and Jacuzzi,

football, tennis, volleyball and go-carts and even ice skating. There are picnic areas or dine at the restaurant (from US$8).

🎟 Day membership Mon–Fri US$15

⊗ INTERCULTURA COSTA RICA
Apdo 1952-3000
Heredia
Tel 506 260 8480
www.spanish-intercultura.com
This school offers language tuition in all levels from beginner upwards, with homestays and cultural activities.

🎟 From US$260 week without homestay, US$370 with accommodation

OROSÍ

⊗ BALNEARIO DE AGUAS TERMALES
300m (325 yards) south and 150m (170 yards) west of Orosí church, next to the Orosí Lodge
Tel 506 533 21 56
There are two outdoor swimming pools here, a restaurant, and basketball court, with plenty of space for sunbathing. Thick unruly vegetation makes it good for early morning bird- and butterfly-watching.

🕐 Wed–Mon 7.30–4
🎟 US$2

POÁS

⊗ DOKA ESTATE
Sabanilla de Alajuela
Tel 506 449 5152
www.dokaestate.com
The lower slopes of Poás Volcano are cloaked in coffee bushes. At Doka Estate, visitors can learn about production and processing of Costa Rica's main crop at the country's oldest *finca* and mill. Folkloric shows add a dramatic dimension and an open-air restaurant with spectacular views serves traditional fare.

🕐 Mon–Sat 9.30–1.30
🎟 US$15

WHAT TO DO

✪ LA PAZ WATERFALL GARDEN
Vara Blanca
Tel 506 225 0643
www.waterfallgardens.com
A lushly forested valley forms a dramatic setting for this theme park named for the spectacular waterfalls that crash through the gorge. A huge butterfly enclosure, a serpentarium exhibiting all manner of snakes, a walk-through frog garden, and a hummingbird garden are among the other attractions.
🕐 Daily 8.30–5.30
💲 Adult US$25, child US$1

SARCHÍ

⊕ FÁBRICA DE CHAVERRI
PO Box 19-4150
Sarchí
Tel 506 454 4411
The heart of Sarchí is to the north but there are workshops in both parts of town. Arriving from the south you come first to Fábrica de Chaverri. The family-run operation was established in 1903 and has seen four generations of Chaverris produce hand-painted oxcarts. A full-size cart costs US$320–360, but smaller options are available for less. Worldwide flat-pack shipping can be arranged.
🕐 Daily 8–6

⊕ PLAZA DE LA ARTESANÍA
Sarchí Sur
Tel 506 454 3430
This shopping complex set in a pleasant courtyard has an expensive but wide selection of arts and crafts. Shipping can be arranged for larger items. There are restaurants, coffee shops, an ice-cream parlour and a bank, as well as souvenir shops, many with imported Guatemalan crafts.
🕐 Daily 9–6
💲 US$5–360

TURRIALBA

✪ RIO LOCOS TROPICAL TOURS
Apdo 285-7150

Turrialba
Tel 506 556 6035
www.whiteh2o.com
Not the biggest white-water rafting operation in Costa Rica but, they claim, the friendliest. Tico-run, and with a lot of experience.
💲 US$55–125 per day

✪ RAINFOREST WORLD
Turrialba
Tel 506 556 0014
www.rforestw.com
One of a couple of small local operators that offers cross-cultural tours with bilingual guides aimed at low-impact tourism, combining two-days rafting on the Pacuare River with camping in the Huacas Canyon. There are trips to their private jungle reserve and scenic "float trips" for those who don't enjoy the rapids experience.
💲 One-day trips US$90 per person; custom tours also available

FESTIVALS

EL DÍA DEL BOYERO
Escazú
March
One of the outstanding features of Escazú is the Día del Boyero (Day of the Oxcart Driver), on the second Sunday of March, which is one of the country's largest festivals. It fills the sleepy streets with oxcart parades accompanied by traditional music and dancers.

JUAN SANTAMARÍA DAY
April 11
Alajuela celebrates the life of the town's most famous son, the young drummer boy Juan Santamaría, who became a national hero when, during the Battle of Rivas in 1856, he torched the headquarters of the reviled American soldier William Walker. To commemorate the event, there is a week of general celebration, bands, concerts and dancing.

✪ SERENDIPITY ADVENTURES
Turrialba
Tel 506 558 1000
In USA tel 877 507 1358
www.serendipityadventures.com
Serendipity provide hot air balloon tours in the Turrialba area, or to the north around Naranjo or Arenal Volcano, in addition to adventure and nature tours, including an eight-day trip that combines canyoning, rafting, horseback riding and motorcycling. A four-day Cabécar Indian trail tour ventures into the Talamanca foothills.
💲 8-day tour from US$2,330; balloon trips from US$280 per person

✪ TICOS RIVER ADVENTURES
Turrialba
Tel 506 556 1231
www.ticoriver.com
This company specializes in one-day rafting trips along the 31km (19-mile) Pacuare rapids, which combine exhilarating stretches of class IV rapids with scenic interludes. Three-and four- day trips to Chirripó are offered mid-June to December.
🕐 Leave at 9am and return at 4pm

VARA BLANCA

✪ POÁS VOLCANO LODGE
El Cortijo Farm
Vara Blanca
Tel 506 482 2194
www.poasvolcanolodge.com
Professional and welcoming, accomplished English horse-woman Emily Cannon runs half-day guided horseback tours. The tour begins on the northern slope of Barva Volcano, passing though scenic backcountry and highland trails fringed with forests on the edge of Braulio Carrillo National Park. The forests teem with birdlife and you may spot signs of tapir, ocelots or jaguars. The horses are well cared for and Emily is knowledgeable about the Poás area and Costa Rica as a whole.
🕐 Daily 8.30–1.30
💲 US$60 minimum two people

NORTHERN REGION

KEY TO SYMBOLS

- 🏠 **Shopping**
- 🎭 **Entertainment**
- 🍸 **Nightlife**
- ⚽ **Sports**
- 🎯 **Activities**
- 💗 **Health and Beauty**
- 🧒 **For Children**

BOCA TAPADA

🎯 LA LAGUNA DE LAGARTO LODGE

Boca Tapada
Tel 506 289 8163
www.lagarto-lodge-costarica.com

Some 40km (25 miles) from the Río San Carlos, the Laguna de Lagarto, a member of The Ecotourism Association, is frequently recommended for its wildlife watching. The lodge looks directly out to the rainforest and a private reserve of 500ha (1,235 acres) where you can roam along 15km (9 miles) of trails with a guide or head out on your own. Some 365 bird species, including the great green macaw, have been recorded on the property. From the lodge you can take canoeing trips on nearby lagoons, a boat trip to the San Juan River on the border with Nicaragua, or go horseback riding. The hotel is off the beaten path so these activities are not convenient for non-guests.

FORTUNA

🎯 ARENAL HANGING BRIDGES

Tel 506 479 9686
www.puentescolgantes.com
www.hangingbridges.com (in English)

This attraction in the Fortuna region offers a complex of gentle trails that wander through 250ha (617 acres) of primary forest and across a series of steel suspension bridges that provide good wildlife spotting and views of Arenal Volcano. Access is via a sharp right turn past the Arenal dam on the Fortuna–Nuevo Arenal road.

🕐 Daily 7.30–4.30
🎟 Adult US$20, child US$10; guided tours and night tours: US$30

🎯 ARENAL RAINFOREST RESERVE

El Castillo
Tel 506 479 9944
www.arenalreserve.com

A Sky Tram ride up a mountainside ends at a lookout with views over Lake Arenal and Arenal Volcano. From here enjoy a canopy tour with

Stay overnight at La Laguna de Lagarto Lodge

almost 5km (3 miles) of zipline—the longest single line is 700m (2,310ft) long! More sedentary trails lead through the rainforest reserve. Snake and butterfly exhibits round out the attractions.

🕐 9–8
🎟 US$40

MONTEVERDE

🏠 ARTS AND CRAFT COOPERATIVE

Casemcoop R. L. (CASEM)
Opposite Stella's Bakery
Tel 506 645 5190

Just over halfway up the road to the reserve, close to El Bosque restaurant, is CASEM, founded in 1872 by women of the Monteverde area who help provide for their families by working from their homes. The cooperative now sells embroidered shirts, T-shirts, wooden and woven articles and baskets. The shop next door sells Costa Rican coffee and you can also get used coffee sacks as an unusual souvenir, if they have any. More than 140 craftspeople are represented.

🕐 Mon–Sat 8–5, Sun 10–4

🏠 BROMELIAS BOOKSTORE AND GALLERY

75m (80 yards) east of Stella's Bakery
Tel 506 645 6272

Some 3km (2 miles) east of Santa Elena, is Bromelias, owned by Patricia Maynard. The gallery represents several local artists and craftsmen with a myriad collection of paintings, batik, stained glass, indigenous musical instruments and jewelry. The arty vibe extends to the alpine-style restaurant festooned with arts and crafts where they serve wonderful home-made chocolate and banana cake, sandwiches and teas. Yoga classes can also be arranged.

🕐 Daily 9–5

🏠 LA CASCADA

Just before the petrol station on the road to Monteverde
Tel 506 645 5186

On the road to Monteverde, La Cascada is the place to head for serious partying until the early hours. Very popular in high season, it may be low key in the early evening, but by 10pm it positively throbs with visitors and locals dancing to live music courtesy of local bands or DJ. Admission price varies accordingly. As well as beer, spirits and cocktails, fast-food bar snacks are served.

🕐 Thu–Sat 9pm–2am
🎟 US$1.50–6

★ LA TABERNA
1km (0.6 miles) from Santa Elena
Tel 506 645 5883
The Taberna, close to the Serpentarium, is a good place to enjoy an early drink on the outdoor terrace, or more ebullient socializing and dancing after 9pm. Infectious beats stir locals and visitors to some serious hip gyrating with a Latin musical repertoire including salsa, son and merengue, although '80s rock usually competes for the airwaves by the early hours. There is a restaurant serving snacks, sandwiches and burgers, and some below-average fish and meat dishes.
🕒 Wed–Sun 11am–2am

★ DESAFÍO EXPEDITIONS
Opposite the supermarket in Santa Elena
Tel 506 645 5874
www.monteverdetours.com
Desafío is a highly recommended tour operator that runs a selection of tailor-made horseback tours in the Monteverde area. Excursions include two-hour secondary forest and farm rides, a good option for novice riders, US$15–20; a four-hour ride which also includes a two-hour hike to the breathtaking 91m (300ft) San Luís Waterfall, US$53; or for the more dedicated, a two-day trip to Fortuna. Helmets are only provided for children and it is worth noting that English-speaking guides tend to be available only on the larger group tours. Prices are cheaper the larger the group.

Desafío also runs white-water rafting trips on the rapids of the class III–IV Río Toro. Trips depart at 8.30am and return at 3.30pm and cost US$80 per person, including equipment and hotel transportation in the Arenal area. Half days on the Arenal River, US$55, are much tamer with more relaxed interludes that allow for wildlife spotting and even for

swimming alongside the raft. For first-time rafters, the class I/II San Carlos River half-day trip is advised, US$45. All guides are bilingual. Remember to call ahead and be aware that river trips are subject to weather conditions being suitable on the day.

★ ECOLODGE SAN LUÍS
San Luís
Tel 506 645 8049
www.ecolodgesanluis.com
Affiliated with the University of Georgia , this educational facility is part research station and part ecological forest reserve. Guided birding and nature hikes—including to a waterfall—plus horseback rides are among the draws, and visitors seeking a more in-depth of local ecology can partake in lectures and intensive study courses. A night walk is a not to be missed.
🕒 Daily 8–5
🎫 US$3 self-guided trail hike, US$10 horseback ride

★ JEWELS OF THE RAIN-FOREST
Selvatura
www.selvatura.com/jewels.html
The world's largest private insect collection is displayed in exotic, colorful detail. Entomologist Richard Whitten is usually on-hand to tell fascinating anecdotes as you admire the many thousands of butterflies, moths, beetles, etc. from around the world, all exquisitely choreographed by Richard's wife, Margaret. Fascinating videos are screened in an auditorium.
🕒 7–5
🎫 US$10

★ SABINE'S SMILING HORSES
Pensión Santa Elena
Tel 506 645 6894
www.smilinghorses.com
Another recommended riding stables, Sabine's places a clear emphasis on fit and healthy horses. Horseback tours from

two to five hours and multi-day riding holidays are organized and include the Monteverde to Arenal tour, beach rides, full moon rides, tours to the San Luís waterfall, and the most popular excursion, the Campesino Secret Trails, crossing through farmland and cloud forest for three hours.
🐴 Three-hour ride US$40

PUERTO VIEJO DE SARAPIQUÍ
★ SARAPIQUÍ CONSERVATION LEARNING CENTER
Tel 506 766 6482
www.learningcentercostarica.org
At Selva Verde, this long-established eco-lodge works to ensure that the local community get to learn about and benefit from the secrets of the rainforest. Extending this education about the rainforest locally is an essential link if the desire to reduce deforestation is to be effective at the grassroots level. A good library is available in the Learning Center, and there is a volunteer program teaching English.

LA VIRGEN
★ RANCHO LEONA
La Virgen
9km (5 miles) north of San Miguel
Tel 506 761 1019
www.rancholeona.com
Some 9km (5 miles) north of San Miguel is La Virgen, and one good reason to stop is Rancho Leona. The main attraction is excellent kayaking on the Río Sarapiquí and excursions are available from beginner to advanced level with two nights' accommodation included in the all-inclusive price of US$75. There is a quiet patio for reading in the lush gardens, an Indian-style sweat lodge and in-depth local knowledge of all the nearby attractions, all fueled by a healthy but filling menu of dishes served in the open-air restaurant.

GUANACASTE

CAÑAS

✪ SAFARIS COROBICÍ
Cañas
Tel 506 669 6091
www.nicoyai.com
This company specializes in scenic rafting trips which focus less on the thrills and spills and more on contemplation of the natural setting, improving the chances to see wildlife: a good option for all the family.
🕐 Hourly trips 7–3
💵 US$35 for 2 hours, US$60 for 4

ISLA DEL COCO

✪ OKEANOS AGGRESSOR
Tel 506 228 6613
Toll free in the US on 800-348-2628
www.aggressor.com
Coco Island is heralded as the apogee of diving in Costa Rica, and is one of the most exciting dive spots in the world, primarily due to the huge numbers of hammerhead sharks in the area. Owing to the cool water and strong currents, dive operators advise that the island is not suitable for beginners. *Okeanos Aggressor* is a 33m (110ft) vessel with comfortable berths for 22 guests. Departing from Puntarenas on the 30- to 36-hour trip, the *Aggressor* offers 8-day and 10-day charters all year.
💵 From US$2,695 for 8 days, US$3,095 for 10 days, per person

LIBERIA

✪ AFRICA MÍA
7km (4.5 miles) south of Liberia
Tel 506 661 8161
www.africamia.net
Making the most of Guanacaste's African-like savanna, this theme park opened in 2006 as a re-creation of the East African plains, with zebras, ostrich and antelope roaming the grassy terrain. Tours are offered in a safari-style bus.
🕐 8–6
💵 Adult US$15, child US$10

MIRAVALLES

✪ LAS HORNILLAS VOLCANIC ACTIVITY CENTER
7km (4.5 miles) northeast of Guayabo
Tel 506 839 9769
www.lashornillas.com
Mudpools bubble and steam

Going overboard: a diver on a Rich Coast Diving trip

vents hiss in this small but very active volcanic crater, where you can bathe in therapeutic mineral clays. Horseback rides lead to waterfalls in the adjacent forest reserve.
💵 US$30 for 2-hour tour

PARQUE NACIONAL RINCÓN DE LA VIEJA

✪ HOTEL HACIENDA GUACHIPELÍN
Parque Nacional Rincón de la Vieja
Tel 506 666 8075
www.guachipelin.com
This cattle ranch, bordering Rincón de la Vieja National Park, focuses on sustainable tourism. It offers a range of activities in a stunning natural setting. A one-day Guachipelín adventure pass covers all the activities and attractions, from snorkeling to horseback riding and visits to waterfalls.
💵 Guachipelín adventure pass US$75

PLAYA AZUL

♥ LA VIDA SPA
The Sanctuary Resort
Playa Azul
Nosara
Tel 506 682 8226
www.thesanctuaryresort.com
Aimed at burned-out executives, La Vida Spa offers treats such as Swedish massages, facials, manicures, pedicures and holistic treatments, including reiki. Seven themed pools feature various treatments: the Polynesian pool is filled with green tea and ginger; the Costa Rican pool has warm, mineral-rich Costa Rican mud. Rooms cost from US$175 per night.

PLAYA CONCHAL

⚽ GARRA DE LEÓN
Playa Conchal Beach and Golf Resort
Playa Conchal
Tel 506 654 4123
www.solmelia.com
Garra de León is, in the resort's own words, an "eco-golf experience course," with broad fairways and Pacific views. The par-72 course offers four sets of tees. The cart is included in the price and private instruction is offered.
💵 18 holes in high season from US$150 for guests, non-guests US$195. Guests age 17 and under play free.

PLAYAS DEL COCO

✪ FLOR DE ITABO HOTEL
PO Box 32
Playas del Coco
Tel 506 670 0292
www.flordeitabo.com
While Playa Flamingo to the south gets the main sportfishing business, the Flor de Itabo hotel in Coco has a good reputation with professional

WHAT TO DO

captains and all the gear if you want to charter a boat. A variety of multiday big game fishing trips can be arranged. 🚤 Boat charter from US$650 per day; 6-days big game fishing from US$774 per person for group of 4

⭐ DEEP BLUE DIVING
Beside Hotel Coco Verde
Playas del Coco
Tel 506 670 1004
www.deepblue-diving.com
Most tour operators offer very similar diving excursions from Coco: A two-tank morning or afternoon dive starts at US$70. Resort courses (ie unqualified) are US$95, and PADI training is also available, with open water certification costing US$320. Prices include tanks, weights and guides, normally for at least two people.

⭐ RICH COAST DIVING
Tel 506 670 0176
In the US and Canada 1-800-4-DIVING
www.richcoastdiving.com
Rich Coast is run by experienced divemasters Martin and Brenda van Gestel. It offers packages, direct or booked through hotels in Coco, starting from two-tank dives at US$70. Dives at Las Islas Catalinas cost US$95. There are also fishing, sailing and snorkeling trips.

PLAYA FLAMINGO

⭐ BLUE DOLPHIN SAILING
Playa Flamingo
Tel 506 653 0867
www.sailbluedophin.com
This family business offers half-day snorkel trips, including instruction from well-informed guides. Romantics take sunset or full moon sails. 🕐 Daily 9–1.30 🚤 Half-day adult from US$75, child (2–11) half price; sunset sails US$60

⭐ SHANNON SAILING
Las Brisas Center 1
Playa Flamingo
Tel 506 653 8437
www.flamingobeachcr.com
Cruising yacht *Shannon* has hosted nautical adventures off

Guanacaste since 1991, allowing close encounters with the region's abundant marine life, including dolphins, rays and whales. The half-day snorkeling and sunset cruise includes a sail to Playa de Amor and guided snorkels. There are surfing trips to Ollie's Point, "extreme sailing," and live-aboard diving expeditions to Isla del Coco. 🚤 Sunset cruise US$75

⭐ FLAMINGO EQUESTRIAN CENTER
Calle Antigua
Playa Flamingo
Tel 506 654 4089
http://equestriancostarica.com

The Blue Dolphin yacht sets out from Playa Flamingo

Bilingual instructor Amanda Gardner offers a wide range of classes in basic horsemanship, dressage and jumping for all ages and levels. Workshops are held throughout the year. 🚤 Horseback ride US$30 per person

PLAYA GRANDE

⭐ LAS BAULAS NATIONAL MARINE PARK
Playa Grande
Tel 506 653 0470
Turtle-watching tours depart from Tamarindo and other northwestern beaches from November to March to Playa Grande. Trips leave late afternoon and must be organized through hotels. Reservations

can be made at Las Baulas Marine Park. During the nesting season, you must be accompanied by licensed guides on the beach at night. 🚤 US$16 plus park entrance and guide

PLAYA HERMOSA

⭐ DIVING SAFARIS OF COSTA RICA
Playa Hermosa
Tel 506 453 5044
Fax 954 351 9740
www.billbeardcostarica.com
One of the longest-running dive operations in the country, the company offers all the standard dive options and some good packages mixing aquatic activities with land-based options. Most dives are within a 30-minute radius, with abundant marine species, including the promise of whale sharks. 🚤 From US$224 for 4-night packages

PLAYA JUNQUILLAL

⭐ PARADISE RIDING
Playa Junquillal
Tel 506 658 8162
www.paradiseriding.com
Guanacaste is *sabanero* heartland, and many ranches have turned to tourism and offer horseback riding tours. Criollo horses are available for all levels and most rides require no previous experience. Tours are from two hours to longer beach gallops. Guides are professional and bilingual. 🚤 US$25 for 2 hours, US$55 for 4 hours

PLAYA PANAMA

⭐ MARLIN AZUL DEEP SEA FISHING
Playa Panama
Tel 506 6 042170
http://costa-rica-sport-fishing.com
A subsidiary of Resort Divers, Marlin Azul offers sportfishing tours and charters and flyfishing. Half-day trips allow for four fishermen and two non-fishermen. Catch and release techniques are practised, with the exception of some fresh fish being kept for dinner, and

includes sailfish, marlin, wahoo, tuna and red snapper. Fishing bait and tackle is provided unless you are flyfishing (May to August).

🎣 Half-day trips US$550 per boat, full day US$800

⭐ RESORT DIVERS OF COSTA RICA

Playa Panama
Tel 506 672 0103 or 506 672 0106
www.resortdivers-cr.com

Resort Divers offers daily half-day two-tank dive trips which leave at 8.45am. Each dive is guided (bilingual) and limited to a group of no more than six divers. There are local dive sites and trips farther afield to the Catalina Islands and Isla de Murcielagos where bull sharks, cow-nosed rays and eagle rays proliferate. Puffer fish, parrot fish and sleeping turtles can also be glimpsed on a night dive. Scuba courses are also offered ranging from PADI open-water courses, to advanced and rescuer courses. The Discover Scuba Diving course provides novices with an idea of the excitement of diving.

🎣 Half-day from US$65

PLAYA TAMARINDO

🖼 COSTA RICA ART AND PAINTINGS

Playa Tamarindo
Tel 506 653 0241
www.natalyn.com

The work of Tamarindo artist Natalie Lynn is divided into several themes, including nature, wildlife and Mayan symbolism, inspired by her trips to the Guatemalan jungle. Check out her work online and then contact her in Tamarindo for a private appointment.

🎣 US$1,500–10,000

🖼 LA GALERÍA

Hotel Portofino
Playa Tamarindo
Tel 506 653 0578

This small gallery forms part of the Hotel Portofino, 100m

(110 yards) from the road to Langosta. You will find the work of contemporary Costa Rican artists and traditional arts and crafts here.

🍸 CRAZY MONKEY BAR

Tamarindo Vista Villas
Playa Tamarindo
Tel 506 653 0114
www.tamarindovistavillas.com

At the entrance to town, on the main road, this lively bar is a popular hang-out among the local surfing community, with frequent live music of Latin, rock, jazz or blues and amazing sunset vistas from its elevated vantage point. Meals come in large portions and the

A seahorse at Playa Hermosa, seen on a Bill Beard safari

sociable and unpretentious vibe makes it a good place to meet people and talk beach breaks and swells.

🕐 Daily 10–10

🍸 NIBBANA

200m (220 yards) from La Rotunda
Playa Tamarindo
Tel 506 653 0447
www.nibbana-tamarindo.com

This beachside bar-restaurant, just behind Century 21 on the main road, has a Caribbean vibe by day with reggae playing. In the early evening, it plays host to surfers and livens up with searing cocktails and an ebullient party spirit. Pizzas, salads, sandwiches and fruit

cocktails provide light refreshment until 6pm, and in the evening meat and seafood dishes are served. There is live music at sunset every Sunday, and an internet café.

🕐 Daily 7am–12am

🍸 PASATIEMPO

Take the left fork 100m (110 yards) before La Rotunda
Playa Tamarindo
Tel 506 653 0096
www.hotelpasatiempo.com

Set back from the main road, a 10-minute walk from the heart of town, this buzzing bar-restaurant in a rancho setting (▷ 201), has large TV screens showing sports, a pool table and wide-ranging music. One of Tamarindo's best nights is Pasatiempo's Tuesday night open mike jamming session.

🕐 8am–midnight

🍸 ZULLYMAR

Beachfront, opposite main roundabout
Playa Tamarindo
Tel 506 653 0023
http://zullymar.com

In the heart of town, Zullymar is a Tamarindo landmark, popular for its ocean views, breezy open-plan setting and lively atmosphere rather than its bland cuisine. For an afternoon beer, watching the surfers in action, it is hard to beat.

🕐 Daily 11–10

⭐ AGUA RICA DIVING CENTER

Centro Commercial Diriá
Tel 506 653 0094
www.tamarindo.com/agua

This professional and relaxed dive center runs PADI certification courses. Pacific coast diving trips in the Tamarindo area are offered, but the zenith of Costa Rican diving is without doubt a live-aboard diving excursion to Isla del Coco, which is also offered by Agua Rica. Multilingual guides provide excellent information.

🕐 Mon–Sat 9.30–6.30, Sun 3.30–6.30
🎣 5-hour trip to Catalina Islands US$95

WHAT TO DO

🌀 CASAGUA HORSES
Finca Casagua
In front of Rancho Cartagena, between
Portegolpe and Lorena
Tel 506 653 8041
www.tamarindo.com/casagua
On the main road between
Belen and Tamarindo, Casagua
Horses is expertly run by
American/Tico couple Kay
Dodge de Peraza and Esteban
Peraza. All ages and levels are
welcome, and you can chose
between Western- and English-
style saddles. Tours range from
countryside trails where you
can see howler monkeys to
the adults-only Cantina tour,
which gives you the chance to
play cowboy, riding along the
old oxcart trails and visiting
wild west towns. If you are
staying in Costa Rica for a
while, you can improve your
horsemanship with private lessons and even learn the high
stepping *tope*, Spanish-style.
🐎 1–2 hour tour from US$25

🌀 MANDINGO SAILING
Tamarindo Diriá Hotel
200m (220 yards) from La Rotunda
Playa Tamarindo
Tel 506 831 8875
www.tamarindosailing.com
Mandingo Sailing is run by
German couple André and
Maria Hammerschmidt, who
offer cruises and snorkeling
trips on board their schooner
yacht, the *Lemuria*. Romantics
are welcomed for the sunset
cruise. On board you can look
for cavorting dolphins, enjoy a
glass of wine and wait for the
heavenly Tamarindo sunset.
From December to March you
may see breaching humpback
whales and sperm whales. Or
spot puffer fish, rays and reef
fish on a sail and snorkel trip.
🐎 Sunset cruise US$50 per person;
half-day snorkel trip US$50 per person

🌀 TAMARINDO BEACH CIGAR LOUNGE
On the Playa Langosta road
Playa Tamarindo
Tel 506 653 0862
The aroma of fresh tobacco

leafs draws you into this handsome cigar lounge with an
adjunct room where skilled
rollers turn raw leafs into fine
cigars for export. The walk-in
humidor displays several
unique homegrown brands,
such as La Flor de Palmares,
boxed in a charming miniature
carreta, or Costa Rica oxcart;
and the Espresso, a flavorful
robusto made of leaves aged
with roasted espresso beans.
📷 Rollers: 8–5, bar: 4pm–midnight

🌟 TAMARINDO SPORT FISHING
300m (330 yards) west of the entrance
to Tamarindo airstip
Playa Tamarindo
Tel 506 653 0090
www.tamarindosportfishing.com
Tamarindo is famed for its
world-class sportfishing and
veteran skipper Randy Wilson
offers professional crews and
facilities. Catches, using his
special catch and release technique for the conservation-
minded angler, include marlin.
🐎 Half-day trip from US$675, day trip
from US$1,200

PUNTA ISLITA

◐ CASA SPA PUNTA ISLITA
Punta Islita
Tel 506 661 4044
www.hotelpuntaislita.com

Near to Corozalito on stunning
Punta Islita, this spa resort
offers more than 30 treatments that combine traditional
therapies with the ancient
beauty skills of the Chorotega
indigenous groups. Modern
Cleopatras can try the milk and
honey massage, while the Piña
Colada pedicure is a must for
hike-ravaged feet. For all-out
indulgence, finish with lunch at
the 1492 restaurant. This spa
does not cater to non-guests.
🐎 5-night yoga package from US$715

ROSARIO

🌀 TEMPISQUE SAFARI
Rosario
Tel 506 689 1069
This 90ha (222-acre) cattle
finca and forest reserve on the
banks of the Río Tempisque
doubles as a wildlife rescue
and breeding center.
Crocodiles splash around in a
lagoon, scarlet macaws roost
in the treetops, and a zoo
includes white-ale deer, peccaries, wild cats, capybaras and
monkeys. There's even an
ostrich! Tours are by cart pulled
by water buffalo, and include a
boat trip along the banks of
Palo Verde National Park.
📷 Daily 9–4
🐎 3-hour tour US$45 per person

SANTA CRUZ

⚐ HACIENDA PINILLA
Playa Langosta
Tel 506 680 3000
www.haciendapinilla.com
Less than one hour by car from
Liberia's airport, this par-72
links golf course on the Pinilla
hacienda has "the best greens
in Central America," claims the
course's PGA head golf professional David R. Vallejos. Four
sets of tees cater to players of
different abilities. Clubs and
shoes are available for rental
and the club provides lessons.
The clubhouse has bar and
grill for post-game drinks.
🐎 18 holes: US$75–85 for hotel
guests; US$125–50 for non-guests, cart
included

FESTIVALS AND EVENTS

LIBERIA FIESTAS
First week of March
Tel 506 666 7171
A series of events in Liberia
featuring Guanacaste folklore,
rides and concerts.

ANNEXATION OF GUANACASTE
Liberia
July 25
Guanacaste's decision in 1824
to be part of Costa Rica rather
than Nicaragua is celebrated
with fiestas in Liberia, folk
dances, parades, bullfights,
cattle shows and concerts.

CENTRAL PACIFIC AND NICOYA

CABUYA

♡ LOS ALMENDROS
Between Montezuma and Cabuya
Tel 506 642 0378
www.somaritmocostarica.com
Some 3.5km (2.2 miles) from Cabo Blanco National Park, this beachside studio and lodge offers classes for individuals interested in health, spirituality and movement arts professions with tai chi, yoga, singing, theater and Latin American dance classes.
🔲 Workshops from US$7 per hour

DOMINICAL

🎭 THE DOMINICAL LITTLE THEATER GROUP
Hotel Roca Verde
1km (0.6 mile) south of Dominical
Tel 506 787 8007 (Hotel Roca Verde tel 506 707 0036)
www.dominical.biz/theater
A short walk from the middle of town, Hotel Roca Verde hosts the varied theatrical programs of the English-speaking Dominical Little Theater group, including off-Broadway classics such as *The Fantasticks*. Each production is an international ensemble with aspiring Costa Rican thespians and the odd English actor. Shows usually start at 8pm with a Sunday showing providing a synopsis in Spanish. Call Hotel Roca Verde for current show information.
🔲 Tickets from US$3

🎭 CINEMA ESCALERAS
Dominical
www.cinemaescaleras.com
Started by movie-lovers Harley and Kimberley Toberman in 2003, this bijoux cinema, on a mountainside with great sunset views, shows classic movies every Friday. Saturday night is Spanish movie night.
🎬 Fri, Sat 5pm dinner, 6pm movie
🔲 No charge, but 2,000 colones donation appreciated

✪ ASOCIACIÓN DE AMIGOS DE LA NATURALEZA DEL PACÍFICO CENTRAL Y SUR (ASANA)
Tel 506 787 0254 (Franklin Sequeira)
Tel 506 787 0001 (Jack Ewing)
www.asana.o.cr
The Association of the Friends

A scene from The Fantasticks *by Dominical's Little Theater Group*

of Nature for the Central Pacific and Southern region is a conservation group that offers a volunteer program developing a wildlife corridor project—the Tapir Biological Corridor—from Manuel Antonio to the Osa Peninsula. You'll work on trail maintenance, tree planting and other tasks. Turtle protection projects are also offered.
🔲 US$75 per week, including food and accommodation

ISLA TORTUGA

✪ CALYPSO TOURS
Apt 1053 1007
San José (for reservations)
Tel 506 256 2727
www.calypsocruises.com

Off the southeastern tip of the Nicoya Peninsula, a handful of sand-fringed islands are easily visited from the peninsula, Puntarenas or San José. The most popular is a luxury cruise to Isla Tortuga, a pair of small uninhabited islands just off the peninsula to the south of Curú, with beautiful white sand beaches, and crystal clear water ideal for swimming, snorkeling and other aquatic activities. As it's one of the most popular trips in Costa Rica, don't expect to have the place to yourself.
🔲 Day trips US$99 with lunch

JACÓ

♀ OZ SPORTS BAR
Calle La Central
Playa Jacó
Tel 506 643 2162
One of Jacó's more stylish nightspots, this is a popular hang-out among weekending Joséfinos and expatriates. The minimalist design is light and airy, and the large circular bar is flanked by two wide-screen TVs showing round-the-clock sports entertainment. There are also pool tables, pinball machines and videos. Live music is on Friday nights with a good range of *bocas* to keep you going until dinner.
🎬 11am–2.30am

✪ WATERFALLS CANOPY TOUR
Playa Jacó
Tel 506 643 3322
www.waterfallscanopy.com
On the road to Herradura, 4km (2.5 miles) from Jacó, the Waterfalls Canopy Tour is owned and run by biologist Luis Fonseca. After the adrenaline rush of the canopy tour, there is a 27m (90ft) rappel, Tarzan swing and tree houses. Guided or self-guiding trails can be followed. Night canopy tours are for a minimum of 10 people. Full-day tours are available from San José, which

WHAT TO DO

include a butterfly tour, frog tour and crocodile-watching at the Río Tarcoles.

🖐 2-hour canopy tour US$65

MANUEL ANTONIO

⭐ AMIGOS DEL RIO
Manuel Antonio
Tel 506 777 0082
www.amigosdelrio.net
Amigos del Rio offers rafting trips along the challenging Upper Savegre River for all levels of experience. White-water kayaking and ocean kayaking around Manuel Antonio can be arranged, as can jungle tours in Humvee vehicles. Amigos del Rio's guides are knowledgeable and professional.

🖐 Full day US$99

⭐ SEA GLASS SPA
Manuel Antonio
Tel 506 777 2607
www.seaglassspa.com
Try a range of alternative and traditional techniques with qualified therapists at this US-owned spa. Packages include hot-stone massages for US$90 and four-hands massages for US$155. Reservations required.

🖐 Aloe wrap US$80

MONTEZUMA

📖 LIBRERÍA TOPSY
Opposite the Bakery Café
Montezuma
Tel 506 642 0576
This bookstore has a good collection of multi-language fiction, predominantly English, and other reading matter to buy, rent or exchange, along with international newspapers and magazines. A collection of Latin American literature includes works by Gabriel García Márquez and Pablo Neruda. You can buy stationery, including maps and travel journals.

🕐 Mon–Fri 8–4, Sat–Sun 8–noon

⭐ LOS MANGOS HOTEL
Montezuma
Tel 506 642 0076
www.montezumayoga.com
Nicoya's New Age explosion has hit the Los Mangos Hotel,

on the road out of town towards Cobaya. Hatha Vinyasa yoga classes are held in an open-air pavilion amid dense jungle. All levels are catered to in 90-minute classes. One-on-one classes can be arranged on request.

🕐 Sun–Fri 9.30am
🖐 Single class US$12, 10 classes US$100

OROTINA

⭐ THE ORIGINAL CANOPY TOUR
Orotina
Tel 506 291 4465
www.canopytour.com
Mahogany Park near Orotina is home to this Original Canopy

Post-surfing relaxation at the all-female Del Mar Surf Camp

Tour franchise with a 3.5-hour tour going through three different ecosystems. The third platform rests on a strangler fig over 30m (98ft) in height which links to a fourth on a 44m-high (144ft) kapok tree.

🕐 Daily tours at 8, 10, 12, 2.30
🖐 US$45; all-inclusive trip from San José US$60

PLAYA HERMOSA

⭐ DEL MAR SURF CAMP
Hotel Terraza del Pacífico
Playa Hermosa
Tel 506 385 8535
www.costaricasurfingchicas.com
The only all-female surf camp in Costa Rica, the Del Mar offers all-inclusive packages

with accommodation at Hotel Pacífico, surfing lessons from female instructors, all equipment, massage and yoga. Beginners should be aware that Hermosa's waves can be large and powerful.

🖐 3 days US$970, 10 days US$1,440

⭐ HOTEL TERRAZA DEL PACÍFICO
Playa Hermosa
Tel: 506 643 3222
www.terrazadelpacifico.com
On the surfing mecca of Playa Hermosa, just south of Jacó, the specialized surf hotel, Hotel del Pacífico, attracts surfers from all over the world over to its events, including the spectacular night surf contest, where stretches of Hermosa beach are illuminated.

QUEPOS

⭐ BLUE FIN SPORTFISHING CHARTERS
Apdo 223-6350
Quepos
Tel 506 777 1676
www.bluefinsportfishing.com
This operator offers full- and half-day sportfishing charters. The conditions are excellent with waters teeming with dorado, marlin and tuna. A range of boats is available and all charters include IGFA tackle, safety kit and a bilingual captain.

🕐 Leave at 7am, return 6pm
🖐 US$475–945

⭐ BRISAS DEL NARA
Quepos
Tel 506 779 1235
www.horsebacktour.com
In the foothills of the Cerro Nosara, 10 minutes from Quepos, the Brisas del Nara offers full- and half-day guided horseback-riding tours through the forest. Tours include swimming in the forest, picnics at the Quebrado Arroya waterfall and scenic trails. Pick-ups can be arranged from your hotel and children less than four years old can ride with their parents.

🖐 Full day US$55

✪ CANOPY SAFARI
PO Box 351
Quepos
Tel 506 777 0100
www.canopysafari.com
Canopy Safari was the first
such operator in the southern
region. With an ecologically
sensitive ethos, canopies are
constructed to ensure that the
environmental impact is
minimal. As well as the white-
knuckle rush of zipping
through the canopy, the well-
organized excursion includes
hiking, swimming, breakfast or
lunch and refreshments.
Friendly guides inform about
the flora and fauna.
🕔 Half-day trips (5 hours) from US$65

✪ IGUANA TOURS
Quepos
Tel 506 777 2052
www.iguanatours.com
Iguana Tours was the first
professional tour operator in
Quepos and offers excellent
and challenging kayaking tours
along the stunning Manuel
Antonio coastline. For a quieter
trip, you can meander through
the inland waterways for five
hours, with mangrove areas
and prolific wildlife. A seafood
lunch is included.
🕓 Tours depart 8–1 or 1–2
🕔 US$65

✪ RAINMAKER CONSERVATION PROJECT
17km (10.6 miles) from Parrita in the
village of San Rafael Norte
Office in Quepos: tel 506 777 3565
www.rainmakercostarica.com
The Rainmaker Conservation
Project aims to protect the Fila
Chonta mountain range on
Costa Rica's Pacific side. Virgin
rainforest almost entirely, the
privately owned reserve contains more than 70 percent of
all the species of flora and
fauna found in Costa Rica. The
Rainmaker Canopy Walk consists of six sections totalling
250m (270 yards) linking platforms attached to trees,
providing close encounters
with this pristine wildlife

haven. Rainmaker operates
sustainable tourism and the
canopy design precludes
harmful impact on the forest.
🕓 Daily 7.30–6, tours 8–3
🕔 US$70 including meals

✪ RANCHO SAVEGRE
Quepos
Tel 506 723 8522 or 506 834 8687
www.costaricahorsetrek.com
Rancho Savegre, a cattle range
covering 810ha (2,000 acres)
some 15km (9 miles) from
Quepos, offers a wide variety
of guided riding tours, from
beach gallops to rainforest
treks and rides to coffee plantation towns. Well-cared-for
horses are available to suit

*Watch the sunset from the
beachside La Vela bar*

beginners and accomplished
riders. Wear long trousers and
sneakers or boots—no sandals.
🕓 7.30am–1.30pm
🕔 3-hour ride US$65

SÁMARA

🍷 LA VELA BEACH BAR AND COCKTAIL LOUNGE
300m (330 yards) east of the Correo
Sámara
Tel 506 656 0418
Right on the beach, this bar/
lounge, run by friendly Italian
couple Marco and Regina, is
rather incongruous, with its
sleek decor. A range of light
appetizers, including leafy
salads and bruschetta, and a
monumental cocktail list are

served in a relaxed environment by the sea. It is rather
pricy, but worth it for a sunset
drink.
🕓 Wed–Mon 4pm–midnight

SANTA TERESA

✪ LUZ DA VIDA RESORT
Santa Teresa
Tel 506 640 0320
www.luzdevida-resort.com
This holiday village embodies
the relaxed escapism and
healthy mindset for which
Santa Teresa has become
known. Activities on land and
sea can be arranged, from surfing classes to yoga, deep-sea
fishing, waterskiing and horseback riding on the beach.
🕔 Doubles US$95–130

TÁRCOLES

✪ JUNGLE CROCODILE SAFARI
Tárcoles
Tel 506 637 0586
www.junglecrocodilesafari.com
Prepare for a thrilling ride up
the Río Tárcoles with the
prospect of witnessing your
guide actually hand-feed a
giant crocodile! Early morning
is best, when the crocs sun
themselves on the banks.
Roseate spoonbills, whistling
ducks, egrets and even scarlet
macaws are among the many
bird species typically seen
close up.
🕓 8.30, 10.30, 1.30 and 3.30
🕔 US$35

FESTIVALS

FESTIVAL OF THE VIRGIN OF THE SEA
Second week of July
Puntarenas
Ends with a parade of brightly
decorated boats sailing out
into the gulf.

FIESTA DE LA YEGÜITA
12 December
Nicoya
Parades, dancing, fireworks,
bullfights and music.

SOUTHERN REGION

BAHÍA DRAKE

✪ CAÑO DIVERS
Pirate Cove Hotel
North end of Bahía Drake
Tel 506 834 1226
www.piratecovecostarica.com
You may see sharks and rays
when diving in Drake Bay with
Caño Divers. You can arrange
your dive through your hotel.
🤿 2-tank diving day US$110

✪ DIVINE DOLPHIN
Delfín Amor Eco Lodge
1km (0.6 mile) west of Bahia Drake
Tel 506 394 2632 or 506 847 3131
www.divinedolphin.com
A short car ride from Bahía
Drake, the Delfín Amor com-
plex offers dolphin-watching.
See hotel listing (▷ 205).
🤿 Packages from San José, US$1,200

PAVONES

🏛 ARTE NATIVO
400m (440 yards) south of Supermares
Tel 506 821 6563
Opposite Esquinas, Arte Nativo
sells locally made art and jewelry. Owner Candyce Speck
offers the only internet service
in town (access 8–8).

PLAYA SAN JOSECITO

✪ CASA ORQUÍDIAS
LAND SEA TOURS
Playa San Josecito
Tel 506 829 1247
Some 30 minutes by water taxi
from Golfito at Playa San
Josecito, you can visit Casa
Orquídeas, a family-owned
botanical garden with a collec-
tion of herbs, orchids and local
plants and an entertaining,
hands-on tour explaining their
medicinal properties.
🕐 Sat–Thu, mornings only, 8.30 tours
🤿 US$5 per person, min 4 people

PLAYA ZANCUDO

✪ GOLFITO SPORT FISHING
Playa Zancudo
Tel 506 776 0007
www.costaricafishing.com
On the narrow peninsula of
Zancudo, angling opportunities

abound. Golfito Sport Fishing
offers offshore fishing for marlin, dorado, wahoo and tuna
and inshore fishing for roosterfish, snapper and grouper.
🕐 Peak season Dec–Jun
🤿 3-day all-inclusive trip US$2,785

SAN ISIDRO DE EL GENERAL

✪ CENTRO BIOLÓLOGICO LAS QUEBRADAS
San Isidro de El General
Tel 506 771 4131
www.ecotourism.co.cr
The community-protected
reserve of Centro Biológico las

*Divine Dolphin: a spinner
dolphin leaps out of the ocean*

Quebradas is a 2.5km (1.5-
mile) walk from Quebradas.
The Centro protects the birds,
bromeliads and butterflies of
the Quebradas River basin.
🕐 Tue–Fri 8–2, Sat, Sun 8–3
🤿 US$6

✪ LOS CUSINGOS
Quizarrá de Pérez Zeledón
San Isidro de El General
Tel 506 200 5472
www.cct.or.cr
Some 30 minutes southeast of
San Isidro by car is this small
bird reserve, home to Costa
Rica's eminent ornithologist,
Dr. Alexander Skutch, co-
author of *A Guide to the Birds
of Costa Rica*. Visits to the
76ha (188-acre) reserve are by

appointment only and limited
to students, researchers,
naturalists and birdwatchers.
🕐 7–4
🤿 US$10 per person

✪ SELVA MAR
Calle 1, Avenida 2–4
San Isidro de El General
Tel 506 771 4582
www.exploringcostarica.com
In the San Isidro de El General
area, white-water rafting is a
popular activity. The El General
river is the largest white-water
river in Costa Rica, with more
than 166km (103 miles) of
suitable streams. While the valley is scenic, the novice rafter
tends to head for the forested
sections of the Pacuare and
Reventazón rivers, leaving the
General's class III–V rapids to
the specialists. A variety of rafting trips can be organized
locally through Selva Mar.
🤿 1-day trip US$95 per person

SAN VITO

🏛 FINCA CÁNTAROS
On the road south to Ciudad Neily
San Vito
Tel 506 773 3760
www.fincacantaros.com
Finca Cántaros specializes in
local arts and crafts, including
Chorotega pottery, woven textiles and hand-crafted wooden
products from the Guaymí and
Boruca, and coffee fresh from
the harvest in the Coto Brus
valley. Cántaros is one of the
best craft shops in Costa Rica.
🤿 From US$2

VALLE DE LOS SANTOS

✪ FINCA EDDIE SERRANO
MIRADOR DE QUETZALES
Pan-American Highway km70
Tel 506 381 8456
This is the place to see the
resplendent quetzal; a sighting
is almost guaranteed. A short
trail leads 3km (2 miles)
through forests of giant oak to
waterfalls and a look-out point.
🤿 2-hour tours US$6

THE CARIBBEAN LOWLANDS

BARRA DEL COLORADO

✪ ARCHIE FIELDS RIO COLORADO LODGE

PO Box 5094, 1000 San José (mailing address)
Tel 506 710 6879
www.riocoloradolodge.com
Fishing packages, expertly run by Dan Wise, can be organized from this lodge. Where the Colorado River flows into the Caribbean sea, you can fish for snook and the prize of all game fish—tarpon. Trips take place with experienced guides in jungle rivers and lagoons. Night turtle-watching tours are available July through September.
🕐 All year; peak season Jan–Mar
🚤 Day fishing US$400; 5-night package from US$1,507; 7 nights US$2,287

✪ CASA MAR

2634 West Orangethorpe Avenue, Suite 6 Fullerton, California (mailing address)
Tel 506 381 1380
Toll free in the US tel 800 543-0282
www.casamarlodge.com
With an idyllic setting on the river, the rustic Casa Mar lodge sleeps 24 people and offers excellent conditions for catching monumental tarpon and snook; lodge owner and local legend Bill Barnes is the current world record holder for catching an 11.8kg (26 lb) snook on a fly rod. Each night you can dine on the fresh catch of the day. Contact the California office to arange a visit.
🚤 A 5-night package US$2,250; 7-night package US$3,195

✪ SILVER KING LODGE

Barra del Colorado
Tel 506 381 1403

In the US tel 1-800 947-3747
www.silverkinglodge.net
Widely regarded as the most luxurious lodge on the north Caribbean coastline, the Silver King Lodge offers impressive fishing using 10 v-hull boats in open water and unsinkable Carolina skiffs in inland waters. They also accommodate nature tourism and non-fishing guests. It's a great place to stay with a good restaurant, a bar, free laundry, a pool and use of kayaks.
🚤 Day fishing US$550 including accommodation, meals and drinks

A tarpon caught on a Silver King Lodge fishing trip

CERRO MUCHILLA

✪ SELVA BANANITO LODGE

Apt 2333-2050, San Pedro
Tel 506 253 8118
www.selvabananito.com
Some 20km (12 miles) south of Puerto Limón, heading inland at Bananito, a challenging road leads to extreme seclusion. Selva Bananito is a remote family-run rainforest lodge, close to Cerro Muchilla on the border of La Amistad Biosphere Reserve. You can enjoy activities such as tree climbing and rappelling, mountain biking, hiking, waterfall swimming, horseback riding or birdwatching. They'll pick you up or provide a map if

you want to drive. Tours are included on package deals, or you can visit for the day.
✪ Activities range from US$20–45; 3-day all-inclusive rates from US$355

GUÁPILES

🛍 GALLERY AT HOME

Guápiles
Tel 506 710 1858
Patricia Erickson has gained national recognition for her paintings. Bamboo furniture and sculptures are made by Patricia's husband. Call ahead for an appointment.
🕐 Tours depart 8–1 or 1–2
🛍 US$200–2,000

✪ RÍO DANTA RESTAURANT AND RESERVE

Grupo Mawamba
PO Box 10980-1000
Guápiles
Tel 506 710 2626
www.grupomawamba.com
Río Danta Restaurant and Reserve is on Highway 32, 6km (3.5 miles) after the junction at Santa Clara that heads north to Puerto Viejo de Sarapiquí. In addition to being a good stopover for tours to Tortuguero, the reserve's nature trails meander through primary forest where you can see poison-arrow frogs and birds. The gardens are bright with heliconias and bromeliads among soaring palm trees.
🚤 Nature trails US$4

✪ TROPICAL MAGIC CANOPY TOUR

Guápiles
Tel 506 392 2088
North from San José along Highway 32 to Puerto Viejo de Sarapiquí is the Tropical Magic forest canopy tour, which has nine platforms with wires passing over the secondary forest of a former *finca*. You can take a dip in the nearby swimming pools on the river, or explore a few trails. It makes a pleasant, low-key

change from the high-profile canopy tours.

US$40

MANZANILLO

⭐ AQUAMOR
Manzanillo
Tel 506 759 9012
www.greencoast.com/aquamor
The Talamanca Dolphin Foundation (tel 406 586 5084, www.dolphinlink.org) and Aquamor have trained local captains and guides in dolphin etiquette to keep the impact of dolphin-watching in the area to a minimum. Volunteer programs require a commitment of at least one week, and charge from US$6 per night camping in the community of Gandoca. Lodging with local families is also available. As well as dolphin-watching, Aquamor also runs a PADI diving school and hold kayaking and snorkeling trips.
Dolphin watching US$54, diving from US$48, snorkeling from US$19

⭐ TARPONVILLE
Manzanillo
Tel 506 759 9115
www.tarponville.com
The only fishing lodge along the southern Caribbean coast of Costa Rica taps the virtually untouched waters of Gandoca lagoon, where anglers are guaranteed exciting fights with feisty tarpon. March to May and September to October are the best months. The lodge has simple yet adequate accommodations and sits in the midst of Gandoca-Manzanillo Wildlife Refuge.
5-day fishing package from US$1,675

MATINA

⭐ PACUARE NATURE RESERVE
Adventure Life Journeys
Matina
Tel 800-344 6118 (toll free USA)
Outside US: 506 541 2677
Between the Caribbean lowlands and the Talamanca mountains, a few kilometers

(a couple of miles) east of Matina, the 800ha (1,976 acres) of the Pacuare Reserve contain amazing biodiversity, produced by high rainfall and altitudes between 100m and 700m (330ft and 2,300ft). The privately owned reserve has 6km (3.5 miles) of virgin beach that protects the nesting sites of marine turtles. Leatherbacks nest from March to June, with green turtles arriving between June and August. A volunteer program run by Adventure Life Journeys in conjunction with Rainforest Concern (www.rainforestconcern.org) has a minimum stay of one week in a lodge overlooking the

Guests at Río Parismina Lodge get ready for a fishing trip

beach. The reserve is also a secluded spot for birdwatching.
Volunteering US$100 per week

PARISMINA

⭐ RIO PARISMINA LODGE
Parismina
Tel 506 824 4442
www.riop.com
This fishing lodge has 12 cabins, a restaurant, bar and pool at the mouth of the Parismina River. The fishing tours led by experienced English-speaking guides take place aboard an ocean-going craft making catch-and-release fishing for snapper, tuna and wahoo in the choppy coastal waters an alternative to exploring inland

canals. Horseback riding and river cruises are available.
Weekend fishing packages start at US$1,850 per person, week-long packages cost US$3,100

PUERTO VIEJO DE TALAMANCA

⭐ ATEC
Main street in Old Harbor
Puerto Viejo
Tel 506 750 0191
www.greencoast.com/atec.htm
The non-profit Talamanca Association for Ecotourism and Conservation (ATEC) promotes projects in the Puerto Viejo area to encourage Talamanca's cultural and ethnic diversity. Activities include daytrips to the KeKöLdi indigenous reserve and overnight stays in the Talamanca reserves, including accommodation with local families and canoe trips.
From US$33

⭐ CACAO TRAILS
Hone Creek
Tel 506 756 8186
www.cacaotrails.com
This multi-themed facility opened in 2006 and serves to educate visitors with a demonstration of chocolate production. Other static exhibits include displays on chocolate and pre-Columbian culture, snakes in glass cages, plus a botanical garden. You can glide through an adjacent lagoon in search of wildlife.
Daily 9–5
US$20

⭐ FINCA LA ISLA BOTANICAL GARDEN
On the road to Cahuita, just north of Playa Negra
Puerto Viejo
Tel 506 750 0046
www.greencoast.com/garden.htm
This abandoned chocolate *finca* has been converted into an experimental farm offering tours and hikes on rainforest trails. The *finca* covers sections of rainforest and areas of crops and spices, including pepper, cinnamon and vanilla. Trails

lead through the forest, where various species of poison-dart frogs hop about underfoot.

🕐 Fri–Mon 10–4

🎫 Entrance: US$5; 2.5 hour tour: US$10

SIQUIERRES

⭐ BANANERO ESPERANZAS

Hwy 32, Siquierres
Tel 506 768 8683
www.bananatourcostarica.com

Banana plantations swathe the Caribbean lowlands. To learn about production and processing, take a tour at Standard Fruit Co.'s Esperanza packing plant, where guides lead you into the banana fields and packing facility.

🕐 Mon–Sat 9–5

🎫 US$10, tours by pre-arrangement

TORTUGUERO

⭐ BARBARA HARTUNG TINAMON TOURS

Tortuguero
Tel 506 709 8004
www.tinamontours.de

Barbara Hartung, an English-, German- and Spanish-speaking biologist, is frequently recommended for boat tours in Tortuguero, where she has lived for a decade. These independent tours are an antidote to mass tourism. You'll move silently in a dugout canoe on the waterways to observe the prolific wildlife. Barbara, an entomology expert, also takes groups on rainforest hikes.

🎫 US$5 per person per hour

⭐ CAÑO PALMA RESEARCH STATION

Tortuguero
Tel 506 381 4116 (in Canada tel 905-831-8809)
www.coterc.org

The Canadian Organization for Tropical Education and Rainforest Conservation owns the Caño Palma Biological Station, north of Tortuguero, which provides leadership in education, conservation and research. A volunteer program offers

FESTIVALS AND EVENTS

THE SOUTH CARIBBEAN MUSIC FESTIVAL

March–April
Playa Chiquita Lodge
5km (3 miles) south of Puerto Viejo
Tel 506 750 0062
www.playachiquitalodge.com

Each year the South Caribbean Music Festival assumes the mantle for the promotion of the region's cultural heritage, with a showcase for the fusion of Costa Rican musical genres, including reggae and Calypso traditions. In addition to the pivotal musical focus, there are children's drama productions, short Costa Rican movie showings and displays of arts and crafts. Events take place on Fridays and Saturdays and running parallel to the shows are a series of artistic workshops.

PUERTO LIMÓN CARNAVAL

October

Carnival, or *carnaval* as it is known in Puerto Limón, takes place on October 12 with the preceding days building up to the big El Día de la Raza. The town suddenly becomes desirable as sedate highlanders flock to the Caribbean to join the music and dancing. The costumes are out in full for Costa Rica's biggest celebration and a moment of genuine unity of Tico and Caribbean influences. Celebrations reach their zenith with the Grand Desfile, or great parade, on the Saturday, when Afro-Caribbean culture is revealed in an exuberant tassle-shaking spectacle. Leave your valuables safely at your hotel.

basic rooms and meals. It's a good place for serious naturalists or just for unwinding.

🎫 US$100 / week, 2 weeks minimum

⭐ CARIBBEAN CONSERVATION CORPS AND TURTLE SURVIVAL LEAGUE

John H. Phipps Biological Field Station
Tortuguero
Tel 506 709 8125
www.cccturtle.org

This non-profit organization was founded in 1959 and has improved the survival outlook for several species of sea turtle. Many volunteer opportunities exist to help save rare sea turtles, such as working in information booths. If more hands-on work is what you are looking for, you can sign up for the CCC Participant research program. The adopt-a-turtle program allows you to track its migration on the internet.

🕐 Leatherback turtle project Mar–Jun; Green turtle project Jun–Nov

🎫 1 week US$1,554; 2 weeks US$1,999

⭐ EDDY BROWN SPORT-FISHING

Tortuga Lodge, Tortuguero
Tel 506 834 2221

Brothers Eddy and Roberto Brown know where the tarpon play and arrange fishing trips in the lagoons and in the rivermouths offshore. Snook, wahoo and tuna are also prime gamefish awaiting your lure. The Brown's use 8m (26-ft) and 8.5m (28-ft) Bimini tops.

🎫 US$50 per hour; US$395 full day

⭐ RIVERBOAT FRANCESCA

Tortuguero
Tel 506 226 0986
www.tortuguerocanals.com

Jungle river fishing is excellent in the Tortuguero area, with snapper, snook, black bass and guapote. Three-day tours are arranged with fishing trips in the morning and afternoon, including meals, park fees and transfers from San José. Marlin, tuna and wahoo can be fished on the salt river trips.

🎫 River fishing from US$40 per hour

Out and About

This chapter describes two walks and six drives that explore Costa Rica's varied scenery. The locations of the walks and tours are marked on the map on page 158, where you will also find a key to the individual maps. For both walks and tours it is advisable to buy a detailed map of the area before you set out.

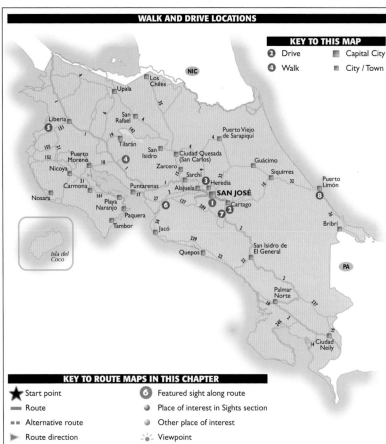

WALK AND DRIVE LOCATIONS

KEY TO THIS MAP
- **2** Drive
- **4** Walk
- ■ Capital City
- ■ City / Town

NIC

Los Chiles
Upala
San Rafael
Liberia **5**
Tilarán **4**
San Isidro
Ciudad Quesada (San Carlos)
Puerto Viejo de Sarapiquí
Puerto Moreno
Nicoya
Zarcero
Sarchí
Guácimo
Siquirres
Puerto Limón
Carmona
Puntarenas
Heredia **3**
Alajuela
SAN JOSÉ
Cartago
8
Nosara
Playa Naranjo
6
1
7
Bribrí
Paquera
Tambor
Jacó
Quepos
San Isidro de El General

Isla del Coco

PA

Palmar Norte

Ciudad Neily

KEY TO ROUTE MAPS IN THIS CHAPTER

- ★ Start point
- ▬ Route
- ▪▪ Alternative route
- ▶ Route direction
- **2** Walk start point on drive
- **6** Featured sight along route
- ● Place of interest in Sights section
- ● Other place of interest
- ☀ Viewpoint
- $\overset{621}{\blacktriangle}$ Height in metres

OUT AND ABOUT

A torch flower, the neo-Gothic La Merced church and the active Volcán Poás: Sightseeing in Costa Rica never gets repetitive. You'll see all these sights on the following drives and walks.

1. Walk
San José's Squares
(▷ 159–161)

2. Drive
Orosí Valley (▷ 162–163)

3. Drive
Volcán Poás and the Central Highlands (▷ 164–167)

4. Walk
Monteverde (▷ 168–169)

5. Drive
Guanacaste's Northwestern Beaches (▷ 170–171)

6. Drive
The Pacific Coast Road
(▷ 172–173)

7. Drive
The Route of the Saints
(▷ 174–175)

8. Drive
The Caribbean Coast Road
(▷ 176–177)

SAN JOSÉ'S SQUARES

A walk through San José reveals a street culture of chaos and clutter where solitary gestures to architectural style stand serene. Colonial-style treasures nestle amid lush patios, kaleidoscopic markets bombard the senses and modern monoliths thrust from squares where Joséfino life ebbs and flows. Leafy parks provide the perfect place to relax.

THE WALK

Length: 3.5km (2 miles)
Allow: a morning
Start: Mercado Central
End: Plaza de la Cultura

If you want to see the city wake you'll have to be ready by 6am. For the human dawn chorus, the tour begins at the Central Market, which takes up a whole block bordered by Avenida Central–1 and Calle 6–8.

1 The Mercado Central throbs with a cacophony of sights, smells and tastes. It sells everything from cheese, spices, fruit, vegetables, dried and fresh flowers through to leather sandals, saddles, bridles and simple tourist gifts. The honey is particularly recommended. You can breakfast on tortillas or empanadas and coffee at one of the many stand-up bars, or take a more leisurely sit-down option. The seriously cheap food and drinks are generally cleanly prepared with a turnover so quick the food doesn't have time to go off.

Leave the market on Avenida 1, and continue east for two blocks to the Central Post Office.

2 The battleship-green Correo Central, understated and often overlooked, seems perfectly balanced in proportion and setting. Behind the elegant facade, the echoing halls of post boxes are a bit daunting, but upstairs is the interesting Museo Postal Telegráfico Filatélico de Costa Rica. The Café del Correo is a splendid café that retains some

The Mercado Central is the bustling heart of San José

The exterior of the Central Post Office on Avenida 1

period pieces and serves coffee and cakes. An ICT office is inside the post office, to the right of the main entrance (8–4). Outside the post office, under the shade of fig trees, Joséfinos have their shoes polished, catch up on the gossip or read *La Nación*.

Leave the post office, turn right and walk one block to the pedestrian thoroughfare of Avenida Central, cross over and then walk one block to Parque Central, bordered by Avenida 2

3 Parque Central, surrounded by traffic, has an insipid yellow bandstand in the middle. All Joséfino life seems to pass through. Poised to the east is the Catedrál Metropolitana,

while to the north, on Avenida 2, is the Teatro Melico Salazar.

Head back north one block onto Avenida Central. Perpetually bustling with people rushing around the shops, banks and department stores, this is one of the main arteries of the city. Three blocks east along Avenida Central is Plaza de la Cultura, the heart of the city.

4 Plaza de la Cultura is dominated by the Gran Hotel de Costa Rica, one of Costa Rica's oldest hotels. A coffee on the terrace of Café 1930 is the ideal vantage point to view the smaller Parque Mora Fernández, prettily landscaped and merging into Plaza de la Cultura. Amid the pigeons,

OUT AND ABOUT

A gold breast-plate in the Museo de Oro Precolumbino (above).

Several attractions including two museums are situated around the Parque Nacional (left)

Joséfino opportunism rages, from photographers toting cameras to a persuasive medley of shoe shiners and buskers. The Teatro Nacional stands in majestic contrast to such urban prose, while on the east side of the square you can contain your avarice at the underground Museo de Oro Precolumbino.

From Plaza de la Cultura head east for six blocks along Avenida Central until you reach the bleak Plaza de la Democracía.

5 Plaza de la Democracía was created in 1989 to celebrate the centenary of Costa Rican democracy. Devoid of water or greenery, the only point of interest is the statue of José Figueres. Lining the western side of the square is a shaded craft market selling hammocks, pictures and wood items. The eastern flank is dominated by the muscular Bellavista Fortress, which now houses the National Museum.

Behind the National Museum, a pedestrian walkway leads south where some restored early 20th-century houses contain cafés with outdoor seating. One block north of the museum is the Palacio Nacional, where parliament sits, surrounded to the north by the Parque Nacional.

6 The Parque Nacional is packed with palm trees surrounding the Monumento Nacional, a statue representing the five Central American republics ousting the North American filibuster William Walker, and the abolition of slavery in Central America. A statue of national hero Juan Santamaría donated by the Sandinista Government of Nicaragua stands in the southwest corner of the park. On the north side, the National Library hides behind a modern exterior. At the northwestern corner of the park is the Museum of Contemporary Art and Design. One block east of the square is the Museo de Formas, Espaco y Sonidos, housed in the old Atlantic Railway station. Visitors to the museum are welcome to explore the old railway cars on the long-abandoned tracks.

From Parque Nacional head west down Avenida 3 back toward the

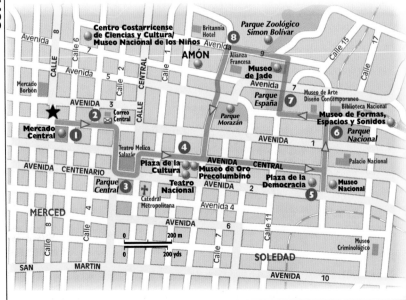

The Monumento Nacional celebrates the defeat of William Walker (above)

middle of town, along the southern side of Parque España.

❼ By day, Parque España is a refreshingly calm square; on Sunday it normally hosts an outdoor market. Directly north of the square, beside the entrance to the Instituto Nacional de Seguros (INS), is Costa Rica's finest museum, the Museo del Jade. To the west, Parque Morazán is overshadowed by the Aurola Holiday Inn. Take the elevator to the top-floor casino for views of the city.

From Parque España take Calle 11, which runs alongside the INS Building north for one block. Tucked behind the two parks defined by the blocks between Calle 1 and Calle 15 and Avenida 7 and 11 are the historic districts or *barrios* of Amón and Otoya.

❽ During the 19th and early 20th centuries, Amón and Otoya barrios were the residential districts of the coffee élites. Along undulating streets, colonial-style mansions, with verdant balconies, recall a French colonial quarter. At pioneer hotels, like the Britannia on Calle 3 and Avenida 11, and Sportsmans Bar, on Calle 13 and Avenida 9–11, flashes of Caribbean-style architecture fuse with sedate Victorian style. On Avenida 9, between

Pretty in pink: the historic exterior of the Hotel Britannia in the district of Amón

Calle 3 and 7, the brick walls are decorated with ceramic tiles depicting rural scenes.

From Avenida 7 heading south along Calle 5 for four blocks and then one block west will bring you back to Plaza de la Cultura.

PLACES TO VISIT
Barrios Amón and Otoya
▷ 62–63

Mercado Central
Avenida Central–1 and Calle 6–8
🕓 Mon–Sat 6am–8pm

The National Theater (above). The gate to the Museum of Contemporary Art and Design (left)

Museo Postal Telegráfico Filatélico de Costa Rica
Calle 2, Avenida 1–3
☎ 506 223 9766, ext 205
🕓 Mon–Fri 8–5

Museo del Jade ▷ 64

Museo de Oro Precolumbino
▷ 65

WHERE TO EAT
Café 1930
Terrace of the Gran Hotel
Plaza de la Cultura
☎ 506 221 4000

Café del Teatro Nacional
Teatro Nacional
Plaza de la Cultura
☎ 506 221 3262

Café Posada del Museo
▷ 182–183
Avenida 2, Calle 17
☎ 506 257 9414

OUT AND ABOUT

OROSÍ VALLEY

East of Cartago, a mosaic of coffee plantations rises and falls, dotted with peaceful villages where colonial churches, surreal sculptures, pirate legends and the curiosities of Costa Rican daily life provide an engaging circular tour. You will also venture to the border of little-visited Tapantí-Macizo de la Muerte National Park.

THE DRIVE

Length: 36km (22 miles)

Allow: a day

Start/end: Cartago/Tapantí National Park

Cartago, gateway to the southeastern corner of the Central Valley, lies under the looming massif of Volcán Irazú, 20km (12 miles) from San José. Exploring the town, go first to the Basílica de Nuestra Señora de Los Angeles, one of the finest churches in the country, 1km (0.6 mile) east of the central park. It holds La Negrita, an indigenous image of the Virgin Mary less than 15cm (6in) high, which draws pilgrims from all over the country. Cartago's other attraction, La Parroquía, locally known as Las Ruinas, stands next to the central park. Founded in 1575, it was Cartago's first parish church. Earthquakes meant the church had to be rebuilt several times and it was finally abandoned in 1910.

Take Highway 10 southeast of Cartago for 8km (5 miles) to Paraíso, where the road falls away to the hidden secrets of the Orosí Valley, surrounded by steep-sided mountains rising up to cloud level. At Paraíso, the road diverges to go east follow-

Looking over the Cachí Dam from the coffee-clad hillside

ing the northern shore of the lake to Ujarrás, or south to Orosí. Where the road drops past a look-out post, follow the signs for Ujarrás, about 7km (4 miles).

❶ Ujarrás is famous as the site of Costa Rica's first colonial church, built between 1570 and 1580. Legend has it that in 1666, English pirates were seen off by Ujarrás's citizens, aided by the Virgin. This event is celebrated annually on April 16 or the closest Sunday when the saint is carried in procession from Paraíso to the ruined church.

Continue east from Ujarrás. The valley floor here is flooded by the waters of Lago Cachí created by the Cachí Dam, which blocks the river before flowing to the whitewater rafting spot on the Río Reventazón. Just 2km (1 mile) away is the small town of Cachí and its nearby attractions.

❷ The Presa de Cachí (Cachí Dam) is not impressive unless it's releasing water, but it is a natural stopping point before heading along the southern shore to the Casa del Soñador (the Dreamer's House), where Hermes and Miguel Quesada carve figurines using twisted old coffee plant roots and driftwood. A short walk away, on the lake shore, is La Casona del Cafetal, a popular eatery.

Just 3km (2 miles) from Cachí continuing east around the lake is the star of the valley, Orosí.

❸ Orosí is best known for the 18th-century Parroquía de San José, built by Franciscan missionaries. The church has weathered countless tremors, clearly apparent in the pitched roof that has warped over the centuries. Across the cloister, the Museo de Arte Religioso displays religious objects in the former monastery. In town there are hot springs next to Orosí Lodge, and more in Los Patios, just south of town.

A short way south of Orosí the road splits; the left fork crosses the Río Orosí. The right fork leads towards Tapantí-Macizo de la Muerte National Park, 9km (5 miles) from the main road. Go over the Río Macho bridge, take the first right turn and continue along the road for 3km (2 miles) until you reach the private reserve of Monte Sky.

❹ Monte Sky is a mountain retreat bordering the Tapantí National Park. The refuge was established in 1985 and more

Ujarrás beat the pirates but its church fell victim to earthquakes

OUT AND ABOUT

Orosí's church has survived countless quakes

The Dreamer's House on Lake Cachí

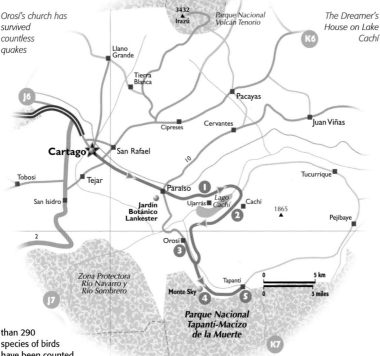

than 290 species of birds have been counted. Monte Sky Space can accommodate up to 20 people. Hiking trails lead through forest and there is a museum.

Tapantí-Macizo de la Muerte National Park is 2km (1 mile) east, signposted from Orosí.

5 Tapantí-Macizo de la Muerte, established in 1994, covers 58,000ha (143,260 acres) of one of the wettest parts of the country. Visitor numbers are still low. The park protects the Río Orosí basin which feeds the Cachí Dam hydroelectric power plant. The south boundary of the park

joins with the Chirripó National Park, extending the protected area that makes up La Amistad International Park.

PLACES TO VISIT

Parque Nacional Tapantí-Macizo de la Muerte ▷ 75

Museo del Arte Religiosa
Orosí Church
☎ 506 533 3051
🕐 Tue–Sat 1–5, Sun 9–12, 1–5
💷 US$1

Monte Sky
PO Box 235–1150
☎ 506 231 3536

WHERE TO EAT

La Casona del Cafetal
Lago de Cachí
☎ 506 533 3280
On the lake's south shore, La Casona del Cafetal draws Sunday crowds to its US$14 buffet.
🕐 Daily 11–6
🍴 L US$32, Wine from US$18

PLACE TO STAY

Orosí Lodge
Orosí Valley
☎ 506 533 3578
www.orosilodge.com
This lodge, with seven rooms, is one hour east of San José, in the Orosí valley.
🍴 US$40–48

OUT AND ABOUT

VOLCÁN POÁS AND THE CENTRAL HIGHLANDS

The central part of Costa Rica has a rich, volcanic soil and a benign climate. This drive goes through fertile, farming valleys into hills carpeted with coffee plantations. Crowning it all is the lunar landscape of Volcán Poás.

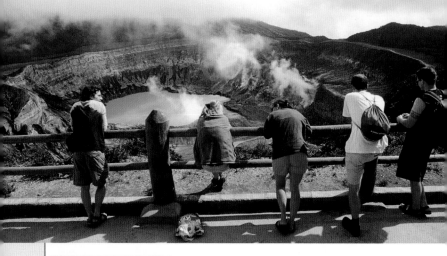

Smoke on the water: looking into the crater of Volcán Poás

OUT AND ABOUT

THE DRIVE	
Length: 73km (44 miles)	
Allow: 1–2 days	
Start/end: San José	

Leaving San José, take the Pan-American Highway west for 5km (3 miles) until the Alajuela exit. A line of villages huddles on the western slopes of Volcán Poás.

The town of Alajuela (▷ 69), capital of the Alajuela province, once fought to rule the region. Now a quiet market town, the main feature is the Central Plaza, shaded by mango trees. Five blocks east is the church of La Agonia, damaged in the 1910 earthquake but since restored. North of the plaza is the Museo Histórico Juan Santamaría, celebrating Alajuela's national hero.

From Alajuela, drive for 9km (5.5 miles) to San Isidro. Take a left turn and follow the signs for Sabanilla. Some 2km (1.25 miles) north of San Luís is the Doka Coffee plantation. En route the views are spectacular, shifting and changing with the light.

1 On the slopes of the Poás Volcano, the 242ha (600-acre) privately owned Doka Coffee Estate has been in the same family for three generations. Set at 1,372m (4,500ft), it is often lauded as one of Costa Rica's most beautiful coffee plantations. Tours, twice daily, show you the traditional coffee production process from nurturing seedlings, growing bushes and harvesting the beans to the peeling process, fermentation, drying and roasting. The estate's coffee shop, Casa del Café, has great views

Left, Poás's red-roofed church

and as well as enjoying a cup of their brew, you can buy roasted beans to take home.

Leaving the Doka Coffee Estate, continue north along route 130 passing through coffee country, following the signs for Poás Volcano. Gently undulating hills rise slowly towards the volcanic slopes of Poás. As you climb from Alajuela, the warmth gives way to freshness and then a slight chill. The scenic Laguna Fraijanes lies 15km (9 miles) from Alajuela, 3km (2 miles) from the Doka Coffee Estate.

2 Laguna Fraijanes is an 18ha (44.5-acre) area of forests dotted with strawberry fields, flowers and grasslands. Look-outs over this popular recreational area offer scenic views of the landscape. There are horses, hiking trails, fishing, playgrounds, campfire sites and cabins for rent. The main attraction is the Fraijanes lagoon, a small volcanic lake with icy water, which makes a lovely place for a picnic. The lagoon dates from 1889 when Volcán Poás set off an earthquake that

The view of the highlands from a ranch near Poás

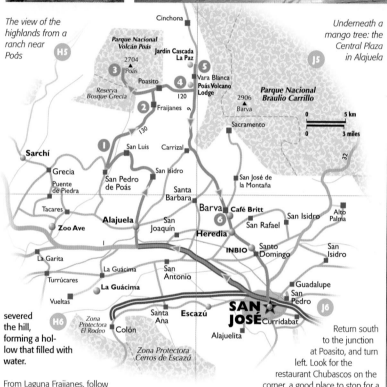

Cinchona

Parque Nacional
Volcán Poás
Jardín Cascada
La Paz

2704
▲ Poás

Poasito

5

Vara Blanca
Poás Volcano
Lodge

Reserva
Bosque Grecia

120

2

130

Fraijanes

San Luis

Carrizal

Sarchí

Grecia

San Isidro

Puente
de Piedra

San Pedro
de Poás

Santa
Barbara

Tacares

Barva

Café Britt

San Isidro

Alto
Palma

Alajuela

San
Joaquín

Heredia

San Rafael

Zoo Ave

INBIO

Santo
Domingo

San
Isidro

La Garita

La Guácima

San
Antonio

Turrúcares

La Guácima

Vueltas

Zona
Protectora
El Rodeo

Santa
Ana

Escazú

SAN
JOSÉ

Guadalupe
San
Pedro

J6

Colón

Alajuelita

Curridabat

Zona Protectora
Cerros de Escazú

2906
▲ Barva

Sacramento

Parque Nacional
Braulio Carrillo

San José de
la Montaña

0   5 km
0   3 miles

32

Underneath a mango tree: the Central Plaza in Alajuela

J5

H5

3

4

I

1

H6

severed the hill, forming a hollow that filled with water.

From Laguna Fraijanes, follow route 30 for 8km (5 miles) to a three-way junction (a right turn heads to Poasito); continue north following signs for Volcán Poás, 37km (23 miles) from Alajuela. Try to be there before 10am when clouds engulf the volcano.

❸ Volcán Poás is the highlight of the 5,601ha (13,835-acre) Volcán Poás National Park. The world's largest geyser-type crater, it has a rim measuring 1.5km (1 mile) in circumference. The park is mostly stunted cloud forest, packed with bromeliads, moss and vines, and is home to a large

number of bird species. The restless volcano puffs and belches, giving off pungent fumes, so visitors spend no more than 30 minutes at the crater. The Sendero Boto trail leads off from the crater to a small lagoon, Laguna Boto, in the crater formed by the Poás Volcano 8,000 years ago. This is one of the few national parks in Costa Rica that is suitable for visitors with disabilities, with wheelchair access to viewing platforms.

The view from Casa del Café: conditions are perfect for coffee

Return south to the junction at Poasito, and turn left. Look for the restaurant Chubascos on the corner, a good place to stop for a fresh fruit *licuado* made with organic local strawberries, and follow signs for Vara Blanca, (6km/3.5 miles). Some 200m (220 yards) before the Vara

Blanca junction, signs on the left indicate Volcán Poás Lodge, down a 1km (0.6-mile) dirt track.

❹ Poás Volcano Lodge makes an ideal base to explore Poás Valley. In addition to following the lodge's trails you can take horseback-riding tours of the La Legua valley, which begin on Volcán Barva's slopes and continue along the edges of Braulio Carrillo National Park (▷ 72–74). The park contains 600 species of trees, 500 bird species and many native mammals. The most readily identified plant is the giant-leaved *Gunnera*, also known as "poor man's umbrella."

When you leave the lodge, turn left and continue for 200m (220 yards) to the Vara Blanca gas station, turn left again and continue for 5km (3 miles). The nature park and wildlife refuge of La Paz Waterfall Gardens are on the left.

❺ La Paz Waterfall Gardens are a nature park and wildlife refuge with 3.5km (2 miles) of self-guiding trails. They wind through forests to five water-falls, with viewing platforms, upstream along the Río Paz. One of the major attractions is the butterfly garden with over 4,000 species, and the world's largest butterfly observatory.

From La Paz Waterfall Gardens, return to the Vara Blanca gas station and take route 120 south, signposted Heredia, via Carrizal, for 21km (13 miles) to the underrated town of Barva, 3km (2 miles) north of Heredia. Lines of coffee bushes run up and down the contours of the slopes.

❻ Barva is usually bypassed en route to Poás. Peaceful and historic, the main attraction is the inspiring, whitewashed church of San Bartolomé, built in the mid-16th century and flanked by single-floor adobe houses. The Museo de la Cultura Popular has exhibits of adobe construction tech-niques, which reveal the town's colonial heritage.

From Barva it is 3km (2 miles) south on route 120 to Heredia, ▷ 70, and then 11km (7 miles) south on Highway 3 to San José.

Waterfalls (left) at La Paz.
Forest and farming in the highlands (above)

WHERE TO EAT

Restaurante Colbert
Vara Blanca
☎ 506 482 2776

WHERE TO STAY

Poás Volcano Lodge
PO Box 1935-3000, Heredia
☎ 506 482 2194
www.poasvolcanolodge.com
💲 US$75, including breakfast

PLACES TO VISIT

La Paz Waterfall Gardens
☎ 506 225 0643
www.waterfallgardens.com
🕐 8.30–5.30, last entry 4
💲 Adult US$25, child (under 12) US$15

Doka Coffee plantation tour
☎ 506 449 5152
www.dokaestate.com
🕐 Tours Mon–Fri 9.30, 1.30, Sat 9.30
💲 US$15

Laguna Fraijanes
☎ 506 482 2176/66
🕐 Daily 6am–sunset
💲 US$1

Museo de la Cultura
Barva
☎ 506 260 1619
🕐 Mon–Fri 8–4, Sat, Sun 10–4
💲 US$1.50

A horseback-riding tour departing Poás Volcano Lodge

MONTEVERDE

You must not miss spending a day at the famous Monteverde Cloud Forest Reserve. A network of well-maintained and mapped trails can be linked together to form a walk of almost any length in this magical forest in the clouds. A guide will know where to go to maximize the fantastic wildlife-viewing opportunities.

THE WALK	
Length: from 2km (1 mile)	
Allow: a day	
Start/end: the park headquarters	

The main trail system in Monteverde forms a rough triangle, and that is its name: El Triangulo. From the entrance to the reserve, four trails, including the Bosque Nuboso Trail, the Rio Trail and the Pantanoso Trail, link up to form the boundary of the triangle. Individual trails are occasionally closed for repair, and there is no guarantee that any specific trail mentioned here will be open at the time of your arrival, depending on conditions.

The most popular trail is the 1.9km (1-mile) Bosque Nuboso trail, due to the 27 points along the trail that correspond to information in a self-guiding pamphlet (US$2 in the Reserve's souvenir shop), making it the best trail to explore without a guide. This trail forms the southern edge of the triangle, terminating where it joins the Brilliante Trail, which then takes a northeasterly tack along the line of the Continental Divide as it passes through Monteverde.

*Above, shafts of sunlight penetrate the tree canopy at Monteverde
Left, a banded orange Heliconian butterfly*

At, or near, self-guided point 4 on Bosque Nuboso, just a few hundred meters from the entrance, many guides pause with their groups, set up their tripods and point their telescopic viewers at aguacate trees just off the trail. Here, frequently, they spot one or more quetzals perched, preening or feeding on the aguacate fruit. This type of avocado has a big seed and little flesh, so quetzals eat great quantities of them.

On the northern side of the triangle, the Rio Trail winds along parallel to a small river, eventually reaching a *mirador*, or look-out, with a splendid view of a waterfall. En route, your guide will point out where the forest turns from secondary growth (an area that has been cleared or logged within the last 75 years) into primary growth, where the trees have never been cut and the largest are up to 150 years old. The guide will identify orchids and other epiphytes, spot and name every bird within sight and talk cloud forest numbers: 150 types of fern, 3,480mm (98in) of rainfall annually, 765 types of tree, 216 mammals including 110 different bats, among them three vampire species. He will tell you interesting facts: that hummingbird hearts beat 800 times per minute and that there are 80 types of avocado in Monteverde alone.

And when you return from your walk—times, distances, trails and directions are dictated by many factors including the location of other guided groups, trail conditions and animal sightings—he might march you off on another trail because a couple of quetzals have been spotted there.

But even without a quetzal sighting, the combination of the guide's insight and the visual splendor of the forest, make this one of the most memorable places to walk in Costa Rica.

A Lycaste Brerspatina orchid

You can spot red-eyed tree frogs

OUT AND ABOUT

TIPS

- Spend the night in the area and arrive early. Those first in at 7am have the best chance of seeing wildlife and will certainly see larger numbers of birds
- Use a guide (from US$15 per person). You can share the cost by going with a group. Given the difficulties of spotting wildlife and the crowded conditions, guides are crucial to understanding the reserve's ecosystems. They can't guarantee sightings, but will know, for example, the locations of the aguacate trees where quetzals gather. Guides are uniformly multilingual and knowledgeable about the forest.
- Dress appropriately: it is often cloudy, misty and windy. It can be quite cool so take a light raincoat, a hat or hooded poncho, and shoes with good

A turquoise-browed motmot

grips; rubber boots can be rented (US$1). Some trails are finished with textured brick, but there are plenty of slippery patches.
- Take binoculars. If you have a pair, you won't have to wait in line for a look through a guide's telescope. If you are taking a camera, make sure it is semi- or fully waterproof and has a zoom.

You'll benefit from using a guide

PRESERVING MONTEVERDE

As one of the most popular tourist destinations in Costa Rica, Monteverde can get swamped by visitors. Without limits the foot traffic would be very damaging, so the reserve's managers have limited visitors to a maximum of 160 per day, and the roads in the region remain unpaved, to deter day-trippers. Even this is a large number for such a small reserve and it puts a physical strain on the trails, stretches of which may be closed for repair, making some areas inaccessible. The limit has also generated anxiety around the entrance, as guides and tourists scramble to get in first. But despite its popularity, Monteverde remains an inspiring place to visit.

GUANACASTE'S NORTHWESTERN BEACHES

Guanacaste's remote beaches have become more popular since the opening of the international airport at Liberia. This tour takes in some of the best. You can choose which to see and where to stop. Take your time and spend a couple of days in the area.

THE DRIVE
Length: 96km (60 miles)
Allow: a day
Start/end: Playas del Coco/Tamarindo

Head west from Liberia for 20km (12 miles) to a main junction at Comunidad. Take the right fork and follow signs for Playas del Coco, Playa Panama and Playa Hermosa. Continue past Sardinal for another 14km (8 miles) until you come to another junction; follow signs to the right. The first turnoff leads to Playas del Coco.

❶ Playas del Coco is the original beach escape for Joséfinos. Laid-back during the day, the pace picks up by night. The narrow, dark sand beach, while pleasant, is nothing special. The town has become a busy hub, with operators offering diving and sportfishing trips.

At the entrance to Playas del Coco a street to the left heads south, with a sign for Ocotal; look for the dive shop on the corner. Take this road to a T-junction, then turn right. Follow the signs to Ocotal, and take the left-hand turn when you get to the junction bisected by a large tree. It is 3km (2 miles) from Coco to Ocotal.

❷ Playa Ocotal is a more secluded bay than its northern neighbor, without the easy access. The rocky headlands have made it a rewarding dive

Many of the Pacific's breaks are best suited to skilled surfers

site. Snorkeling at the southern stretch is excellent when the water is clear and it is a good place for a swim. From here you have two options.

You can return to the main road leading from Highway 21 to Playas del Coco and continue for 10km (6 miles). A right spur heads north to Playa Hermosa, which can be reached from two side roads from the main road.

❸ Playa Hermosa, on the southern tip of Bahía Culebra, is a golden beach good for swimming and general water sports. With a west-facing beach, the sunsets are impressive, and cruises are popular at twilight. The beach has no village, but this is a pleasant place for a lunch break.

Some 5km (3 miles) past Playa Hermosa, you come to the most northern of the Guanacaste beaches, Playa Panama.

❹ The development of Playa Panama and the Bahía Culebra is driven by the state sponsored Papagayo Project. It has seen the transformation of this scenic bay into a collection of mega-resorts and high-rise apartments. With investment by Mexican and European companies, the place is fast becoming the largest leisure city in Central America. The effect that such development will have on the area, and the demand for water in the country's driest region, has led to much criticism from environmentalists. On the northern side of the bay, accessible by boat, the pre-Columbian site of Nacascolo may interest dedicated explorers of ruins.

Or, after visiting Playa Ocotal, return to the main junction at Comunidad then head south for 11km (7 miles) to Belén. From Belén, it is a 24km (15-mile) drive to the village of Huacas,

and several popular beaches to the north, west and south. At Huacas, take the northern fork. The road follows the coast past Playa Conchal, Playa Brasilito, Playa Flamingo, Playa Potrero and distant Playa Pan de Azúcar.

❺ The white bay of Playa Conchal, or Shell Beach, made up of countless tiny shells, is good for swimming and snorkeling in its clear waters.

The hotel behind the beach makes direct access difficult; it is easier to approach Playa Conchal from Playa Brasilito to the north.

❻ The beach at Playa Brasilito is not overly attractive, but good transport and a range of services make it a useful base if you want to explore this part of the coast on a tight budget.

If you've had enough driving for one day, head straight for Playa Grande (see **❾**) at the point. Otherwise, continue through Brasilito and take the paved road as it turns right and continue on for 3km (2 miles) following the signs for Playa Flamingo. Turn left along the beach heading towards the group of hotels on the mountainside to the left.

❼ Playa Flamingo is the sportfishing capital of the peninsula; however, its large marina was closed down by health authorities in 2006. Once-beautiful white (originally known as Playa Blanca) sand beaches have suffered from development, but the town has a good collection of services and comfortable hotels. Nestling in the hills are the homes of the Hollywood glitterati. Despite the name there are no flamingos here.

Just before Flamingo beach there will be a turnoff to the right with signs pointing to Playa Potrero. Continue along the 3km (2-mile) dirt road, which is in relatively good condition.

Stunning beach scenery is the backdrop to watersports such as boating in the surf or game fishing

8 The dark sand beach of Playa Potrero beyond the rocky headland stretches north from Playa Flamingo. A pleasant 3km (2-mile) walk north of Potrero is Playa Penca and, beyond it, the forest-fringed sandy bay of Pan de Azúcar

Return to the main highway 21, back at the Huacas junction, which leads straight ahead to Matapalo and after 9km (5 miles) to Playa Grande (▷ 99). The last 5km (3 miles) are on an unpaved road.

9 Playa Grande is a quiet, extensive beach area, popular with surfers and leatherback turtles. Along the coast of a small peninsula created by the Tamarindo Estuary, 485ha (1,198 acres) of beach and mangroves are protected in the Parque Nacional Marino las Baulas de Guanacaste.

From Playa Grande it is a delightful 30-minute walk south to Tamarindo. At high tide you will need to take a short river taxi ride across the estuary (US$1).

10 The hectic surf town of Playa Tamarindo is very popular. The expatriate community is serviced by restaurants, bars and shops lining the main street. Heading south, beyond the headland is the idyllic Playa Langosta. To avoid crowds, stay in Playa Grande.

WHERE TO EAT

Tequila Bar and Grill
200m (220 yards) before the beach
Playas del Coco, ▷ 187
☎ 506 670 0741

Marie's
Playa Flamingo, ▷ 187
☎ 506 654 4136

Great Wattini's
Hotel Bula Bula
Playa Grande
☎ 506 653 0975

THE PACIFIC COAST ROAD

This is a fascinating journey down the Pacific coast from the resorts of Jacó, Quepos and Manuel Antonio to plantations in the far south. Getting lost is difficult: You follow one road down the coast. The road runs parallel to the coastline, but only occasionally touches it.

THE DRIVE

Length: 230km (143 miles)
Allow: 2–3 days
Start: Orotina
End: Palmar Norte

Starting in Orotina, Highway 34, the *costanera* (coastal road) begins smoothly; the section from here to Jacó (40km/25 miles) is some of the best road in Costa Rica. On this stretch the road winds through the coastal hills. It's easy to go fast, and there are often police waiting to write out tickets, so watch your speed.

❶ From the Río Tárcoles bridge you can see some of the country's best free entertainment. Park your car on the south side of the bridge close to the police kiosk (avoid leaving valuables in it) and look over the side to watch the crocodiles in the water below.

Carry on down the road to Parque Nacional Carara at Km22.

❷ Carara National Park is one of the country's most popular and accessible. Its primary forest contains more than 750 plant species. The park also protects pre-Columbian archaeological sites, some of which date back to 300BC. At the southern end of the park, close to the rangers' station, are a couple of self-guiding trails, of just over 1km (0.6

Look down from the Río Tárcoles bridge to see the crocodiles

mile), where you may see scarlet macaws, spider monkeys and poison-arrow frogs.

At Km40, take the turn that heads west to Jacó.

❸ Jacó is a busy, if mediocre, surf spot (▷ 102). A little way beyond Jacó, a road leads to the huge, ferocious waves of Playa Hermosa.

A short distance farther down the road a turning goes to Playa Hermosa. Continue south on a good road with sea views. Down the coastline at Punta Guapinol, there's a convenient stopping point. The road continues past the secluded Esterillos beaches and to Parrita, from where a rusty one-lane bridge marks the beginning of the palm oil plantations that stretch south to Río Savegre. The oil from the palms is used in ice cream, mayonnaise, baked goods and detergents. At Km89 an old bridge marks a turnoff west to Quepos and Manuel Antonio National Park. This is a good place to spend a night.

❹ Quepos has successfully moved beyond a dependency on banana exports to provide for visitors. The restaurants and bars along the seafront jostle with the sportfishing outfits.

South from Quepos, a 7km (4-mile) road snakes over the rocky Punta Quepos peninsula past luxury hotels and smart restaurants to Parque Nacional Manuel

Nauyaca waterfall at Dominical

Antonio. Mid-price hotels are a short walk back from the beach.

❺ Manuel Antonio National Park is, justifiably, one of the most visited parks in the country. Glorious white sand beaches backed by jungle, and close encounters with monkeys and other wildlife draw visitors. The Rainmaker Project (▷ 152) is also here.

The road from Quepos ends at the park, so return to Quepos to rejoin the main road. South of Quepos the road becomes a pot-holed, washboard boneshaker. Progress is slow. You will pass more palm oil plantations, and a processing factory at Finca Llorana. After the Río Savegre crossing (Km18) there's a shift to bananas. The western slopes of the Central Mountains encroach on the coast, pushing the road up to the shoreline at Matapalo. The bumps persist for another 26km (16 miles) past Hacienda Barú (▷ 102) to Dominical.

❻ Dominical, like Jacó to the north, has a reputation as a surf destination, albeit a more laidback option. Activities range from surfing to hiking, horseback riding and fishing. There's a diversion from Dominical to the 50m-high (164ft) Nauyaca Waterfalls, 10km (6 miles) on the road to San Isidro de El General.

Follow Highway 10 south again. It reverts to paving and remains largely smooth. At Km6 from Dominical a road turns toward the shore to Rancho La Merced.

❼ Rancho La Merced is a working cattle ranch and wildlife refuge south of Uvita, with more than 500ha (1,235 acres) of tropical rainforest as well as mangrove estuary. The area can be explored, ideally on horseback, with trips going to the beach, the mangroves or around the ranch. Walking tours go to nearby waterfalls.

OUT AND ABOUT

A typical house on the palm plantations

Looking out over Playa Hermosa to Ballena marine park

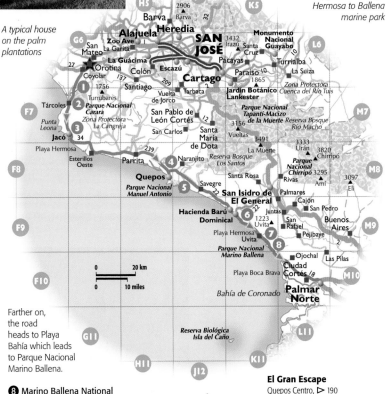

Farther on, the road heads to Playa Bahía which leads to Parque Nacional Marino Ballena.

❽ Marino Ballena National Park is a starting point for boat trips to see dolphins and whales, at the right time of year (December to April and August to October).

From Playa Bahía it's a short distance south through the coastal communities of Ojochal with several stylish accommodation options. Spend the night at one, then rejoin the Pan-American Highway at Palmar Norte.

PLACES TO STAY

Si Como No
2.5km (1.5 miles) from Manuel Antonio
National Park entrance, ▷ 203
☎ 506 777 0777
www.sicomono.com

Mono Azul
Apdo 297
Manuel Antonio, ▷ 203
☎ 506 777 2572
www.monoazul.com

WHERE TO EAT

Pacific Bistro
75m (82 yards) north from Jacó's downtown bridge, ▷ 189
☎ 506 643 3771
⏰ Wed–Mon 6pm–10pm

El Gran Escape
Quepos Centro, ▷ 190
☎ 506 777 0395
www.elgranescape.com
⏰ Wed–Mon 6am–11pm

San Clemente Restaurant
On the main road in Dominical, ▷ 189
☎ 506 787 0055

PLACES TO VISIT

Rainmaker Project
North of Manuel Antonio, ▷ 152
☎ 506 777 3565
⏰ Daily 8–3

Hacienda Barú
2km (1.25 mile) north of Dominical
☎ 506 787 0003

THE ROUTE OF THE SAINTS

An easy drive from San José enables you to explore the cluster of coffee-producing villages that huddle on the lowlands slopes of the Talamanca Mountains. History failed to record the reasons, but the spirituality of the region lives on with each town named after a saint, and each with a church of differing design.

THE DRIVE

Length: 41km (24.5 miles) from the Pan-American Highway turnoff

Allow: a day

Start/end: San José or Cartago taking the Pan-American Highway (Highway 2) south through the Talamanca Mountains

From the Pan-American Highway, take the turning west at km51, south of Empalme, signposted to Santa María. It's a good road, twisting and turning through pastureland and passing clapboard houses to provide that frontier spirit. Eventually it opens up to reveal Santa María de Dota in the Río Pirrís valley (14km/8 miles).

❶ In Santa María de Dota stop outside the church. A simple town of just a few thousand residents, it revolves around the main square. Here the focal point is the boxy lime-green church basking on the plaza. Inside, an engaging fusion of religious ideas prevails, with pagan symbols mixed with Christian ones.

From the plaza in Santa María de Dota, head away from the church and take the road straight ahead, signposted San Marcos (it would have been the first right on entering the square).

Sunday best: the church in San Marcos de Tarrazú, above., and, right, the interior, complete with icons of local saints, left

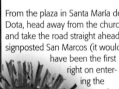

An easy drive winds down the steep slopes of the Río Pirrís. After 6km (3.5 miles) turn left to San Marcos de Tarrazú.

❷ San Marcos de Tarrazú has a more traditional church and even on dull days the cream-painted building looks sunlit. Perched on the hilly slopes, the village appears as if it might be auditioning for a John Ford western. A combination of altitude, soil, sunlight and rain conspires to make conditions ideal for growing superlative coffee. Unpaved roads connect coffee estates with the towns of Santa María,

San Pablo and San Marcos. One of the most renowned estates, Umaña lies 1km (0.6 mile) from San Marcos, and has been run by the Umaña Jimenez family since the 1890s. While there's little do in San Marcos itself, it is a charming place to stop for refreshment.

Leaving San Marcos's square, continue past the church, going left at the T-junction and follow the road that bends round behind the church. Cross over a couple of roads, climbing a small section of hill, then turn left, signposted San Pablo de

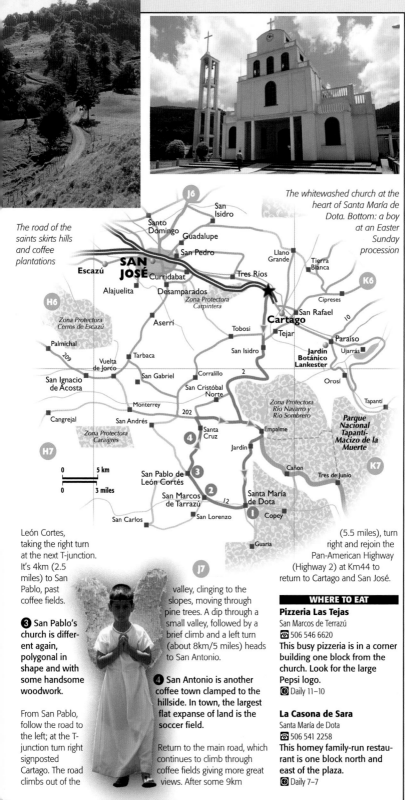

The road of the saints skirts hills and coffee plantations

The whitewashed church at the heart of Santa María de Dota. Bottom: a boy at an Easter Sunday procession

León Cortes, taking the right turn at the next T-junction. It's 4km (2.5 miles) to San Pablo, past coffee fields.

❸ San Pablo's church is different again, polygonal in shape and with some handsome woodwork.

From San Pablo, follow the road to the left; at the T-junction turn right signposted Cartago. The road climbs out of the valley, clinging to the slopes, moving through pine trees. A dip through a small valley, followed by a brief climb and a left turn (about 8km/5 miles) heads to San Antonio.

❹ San Antonio is another coffee town clamped to the hillside. In town, the largest flat expanse of land is the soccer field.

Return to the main road, which continues to climb through coffee fields giving more great views. After some 9km (5.5 miles), turn right and rejoin the Pan-American Highway (Highway 2) at Km44 to return to Cartago and San José.

WHERE TO EAT

Pizzeria Las Tejas
San Marcos de Terrazú
☎ 506 546 6620
This busy pizzeria is in a corner building one block from the church. Look for the large Pepsi logo.
🕐 Daily 11–10

La Casona de Sara
Santa María de Dota
☎ 506 541 2258
This homey family-run restaurant is one block north and east of the plaza.
🕐 Daily 7–7

OUT AND ABOUT

THE CARIBBEAN COAST ROAD

From Puerto Limón, the road south runs close to the sea for over 80km (50 miles) past palm-fringed beaches. This drive follows it south to the Refugio Nacional de Vida Silvestre Gandoca-Manzanillo, and has interesting diversions into the Talamanca Mountains.

THE DRIVE	
Length: 89km (55 miles)	
Allow: 1–2 days	
Start: Puerto Limón	
End: Manzanillo	

This drive follows the coast road south, past tempting beaches, toward the border with Panama.

Raw, unpolished and challenging, Puerto Limón juts out from a monotonous coastline, and throbs with the dubious energy endemic to many port towns. Limón's fortunes have ebbed and flowed since it first became the melting pot for the influx of workers who arrived to build the railroads.

An optional short diversion is to travel north of Limón to Playa Bonita, 5km (3 miles), following the coastline, and less than 2km (1.25 miles) farther north to the town of Portete. Farther on over the hill, 7km (4 miles) west is Moín.

① Playa Bonita has the best beaches close to Limón. A handful of houses form the town of Portete where fishing boats are moored in the bay. Moín has the international docks where modern-day banana boats are loaded with the 2.1 million tons of bananas Costa Rica exports each year.

West of Limón, a 30-minute drive along a paved road takes you to Highway 32 and starts the 43km (26-mile) coastal journey south to Cahuita. A thin line of palms breaks the view of the beautiful beaches; though they are marred by the dangerous currents found along the coastline north of Cahuita. Some 20km (12 miles) south of Puerto Limón, head inland at Bananito and take the rough road (four-wheel-drive essential) leading to secluded Selva Bananito Lodge. Reaching it involves crossing four rivers. In January 2005 and 2006 storms severely damaged many roads in the Caribbean Lowlands; before setting out call ahead to verify that roads and bridges are passable.

② Selva Bananito is a relaxing, family-run rainforest lodge with cabins made from earthquake-salvaged hardwoods. Balconies, complete with hammocks, have spectacular views to the mountains. Without electricity, evenings are lit by candles and days start with the sun and the dawn chorus of the rainforest. Only make this detour if you plan to spend the night and take two days rather than one for this drive.

Back on the main road, a short way north of Penshurst **③**, a road heads inland climbing the Estrella Valley eventually arriving at Hitoy Cerere Biological Reserve—a tough drive that requires a full day (▷ 126). Blink and you'll miss Cahuita, hidden down a road off Highway 36, 10km (6 miles) south of the petrol station at Penshurst.

④ Cahuita, perched on a craggy peninsula, has a population of 4,200, imbued with the laissez-faire Caribbean lifestyle. Heading north out of town, a dirt road shadows Playa Negra. South of town, a small creek leads to the golden sands that mark the northernmost point of Cahuita National Park, home to some of the best coral reefs in the country.

From Cahuita it may be possible to walk along the beach at low tide to Puerto Viejo (best not tried alone) or take the coast road 17km (11 miles) south to Puerto Viejo de Talamanca.

⑤ Puerto Viejo de Talamanca is an intriguing blend of indigenous and Afro-Caribbean cultures. A former fishing village, it is a mêlée of bright shacks, cosmopolitan restaurants and rustic lodges, all woven through the forest that lines the rugged beach. It's Costa Rica's top destination for young, party-seeking visitors.

At Hotel Creek, north of Puerto Viejo, the paved road heads into the hills to the village of Bribrí.

⑥ Bribrí is only of interest to visitors because it has a bank. The town is at the foot of the Talamanca Mountains and the Talamanca Indian Reserve. Access to the park is limited, the most viable option being to plan a trip with ATEC in Puerto Viejo (▷ 155).

From Puerto Viejo, the road south to Manzanillo provides a wide range of accommodations.

Schoolchildren in a park in Puerto Limón (left). Beachcombing at Punta Uva (right)

OUT AND ABOUT

Inside Gandoca-Manzanillo Wildlife Refuge

Local boat owners at Puerto Viejo offer boat rides and snorkeling trips

The strip is developing quickly, despite the restriction of the Gandoca-Manzanillo Wildlife Refuge and sections of the KeKöLdi indigenous reserve. Several sandy beaches provide a quieter retreat. Some 4km (2.5 miles) away from Puerto Viejo, past Playa Cocles is Punta Cocles. Playa Chiquita, a further 2km (1.25 miles) away, has several hotels. Next is Punta Uva (Grape Point). The road south ends in Manzanillo, 12km (7 miles) from Puerto Viejo.

❼ Manzanillo is nothing more than a turning point for buses, but plenty of activities are available here. Aquamor runs diving and kayaking trips out of Manzanillo and has estab-

lished more than 100 dive sites, including diving trips to the Gandoca lagoon.

Manzanillo is followed by the white sand beaches and rocky headlands of Punta Mona and then the Gandoca-Manzanillo Wildlife Refuge at the southeastern corner of Costa Rica.

❽ The wonderland of Refugio Nacional de Vida Silvestre Gandoca-Manzanillo contains some of Costa Rica's most significant wetlands. Waterways and forests teem with birdlife

and mammals, while the coastal waters protect significant endemic species of coral.

WHERE TO EAT

Miss Edith's
75m (82 yards) north of the police station in Cahuita, ▷ 192
☎ 506 755 0248

La Pecora Nera
2km (1.2 miles) south of Puerto Viejo
Playa Cocles
☎ 506 750 0490
🕐 5.30pm–midnight

Maxi's
On Manzanillo's beach
☎ 506 759 9081
A local institution serving fresh fish to hip, people-watching diners. The sea views are great.
🕐 Daily 11.30–10.30

OUT AND ABOUT

Tour operators in San José offer all-inclusive trips throughout the country. Trips range in length from half a day to all-inclusive packages for up to a week or longer. It is possible to do most of the activities independently by public transport or using a rented vehicle, but rarely within the same time frames. The disadvantage is having to adhere to an itinerary.

Companies listed here are capable of organizing any of the tours included below, and creating custom tours.

COSTA RICA EXPEDITIONS
Avenida 3, Calle Central–2
Tel 506 257 0766
www.costaricaexpeditions.com
Costa Rica's first travel company offers upscale wildlife adventures and owns Tortuga Lodge on the Caribbean coast, Corcovado Lodge Tent Camp on the Osa Peninsula and Monteverde Lodge near Santa Elena. Options include rafting. Open daily 5.30am–9pm.

COSTA RICA TEMPTATIONS
Apdo 1199–1200 San José
Tel 506 508 5000
www.crtinfo.com
This reputable, locally-owned tour operator offers a full range of tours and a reservation service.

EXPEDICIONES TROPICALES
Calle 3, Avenida 11–13
Tel 506 257 4171
www.expedicionestropicales.com
Friendly staff talk through the full range of one- and two-day tours. One of their most popular tours is The Best of Costa Rica. Open daily 6am–10pm.

HORIZONTES
Calle 28, Avenida 1–3
Tel 506 222 2022
www.horizontes.com
One of Costa Rica's best tour operators offers a range of services from car rentals, to trips focusing on natural history, birdwatching, culture, photography and adventure. English, Spanish, Italian, German and French spoken. Open Dec–Apr Mon–Fri 8–5.30, Sat 9–12.

SWISS TRAVEL SERVICE
Branches in all major hotels
Tel 506 282 4898
www.swisstravelcr.com
The Swiss Travel Service will arrange almost anything. Their Birdwatcher's Paradise day-trip for birders is popular.

TAM TRAVEL
4 branches, 1 in San José Palacio Hotel,
Tel 506 256 0203
www.tamtravel.com
Try Tam Travel for local tours such as the Poás Volcano Tour, which can be combined with a visit to the Doka Coffee Estate.

SPECIAL INTERESTS

AGUAS BRAVAS
Tel 506 292 2072
www.aguas-bravas.co.cr
Specializing in white-water rafting on several rivers, Aguas Bravas also arranges other activities including horseback riding and mountain biking.

ARMO TOURS
Calle 9, Avenida 6
Tel 506 257 0202
www.armotours.com
Righly recommended for national tours; German, French, English and Italian spoken.

AVENTURAS NATURALES
Avenida Central, Calle 33–35
Tel 506 225 3939
www.adventurecostarica.com
This respected tour operator specializes in white-water rafting. For rafters with an interest in natural history, this is the best company.

CALYPSO TOURS
Edificio Las Arcadas, next to the Gran Hotel Costa Rica
Tel 506 256 2727
www.calypsocruises.com
Calypso are the originators of the Pacific Island Cruise with day trips from US$99.

CENTRAL AMERICAN TOURS
Paseo Colón
Tel 506 257 3529
www.catours.net
Will help with full trip planning service and day tours.

COSTA RICA OUTDOORS
Apdo 199-6150, Santa Ana
Tel 506 282 6743
www.costaricaoutdoors.com
Specialists in outdoor activities, notably fishing. Owned and operated by local fishing expert, Jerry Ruhlow.

COSTA RICA SUN TOURS
Apdo 1195–1250 Escazú
Tel 506 296 7757
www.crsuntours.com
Regular departures on many of the normal tours including Arenal, Monteverde, Manuel Antonio, Corcovado and Tortuguero.

ECOLE TRAVEL
Calles 5/7, Avenida Central,
Tel 506 223 2240
www.ecoletravel.com
This agency offers tours to Tortuguero, Corcovado and tailor-made excursions off the beaten track.

GREEN TROPICAL TOURS
Calle El Rodeo, Apdo 675-2200
Coronado
Tel 506 229 4192
www.greentropical.com
Specializing in tailor-made itineraries with many of the normal tours and some to less widely visited areas.

ORIGINAL CANOPY TOUR
Avenida 9, Calle 3a
Tel 506 291 4465
www.canopytour.com
The pioneers of the canopy tours with installations at Monteverde, Mahogany Park by Orotina, and Drake Bay. Their original Canopy Tour at Tabacon is closed indefinitely. Rates from US$45 per person.

RÍOS TROPICALES
Calle 38, between Avenida 3 and 5
Tel 506 233 6455
www.riostropicales.com
Specialists in white-water rafting on the Pacuare, Sarapiquí, Reventazón, General and Corobicí rivers, also sea kayaking. Ríos Tropicales are careful to assess rafters' abilities.

SIMBIOSIS TOURS
Apdo 6939-1000
San José
Tel 506 290 8646
www.turismoruralcr.com
The reservations arm of Cooprena, a network of community-owned lodges.

OUT AND ABOUT

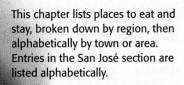

This chapter lists places to eat and stay, broken down by region, then alphabetically by town or area. Entries in the San José section are listed alphabetically.

Eating and Staying

EATING OUT IN COSTA RICA

Thanks to the influx of nationalities from around the globe, dining in Costa Rica is a form of culinary globetrotting. With such a variety of cuisines, especially in larger towns, you can try national delights one day, and familiar dishes from around the world the next. Tastes vary in Costa Rica from the spicy cuisine of the Caribbean to plainer dishes in the highlands. One thing is certain: you won't taste better coffee anywhere.

Fresh produce, such as these fish on the Caribbean coast (left), is served in beachside bars and restaurants (middle, Samasati Nature Retreat). But sometimes all you need is a cold refresco (right)

EATING

RESTAURANTS

Restaurants in Costa Rica meet the needs of *locals* and visitors. Local restaurants tend to do most of their business at lunchtime when *comida típica* (typical food) is served at a cost of a few dollars: a salad starter, rice and beans served with chicken or beef for the main course, and a sometimes rather strange-looking dessert, rarely attractive, but always filling.

More trendy restaurants improve the level of service, setting, food and, naturally, the price. You'll find almost anything your palate desires in San José and in the more popular locations around the country, including French, Italian, Asian, Pacific fusion and seafood. In less tourist-oriented places, you will find regional dishes and more limited menus.

At food stands in markets you will find basic, but very often tasty, food is available.

REGIONAL DISHES

Many people return from Costa Rica enthusing about *gallo pinto*, the ubiquitous staple dish of rice and beans. However, each region yields a variety of gastronomic treats. In the Central Highlands for example, blackberries and strawberries flourish and in the *sabanero* heartland of Guanacaste, *tamales*—corn maize based pasties mixed with chicken, meat or vegetables—fuel the rural worker and visitor alike.

The oceans teem with marlin, dorado, yellowfin tuna, snapper and wahoo. Along the Caribbean coast, you'll find spicy chicken and desserts prepared in coconut milk.

To start the day, rice and beans come with eggs, sour cream and tortillas, and tropical fruits to try include pejibaye, a palm fruit with a soft spiky exterior. *Cajetas* is a sweet spread added to everything from slabs of bread to tortillas. Another favorite is *tres leches*, a light sponge cake drenched in condensed milk.

LOCAL DRINKS

Costa Ricans don't indulge heavily in drinking. On Friday and Saturday nights the streets are not filled with people moving from one bar to another—but the bars are nonetheless lively. Once you've tapped into the local happening bar, beer is the drink of choice with Imperial and Pilsen being the most popular lagers and Bavaria a darker malty option. Fruit juices, either straight or with water, are also popular, as are *refrescos*, soft drinks.

The spirit of choice and convenience is *ron*—the Spanish word for rum. Other spirits and good quality wines find their way to the tables of bars and restaurants as the price rises.

The sugar-cane based, falling-over juice found in dive-bars is *guaro*, guaranteed to provide a sore head and a night you won't forget, even if it is only for the headache the following day.

Café Rica is a coffee-based liquor, true to the country's coffee-producing origins.

Although you're not going to rhapsodize about the country's traditional cuisine in a postcard home, local food can be very tasty. The best dishes are often the simplest, with fresh fish and fruit being Costa Rican cuisine's greatest strengths. The national diet is based on combinations of rice, beans and meat or fish. This menu reader describes some of the local dishes and foods that you will find on restaurant menus. Menus in tourist areas will usually have a description of the dishes in English alongside the Spanish name.

Local restaurants, called sodas *are a fixture on most main streets. Most serve traditional dishes based on rice and beans (middle). For self-catering, street markets are an inexpensive source of fresh food (right)*

MEAT DISHES
Arroz con pollo rice with chicken
Carne/bistek meat/steak
Casados standard national lunchtime dish of rice, beans with meat, chicken or fish and a bit of salad
Cerdo pork
Chicharrón deep-fried pork skin cooked until crispy
Cordero lamb
Empanadas deep-fried tortilla stuffed with meat or chicken
Pato duck
Pavo turkey
Perdiz partridge
Pollo chicken
Ternera veal

FISH AND SEAFOOD
Those who go out on a game fishing trip will often bring some of the catch, such as tuna or swordfish, back to be cooked for the evening meal.
Atún tuna
Camarón prawn
Ceviche raw fish marinated in lemon, coriander and normally absolutely divine
Corvina sea bass
Langosta lobster
Mariscos seafood
Pescado fish
Pez espada swordfish
Pulpo octopus

SIDE DISHES
Arroz rice
Bocas small dishes for nibbling which may be meat, chicken or fish in various forms
Gallo pinto rice and black beans, which in the Caribbean has the distinctly pleasurable addition of coconut milk
Patacones mashed plantain deep fried and normally served with beans
Plátano plantains, or savory banana, often fried
Tamales a cornstarch–cornflour–based pastie mixed with chicken, meat or vegetables served in a plantain leaf
Tortillas cornflour pancake

DESSERTS
Cajetas a delightful, tooth-achingly sweet spread
Cajeta de leche thick, fudge-like milk pudding
Dulce de leche baked sweet milk
Helados ice cream
Miel de abeja glorious Costa Rican honey
Tres leches sponge cake soaked in sweet milk

FRUIT
In addition to the usual tropical fruits—in particular several different types of mango—Costa Rica supplies some unusual ones you may not have met before.
Aguacate avocado
Cas bitter tasting straight from the fruit, but when mixed with honey or sugar it makes a great *refresco* (soft drink)
Fresa strawberry
Limón lemon
Manzana apple
Naranja orange
Pejibaye almost unique to Costa Rica, it's a popular fruit from a palm tree with a soft spikey outside. Sold by the bagload along the roadside, some people love it, for others it's more effort than it's worth
Platano banana
Tamarindo a date-like fruit that is refreshing to the core when pulped and mixed with ice-cold water
Uva grape

VEGETABLES
Ajo garlic
Judías beans
Patata potato
Pimientos red/green peppers

DRINKS
Agua water
Café coffee
Cerveza beer
Leche milk
Vino wine

EATING

SAN JOSÉ

Fine restaurants tend to be found in or near good hotels west of downtown, on or around Paseo Colón and Parque Sabana, or to the north in the districts of Amón, Otoya and farther east in the residential suburbs of Los Yoses. One of the local dining habits peculiar to San José and Costa Rica is the omnipresent *soda*—the national version of a fast-food outlet, without the boring uniformity of US fast-food versions—found on many street corners. The city also has an array of cafés and bakeries where you can stop for coffee or light refreshments.

PRICES AND SYMBOLS

The restaurants are listed alphabetically (excluding El, Le and La). The prices given are for a two-course lunch (L) and a three-course dinner (D) for one person, without drinks. The wine price is for the least expensive bottle.
For a key to the symbols ▷ 2.

BAKEA

Calle 7, Avenida 11, Casa 956, Barrio Amón
Tel 506 221 1051
In a restored colonial home in Barrio Amón, two blocks north of Parque Morazán, this sleek restaurant-bar fuses colonial elegance and contemporary style. The Expressionist art on the walls and faultless service from the staff provides the perfect backdrop for chef Camille Pérez's eclectic menu—a blend of Asian, Mediterranean and Caribbean dishes. Main dishes include a zingy chicken with orange and ginger sauce and filet mignon. You can get a good value three-course lunch during the week for US$15, and late night snacks.
🕐 Tue–Sat 12–12 🍽 L US$15, D US$22, Wine US$19

EL BALCÓN DE EUROPA

Calle 9 and Avenida Central–1
Tel 506 221 4841
Two blocks east of Plaza de la Cultura, this charismatic Italian restaurant dates back to 1909; it is the oldest in Costa Rica. With dark wood-paneled walls, covered with photos, the setting and ebullient atmosphere compensate for a hit-and-miss menu. Well-priced pasta dishes are reliable, but some of the meat and fish dishes, the Spanish-style steak excepted, can be on the small side.
🕐 Sun–Fri 11.30–10
🍽 L US$15, D US$18, Wine US$15

CAFÉ DEL TEATRO

Teatro Nacional,
Plaza de la Cultura
Tel 506 221 3262
www.teatronacional.go.cr

The National Theater's coffee shop combines neoclassical grandeur and impeccable service to make an unmissable San José experience. Polished marble tiled floors and tabletops, chandeliers and ceiling frescoes have been elegantly restored. Excellent coffee is served and for snacks and lunches there are sandwiches, cakes, fresh juices and salads. It's expensive but worth it.
🕐 Mon–Fri 10–5, Sat 9–4, Sun only during performances
🍽 Coffee and cake US$4.50

CAFÉ MUNDO

Calle 15, Avenida 9
Barrio Amón
Tel 506 222 6190
In a converted mansion in Barrio Amón, north of Parque España, this hip, gay-friendly Italian restaurant is popular with fast-lunch business workers by day and bohemian Ticos, visitors and expatriates in the evenings. The porch is a lovely setting for the excellent value *plato del día* (US$4). The extensive repertoire of pastas includes fettuccini with vegetables and shrimp sauce, and penne with chicken and vodka. There are pizzas big enough to share, and tomato and herb bread served with olive oil. Hidden behind a wall, the café is easy to miss;

look for the open gate on the corner.
🕐 Mon–Thu 11–11, Fri 11am–midnight, Sat–Sun 5–midnight
🍽 L US$16, D US$21, Wine US$17
🚶 200m (220 yards) east and 100m (110 yards) north of the INS building

CAFÉ 1930

Gran Hotel Costa Rica
Avenida 2, Calle Central
Tel 506 221 4000
On the Parque Mora Fernández, the terrace café of the renovated Gran Hotel is a San José institution. The renovation has expanded the café,

which remains one of the most popular people-watching spots in town. Main course dishes can be bland and overpriced. For light lunches and late-night munchies, however, the club sandwiches, salads and breakfasts are more than satisfying.
🕐 24 hours
🍽 L US$9, D US$22, Wine US$16

CAFÉ POSADA DEL MUSEO

Avenida 2, Calle 17
Diagonal to the National Museum
Tel 506 257 9414
This bohemian restaurant and art gallery is welcoming, with comfortable terrace seating outside. The menu includes Argentinian dishes like *torta de ricotta*, *torta de espinacas* and *alfajores*. The excellent three-course set lunches draw the suits, and monthly evening gatherings are popular with artists. A two-minute walk from the National Museum, this restaurant

merits a stop for dinner or a coffee.

◎ Mon–Thu 7–6, Fri–Sun 9–11
🖫 L US$5, Wine US$14

LA COCINA DE LEÑA

El Pueblo Commercial Center
Tel 506 223 3704
www.lacocinadelena.com
A five-minute taxi ride from Plaza de la Cultura takes you to a popular restaurant among gilded Joséfinos. This is Costa Rican *comida típica* at its finest. The house specials are tenderloin and Creole chicken broiled with a special sauce. Lighter options include tuna and palm heart salad and *tamales*. The rustic taverna setting buzzes at the weekend with families and couples. Reservations are advised.

◎ Daily 11–11
🖫 L US$15, D US$26, Wine US$17

LA ESQUINA DE BUENOS AIRES

Calle 11, Avenida 4
Tel 506 223 1909
Replicating a genuine Argentinian *bodega*, this intimate bar-restaurant is festooned with period prints and infused with the rhythms of tango, drawing a sophisticated local crowd and expatriates in the know. The wide-ranging menu includes onion soup, and shrimp and avocado salad. The filet of sole in blue cheese with boiled potatoes is superb, and the wine list draws heavily from the homeland.

◎ Mon–Thu 11.30–3, 6–10.30; Fri 11.30–3, 6–11; Sat 12.30–11; Sun 12–10
🖫 L US$15, D US$20, Wine US$18

GRANO DE ORO

Calle 30, between Avenida 2 and 4
Tel 506 255 3322
www.hotelgranodeoro.com
Just off Paseo Colón, the Hotel Grano de Oro's exciting new restaurant combines elegance with inventive Mediterranean cuisine. The tranquil courtyard patio is perfect for a light lunch, while, in the evenings, the intimate candlelit restaurant provides a romantic setting. Appetizers include fried Camembert with hot blackberry sauce and leafy salads. For a main course, try caramelized chicken breast with dried fruits or one of the highly rated, but good value, seafood

dishes, such as jumbo garlic shrimp and sea bass.

◎ Daily 7am–10pm
🖫 L US$22, D US$30, Wine US$18

JÜRGEN'S RESTAURANT

Barrio Dent, 200m (220 yards) north of Subaru dealership
Hotel Boutique Jade
Tel 506 283 2239
Tucked away in a quiet residential quarter of Los Yoses, this elegant hotel-restaurant represents sophisticated dining at its best. Contemporary art pieces and floral displays complement the menu, which has a French influence. Appetizers include mussels Rockefeller, and entrees range from *tilapia* with mustard sauce to pork in wine sauce. Service is mustard-keen, and there's a cigar lounge.

◎ Mon–Fri 12–2.30, 6–10; Sat 6–11
🖫 L US$18, D US$26, Wine US$20

MACHU PICCHU

Calle 32, Avenida 1–3
Tel 506 222 7384
This Peruvian restaurant, one block north of Paseo Colón, is an old San José haunt that is popular with tourists. With a spartan dining room and walls hung with a few tokens to the Inca theme, it is the delicious, inexpensive food that is the star here. The seafood menu includes sea bass *a lo macho* (a fillet drenched in Peruvian *aji*). There are appetizers such as octopus cracklings and *ceviche* and superb pisco sours.

◎ Mon–Sat 11–3, 6–10
🖫 L US$8, D US$12, Wine US$6

NEWS CAFÉ

Hotel Presidente
Avenida Central, Calle 7
Tel 506 222 3022
www.hotel-presidente.com
This American-style sports bar-restaurant is a tourist magnet and, while it may have little to do with Costa Rica, it is a reliable downtown option for lunch or a cool beer in the bar. The interior is snug with TVs in the corner and plenty of newspapers. The burgers are peerless, and there are sandwiches, wraps and salads.

◎ Daily 6am–midnight
🖫 L US$12, D US$16, Wine US$15

LA OASIS

Hotel Santo Tomas
Avenida 7, Calle 3–5
Tel 506 255 0448

The Santo Tomas Hotel restaurant in Barrio Amón, with its poolside dining room, is a soothing antidote to San José's urban jungle. The international menu satisfies most tastes, with grilled pesto tuna, chicken breast with caper sauce, and filet mignon. Save space for desserts such as crêpes, mousse or apple pie. There is also a fine wine list.

◎ Tue–Sat 4–11, Sun 3–10
🖫 D US$21, Wine US$18

LA PIAZZETTA

Paseo Colón, Calle 40
Tel 506 362 3000
A brief walk from Parque Sabana, this Italian restaurant serves regional dishes in a modern building. Appetizers include snails with garlic, and mussels and lemon oysters. Various pasta dishes include linguine with salmon and mascarpone, and there is a varied repertoire of southern Italian fish and meat dishes.

◎ Mon–Fri 12–2.30, 6.30–11, Sat 6.30–11
🖫 L US$15, D US$22, Wine US$22

TIN JO

Calle 11, Avenida 6–8
Tel 506 221 7605
Four blocks south of Plaza de la Cultura, in front of the Lucho Barahona theater, is Tin Jo, one of San José's most popular restaurants. It serves Asian cuisine from steamed Vietnamese chicken to teriyaki salmon, with plenty for vegetarians. At Sunday lunch it is packed with Costa Rican families. Take a taxi in the evenings; the neighborhood can be unsafe after dark.

◎ Mon–Thu 11.30–3, 5.30–10, Fri, Sat 11.30–3, 5.30–11, Sun 11.30–10
🖫 L US$18, D US$24, Wine US$17

EATING

CENTRAL HIGHLANDS

In contrast to the international haute cuisine of the capital, in the satellite towns of Alajuela, Heredia and Cartago fast food-style restaurants predominate. They do most of their business at lunchtime, serving up hearty portions of national dishes. For a quintessential Costa Rican cultural experience, try one of the ubiquitous *sodas*, where you can buy a midday *plato del día* or *casado* for around US$2.50. Nestling among the slopes of Volcán Poás, organic fruit and vegetable farms assure a supply of fresh produce—delicious strawberry and blackberry *licuados* are available in cafés and restaurants that afford spectacular views over coffee plantations. For more sophisticated dining, Escazú has the most memorable dining options.

PRICES AND SYMBOLS

The restaurants are listed alphabetically (excluding El, Le and La). The prices given are for a two-course lunch (L) and a three-course dinner (D) for one person, without drinks. The wine price is for the least expensive bottle.
For a key to the symbols ▷ 2.

ALAJUELA

EL AMBROSIA
Calle 2, Avenida 5
Alajuela
Tel 506 440 3440
Quality restaurants are rare in Alajuela, but this café has patio seating and an upbeat ambience. There is a range of coffees and sandwiches, pastries and cookies. At lunch, it is usually busy, drawing the local business crowd for a good-value *plato del día*. Credit cards are not accepted.
🕐 Mon–Sat 9–6.30
🍷 L US$4, no wine served

CERUTTI
San Rafael de Escazú
Tel 506 228 4511
Rated by some as one of the best Italian restaurants in Costa Rica, Cerutti is popular with visiting glitterati, politicos and expatriates. Italian cuisine, including fresh pasta dishes, seafood and fish and meat dishes, is served with panache in a serene 100-year-old house. Understated elegance predominates with crisp white tablecloths and glimmering silverware. Reservations are advised.
🕐 Wed–Mon 12–3.30, 6.30–11
🍷 L US$15, D US$24, Wine US$20

LA LUZ
Hotel Alta
Alto de las Palomas
Escazú
Tel 506 282 4160
Considered by many to be one of the best restaurants in Costa Rica, this elegant hotel restaurant serves fusion food with Asian and Caribbean tastes. Ironwork chandeliers and heavy wood beams set the tone and the valley view is superb. Appetizers include macadamia-encrusted chicken strips and entrees feature a monumental seafood platter with jumbo shrimps covered with bacon, mussels and squid. For meat-eaters grilled tenderloin with strawberry sauce is a must. For dessert, the crème brûlée is superb.
🕐 Mon–Sat 6–3, 6–10, Sun 9–4
🍷 L US$26, D US$34, Wine US$20
🚗 On the road to Santa Ana

LE MONASTÈRE
Old road to Santa Ana
Escazú
Tel 506 289 4404
www.monastere-restaurant.com
In the hills of Escazú, this restored monastery is the most romantic dining room in the Central Valley. French-Belgian cuisine includes salmon with rose petals and caviar, duck foie gras, mahi mahi with Cajun shrimp and wild boar stew with truffles. Dining under the gaze of marble statues and staff dressed in full monks' habits, this is a memorable experience, although the food itself is sometimes a let-down.
🕐 Mon–Wed 7–10.30, Thu–Sat 7–11
🍷 L US$23, D US$30,
🚗 On the Santa Ana road from Escazú, turn left at the Multicentro Paco and follow the green crosses.

TIQUICIA
Escazú
Tel 506 289 5839
Nestling in the hills south of Escazú, Tiquicia serves traditional food. It's quite an adventure to get here, and the views are unbeatable day or night. In a rustic setting, Tiquicia is an institution and would be more so if the hours weren't so erratic. It's advisable to call ahead and check. Get a taxi or a four-wheel-drive vehicle if going after rain. A troupe of traditional dancers sometimes performs.
🕐 Tue–Fri 5–1am, Sat noon–1am, Sun 12–6
🍷 L US$18, D US$25, Wine US$17

LA GARITA

FIESTA DEL MAÍZ SODA/RESTAURANT
Jacó road
La Garita
Tel 506 487 5757
If you're exploring the area west of Alajuela by car, this *soda* merits a visit. The restaurant also concentrates on corn, producing tasty dishes. The decor is unprepossessing, but it is popular as a stopping place for weekenders on their way to and from Jacó beach. Credit cards are not accepted.
🕐 Tue–Thu 10–8, Fri–Sun 7am–9pm
🍷 L US$5, D US$8, Wine US$9
🚗 On the left-hand side of the road, just after leaving the town of La Garita on the way to Jacó

HEREDIA

FRESAS
Calle 7, Avenida 1
Heredia
Tel 506 262 5555
This open-plan diner beside a noisy traffic nexus serves everything you could want for a quick lunch, including snacks, sandwiches, full meals, fresh fruit juices and, not surprisingly, plenty of strawberries (*fresas*). They will also deliver. Credit cards are not accepted.
🕐 Daily 8am–midnight
🍷 L US$7.50, D US$10

LE PETIT PARIS
Calle 5, Avenida Central–2
Tel 506 262 2564
Three blocks from the Parque Central, this is a little piece of France in the heart of Heredia.

EATING

Amid Doisneau photographs and 1930s posters of Paris, the ambience changes between the bar, restaurant and leafy patio. The menu is mainly French, but pizza and pasta dishes are also served.

🅒 Mon–Sat 12–10pm
🍽 L US$10, D US$15, Wine US$15

VISHNU
Calle 7, Avenida Central–1
Heredia
Tel 506 237 2526
One block from the University, vegetarian dishes at great prices are served in this spotless diner. On weekdays, office workers and students pack in for the value *plato del día* (US$3), which includes a main course dish, salad, soup, fruit

juice and dessert. The quasi-legendary vegetarian burger (US$2) is guaranteed to satisfy even the most ardent carnivores. It's difficult to walk past the glass cabinets displaying gooey brownies, *empanadas de piña*, coconut cake and wholemeal and tomato breads. There are also many branches of Vishnu in San José.

🅒 Mon–Sat 9–6
🍽 L US$4

MONTE DE LA CRUZ
BAALBEK BAR AND GRILL
Los Angeles de San Rafael, 500m (550 yards) below El Castillo Country Club
Tel 506 267 6482
This Lebanese restaurant on the slopes of Barva Volcano

draws the cognoscenti as much for the views as for the excellent Levantine fare, such as *mehshe* (chicken and rice in cabbage), and grilled eggplant. The menu—complemented by a large wine list—also has international staples such as T-bone steaks and grilled salmon. Choose from the elegant downstairs restaurant or more intimate booths upstairs, where hookahs are smoked by diners reclining in sumptuous sofas.

🅒 Tue–Sat 12–12
🍽 L US$12, D US$23, Wine US$20

OROSÍ VALLEY
BAR-RESTAURANT COTO
Orosí
Tel 506 533 3032
In the middle of the small town of Orosí, beside the soccer field, with views of the mountains and the small restored church, this rancho-style bar-restaurant and *parillada* (grill) is welcoming serves simple but tasty Tico dishes. Meat is the specialty; there is a good-value *casados*, fried fish, heart of palm salads and homemade *flan de coco* for dessert. By day, the TV and children's soccer matches are the lunchtime entertainment, while in the evening there is often live music.

🅒 Daily 8am–midnight (or until the last person leaves)
🍽 L US$6, D US$10, Wine US$16

LA CASONA DEL CAFETAL
Lago de Cachí
Orosí Valley
Tel 506 533 3280
On the southern shore of Lake Cachí, La Casona del Cafetal is a popular place to eat, open every day, but drawing crowds of locals and tourists on Sundays to its all-you-can-eat buffet for US$15. The à la carte menu starts at around US$6. It's a beautiful setting and after lunch you can take a horse-drawn carriage round the coffee plantation before heading east towards the town of Orosí.

🅒 Daily 11–6
🍽 L US$15, Wine US$18

OROSÍ LODGE CAFÉ
Orosí
Tel 506 533 3578
www.orosilodge.com
The excellent German-run Orosí Lodge has a relaxed and

welcoming European-style café with mesmerizing views overlooking the lush valley. It is a lovely spot to eat breakfast and you can birdwatch while you enjoy homemade granola, fruits, croissants and bagels, and a very satisfying scrambled eggs with cheese and bacon served in the frying pan with fresh baked bread. In the late afternoon banana cake, apple strudels and carrot cakes to die for pop out of the oven, then the candles are lit, the jukebox plays everything from French hits to salsa and the lights in the valley glitter in the distance.

🅒 Daily 7–7
🍽 Breakfast US$5, coffee and cake US$4

VOLCÁN POÁS
JAULARES
1km (0.6 miles) south of Fraijanes, on the San Pedro–Poás road
Tel 506 482 2155
www.jaulares.com
A good lunchtime stop en route to Poás Volcano, Restaurante Jaulares is steeped in a traditional farmstead ambience. It is known for its *comida típica* dishes prepared on a wood-burning stove. The black bean soup and succulent jalapeño steak draw the locals, along with excellent daily *casados* (set lunches). Friday nights are the best time to visit, when local musicians perform.

🅒 Mon–Sat 10–10, Sun 8–6
🍽 L US$5, D US$12, Wine US$14

MI CASITA
Vara Blanca road
Tel 506 482 2629
Wonderfully positioned with stunning views to Poás Volcano, this welcoming restaurant serves huge platters of fresh food at great prices. The broad menu includes sizzling chicken fajitas, pasta, *casados* and homemade cheese tortillas with sour cream. There is a delicious *tres leches* cake for dessert. Don't leave without trying a *jugo de mora*, thick fruit juice made with local blackberries. Owner Rodolfo also has some Austrian-style chalets for rent (▷ 197).

🅒 Mon–Fri 7am–midnight, Sat–Sun 7am–2am
🍽 L US$8, D US$13, Wine US$10

EATING

NORTHERN REGION

All-inclusive lodges proliferate in the northern lowlands, particularly in the Monteverde and Lake Arenal areas, with cuisine ranging from Costa Rican dishes to international cuisine in the smarter hotels. Santa Elena and Fortuna are economical bases for Monteverde and Arenal respectively and are stocked with rustic open-air restaurants, hip pizzerias and holistic cafés where you can feast on innovative fish and meat dishes, pizza, pasta and vegetarian choices.

ARENAL

RESTAURANTE HELICONIAS
Hotel Arenal Kioro
10km (6 miles) west of La Fortuna
Tel 506 461 1700
www.hotelarenalkioro.com
With unrivaled grandstand views of the volcano, this smart hotel-restaurant with vast picture windows is the place to enjoy superlative international cuisine. An octopus cocktail appetizer and sea bass in caper sauce are among the treats. Service is exemplary.
🅖 Daily 6.30am–10pm
🍷 L US$16, D US$26, Wine US$15

TOAD HALL
La Unión de Arenal
Tel 506 692 8020
www.toadhall-gallery.com

Toad Hall café, a 45-minute drive from Fortuna, serves a mix of fresh food with home-grown salads, fruit juices and divine chocolate brownies. The views of the lake and volcano are great and its gift shop is one of Costa Rica's best.
🅖 Daily 8–4
🍷 L US$10

MONTEVERDE

CAFÉ FLOR DE LA VIDA
Cerro Plano
Monteverde
Tel 506 645 6328
Below Hotel El Establo, the holistically hip "flower of life" café serves excellent vegetarian food in an airy, open-plan restaurant. Fresh fruit, bagels or more traditional *gallo pinto* is available for breakfast. For lunch and dinner choose from pasta dishes, soups, salads and pizza. Scrumptious cakes are served with tea or coffee all day long. Live music is often played in the evenings. Credit cards are not accepted.
🅖 Daily 7am–10pm
🍷 B US$7, L US$14, D US$23

PIZZERIA DE JOHNNY
On the Santa Elena–Monteverde road
Monteverde
Tel 506 645 5066
En route to the national park, 1km (0.6 mile) from Santa Elena, restrained elegance prevails at the long-established Johnny's, often lauded as the best restaurant in the region. Good wood-oven pizzas, in a range of sizes, are liberally topped with fresh ingredients, and appetizers include garlic mussels and bruschetta. There is a good wine list, and for lighter fare, or a lunchtime snack, choose from a selection of sandwiches. A balcony has several outdoor tables.
🅖 Daily 11.30–9.30
🍷 L US$10, D US$16, Wine US$16

RESTAURANT DE LUCÍA
On the road to the Monteverde Butterfly Garden
Tel 506 645 53 37
Across the street from José and Lucia's Hotel de Lucia Inn, Lucía's is a piece of Italy that has received countless recommendations. Tasty vegetarian cuisine, including lasagne and tortillas, are served alongside meat and fish dishes in a relaxed and informal setting. The daily specials of fish and meat are brought to your table

and cooked to taste. Reservations advised.
🅖 Daily 7am–9pm
🍷 L US$13, D US$20, Wine US$18

EL SAPO DORADO
Apartado 9-5655
Monteverde
Tel 506 645 5010
www.sapodorado.com
Costa Rican and Quaker traditions fuse with aplomb at the widely recommended restaurant of the El Sapo Dorado Hotel on the Monteverde road. Global and national dishes merge vegetarian options with Tico dishes and organic produce is used in each inventive meal. Serene views over Nicoya from the terrace extend the sense of well being. If you have specific dietary needs, call ahead and the staff will be happy to oblige.
🅖 Daily 6.30–9.30, noon–3, 6–9.30
🍷 B US$7.50, L US$14, D US$20, Wine US$18

SANTA ELENA

MORPHOS
Opposite the supermarket
Santa Elena
Tel 506 645 5607
Upbeat Morphos, one of the most consistently recommended restaurants in Santa Elena, serves a selection of daily specials featuring fish and meat staples in abundant portions. The dining room is a social hub by day with hungry hikers devouring sandwiches, while candlelit tables add romantic appeal by night.
🅖 Daily 11–10
🍷 L US$10, D US$18, Wine US$15

GUANACASTE

Home to the most cosmopolitan residents in Costa Rica, northwest Guanacaste offers some of the most varied dining in the country. At stunning beachside settings, with views of melting sunsets, everything from Thai to Mexican can be found with seafood specials forming the chalkboard menus. At resorts you will find some of the most expensive prices in the country (although not by international standards). Family oriented areas such as Tamarindo cater to children. While most establishments tend to be American owned, you don't have to stray too far to find a local *soda*, where you can enjoy cheap and satisfying *casados*.

PRICES AND SYMBOLS

The restaurants are listed alphabetically (excluding El, Le and La). The prices given are for a two-course lunch (L) and a three-course dinner (D) for one person, without drinks. The wine price is for the least expensive bottle.
For a key to the symbols ▷ 2.

LIBERIA

PIZZERIA DE BEPPE
Avenida Central, Calle 10
Liberia
Tel 506 666 0917
A Liberian institution in a verdant setting, Pizzeria de Beppe serves excellent pizzas with a large choice of toppings, including vegetarian options. They're cooked in a wood-fired oven and make a tasty lunch. The restaurant is also open for breakfast. In order to compete with the new restaurants and cafés opening in booming Liberia, prices are kept low.
🅖 Daily 10–10
🍴 L US$6, D US$10

RESTAURANTE PASO REAL
Avenida Central
Tel 506 666 3455
Facing the plaza in the heart of the city, this friendly seafood restaurant is a great place to select from a wide-ranging menu that spans King Neptune's larder. The ceviche is excellent, as are the Mexican-style shrimp jalapeños and the fish with brandy sauce. The fish of the day can be anything from mahi mahi to red snapper. The spacious indoor restaurant has a large-screen TV and can get noisy when packed with a local clientele; the place to be is the narrow patio terrace overlooking the square.
🅖 Daily 11–10
🍴 L US$12, D US$20, Wine US$12

PLAYAS DEL COCO

TEQUILA BAR AND GRILL
200m (220 yards) before the beach
Playas del Coco
Tel 506 670 0741
On the main road down to the beach, this gregarious bar-grill with a raw *tequilera* edge packs in locals and tourists for its reasonably priced menu of piquant Mexican fare, ranging from sizzling hot plates of chicken and beef fajitas to seafood tacos and *chilaquiles* (tortilla strips cooked with meat and vegetables). If you are planning a lively night in Coco, the bar is worth a visit alone for its margaritas and tequila chasers. Credit cards are not accepted.
🅖 Thu–Tue 11–10
🍴 L US$11, D US$15

PLAYA FLAMINGO

MARIE'S
Playa Flamingo
Tel 506 654 4136
Marie's, right on the beach, is one of Flamingo's most highly regarded restaurants. In the evening, a chalkboard of specials includes the catch of the day. Appetizers include ceviche and brilliant-green avocados stuffed with succulent shrimp. For breakfast, try the papaya pancakes with a bright orange flush. For a quick, satisfying lunch there are good value *casados*, fajitas and burritos. With a relaxed natural setting, excellent service and good prices, this is beachside dining at its best.
🅖 Daily 7am–10pm
🍴 B US$5, L US$11, D US$19, Wine US$13

PLAYA GRANDE

GREAT WALTINI'S
Hotel Bula Bula
Tel 506 653 0975
www.hotelbulabula.com
Run by American owners Wally and Todd, Great Waltini's is the liveliest dining spot in Playa

Grande, drawing local expatriates for killer cocktails at the bar: the Jumbo-sized "Waltini Martini" and "Bert's Jumbo rum punch" will put you on your back! Fusing influences from throughout the Americas, the menu has everything from quesadillas and crabcakes to such entrees as filet of ahi tuna sauteed with white wine and garlic butter. Leave room for the "Siberia" chocolate drink dessert.
🅖 Tue–Thu 5.30–8.30, Fri–Sat 5.30–9
🍴 D US$22, Wine US$18

PLAYA HERMOSA

LA FINISTERRA
100m (110 yards) uphill from the Hotel
Playa Hermosa
Tel 506 670 0227
www.finisterra.net
Overlooking Playa Hermosa, with lovely views framed by tamarind trees, this open-air balcony restaurant is a great place to escape the heat. Chef "Eduardo" does a fine job preparing nouvelle Costa Rican cuisine using fresh ingredients. Daily specials might include filet mignon with peppercorn sauce, and international staples such as caesar salads and home-made pasta dishes are represented.
🅖 Daily 10–10
🍴 L US$12, D US$24, Wine US$18

GINGER
200m (220 yards) inland of the beach on the Playa Panama road
Tel 506 350 2922
Dramatically contemporary, this open-air tapas restaurant beneath a cantilevered glass canopy looks almost too hip to be true. The invitingly chic dining space wraps around a trapezoidal bar where all-too-diminutive cocktails are served. Canadian chef Anne Hegney Frey, however, delivers mouthwatering tapas with a light touch: fried calamari, exquisite ginger rolls and a

ginger ahi tuna as soft as a sigh. Occasional wine tastings are hosted.

🅒 Tue–Sun 5–10
🅦 D US$32, Wine US$25

PLAYA LANGOSTA

TABOO

200m (220 yards) north of Hotel Barceló, Playa Langosta
Tel 506 653 1422

This French-owned, open-air restaurant, near the end of the Playa Langosta road, serves smallish portions of delicious dishes from a changing menu. Appetizers range from stuffed mussels to tuna salad, while main course options might include chard-wrapped tuna. Dust can be a problem on the unpaved road in summer. The large wine list spans the globe.

🅒 Sun–Fri 12–3, 6–10
🅦 L US$14, D US$28, Wine US$24

TAMARINDO

CAPITÁN SUIZO

Hotel Capitán Suizo
Tamarindo
Tel 506 653 0975

Another chic hotel-restaurant serving nouvelle dishes, this one is under the care of a long-term German resident chef. The curving open-air bar is a great place to sample cocktails and is spacious enough for dining. The adjoining wall-less restaurant is airy thanks to a soaring *palenque* roof. Service is relaxed yet professional, delivering fusion dishes that merge European and Pacific influences and ingredients. A favorite is *tilapia* in caper sauce.

🅒 Daily 7am–9.15pm
🅦 L US$13, D US$26, Wine US$18

DRAGONFLY BAR AND GRILL

100m (110 yards) north of Hotel Pasatiempo
Tamarindo
Tel 506 653 1506
www.dragonflybarandgrill.com

Among the latest in a breed of nouvelle restaurants recently opened in Tamarindo by professional chefs, this one stands out, not least for its canvas canopy "roof" supported by glazed treetrunks and lit by romantic paper lanterns. Asian-fusion is the name of the game. Owner Tish Tomlinson and chef Kevin Mulry have combined talents

to produce an exciting menu ranging from beef satay with ginger soy sauce appetizer to main dishes such as pistachio-crusted mahi mahi and chili rubbed pork chops with chipotle mashed potatoes. Divine!

🅒 Daily 7pm–10pm
🅦 D US$20, Wine $16

JARDÍN DEL EDÉN

Hotel Jardín del Edén
Tel 506 653 0137

The classiest restaurant in town, this delightful and chic thatched mezzanine restaurant overlooks a floodlit multi-tier pool and cascade. The marble-topped bar is a great place for cocktails before settling at a romantic booth or candlelit table to taste Peruvian chef Omar Grados's Pacific fusion delights. Mussel soup with saffron and tenderloin flambé with martini are typical of the revolving menu.

🅒 Daily 12–3, 6–11
🅦 L US$16, D US$32, Wine US$26

KAHIKI RESTAURANT

200m (220 yards) along the road to Playa Langosta
Tamarindo
Tel 506 653 0344

A 10-minute stroll from the middle of town, this American-owned restaurant draped with fairy lights delivers chalkboard specials of artfully presented Asian-fusion fare. Oven-roasted, herb-rubbed pork tenderloin and seared tuna with wasabi cream and shrimp and calamari *ceviche* salads are some of the nightly specials that might appear. The open-air dining area is informally stylish. No reservations. Credit cards are not accepted.

🅒 Wed–Mon 11–2, 5–10
🅦 L US$10, D US$25, Wine US$15

NOGUI'S SUNRISE CAFÉ

On the beachfront, just off rotunda
Tamarindo
Tel 506 653 0029

Right on the beach at the heart of town, this popular Tico-run café serves the best breakfasts in Tamarindo: create-your-own, three-egg omelettes, stuffed tortillas, banana bread topped with cinnamon cream cheese and fresh fruit and pancakes. For lunch there are tacos, pesto pizzas, bountiful salads and

sandwiches, including the best BLT in town. The real draw, however, is the peaceful beachside setting, with just the sound of the waves and fans. Service can be slow when the place is busy, but always gracious.

🅒 Thu–Tue 6am–9.30pm
🅦 B US$5, L US$10

PANADERÍA DE PARIS

Hotel La Laguna del Cocodrilo
Tamarindo
Tel 506 653 0255
www.lalagunadelcocodrilo.com

At the northern end of town, the Panadaría de Paris is the mother of all bakeries in this part of the world. French owners Josette and Claude have brought their Parisienne pastry *savoir faire* to Tamarindo. The aroma of freshly baked bread, croissants, *pain au chocolat*, fruit tarts, cookies and banana bread drifts seductively from the small streetside bakery. For a quick lunch, there are baguettes and slices of pizza or quiche. Come here for afternoon tea at 5pm and you can see Claude feed the crocodiles that swim up the estuary alongside the hotel. Note that credit cards are not accepted.

🅒 Daily 6am–7pm
🅦 B US$3, coffee and cake US$3

STELLA'S

200m (220 yards) past Pasatiempo
Tamarindo
Tel 506 653 0127
www.stella-cr.com

A 15-minute walk away from the beach and the middle of town is Stella's, a longstanding Tamarindo favorite. The open plan hacienda-style dining area focuses upon the eye-catching wood oven, and whitewashed walls are hung with folk art. Colonial-style furnishings complete the theme. A consistently good menu includes wood-oven pizzas, sashimi tuna, mahi mahi with a mango chili salsa, jumbo shrimp skewers, escargots and Middle Eastern platters of tabouleh, hummus and tzatziki served with pita (pitta). Reservations advised during high season.

🅒 Daily 11.30–10
🅦 L US$16, D US$22, Wine US$14
🚐 A shuttle service will pick you up and take you home

EATING

CENTRAL PACIFIC AND NICOYA

In beach resorts from Jacó to Dominical and the southern tip of the Nicoya Peninsula, carbo-rich surf and turf menus fuel two of the region's popular sporting pastimes—surfing and golf. By day, beach bars and restaurants serve up monumental American breakfasts, while by night you can choose from a cosmopolitan cuisine. At each of the beach towns, the setting is as varied as the food. You can dine beneath the stars with the sound of the waves, or before a large TV at an American-style sports bar, or survey the views from hillside restaurants.

PRICES AND SYMBOLS

The restaurants are listed alphabetically (excluding El, Le and La). The prices given are for a two-course lunch (L) and a three-course dinner (D) for one person, without drinks. The wine price is for the least expensive bottle.
For a key to the symbols ▷ 2.

DOMINICAL

SAN CLEMENTE RESTAURANT
On the main town road
Dominical
Tel 506 787 0055
The San Clemente Hotel and Restaurant is a Dominical landmark, the epicenter of expatriate life and a lifeline for brigades of surfers. Walls are festooned with broken surf boards and covered with sporting memorabilia. With a satellite TV showing sports events, pool table and lively banter, it positively throbs. Huge platters of spicy Tex Mex food are served, including burritos, fajitas and nachos, and on all-you-can-eat Taco Tuesday you can satisfy the hungriest appetite for less than a dollar.
🕒 Daily 7am–10pm
🍷 L US$10, D US$15, Wine US$15

JACÓ

PACIFIC BISTRO
75m (82 yards) north from Jacó's downtown bridge
Jacó
Tel 506 643 3771
Pacific Bistro is, arguably, one of the finest gastronomic experiences on the Pacific coast. Chef Kent Green produces an Eastern-inspired menu of chalkboard specials ranging from seared yellowfin tuna steaks to mahi mahi with sake. Each dish is a riot of tastes and textures, while the backdrop is lanterns and cobbled white stonework. The serene location, tucked

away from Jacó crowds is appealing.
🕒 Wed–Mon6pm–10pm
🍷 D US$20, Wine US$16

MANUEL ANTONIO

BARBA ROJA
At the southern end of the Quepos–Manuel Antonio road, before the top of the hill
Tel 506 777 0331
With glorious panoramas of Manuel Antonio, this is one of the area's most popular eateries, as much for the setting as for the daily menu, which specializes in seafood dishes. At 6pm, crowds flock here to pay tribute to the setting sun and enjoy the punchy fruit daíquiris and piña coladas. There are daily happy hours and home-made breakfasts and lunches.
🕒 Tue–Sun 10–10 (often open only for dinner in the low season)
🍷 B US$6, L US$12, D US$20, Wine US$16

MONO AZUL
Apdo 297
Manuel Antonio
Tel 506 777 2572
www.monoazul.com
At the Mono Azul Hotel at the northern end of the road to

Manuel Antonio National Park, the "Blue Monkey" terrace provides a wide, if predictable, menu of pizzas, pastas, salads, fish and meat dishes. Service is assured and the lunchtime *casados* are excellent value.
🕒 Daily 7am–10pm
🍷 B US$3, L US$8, D US$20, Wine US$14

SUNSPOT POOLSIDE BAR AND GRILL
Makanda-by-the-Sea
On the road to Hotel El Parador
www.makanda.com
This small and intimate open-air restaurant is the ultimate in romantic venues: a poolside terrace enveloped by jungle and lit at night by flickering candlelight. The varied lunch menu offers salads, sandwiches and quesadillas, while evening means more creative fare supported by a thoughtful wine list. Fresh-baked foccaccia with home-made herb butter starts off satisfying dinners that can include scallops with blackberry and balsamic reduction. Pizzas from a wood-fired oven are a specialty.
🕒 Daily 11–10
🍷 L US$18, D US$44, Wine US$24

MONTEZUMA

BAKERY CAFÉ
Opposite Librería Topsy
Montezuma
Tel 506 642 0458
This friendly bakery-café at the north end of the village, run by Costa Rican/Swiss couple Luis and Priska Rojas, is a perfect spot for a wake-up call. With a cluster of tables in a natural jungle garden, visited by cheeky monkeys, it combines tranquility with mostly vegetarian food. The café serves breakfast fare ranging from omelettes to *gallo pinto*. Lunches include vegetarian burgers and sandwiches. Credit cards are not accepted.
🕒 Daily 6–6
🍷 B US$5, L US$7.50

NECTAR BAR & RESTAURANT
Florblanca Resort
Playa Santa Teresa
Tel 506 640 0230
www.florblanca.com
At the far north end of Playa Santa Teresa, this beachfront hotel-restaurant could well be the finest on the Pacific coast of Costa Rica. Young Canadian chef Damien Geneau delivers skillfully prepared Pacific-Latin fusion fare served beneath the stars to the sounds of the ocean and hip ambient music to set the tone for a romantic evening. Sushi is served at the laid-back bar during the afternoon. The frequently changing menu is heavy on seafood, but also ranges to such temptations as Chinese five-spice marinated duck breast with caramelized red onion and butter-wilted spinach.
🕐 6.30am–3pm café only, 6pm–9pm main restaurant
🖐 L US$26, D US$35, Wine US$22

EL SANO BANANO
On the main town road
Montezuma
Tel 506 642 0638
www.elbanano.com
At the heart of Montezuma, breakfast and nighttime action pivots around the Healthy Banana restaurant, which serves satisfying meals with a vegetarian slant. Alongside heart of palm salads, lasagne and enchiladas, a daily chalkboard of specials has fish and meat dishes. An 7.30pm dinner accompanies the nightly DVD (free with dinner order) on a drop-down screen.
🕐 Daily 7am–10pm
🖐 B US$5, L US$12, D US$20, Wine US$24

PLAYA HERRADURA
ANFITEATRO SUNSET RESTAURANT
Hotel Villa Caletas
3km (2 miles) north of Playa Herradura
Tel 506 637 0505
The sublime mountaintop setting with staggering views over the Gulf of Nicoya are reason enough to dine at the Anfiteatro restaurant, adorned with gracious antiques and fine art pieces. New Age music lends to the serene mood. Fortunately, this supremely elegant restaurant with an outdoor terrace also delivers

the goods. Only the freshest ingredients go into the creative dishes, which might include a beef tenderloin carpaccio appetizer, and a main course of marlin with coconut milk and rum sauce. A month-long gastronomic festival is held in mid-summer.
🕐 Daily 7am–10pm
🖐 B US$10, L US$18, D US$36, Wine US$28

QUEPOS
CAFÉ MILAGRO
On the seafront at north end of town
Quepos
Tel 506 777 1707
www.cafemilagro.com
This smart café serves great coffee, breakfasts, light meals,

pastries and cakes, with books and newspapers also for sale. Snacks include delicious bagels, banana bread, brownies and sandwiches. Don't leave without trying the Skippy shake: chocolate ice cream blended with peanut butter. There's a tranquil garden patio at the rear.
🕐 Daily 6am–10pm
🖐 B US$5, L US$9

EL GRAN ESCAPE
Quepos Centro
Tel 506 777 0395
www.elgranescape.com
On the main seafront road, El Gran Escape is one of Quepos's long standing restaurants. A sportfishing theme prevails with the breezy open-plan dining area decorated with marlin sculptures and inflatable sharks. The menu features, not surprisingly, freshly caught fish and seafood with a Caribbean influence: succulent coconut shrimp, seared tuna, tamarind and red pepper snapper. For carnivores, there are 12oz steaks, and a Mexican selection that runs the gamut of burritos, fajitas and chimichangas. There is also a

sushi bar, with all-you-can-eat specials, and a candlelit Italian restaurant next door.
🕐 Wed–Mon 6am–11pm
🖐 L US$14, D US$20, Wine US$18

SÁMARA
LAS BRASAS
Costado de la Plaza del Deporte
Sámara Centro
Tel 506 656 0546
This confident Spanish restaurant, next to the soccer pitch, on the main street running up from the beach, is one of Sámara's most popular, smart eateries. Airy and spacious, with chunky wooden tables and chairs and, often, strolling musicians, it has a lively atmosphere. The house specials include gazpacho, paella, tortilla and for eight people minimum, with advance notice, a whole roasted suckling pig.
🕐 Mon–Sat 12–10
🖐 L US$12, D US$18, Wine US$17

PASTA AND PIZZA A GO GO
Hotel Giada
250m (275 yards) north of Guardia Rural
Sámara
Tel 506 656 0132
www.hotelgiada.net
Just a five-minute walk from the beach, the unpretentious restaurant of Hotel Giada specializes in monumental pizzas. An extensive choice of pasta dishes includes penne with gorgonzola and salmon, and linguine with a shrimp and vodka sauce. For a light lunch, palm heart, avocado and tuna salads and thick fresh fruit licuados (milk shakes) and fresh juices are served. There are streetside tables and more secluded dining to the rear.
🕐 Daily 12–3, 5–10
🖐 L US$8, D US$11, Wine US$14

EATING

SOUTHERN REGION

Owing to the remoteness of Golfito and the national parks and wildlife attractions of the southern region, the vast majority of visitors come here on all-inclusive packages arranged either direct with one of the many classy lodges or on tours with one of the agencies in San José. Consequently, meals tend to be taken on an all-inclusive basis. Most lodges provide a mix of homestyle Costa Rican cooking, while others introduce more international touches.

PRICES AND SYMBOLS

The restaurants are listed alphabetically (excluding El, Le and La). The prices given are for a two-course lunch (L) and a three-course dinner (D) for one person, without drinks. The wine price is for the least expensive bottle.
For a key to the symbols ▷ 2.

MATAPALO

BRISA AZUL

Ecolodge Lapa Rios
Matapalo
Tel 506 735 5130
www.laparios.com

One of the finest ecolodges in Costa Rica serves fine cuisine beneath a soaring thatched *palenque*. The menu changes daily and includes fish, meat and vegetarian dishes. Starters include *ayote* soup (beans with pork loin chunks) and red peppers stuffed with Turrialba cheese. For main courses try the house special, *Osa Bouillabaisse*. Desserts include a traditional *tres leches* and the Drunken Watermelon. There is an excellent wine list featuring Chilean and Uruguayan wines.
⏰ Daily 6.30am–10pm
🍽 L US$31, D US$44, Wine US$21

PARQUE NACIONAL PIEDRAS BLANCAS

ESQUINAS RAINFOREST LODGE

Parque Nacional Piedras Blancas
Tel 506 775 0901
www.esquinaslodge.com

The wildly beautiful Esquinas Lodge, surrounded by Piedras Blancas National Park, is one of the Osa Peninsula's most magical jungle retreats. The restaurant has a stunning setting with views of the jungle and tropical gardens. The menu includes seafood caught daily in the Golfo Dulce, and organic fruit and vegetables.
⏰ Daily 7am–9pm
🍽 L US$29, D US$38, Wine US$19

PUERTO JIMÉNEZ

AGUA LUNA

50m (55 yards) north of the pier
Puerto Jiménez
Tel 506 735 5719
Dining options in Puerto Jiménez are not extensive, but the lively Agua Luna overlooking the bay is the best–and most expensive–restaurant in town. Appealing for its simplicity, with linen tablecloths and tiled flooring, the traditional Cost Rican fare includes daily fish and seafood specials, with an emphasis on freshness rather than culinary wizardry.
⏰ Daily 9am–10pm
🍽 L US$25, D US$32, Wine US$15

CAROLINA'S

Main street
Puerto Jiménez
Tel 506 735 5185
Right in the middle of town, Carolina's serves decent dishes and is recommended for its simple fish and seafood and as a place to find out about tours with Escondido Trex at the rear of the restaurant. For a no-frills lunch, the fish and chicken *casados* are hard to beat, and with plenty of visitors it also makes for a lively hang-out.
⏰ Daily 7am–10pm
🍽 L US$4, D US$12, Wine US$15

SAN ISIDRO DE EL GENERAL

RANCHO LA BOTIJA

San Isidro de El General
Tel 506 770 2146
www.rancholabotija.com
The road to San Gerardo de Rivas, 6km (4 miles) east of

San Isidro, passes Rancho La Botija, a cattle and coffee estate. Its restaurant is set

around a central *trapiche* or sugar mill, with a menu that includes tasty dishes at good prices. Service is friendly.
⏰ Tue–Sun 9–5 for non-guests, unless a reservation has been made for dinner
🍽 L US$12, D US$24, Wine US$16

SAN VITO

HOTEL EL CEIBO

150m (165 yards) east of Parque Central
San Vito
Tel 506 773 3025
On a quiet street, heading east from the middle of town, the spruce Hotel El Ceibo is the best place for a meal in San Vito. Arcades and balconies give a charming feel. A range of traditional Italian cuisine is served, including fresh pasta with a variety of sauces, fish and seafood as well as robust meat dishes.
⏰ Daily 7am–10pm
🍽 L US$10, D US$20, Wine US$14

LILIANA

100m (110 yards) from the plaza
San Vito
Tel 506 773 3080
Right in the middle of town, Liliana is true to the Italian heritage of San Vito, and comes highly recommended for its upbeat vibe and comprehensive menu, which extends to 20 classic Italian dishes. Plentiful portions of homemade pasta, pizza, fish and meat dishes are served with Italian wines.
⏰ Daily 10–10
🍽 L US$8, D US$18, Wine US$18

THE CARIBBEAN LOWLANDS

Doused in spices and seasonings, some of Costa Rica's tastiest cuisine is served in the Afro-Caribbean heartlands of Puerto Viejo and Cahuita. In bright clapboard houses and beachside shacks, homestyle cooking takes the form of piquant fish and meat dishes, with Creole sauces and served with fragrant coconut rice, salads and fried plantains. More internationally inspired dishes can also be found in an increasing number of smarter eateries, but regardless of the cuisine or decor, an infectious laid-back Caribbean style prevails. On the northern Caribbean side, most trips arranged from San José to Tortuguero involve staying at all-inclusive lodges where three rather unimaginative meals a day are served, generally on a buffet-style basis.

PRICES AND SYMBOLS

The restaurants are listed alphabetically (excluding El, Le and La). The prices given are for a two-course lunch (L) and a three-course dinner (D) for one person, without drinks. The wine price is for the least expensive bottle.
For a key to the symbols ▷ 2.

CAHUITA

CASA CREOLE
Hotel Magellan Inn
Playa Negra
Tel 506 755 0035
Attached to the intimate Magellan Inn, this small, unpretentious restaurant occupies a terrace romantically lit at night with candles. Chef Teri Newton uses imagination in melding local ingredients with spicy French Creole flavors. Dishes are artfully presented. The fare includes pâté maison, shrimp martiniquaise, and lobster with corn and ginger vanilla sauce, perhaps followed by tarte tatin or profiteroles. The repertoire of potent cocktails includes a commendable rum-based Rasta's Revenge.
🕐 Daily 6–9
🍷 D US$24, Wine US$20

CHA CHA CHA
Main town road, 100m (110 yards) south from the police station
Cahuita
Tel 506 755 0476
Arguably the finest cooking in Cahuita is served in a refreshingly chic setting one block from the seafront, with fairy lights and flowers set against the crisp white table linen of an open-air dining room. The menu is as varied as it is long, with fusion, Thai, Caribbean and Indian dishes incorporating local ingredients and fresh seafood. Many

people come especially from Puerto Viejo to dine at this small restaurant, so reservations are recommended.
🕐 Tue–Sun 5.30–10
🍷 D US$18, Wine US$15

MISS EDITH'S
75m (82 yards) east of police station
Cahuita
Tel 506 755 0248
Miss Edith has been a legend in Cahuita since she began serving hearty portions of tasty home cooking from the front porch of her house. While Edith, having established the restaurant, now shares the reins with her sisters and daughters, Miss Edith's remains Cahuita's most popular choice for Caribbean and vegetarian food. You should bring your own bottle and be warned that the service is infamously slow. Credit cards are not accepted and reservations are required.
🕐 Mon–Sat 8am–10pm, Sun 12–10
🍷 L US$9, D US$15, no wine served

MANZANILLO

RESTAURANTE MAXI
At the end of the road in Manzanillo
Tel 506 759 9086
Hit this upstairs open-air beachfront bar-restaurant in its groove and you'll have to squeeze shoulder to shoulder through the party crowd that flocks here on weekends and holidays. The vibe is funky and unpretentious, with bare-bones furnishings and Bob Marley's reggae riffs the predominant sound. The menu is heavy on seafood, such as roast red snapper and bargain-priced lobster. Meals are sometimes served on the beach when the crowd overflows the restaurant. Alas, service can be slow and indifferent. Avoid the downstairs soda, which lacks all ambience and draws flies. Credit cards are not accepted.
🕐 Daily 11.30–10
🍷 L US$8, D US$16, no wine served

PLAYA COCLES

RESTAURANTE MEDITERRANEO
Totem Hotel Resort, Playa Cocles
Tel 506 750 0758
www.totemsite.com
New in 2006, this lovely two-story beachfront restaurant exudes a Mediterranean feel. Italian chef Nicolo Baretti is a wizard in the kitchen. Everything is made on site, including the delicious Romagnola *piadina* flatbread and pastas, which take up a good part of the menu. The spinach and riccota cheese ravioli is delicious. Fresh seafoods are a highlight, and there's an oyster bar by day. Pizzas are fired in a traditional oven. Desserts include home-made tropical fruit ice creams and, for a little more decadence, a divine tiramisu. A robust wine list includes a large selection of Italian wines.
🕐 Daily 7am–10pm
🍷 B US$8, L US$12, D US$20, Wine US$16

LA PECORA NEGRA
3km (2 miles) south of Puerto Viejo
Playa Cocles
Tel 506 750 0490
The unpretentious exterior of this Mediterranean restaurant, on the road to Manzanillo, belies its stellar cuisine. The flamboyant character of the Italian chef/owner comes through in each dish. The fresh pasta and pizzas are superb and the daily specials include an inspired selection of fresh fish, seafood and meat dishes, cooked with Italian pizzazz. With prices that are a steal by international standards, and attentive service, La Pecora Negra are not accepted. Credit cards are not accepted.
🕐 Tue–Sun 5.30pm–12; erratic opening hours in the low season, call ahead
🍷 D US$22, Wine US$18

EATING

PUERTO LIMÓN

BLACK STAR LINE
Avenida 5, Calle 6
Tel 506 798 1948
One of the most popular places in town, the Black Star Line restaurant is housed in a rickety wooden building formerly the headquarters of the Black Star Line Steamship Company. It is casual and welcoming, drawing the local Afro-Caribbean community for *casados* (set lunches) of local *comida típica*, such as steamed fish in coconut milk, or goat in a piquant pepper sauce, served with rice, beans and fried plantains. The building still serves as a social center, with occasional live music and dancing. Credit cards are not accepted.
🕐 Mon–Sat 7.30am–10pm, Sun 11–5
🍴 L US$5, D US$10, no wine served

PUERTO VIEJO

AMIMODO
100m (110 yards) from Bambú disco on the road to Manzanillo
Puerto Viejo
Tel 506 750 0257
Within walking distance of Puerto Viejo, stylish Amimodo has been usurped by La Pecora Negra as the top Italian restaurant on the Caribbean. Still, the classic northern Italian menu offers great fresh pasta, including the house special, ravioli stuffed with lobster, and fish, and meat dishes such as beef in apple and plum sauce. Run by an ebullient Italian family, Amimodo's is intimate, with candlelit tables, and entertaining, with an open kitchen and strumming guitarists passing through.
🕐 Thu–Tue noon–11
🍴 L US$14, D US$20, Wine US$17

CAFÉ RICO
50m (55 yards) south of Cabinas Casa Verde, on the northeast side of town
Tel 506 750 0510
Run with savvy aplomb by Roger, a friendly Englishman, this laid-back café is *the* place to breakfast in town. A sand floor, thatch roof and rough-hewn tables and chairs add to the amiably casual setting. Hearty breakfasts include granola with fruit and yogurt, blackberry pancakes, great omelettes and *huevos rancheros*, all at bargain prices. The lunch menu is heavy on scrambles and sandwiches made with delicious whole-wheat bread, and the baked desserts are scrumptious. Have your laundry washed here and you'll get free coffee or tea. Credit cards are not accepted.
🕐 Mon–Sat 5.30am–9pm
🍴 B US$5, L US$10, no wine served

CAFÉ VIEJO
75m (82 yards) from ATEC
Puerto Viejo
Tel 506 750 0817
Right in the middle of town, this smart Italian restaurant serves homemade pasta, large wood-oven pizzas, fish, seafood and beef dishes. The open-plan design doesn't feel

Caribbean, but the atmosphere is relaxed. The food, while a little overpriced, is very good, the presentation artful and the portions generous. Main course dishes include red snapper with capers, tomato and anchovies, and ravioli stuffed with lobster. The vegetarian offerings are limited, but there is a fine antipasti platter. The bar area is a good place for an early evening drink, with great people-watching.
🕐 Wed–Mon 6pm–12
🍴 D US$17

CHILE ROJO
100m (110 yards) east of ATEC
Apt 17-7304
Puerto Viejo
Tel 506 750 0025
On Puerto Viejo's main street, this tiny, German-run restaurant is usually jam packed with lovers of Asian and Middle Eastern food. A list of chalkboard specials complements the lunch and dinner menu, which satisfies all tastes and budgets. With bamboo roofing, clusters of wooden tables and just a few decorative tokens to the theme, the food, served with expeditious grace, is the star. Appetizers include skewers of chicken satay, served with coconut rice and peanut sauce, and for main courses there is tuna seared with black bean sauce, sushi, Thai chicken curry and pita (pitta) stuffed with falafel. Credit cards are not accepted.
🕐 Tue–Sun 2–10
🍴 L US$11, D US$18, Wine by the glass US$2

PAN PAY CAFÉ
100m (110 yards) south from the bus stop, overlooking the beach
Puerto Viejo
Tel 506 750 0081
South of town, the Pan Pay is the most popular breakfast stop in town, drawing hungry people with its buttery croissants, baguettes, cakes and pastries. With a pervading Spanish theme, a medley of American and Tico breakfasts is served together with freshly baked baguettes topped with tomato and drizzled with olive oil. Inside, the stirring flamenco music, book exchange and notice board keep the atmosphere lively, while outside tables overlooking the sea are more relaxed. With excellent prices and just a stone's throw from the bus stop, it is a convenient place to wait for an onward connection. Credit cards are not accepted.
🕐 Thu–Tue 7am–6pm
🍴 B US$4

TORTUGUERO

MISS JUNIE'S RESTAURANT
Tortuguero Village, next to the Natural History Museum
Tel 506 709 8029
In the heart of Tortuguero, Miss Junie's makes a refreshing change from the often bland and mass-produced lodge buffets. The eponymous hostess is renowned in the area for her cheap, abundant and satisfying platters of tasty Caribbean cooking, ranging from jerk chicken to fresh fish in a spicy sauce concoction, served with mounds of rice and beans and fried plantains. Normally, there are just a few meat and fish dishes to choose from—it is rare to find a vegetarian choice, but with advance notice, a special dish can usually be prepared. Credit cards are not accepted.
🕐 Daily 7–2, 6–9
🍴 L US$10, D US$14, Wine US$15

EATING

STAYING IN COSTA RICA

From sumptuous hotels to basic cabins, accommodation options cover all styles and budgets. It is hardly surprising that in Costa Rica the variety and diversity is spectacular. Eccentric and purist designs perched on hillsides providing respite for mind and body; quiet hotels tucked away in secluded private reserves; beachfront properties amid nonstop action; and glorious romantic hideaways: the choice is yours.

Accommodations in Costa Rica range from trendy resorts and luxurious jungle lodges to basic cabins

HOTELS

The high season runs from December to April, with the two weeks around Christmas and the New Year constituting an extra-high high season. Easter week (*Semana Santa* or Holy Week) is a major holiday period in Costa Rica and everything at the beach fills up fast; if you're planning a trip at this time, make reservations early. Outside of these months it is the green season. Discounts at this time are common and can be as much as 50 percent. They vary greatly according to location and some places prefer to close for the low season.

The good hotels fill up in the high season (and some in the green season as well) and reservations are advisable. Mid- and upper-range hotels may require a deposit. Lower budget hotels will also accept reservations and while you may not be able to secure the room, do what you can to check the reservation is being taken seriously. Hotels in almost every price range (except the lowest) offer confirmed reservations via websites and email in addition to telephone. If you plan to arrive late in the evening, let the hotel know.

Service levels vary considerably in Costa Rican hotels; price can be a good indicator of standards.

A few chains have several hotels in the country: Best Western has six hotels in the main tourist areas, and the Barcelo group has half a dozen all-inclusive resorts open and more pending. Marriot and Melia are two other chains with properties distributed throughout the country. Several hotels have grouped together into marketing consortia. One of particular note is the Small Distinctive Hotels of Costa Rica (tel 506 258 0150, www.distinctivehotels.com), with six hotels, including gorgeous Florablanca in Santa Theresa and the charming Grano de Oro in San José, that are small, individual and provide excellent service.

COSTS

Hotels are subject to a 16 percent tax (13.39 sales and 3 percent room tax). Many hotels don't include this tax in the quoted price; check whether it is included in the price you are given. Tax is included in the prices in this guide, unless stated otherwise. Some mid-range hotels and above allow children under 12 to stay in their parents room for free or at a lower rate. Ask when making reservations. Many hotels charge an additional 5–15 percent for using a credit card.

BED-AND-BREAKFAST

Bed-and-breakfast has made relatively little impact in Costa Rica. Those you may find tend to operate in the mid- to high price range.

YOUTH HOSTELS

Hostelling International, the international arm of the Youth Hostel Association, represents 4 hostels in Costa Rica. Visit www.hihostels.com for details. You'll have to be a member of the YHA to take advantage of the low prices. There are several dozen additional hostels unaffiliated with YHA.

HOME STAYS

Cooprena (www.turismoruralcr.com), a national ecotourism cooperative, organizes courses and represents lodges in rural communities.

NATURE LODGES

Nature lodges have become hugely successful in recent years. Often located in remote areas in or close to national parks and reserves, they may take time and effort to reach: a multi-day stay is preferable. Many offer outdoor activities and good dining to non-guests but a lot of the lodges are too remote to be within easy reach.

STAYING

SAN JOSÉ

Hotels in the capital range in size and style from the standard chains of Holiday Inn and Best Western to stylish affairs that reveal the history of a building or district. Lower down the price ladder there are many good choices and you can find hotels of all ranges within the central district of the city. However, the city is small enough to make some of the memorable hotels along and off Paseo Colón to the west, and northwest of the city in Barrios Amón and Otoya accessible. Budget-conscious visitors will find much accommodation around the Mercado Central area and the infamous Coca-Cola Bus Terminal, where safety can be a problem. While security has been increased, visitors staying in these areas should take appropriate precautions.

FLEUR DE LYS
Calle 13, Avenida 2–6
Tel 506 223 1206
www.hotelfleurdelys.com
One block south of Plaza de la Democracía, this restored Victorian mansion is absolutely delightful, with elegant rooms named after native Costa Rican flowers. Each room has a private bathroom, hair-dryer, telephone and cable TV. A French restaurant and a bar will mean the only reason you have to leave the hotel is to visit the Museo Nacional, one block away. There's a tour desk with lots of information. The terrace bar is the perfect place to have a cocktail before relaxing on the porch.
🛏 US$82 room, US$97–135 suites, including breakfast
🛏 31
🅿

GRAN HOTEL COSTA RICA
Avenida 2, Calle Central
Tel 506 221 4000
www.granhotelcostarica.com

This landmark hotel, in the heart of the city on Plaza de la Cultura, was the first purpose-built hotel in Costa Rica. Despite having been remodeled in 2006, the hotel is steeped in history, having hosted a roll call of icons from John F. Kennedy in 1963 to John Wayne. The refurbished rooms are equipped with cable TV, fan and safety deposit box, and there is a laundry and room service. In the lobby, a dining room has replaced the casino, which has been moved to a lower level. The downsized and fenced-in al fresco Café 1930 (▷ 182) remains the best people-watching spot in town.
🛏 US$89
🛏 105, non-smoking available

GRANO DE ORO
Calle 30, Avenida 2–4
Tel 506 255 3322
www.hotelgranodeoro.com

Two blocks south of Paseo Colón, close to Parque Sabana, this lavish 20th-century mansion offers unadulterated luxury and a warm welcome. The wrought-iron beds set off rooms with cable TV, Jacuzzi or sundeck spa, mini bar and ceiling fan. An exciting new addition, opened in 2007, includes an elegant two-tier restaurant that is now the city's most dramatic place to dine (▷ 183). There is also a spa.
🛏 US$90–125 rooms, US$145–250 suites, plus tax, breakfast included
🛏 37 rooms, 3 suites
🅿

HEMINGWAY INN
Calle 9, Avenida 9
Tel 506 221 1807
www.hemingwayinn.com
In the peaceful Amón district, just a 10-minute walk from Plaza de la Cultura, it's no surprise that this colonial house is filled with references to the author. Managed by Canadian Eric Robinson the Hemingway Inn is "Proudly not a Holiday Inn." Each room is simply decorated with cable TV, fans and safety deposit boxes. Extras include airport pick-up taxi voucher, orthopaedic beds, free local calls, small Jacuzzi on the courtyard patio, free internet access, laundry and free luggage storage. Discounts are available for longer stays.
🛏 US$52–62, plus tax, breakfast included.
🛏 17
🅿 US$8 per day

HOTEL AMÓN PLAZA
Avenida 11, Calle 3
Tel 506 257 0191
www.hotelamonplaza.com
Minimalists will retreat from this large, anonymous hotel in the stylish Amón district, designed for the business visitor. The ostentatious lobby sets the tone, lined with marble, crammed with antique furnishings and illuminated by chandeliers. Rooms have internet access, satellite TV, housekeeping, air-conditioning and free local calls. There is a lively 24-hour bar, a café-restaurant, a casino, ballroom and a spa with sauna, Jacuzzi and gym.
🛏 US$120
🛏 80
🅾 📺
🅿

HOTEL BRITANNIA
Avenida 11, Calle 3
Tel 506 223 6667 (US: 1-800-263-2618)
www.hotelbritanniacostarica.com
The landmark Hotel Britannia in colonial Barrio Amón,

STAYING

exudes old-fashioned style. The renovated, pastel-pink, plantation-style mansion dates back to the coffee boom and has retained its character while providing first-class service. A wrought-iron gateway leads to

a tiled porch lined with pillars and, inside, the courtyard reception continues downstairs to the wine cellar, now a rather expensive restaurant. Conservative rooms, in both the original building and a more contemporary new wing, offer all the expected comforts with ceiling fans and large tiled bathrooms.

🏨 US$76–105, plus tax, breakfast included

ℹ️ 23

HOTEL CASTILLO
Avenida 9, Calle 9, behind INS
Tel 506 221 5141
www.hotelcastillo.biz
This 19th-century mansion in Barrio Amón has been restored to offer good-value

accommodations. Each room is different, but all appeal with crisp decor, comfortable beds, cable TVs and bathrooms. Rooms 6, 7 and 8 have fine views across the city and are often reserved in advance. Security is good and discounts are available for longer stays.

🏨 US$54–89, plus tax including buffet breakfast

ℹ️ 12 rooms, 10 villas, 1 suite

🅢
🅟

HOTEL DON CARLOS
Calle 9, Avenida 7–9
Tel 506 221 6707
www.doncarloshotel.com
The family-run Hotel Don Carlos in Barrio Amón, combines colonial character, great facilities and a sense of style. Spacious, spotless rooms each have a bath, cable TV and air-conditioning or fan. The hotel has a collection of artworks; the highlight is a mural of San José in the 1900s by Mario Arroyabe. Staff are friendly and there is information on tours in the area, as well as internet and free local calls. The Annemarie Boutique is one of San José's best souvenir shops.

🏨 US$70–80, tropical breakfast included

ℹ️ 36

🅢
🅟

HOTEL PARQUE DEL LAGO
Paseo Colón, Calles 40/42
Tel 506 257 8787
www.parquedellago.com
This once staid business hotel close to Parque Sabana has emerged from a total remake as one of the city's most sophisticated options. The spacious rooms have divinely comfortable mattresses, cable TV, minibar, coffee-makers, and other accouterments. The restaurant and bar is a chic retreat serving consistently satisfying dishes. Other facilities include a spa, internet room, and business rooms.

🏨 US$95–150

ℹ️ 30

🅟

HOTEL PRESIDENTE
Avenida Central, Calle 7
Tel 506 222 3022
www.hotel-presidente.com
Hotel Presidente is one block from Plaza de la Cultura. Rooms have parquet floors, cable TV, telephone, air-conditioning and safe box. Breakfast is served in the popular News café (▷ 183), which sells international newspapers. There is also a sauna and Jacuzzi, travel agency, casino and airport pick-up.

🏨 US$80–299, plus tax, breakfast included

ℹ️ 100 rooms

🅢
🅟

RITMO DEL CARIBE
Paseo Colón and Calle 32, 700m (765 yards) from Coca-Cola bus terminal
Tel 506 256 1636
www.ritmo-del-caribe.com
The eye-catching yellow and blue Ritmo del Caribe, opposite KFC half way along Paseo Colón, is run by a German/Tica couple. Rooms vary, but most are equipped with cable TV and fans, and all but one have a private bath. A small garden has sun loungers. Pick-up from the airport can be organized in advance and there is free internet access and free luggage store. Recommended for backpackers and groups.

🏨 US$25–42, plus tax, buffet breakfast included

ℹ️ 14

ROSA DEL PASEO
Paseo Colón, Calle 28–30
In front of INA
Tel 506 257 3225
http://rosadelpaseo.com
A 10-minute walk from Parque Sabana, this colonial house has a striking bronze and cream facade. A refurbishment of the 104-year-old building extended the hotel to include a small courtyard. Rooms with high ceilings, floorboards, bathrooms and modern comforts are neatly finished, although the Victorian style may be too conservative for some. The master suite has a Jacuzzi and terrace balcony.

🏨 US$75–120, tropical breakfast included

ℹ️ 19

🅟

SANTO TOMAS
Avenida 7, Calles 3–5
Tel 506 255 0448
www.hotelsantotomas.com
Splendidly situated a stone's throw from the Jade Museum, this is a gracefully converted mansion. Rooms vary in size, but all retain period features, including glossy colonial tile or hardwood floors. Cable TV and direct-dial phones are standard. A garden has a small swimming pool with Jacuzzi and cascade, and the colonial-themed Restaurant El Oasis is popular with discerning patrons.

🏨 US$70–104, tropical breakfast included

ℹ️ 20

STAYING

CENTRAL HIGHLANDS

Former coffee *fincas*, architect-designed Gaudíesque confections and Swiss-style lodges with views of coffee plantations provide some atmospheric places to stay in the Central Highlands. In the satellite towns of Alajuela, Heredia and Cartago, you can find rooms for all budgets in bed-and-breakfasts and converted inns which add higher levels of comfort and service. Outside the towns, the smarter lodges are in spectacular, but remote, settings.

ALAJUELA

XANDARI RESORT AND SPA
5km (3 miles) north of Alajuela
Tel 506 443 2020
In the US, toll free 1-800/686-7879
www.xandari.com

With views over the Central Valley, this former coffee *finca*, (ranch) created by Californian architect Sherrill Broudy, is one of Costa Rica's most impressive hotels. The dramatic design is quite stunning and is graced by stained-glass windows, wave-form hardwood ceilings, and artpieces by Sherrill's wife, Charlene. Each of the private villas has a balcony and bathroom. The restaurant uses organic produce from local farmers and fishermen, and the hotel's own plantation. You can explore trails leading to natural waterfalls, dip in the pool or enjoy a spa treatment in the full-service Spa Village, perhaps the finest spa in the highlands.
🏨 US$195–275, plus tax, breakfast included
🛏 22 villas
🏊 Outdoor
🅿

HEREDIA

BOUGAINVILLEA
Santo Tomás de Santo Domingo
9km (6 miles) east of Heredia
Tel 506 244 1414
US toll free 866/880-5441
www.bougainvillea.com
This efficiently run, Dutch-owned hotel has consistently ranked in the top tier of highland hotels. Rooms at the Bougainvillea, 10 minutes' drive out of San José, have a desk, cable TV, air-conditioning, a bathroom and a balcony looking out onto the Central Valley. There are tennis courts, gardens attracting hummingbirds and butterflies and a free shuttle service to San José.
🏨 US$80, plus tax, breakfast included
🛏 81, plus 2 for disabled visitors
🏊 Outdoor

FINCA ROSA BLANCA
1.5km (1 mile) from Santa Bárbara
Heredia
Tel 506 269 9392
www.finca-rblanca.co.cr
This exciting hotel on a bluff overlooking the Central Valley, is capped by the Rosa Blanca suite: a turret with a four-poster bed and floor-to-ceiling windows. Converted from a family home, and surrounded by coffee fields, the hotel is an architectural delight. Rooms are individually themed; most have murals and mosaic-lined tubs. The garden supplies organic produce.
🏨 US$185–280, plus tax, breakfast included
🛏 10 suites
🏊 Outdoor

PEACE LODGE
Vara Blanca
Tel 506 225 0643
www.waterfallgardens.com
Overlooking a lush valley and the nature-based Waterfalls Garden theme park, this deluxe hotel is a one-of-a-kind with its fanciful design. Mammoth-size rooms combine natural stone and timbers to bring nature indoors, notably in the whimsical bathrooms that replicate grottos. Suites have indoor and outdoor Jacuzzis, and all rooms have fireplaces.
🏨 US$195–335
🛏 25
🅿

OROSÍ VALLEY

OROSÍ LODGE
Orosí
Tel 506 533 3578
www.orosilodge.com
The Orosí Lodge is one hour east of San José. Rooms have balconies looking towards Irazú Volcano, bath and a kitchenette. Owners Andreas and Cornelia provide mountain bikes, kayaks and horses for rent, and internet. There are hot springs next door (▷ 185).
🏨 US$48, plus tax
🛏 7
🅿

VOLCANO POÁS

POÁS VOLCANO LODGE
PO Box 1935–3000
Heredia
Tel 506 482 2194
www.poasvolcanolodge.com

High up in the valley, this lodge fuses stonework from the English owner's heritage with the openness of a ranch. and has good views of the volcano. Rooms are spacious and there is internet access and plenty of outdoor activities (▷ 143).
🏨 US$55–125, including breakfast
🛏 9
🚗 From Poasito take right turn toward Vara Blanca. After 6km (3.75 miles), a turnoff to the left is signposted. Sign on gate at El Cortijo farm where the road leads for 1km (0.6 mile) to the house

NORTHERN REGION

In an exhilarating region headlined by Arenal Volcano and Monteverde, many hotels and lodges in the area are experiences in their own right. Santa Elena and Fortuna provide budget bases for Monteverde and Arenal Volcano respectively, with basic cabins and more comfortable pensions. Arenal and Fortuna have a good selection of accommodation options for all different budgets, from lakeside inns, spas and watersport resorts, to rustic *cabinas*. The cheapest accommodation is in Fortuna. While many hotels have volcano views, eruptions usually cannot be seen from town and you will have to pay around US$25 to get to the north side of the volcano to see them. If you have a car, it's worth staying on Lake Arenal's north shore. In the green season many hotels offer discounts. In the mountains, a few hours south of the lake, a dirt road, punctuated by secluded lodges and hotels, leads to the Monteverde's cloud forest reserve.

PRICES AND SYMBOLS

Prices are for a double room for one night. Breakfast is not included unless noted otherwise. All the hotels listed accept credit cards unless otherwise stated. Note that rates vary widely throughout the year. For a key to the symbols ▷ 2.

ARENAL

ARENAL COUNTRY INN
Apt 678 2010
Arenal
Tel 506 479 9670
www.arenalcountryinn.com
With views of Arenal Volcano, this former working hacienda, set among tropical gardens, about a kilometer out of town, has been converted into an inn. The large, fully equipped *cabinas* each have a private bathroom, safety deposit box, flat screen TV, air-conditioning, minibar and private terrace. Breakfast is served in the breezy open-air dining room—once a cattle-holding pen—and you can rest by the large pool before heading out to explore. Facilities for disabled guests are good. The service is excellent and it's probably Fortuna's best inn.
🏨 US$95, including breakfast
🛏 20 bungalows
♿ 🏊 🅿
🗺 On the road to San Ramón, 1km (0.6 miles) before La Fortuna church

ARENAL KIORO
Between Fortuna and Lake Arenal
Tel 506 461 1700
www.hotelarenalkioro.com
Less than one kilometer east of Tabacón, this all-suite hotel, which opened in 2006, is the premier resort in the region; it has unrivaled proximity to the volcano and it is known for its all-round luxury. Occupying a ridgeline at the base of the unnervingly close volcano, the lavishly appointed Kioro is designed to maximize the viewing experience in every regard. The spacious junior suites have walls of glass, rattan furnishings, satellite TV, direct-dial telephones, safes, plus Jacuzzis for indulgent grandstand vistas, and the deluxe marble-clad bathrooms have his-and-hers showers and sinks. The airy and elegant restaurant, serving excellent fusion fare, also has a wall of glass, as do the adjoining bar and the games room and gym. Thermal waters heat twin swimming pools. A list of activities includes horseback riding, mountain biking, fishing and boat tours, but the sumptuous spa is reason enough never to leave the property.
🏨 US$270–300
🛏 53 rooms
🏊 Outdoor
🅿

ARENAL OBSERVATORY LODGE
Between Fortuna and Lake Arenal
Tel 506 692 2070
www.arenal-observatory.co.cr
On the northwest side of the volcano, 4km (2.5 miles) after El Tabacón, a signposted gravel road heads to the Arenal Observatory Lodge. Dating back to 1973, the observatory was once a research station for the Smithsonian Institute, but now has 40 rooms, most with views of the volcano. Lodgings vary from basic rooms, with shared bath, in La Casona farmhouse, to luxurious Smithsonian rooms with glass walls, tiled floors, separate dining areas and queen-size beds. The proximity of the volcano provides stunning views across the Río Agua Caliente valley and Lake Arenal.

🏨 US$90–137, plus tax, includes breakfast, and an early morning guided hike to Arenal Volcano (US$6)
🛏 40
🏊 Outdoor
🅿
🗺 Four-wheel-drive vehicle recommended, but not essential along the stretch of 9km (6 miles) leading to the Lodge (taxi-jeep from Fortuna US$12)

HOTEL LOS HÉROES (PEQUEÑA HELVECÍA)
Lake Arenal
Nuevo Arenal
Tel 506 692 8012
www.hotellosheroes.com
Some 30km (18 miles) from Fortuna, this Alpine-style château is a wonderful blend of Tico hospitality and Swiss patriotism. All the rooms have a private bathroom and views of the lake; some have a terrace. The main restaurant serves fondues and other Swiss classics and a new restaurant revolves through 360 degrees. Devotion to all things Swiss include a 60cm (23.4in) gauge railway with a

couple of diesel engines going up the hillside crossing two bridges and passing through a couple of tunnels for 2km/ 1.25 miles (US$3, three times a day), and a small yet beautiful private family chapel. Credit cards are not accepted.

🛏 US$55–65, including breakfast
🛈 12 rooms, 2 suites
🏊 Outdoor
🅿

LA MANSION MARINA AND CLUB
9km (6 miles) from Nuevo Arenal
Tel 506 692 8018
www.lamansionarenal.com
The romantic La Mansion overlooks Lake Arenal, providing split-level bungalows with different levels of luxury. All rooms have lake-view terraces with sweeping panoramas and come with a CD player (you can borrow discs from the hotel). The price includes luxury breakfast, with champagne, served in your room or in the terrace restaurant which specializes in European cuisine. Horses and canoes are available for guests to rent for a small charge. The impressive Royal Cottage has its own private infinity pool, Jacuzzi and gardens.

🛏 US$175–550 including breakfast
🛈 16 bungalows, 4 suites, 1 cottage
🏊 🏊 Outdoor
🅿
🚗 It is a 45-minute drive from La Fortuna to the Mansion Inn, passing El Tabacón hot springs, then the dam. A dirt road leads straight to the inn, about 9km (5 miles) before Nuevo Arenal

TABACÓN RESORT AND SPA
Tabacón
Tel 506 519 1900
Toll free in US tel 1-877 277 8291
www.tabacon.com
Some 12km (7 miles) from La Fortuna, Tabacón Resort Hotel is on most Arenal tourist agendas for its thermal mineral pools (▷ 78–81). Rooms are spacious, with air-conditioning, cable TV, hair-dryer and bathrobes to slink around in while gazing at the views of the volcano. After visiting the mineral pools (free entry for hotel guests) you can have dinner at the reasonably priced restaurant. The Iskandria Spa provides all manner of beauty and relaxation treatments. Note that

some tour operators won't book guests into this hotel due to its location in the potential path of a lava flow should Arenal experience a sudden major eruption.

🛏 US$175–290, plus tax, including buffet breakfast and free access to the mineral pools
🛈 95 rooms, 11 junior suites
🛎
🅿

LOST IGUANA RESORT
Nuevo Arenal
Tel 506 461 0122
www.lostiguanaresort.com
Heading across the Arenal dam, just past Tabacón, take a right turn onto the dirt road leading to the Arenal Hanging Bridges; you'll find the Lost Iguana along here. This new hotel, built on the side of a landscaped hill, has rooms and a deck designed for maximum views of the volcano. You can even watch Arenal from your bed. Each room and suite is fitted with satellite TV, phones and fans. Suites have whirlpool tubs on their decks and a spa is due to be added. There is also an international restaurant.

🛏 US$135–185
🛈 12 rooms, 8 suites, 2 villas
🛎
🏊

MONTEVERDE
MONTEVERDE LODGE
Monteverde
Tel 506257 0766
www.monteverdelodge.com

Climbing the hill from Santa Elena to Monteverde, a dirt road to the right leads to the Monteverde Lodge, owned by Costa Rica Expeditions. The spacious suites are rustically chic, and all have two double rooms and a private bathroom with solar-heated water. It's a graceful hotel, which impresses from the outside

and has a vast lobby complete with open fire and a dining room with excellent views. The environmental considerations extend to the solar-heated Jacuzzi, set in a glass atrium. Package deals are available, and children under 10 sharing a room go free.

🛏 US$94–125, plus tax
🛈 27
🅿

EL SAPO DORADO
Monteverde
Tel 506 645 5010
www.sapodorado.com
Coming along the gravel road from Santa Elena up to Monteverde, a steep road to the left arrives at the Golden Toad where Tico/US owners reflect the synthesis of Costa Rican and Quaker traditions. Secluded suites each have a private bath with hot water showers: choose from Sunset Suites, overlooking the Nicoya Peninsula, the newest and largest Fountain Suites, with fridge, or Classic Suites, which have an open fire for the cooler months. In the restaurant, vegetarian options merge with traditional dishes. The lodge has its own trail that skirts the Monteverde reserve.

🛏 US$112–122
🛈 30 suites
🅿

LA URUCA
OCCIDENTAL EL TUCANO RESORT AND THERMAL SPA
Aguas Zarcas
Tel 506 460 6000
Toll-free in the US tel 1-800/858-2258
www.occidental-hoteles.com
Just 45 minutes' drive from Arenal Volcano, and less than a mile from Ciudad Quesada, on the road to Aguas Zarcas, 8km (5 miles), is the luxurious El Tucano Resort and thermal spa. Hot mineral and sulfur pools provide various beauty treatments, with a background of tropical forest. There is a large pool, two Jacuzzis, sauna, mini golf, horseback riding and tennis. Each room has a bathroom, telephone, safety deposit box and satellite TV.

🛏 US$75–90 including breakfast
🛈 87
🏊 Outdoor
🅿

GUANACASTE

Since the opening of the international airport in Liberia, the beaches of northwest Guanacaste and surf towns like Tamarindo and Playas del Coco, have developed swiftly. Eccentric designs perch on the hillsides, quiet hotels nestle in private reserves, beachfront properties and glorious romantic hideaways descend in steps of luxury, comforts and services to the simplest, basic rooms. Working haciendas lying close to the less visited national parks of northwest Guanacaste provide all inclusive accommodations as well as offering nature and recreational activities.

PRICES AND SYMBOLS

Prices are for a double room for one night. Breakfast is not included unless noted otherwise. All the hotels listed accept credit cards unless otherwise stated. Note that rates vary widely throughout the year. For a key to the symbols ▷ 2.

PARQUE NACIONAL GUANACASTE

HACIENDA GUACHIPELÍN

Curubandé, 18km (12 miles) east of the Pan-American Highway and 8km (5 miles) west of the park ranger station
Tel 506 666 8075
www.guachipelin.com
This working cattle ranch at the base of the volcano has become one of Costa Rica's leading activity centers providing a back-to-nature experience. Former stables have been turned into comfortable albeit simply appointed rooms with ceiling fans and views. The open-air restaurant serves reasonably priced regional dishes, and a second restaurant draws the public for folkloric music and dance. With a swimming pool and activities that include horseback riding, canyoneering, white-water rafting, and a zipline tour, the hacienda provides an all-round vacation.
📷 US$67 standard, US$75 superior, US$119 junior suite
🛏 34
🍴 🏊 Outdoor
🅿

PLAYAS DEL COCO

FLOR DE ITABO

PO Box 32
Playas del Coco
Tel 506 670 0438 and 506 670 0292
www.flordeitabo.com
On the road leading to the town, 1km (0.6 miles) from Playas del Coco, this Italian-run hotel has accommodations ranging from standard and luxury rooms, to apartments,

bungalows and suites. All have private bathrooms, air-conditioning and cable TV, while deluxe rooms have kitchenettes and master suites have Jacuzzis. Seafood and steaks are served in the restaurant, and the ceramic-tiled pool has a swim-up bar. The hotel specializes in sportfishing and there's also a casino (open 7pm–2am). The hotel offers free transfers from Daniel Oduber Quirós airport in Liberia.
📷 Bungalow US$50, standard double US$85, deluxe suite US$135, apartments (sleeping 6) US$180
🍴 Rooms available 🏊 Outdoor
🅿

LA PUERTA DEL SOL

100m (110 yards) from the beach at the northern end of town
Playas del Coco
Tel 506 670 0195
www.lapuertadelsol.com
Hidden down a side road, there's a family feel to this Italian-run place. The suites all have a living room, bathroom, air-conditioning and fan, telephone and safe box. The pool can be used for free scuba try-outs. Enjoy good homemade pasta in the Italian restaurant.
📷 US$80
🛏 10
🍴 🏊 Outdoor 📺
🅿

PLAYA GRANDE

HOTEL BULA BULA

Playa Grande
Tel 506 653 0975
Near the southern end of the beach, beside the tiny dock for Tamarindo, this lively hotel is set in exquisite gardens with a small pool. Owners Walt and Todd run this place with loving care that extends to the decor and unusual touches, such as fresh-cut flower arrangements in rooms, and batik sarongs provided for around the pool. The restaurant is the finest around, and the bar draws local expatriates. Guests get free use of the hotel's beach club, as

well as free water-taxi rides to Tamarindo.
📷 US$105
🛏 10
🍴 🏊 Outdoor

HOTEL LAS TORTUGAS

Playa Grande
Tel 506 653 0423
www.cool.co.cr/usr/turtles
Close to the turtle sanctuary of Playa Grande, this ecologically conscious hotel has been constructed by owner Louis Wilson to prevent light reaching the beach and affecting nesting turtles. Rooms either have air-conditioning or have been designed to benefit from cross ventilation. The open-air restaurant serves international and local dishes from US$10.
📷 US$50–120
🛏 10
🍴 🏊 Outdoor
🅿

PLAYA HERMOSA

VILLA DEL SUEÑO

The first beach turnoff, on the main road to Playa Hermosa
Tel 506 672 0026
www.villadelsueno.com
Off the main road in Playa Hermosa, the resort is a thoughtfully designed complex of villas amid a riot of tropical vegetation. Popular with families and couples, rooms range from standard and luxury doubles to apartments sleeping up to four people, all with bathrooms and ceiling fans. Dinner is often accompanied by live music. Other amenities include a freshwater pool, tiki-hut-style bar and boutique.
📷 Room US$73, apartment US$130
🛏 15
🍴 🏊 Outdoor
🅿

PLAYA LANGOSTA

CALA LUNA

Playa Langosta
Tel 506 653 0214
www.calaluna.com
The Cala Luna, in a peaceful spot near Playa Langosta, 10

minutes' drive south of the airport, offers unabashed luxury. Each of the villas has a pool, cable TV, telephone, CD player and kitchen. Yoga classes are available by appointment. The Cala Moresca restaurant serves regional and Italian dishes and American breakfasts.

🛏 Rooms US$185 including breakfast, villas from US$470 excluding breakfast
ⓘ 20 rooms, 21 villas
♿ 🏊 Outdoor
🅿

SUEÑO DEL MAR
Playa Langosta
Tel 506 653 0284
www.sueno-del-mar.com
Among tropical vegetation, right on Playa Langosta, this bed-and-breakfast is one of the most charming hotels in Costa Rica. With a rugged Robinson Crusoe setting, the adobe design combines colonialism with contemporary comforts. Each room is decorated with frescoes. Balinese-style bathrooms and four-poster beds add to the air of romance.

🛏 US$195–235, plus taxes, breakfast included
ⓘ 4 rooms, 1 casita
♿ 🏊 Outdoor
🅿

TAMARINDO

BEST WESTERN TAMARINDO VISTA VILLAS
At the northern entrance to town
Tel 506 653 0114
www.tamarindovistavillas.com
At the north side of Tamarindo, this hillside hotel overlooking the ocean has excellent facilities, including a pool with swim-up bar, a Jacuzzi and the Monkey bar-restaurant, a surfer hang-out. The feel is youthful and with bicycles, surf boards and golf clubs for rent, it is a sociable base. The 16 villas all have living rooms and kitchens. Rooms and villas have air-conditioning and TV.

🛏 Double US$159, villa sleeping up to 8 people US$209
ⓘ 17 villas, 12 rooms
♿ 🏊 Outdoor
🅿

CAPITÁN SUIZO
South end of Tamarindo town towards Playa Langosta
Tel 506 653 0075
www.hotelcapitansuizo.com

This Swiss-run beachfront hotel, toward Playa Langosto south of Tamarindo, has stylish rooms in thatched bungalows. Each has a mezzanine sleeping area and is neutrally decorated with a fridge, patio, or a balcony. The restaurant overlooks gardens visited by howler monkeys; paths lead to the pool. The service is faultless.

🛏 US$165, US$185 with air-conditioning, bungalows US$225–360
ⓘ 22 rooms, 8 bungalows
♿ 🏊 Outdoor
🅿

LA COLINA APARTHOTEL
200m (220 yards) east of the main road
Tamarindo
Tel 506 653 0303
www.la-colina.com
Surveying Tamarindo and with fine sea views, La Colina is self-catering accommodation on a grand scale. Everything is big: the bed, the walk-in fridge, the pool. All suites have air-conditioning, fans, telephone, TV and kitchens. For glorious sunsets, hammocks swing below pergolas.

🛏 Apartment suite for 2 US$125, penthouse sleeping up to 4 US$280
ⓘ 15 suites, 3 penthouses
♿ 🏊 Outdoor
🅿

EL JARDIN DEL EDEN
400m (440 yards) uphill from main road
Tamarindo
Tel 506 653 0137
www.jardindeleden.com
Standing on a hill outside the main part of town, this stylish hotel is run by French owner Nicolas Segonne. The villas and rooms are set in gardens. Each room is designed with west-facing windows for views of Tamarindo's sunsets. Sophisticated contemporary furnishings play on regional themes—Tunisia, Japan, Mexico or Bali—while the African-themed rooms have de rigueur zebra skins and leopard-print fabrics, and even huge elephant heads over the beds. The restaurant, while expensive, is one of the best in town, and is the place to come for fine fusion cuisine enjoyed beneath a soaring thatch *palenque* overlooking the floodlit, twin-tier pool. A private path leads directly to the beach.

🛏 US$125, plus tax, breakfast included
ⓘ 2 apartments, 34 rooms
♿ 🏊 Outdoor
🅿

LA LAGUNA DEL COCODRILO
Opposite Tamarindo Villas Tamarindo
Tel 506 653 0255
www.lalagunadelcocodrilo.com
Run by French couple Josette and Claude, this beachside hotel is at the north end of town. Each bright room has a blue-tiled bathroom. Ground level rooms have air-conditioning and terraces with sea views. A path leads to the beach. At 5pm, Claude feeds the crocodiles that swim in the estuary alongside the hotel's garden. For breakfast, the best bakery in town is next door.

🛏 US$75–110
ⓘ 10
♿
🅿

NAHUA
Just south of the road to Playa Langosta
Tamarindo
Tel 506 653 1033
www.hotelnahua.com
This Swiss-run apartment complex is a good option for families looking for a combination of self-catering facilities and proximity to Tamarindo's finest restaurants. Some apartments have air-conditioning, others, a fan; all are spacious, with mezzanine sleeping areas, living space and a kitchen.

🛏 US$49, apartment for 4 people US$59
ⓘ 5 apartments, 2 rooms
♿ 🏊 Outdoor
🅿

CENTRAL PACIFIC AND NICOYA

Jacó is one of the country's major tourist destinations, where accommodations cater both to the surfer, with budget cabins, and to the more moneyed visitor. Some of the region's smartest hotels line the road from Quepos to Manuel Antonio National Park. Hotels fill up quickly in the high season and on weekends so make reservations in advance. Montezuma and Malpais at the southern tip of the Nicoya Peninsula are popular for visitors on a budget with basic, but usually clean, cabins on the beach. Hotels lie to the north and south of town, and require private transport.

ESTERILLOS

XANDARI BY THE PACIFIC
Playa Esterillos Este
Tel 506 778 7070
www.xandari.com
A recently opened sibling to the spectacular Xandari Resort and Spa, this superlative beach hotel utilizes the same winning designs and artsy touches. Luxury villas exude romance and good taste in their use of hardwoods, mosaics, and bright cushions. Generous bathrooms have a wall of glass opening to courtyard gardens, while lounges have a wall of glass offering ocean views. The long lap pool in the formal garden is inviting and the restaurant is the best for miles.
US$245–350
12 villas
Outdoor

ISLITA

HOTEL HACIENDA PUNTA ISLITA
Punta Islita
Tel 506 231 6122
www.hotelpuntaislita.com
Perched upon a headland with dramatic ocean views, Punta Islita is among Costa Rica's top tier of hotels and is justifiably a member of the Small Luxury Hotels of the World. The wall-less lobby lounge beneath a soaring *palenque* is breathtaking and overlooks a sunken bar serving an infinity pool. Rooms are appointed with roughhewn furniture, including draped beds, satellite TV, coffee-maker and minibar.

US$218 rooms, US$350 suites, US$400 *casitas*
20 bungalows, 8 suites, 5 *casitas*
Outdoor

JACÓ

COPACABANA
Jacó
Tel 506 643 3131
US toll free tel 1-866-436 9399
www.copacabanahotel.com
On the beach, at the northern end of town, this complex is one of Jacó's most popular choices. Each airy studio has a shower, air-conditioning and/or fans and a fridge. The pool area has a swim-up bar, and the open-air restaurant serves good food and has plenty of birdlife. By night, the pace is livelier, with whoops from the sports bar. Secure parking is available.
US$99–149
32
Outdoor

MARRIOTT LOS SUEÑOS
800m (875 yards) west from the entrance to Playa Herradura
Jacó
Tel 506 630 9000
Toll free in the US: 1-800/228 9290
www.lossuenosresort.com
A 15-minute drive from Jacó, on unappealing Playa Herradura, Los Sueños Resort is one of the most expensive hotels in Costa Rica. Shameless luxury combines with a huge range of amenities, all set in a forest of 445ha (1,100 acres). The four-floor complex, with casino and gym, is a pastiche of Spanish colonial style. There is a 18-hole golf course and a marina.
US$200–400
211
Outdoor

VILLA CALETAS
9km (5.5 miles) north of Jacó
Tel 506 637 0505
www.villacaletas.com
Looming high above Jacó, with 360-degree vistas, this lavish

hotel is a dizzying cocktail of mock Victorian, Greek, French and Latin styles. Each room and villa is replete with every possible convenience. The Caletas amphitheater hosts concerts and weddings. There are gardens to meander through, a swimming pool, a sumptuous spa and gym with sublime views and two restaurants that serve acclaimed cuisine and there is an 18-hole golf course a 10-minute drive away.
US$165 standard, US$210 villa, US$280–425 suite, plus tax
35
Outdoor

MALPAIS

MALPAIS SURF CAMP
Malpais
Tel 506 640 0031
www.malpaissurfcamp.com
A five-minute walk from rugged Malpais beach, Malpais Surf Camp offers an excellent variety of accommodations for all budgets. Thatched-roof cabins allow for an at-one-with-nature experience, to a soundtrack of howler monkeys and birdlife. Bungalows, grouped around the pool, have patios and tiled bathrooms to satisfy those seeking more comfort and fewer creatures. The lodge serves erratic, but often excellent, meals and is a real social hub in the evenings.
US$30–105
16
Outdoor

STAYING

MANUEL ANTONIO

COSTA VERDE
Manuel Antonio
Tel 506 777 0584
Toll free in the US: 1-866/854-7958
www.hotelcostaverde.com
The World War II aeroplane—decked out as Ollie's Folly Bar—perched at the brow of the hill marks the downhill run to the beach and the imminent arrival of Costa Verde hotel. Checking in at the train carriage reception, you're led to one of five multi-floor apartment blocks with comfortable to luxurious suites all with ocean or jungle views. Trails lead into the forest. You're bound to be woken by howler monkeys as they crash through the trees.
US$104 room, US$135 studio, US$185 penthouse, plus tax
46 rooms, 2 bungalows
2 outdoor
P

MAKANDA BY THE SEA
Manuel Antonio
Tel 506 777 0442
US toll free tel 1-888 MAKANDA
www.makanda.com
One of the best hotels in Manuel Antonio, the studios and villas of Makanda are equipped for pure indulgence and designed with subtle Japanese minimalism. What remains in the split-level studios is a stunning view as the day unfolds from dawn to dusk, seen from the perfectly positioned sofa, hammock or bed. You can wander to the infinity pool, Jacuzzi, or the nearby almost-private beach.
US$265 studio, US$350-400 villa
11
Outdoor
P

MONO AZUL
Apdo 297
Manuel Antonio
Tel 506 777 1548
www.hotelmonoazul.com

Mono Azul is some 5km (3 miles) from Manuel Antonio beach. This characterful hotel has clean, functional rooms with fan, bath and hot water. Luxury rooms have the added comfort of a TV and air-conditioning. The Blue Monkey's appeal lies in the hotel's ecological focus and wide range of services including pools, games room, library, internet café and bar-restaurant (▷ 189). Co-owner Jennifer Rice, a minister, presides over weddings.
US$60-65 room, US$80-135 villa, US$105-135 suites, plus tax
28
Outdoor
Internet café
P

EL PARADOR
Manuel Antonio
Tel 506 777 1414
www.hotelparador.com

Chatty but courteous staff attend your every need at El Parador, some 2km (1.25 miles) from the main Quepos to Manuel Antonio road. Rooms and suites have all the expected comforts and fine views of the ocean and the gardens. A pool and bar, tennis courts and a gym will keep you in trim. There's a free shuttle bus to the beach. Special weekly packages are often available; check the website.
US$180 standard room, US$265 deluxe, US$330 suite, US$920 presidential suite, plus tax, breakfast included
98 rooms, 10 suites
Outdoor
P

SI COMO NO
2.5km (1.5 miles) from park entrance
Manuel Antonio
Tel 506 777 0777
www.sicomono.com
This is one of Costa Rica's most acclaimed hotels. Rooms have ocean or forest views and comforts include a solar-heated Jacuzzi, two pools and wet-bar, and you can dine at the Claro Que Si seafood restaurant or the Rico Tico grill. The spa has a solarium and whirl-pool and a 40-seater cinema. A new addition is the creation of a wildlife refuge in front of the hotel, with a butterfly garden.
US$190-275, plus tax, breakfast included
58
2 outdoor
P

MONTEZUMA

AMOR DE MAR
100m (110 yards) from the estuary bridge on the road to Cabuya
Montezuma
Tel 506 642 0262
www.amordemar.com
A short walk to the south of town lies one of Montezuma's most relaxing hotels. Amor de Mar occupies a craggy cove at the tip of the bay, with manicured gardens that lead from the café-restaurant (excellent for breakfast and light snacks) to the crashing waves of the beach. The lodge-style hotel is immaculate, with a variety of rooms, with or without a bath. For groups of friends or families, there is also a *casita*, formerly the owner's home, which is available by the week.
US$45-90, casita US$170 per day, plus tax
11 rooms, 1 *casita*
P

EL JARDÍN
200m (220 yards) from the beach at the main entrance to the town
Montezuma
Tel 506 642 0074
www.hoteleljardin.com
Stretching up the hill behind Montezuma, El Jardín is a pleasant complex of rooms and villas set in gardens. More expensive rooms have sea views, a balcony and air-conditioning, but all have private bathrooms and ceiling fans, and there is hot water in all but rooms one and two. With friendly staff and efficient service, this is a reliable choice.
US$85-95
15 rooms, 2 villas
Outdoor

STAYING

LOS MANGOS

Montezuma de Cobano
Tel 506 642 0076
www.hotellosmangos.com
This collection of bamboo bungalows lies amid thick forest, a five-minute walk from town. Each bungalow has a ceiling fan, screened windows and its own porch, with hammock. White-faced monkeys are drawn to the abundant mango trees. With a good-sized pool and yoga classes, Los Mangos is a rejuvenating experience.
🛏 Double room US$55, bungalow US$75
ⓘ 10 rooms, 10 bungalows
🅢 🌊 Outdoor

NATURE LODGE FINCA LOS CABALLOS

3km (2 miles) north of Montezuma on the road to Cóbano
Montezuma
Tel 506 642 0124
www.naturelodge.net
Just a five-minute drive away from Montezuma, this blissful eco-lodge crowns the hilltop. Rooms at the Spanish-style ranch have a private bath and a terrace with ocean views. A procession of birdlife passes through the migratory corridor in the jungle below. There is a blue-tiled infinity pool, horse tours and a patio restaurant.
🛏 US$80–130, plus tax
ⓘ 12 rooms
🌊 Outdoor
🅟

YLANG YLANG BEACH HOTEL

800m (870 yards) to the north of town
Montezuma
Tel 506 642 0068
www.elbanano.com
This one-of-a-kind boutique hotel blends the laissez-faire Montezuma ethos with creature comforts. The location is the main draw, overlooking a rugged section of beach, encroached by forest and home to birds and monkeys. Accommodations range from bungalows to double rooms, all with bathrooms, air-conditioning and fans. A freeform swimming pool is fed by a water cascade and there is also a lush garden.
🛏 US$153 rooms, US$175 suites, US$195–220 bungalows
ⓘ 3 beach rooms, 3 beach suites, 7 bungalows,
🅢 🌊 Outdoor
🅟

BELVEDERE

100m (110 yards) from the entrance to town, on the left
Sámara
Tel 506 656 0213
www.samara-costarica.com
This friendly and efficient hotel, in a quiet area a short stroll from the beach, has a family atmosphere. Rooms are placed around leafy patios, all with a bath and solar-heated water. Rooms with fans are cheaper than those with air-conditioning. Facilities include a Jacuzzi and there are apartments for long stays. Aerial tours by ultralight can be arranged.
🛏 US$65, including breakfast
ⓘ 12
🅢 🌊 Outdoor
🅟

FLYING CROCODILE

PO Box 99
Sámara
Tel 506 656 8048
www.flying-crocodile.com
A contender for one of the most original hotels in Costa Rica, the Flying Crocodile takes its inspiration from Catalan architect Antoni Gaudí. Each lodge is a confection of undulating, shimmering and encrusted forms. The hotel doubles as an ultra-light flying center offering soaring tours for US$60. If you prefer to keep your feet on the ground, bicycles, horses and motorbicycles can also be rented.
🛏 US$49–59 shared rooms, US$80–100, air-conditioned rooms
ⓘ 9 bungalows
🌊 Outdoor

HOTEL GIADA

250m (275 yards) north of Guardia Rural
Sámara
Tel 506 656 0132
www.hotelgiada.net
Hotel Giada is a five-minute walk from the beach and has clean, spacious rooms with bamboo furniture. Well managed and friendly, this hotel provides good services for this price category with large beds, cable TV, modern air-conditioning units, fans and bathrooms stocked with goodies. There is a good pizza restaurant, where breakfast is served.
🛏 US$65, including breakfast
ⓘ 24
🅢 🌊 Outdoor
🅟

MIRADOR DE SÁMARA

Sámara
Tel 506 656 0044
www.miradordesamara.com
On a hilltop above Sámara, this dazzlingly white aparthotel has fully equipped apartments and is an ideal choice for families and long-stay visitors. Cool and comfortable, each apartment has a bathroom and

kitchen, and a private balcony. It also has four spacious rooms. There is a freshwater pool if you can't muster the energy to amble down to Sámara beach.
🛏 US$90 rooms, US$105 apartments, including breakfast
ⓘ 4 rooms, 10 apartments
🅢 🌊 Outdoor
🅟

SANTA TERESA

FLORBLANCA RESORT

Playa Santa Teresa
Tel 506 640 0232
www.florblanca.com
You can't get closer to the ocean than staying at what may well be Costa Rica's most fashionable beach hotel. Hidden among lushly foliated grounds, this chic unpretentious retreat defines casual calm and serenity. Imbued with a combination of Balinese and New Mexican architecture, the vast villas have outdoor bathrooms, while lounges with terra-cotta floors open directly to the jungle. The fusion restaurant is one of the finest outside the capital. A twin-tier swimming pool, plus gift shop, TV lounge, and yoga dojo round out the facilities.
🛏 US$375-655
ⓘ 10 villas
🅢 🌊 Outdoor
🅟

STAYING

SOUTHERN REGION

San Isidro de El General is the largest town south of San José and provides the point of access for Costa Rica's highest peak, Cerro Chirripó. In town, budget options are nothing special, but convenient and generally clean. South along the Pan-American Highway, resort-style complexes and lodges are set against a peaceful backdrop. For the two- or three-day ascent of Chirripó, *refugios* with dormitory rooms provide the only accommodations. The wilderness experience of Golfito and the Osa Peninsula is completed by jungle retreats that embody the concept of rustic chic. South from Golfito, Zancudo has the best sportfishing in the country and several lodges provide fishing packages, while Pavones offers one of the world's longest surfing waves.

BAHÍA DRAKE

DELFÍN AMOR
Tel 506 847 3131
www.divinedolphin.com
The Delfín Amor Eco Lodge, 1km (0.6 mile) west of Drake, a short boat journey, is driven by a passion for the dolphins and whales that visit Drake

Bay. Simple cabins have double beds with ocean views. The main draw is the jungle setting with prolific wildlife around you and a sense of wilderness. Jungle trails run through the property and the lodge has its own private beach. Multi-day packages include tours to Corcovado and Caño Island, flights from San José to Drake Bay, transfers and meals.
US$95 per person per night, including all meals, 3 nights US$658 per person, 8 nights US$1,375 per person
6 cabins

DRAKE BAY WILDERNESS RESORT
Tel 506 770 8012
US tel 561 762 1763
www.drakebay.com

In a magnificent location opposite Aguila de Osa, the Drake Bay Resort combines a rejuvenating back-to-nature experience with total comfort and a range of activities and services. Spacious and immaculate tropical cabins, sleeping up to five people, all have queen-size beds, private bathrooms with hot water, porches and splendid ocean views. The ocean-view pool and wild tropical setting complete the sense of well being. There is free laundry service, email access and the resort has its own private dock. A range of packages is available from the standard three-nights accommodation, including all meals, transportation from San José and two guided tours, to more specifically tailored birdwatching, scuba diving, kayaking, mountain biking and fishing tours, and the six night "Week of Paradise" multi-tour combination. Generous discounts are available for children.
Standard 3 night package US$660 per person
20 cabins
Outdoor
P

MATAPALO

BOSQUE DEL CABO
Tel 506 735 5206
www.bosquedelcabo.co
Just a short distance beyond Lapa Ríos, this low-key yet luxurious cliff-top resort competes with less fanfare than the spectacular scenery. The resort is surrounded by rainforest yet has dramatic ocean vistas from the villas that hang suspended over cliffs looking over the Pacific Ocean at the tip of the Osa Peninsula. Scarlet macaws frequent the grounds while monkeys often troop across the rooftops of the ten thatched villas, which have solar-powered electricity, screened-windows, outdoor

garden-showers, and spacious verandas for soaking up the views. Six luxury bungalows have king-size beds. Delicious health-conscious meals are served beneath soaring thatch. Trails include a suspension bridge to a botanical garden, plus Bosque del Cabo has its own zipline canopy tour; and numerous tours, from guided nature hikes to sportfishing, can be arranged.
US$150 standard, US$165 deluxe, US$300–395 *casas*
10 villas, 2 *casas*
Outdoor
P

LAPA RÍOS LODGE
Tel 506 735 5130
www.laparios.com

Around 17km (10 miles) from Puerto Jiménez the road rises steeply to pass over Cabo Matapalo where you will find the Lapa Ríos Lodge, set in a private rainforest reserve covering 400ha (988 acres). Luxurious thatched bungalows were constructed using hardwoods and are equipped with bamboo furniture. Each bungalow has a private deck with views to the ocean or rainforest, and a bathroom with an indoor and an outdoor shower. The open-air restaurant serves international cuisine, complete with a full bar providing cooled drinks you can sip from the observation deck, which has fantastic views. A full range of tours is available and there are yoga classes, massages and a pool to contemplate the paradise. The guiding principals for this eco-conscious hotel ensure that only locals are employed, and tree plantings in previously clear-cut areas ensure the daily presence of monkeys. There are green season discounts.

🛏 US$276 per person, including three meals per day and all taxes
🛏 16 bungalows
🏊 Outdoor
🅿

PARQUE NACIONAL CORCOVADO

CASA CORCOVADO JUNGLE LODGE

Corcovado
Tel 506 256 3181
www.casacorcovado.com

Almost at the San Pedrillo park entrance to Corcovado National Park, in a lush jungle setting, these comfortable thatched bungalows and suites are dotted about a private reserve of 69ha (170 acres). Rustic but impeccably finished, each bungalow has wooden furniture, tiled floors, ceiling fans and beds draped with mosquito nets. A good luxury choice, it offers a variety of tailor-made packages with transfers to and from San José, a choice of tours including hiking in Corcovado, trips to Caño Island, birdwatching, scuba diving and horseback riding.

🕐 Closed Sep 1–Nov 30
🛏 2–7 night packages including meals, tours, taxes, transport and park fees from US$865–1,445
🛏 14 bungalows
🚤 No entry by road; access is by a 1.5hr boat ride from Sierpe

CORCOVADO LODGE TENT CAMP

Apt 6941 1000
San José (postal address)
Tel 506 257 0766
www.costaricaexpeditions.com

A 30-minute walk west along the beach from Carate, the Corcovado Lodge Tent Camp is part of the impressive Costa Rica Expeditions set-up. The 3m (10ft) walk-in tents are on raised platforms, each with two comfortable camp beds and a small front porch, set in a beautiful coconut grove meters from the beach with the rainforest climbing up the hills nearby. Shared bathrooms are a short walk from the tents. Meals are served in a large thatched-roofed dining room, and there's a hammock house for relaxing. The Costa Rica Expeditions team provide bilingual experts to guide you through their 198ha (489-acre) private reserve, which has a wildlife viewing platform some 30m (100ft) above the ground. You can follow trails to wonderful views of the bay or you can go on longer treks to and through Corcovado National Park. Multi-day packages are available from San José or starting locally.

🛏 US$46, 3-day package with meals, transport, taxes and fees from US$678 per person
🛏 16 tents

PIEDRAS BLANCAS NATIONAL PARK

ESQUINAS RAINFOREST LODGE

Tel 506 775 0140
www.esquinaslodge.com
Surrounded by the virgin wilderness of Piedras Blancas National Park (▷ 116), this lodge, financed by the Austrian Government, is a model for sustainable tourism and one of the few not-for-profit ecotourism projects in the country. The 14 snug rooms, with tiled floors, ceiling fans, private baths and mosquito screens, all have verandas overlooking the tropical gardens and forest. The large thatched bar and

restaurant serves local and Austrian dishes and there's a pool for cooling off after a day's hiking. As part of the program to alleviate the economic pressures for logging, the lodge employs local people, and uses all profits to support projects in the small community of nearby La Gamba, such as the repair of the water system, roads and bridges, planting of cash crops, reforestation or environmental education. Multiple tours and activities are offered. Credit cards are not accepted.

🛏 US$105 per person, with meals
🛏 14
🏊 Outdoor
🚗 It's 4km (2.5 miles) to Esquinas from the Pan-American Highway, or arrive from the south via Golfito along a difficult and occasionally impassable road—especially in the wet season

PUNTA BANCO

TISKITA JUNGLE LODGE

Punta Banco
Tel 506 296 8125
www.tiskita-lodge.co.cr
South of Pavones, at the mouth of the Golfo Dulce, is Punta Banco and the incredibly remote tropical retreat of the Tiskita Jungle Lodge. A collection of cabins and rooms set in a private biological reserve spreading over 223ha (550 acres), this is surely the ultimate "escape from it all" lodge in Costa Rica. Cabins are comfortable, with broad balconies and quite spectacular outdoor bathrooms. Hearty national dishes using the freshest fruit and produce are served in the rustic open-air restaurant. Activities include a swimming pool, natural tide pools and trails leading through the nearby primary and secondary rainforest. Trips head farther afield to Corcovado National Park and Sirena across the Gulf. Arriving at Tiskita is normally by chartered plane to the Lodge's private airstrip.

🛏 US$130 including meals, guided walk and taxes, 3-day packages US$1,590 for two people including meals and tours
🛏 16 cabins

THE CARIBBEAN LOWLANDS

Where the Latino lifestyle gives way to the Caribbean culture, the southern Caribbean enclaves of Cahuita and Puerto Viejo cater to a younger, laid-back visitor with inexpensive and mid-range accommodations, ranging from plantation-style houses to idiosyncratically designed cabins and bungalows. Woven quite magically through dense forest and scattered along stretches of rugged coastline, these places, regardless of the price or design, exude an infectious emphasis on chilling out and relaxing. Heading east from Puerto Viejo, a wide range of accommodations has developed along the road to Manzanillo, despite the restriction of the Gandoca-Manzanillo Refuge. Unusually heavy rains frequently wreak havoc on sections of the road from San José to Puerto Limón and from Puerto Limón to Manzanillo.

CAHUITA

MAGELLAN INN
2km (1.2 miles) north of Cahuita on Playa Negra
Tel 506 755 0035
www.magellaninn.com
The Magellan Inn is among the area's smarter options. Each rather simply appointed carpeted room has a neat, tiled bathroom, terrace, ceiling fan and wicker furniture. The garden is filled with the perfume of the belladona lily by day and ilan ilan at night, and is filled with masses of birds. The unimposing pool, nestling in leafy gardens where breakfast is served, is set in natural coral surrounds. There is a bar-restaurant and laundry service is available
🛏 US$69–89, including breakfast
🛌 6
🏊 Outdoor
🅿

SAMASATI LODGE AND RETREAT CENTER
Just south of Cahuita, along Highway 36
Tel 506 224 1870
US toll free tel 1-800/563-9643
www.samasati.com
Visitors seeking no-frills calm should follow the signs to the Samasati Lodge, a relaxing place perched on a hill overlooking the Caribbean. The nine hardwood bungalows, with private bathrooms, all have balconies looking across to the ocean or to the rainforest. For a less expensive option,

there are five double rooms in the guesthouse set among lush gardens. Private houses are also available for longer stays and groups. The vegetarian

restaurant is peaceful and there are walking trails in the forest where over 200 species of birds have been recorded, but the real focus of the retreat is yoga (US$12 per class, meditation (US$5), massage (US$60) and other therapies given in the wonderful setting of the meditation hall, deep within the privacy of the rainforest. A range of packages is available which include transportation, tours and activities.
🛏 US$75 per person guesthouse (shared bath); bungalow US$115 per person
🛌 9
🅿

PLAYA CHIQUITA

LA COSTA DE PAPITO
Playa Chiquita, 1.5km (1 mile) from Puerto Viejo
Tel 506 750 0080
www.lacostadepapito.com
On the beach road between Puerto Viejo and Manzanillo, the Costa de Papito is a delightful collection of individually designed bungalows set in a lush tropical garden of 2ha (5 acres) fringed with jungle. The spacious cabins all have cracked-tile bathrooms and a small balcony complete with hammock, and the attention to detail extends even to the

grain and cut of the wood, which is intrinsic to the design. Breakfast is available, and

bought to your door if requested, and there are bicycles, surfboards and boogie boards for rent, as well as a massage therapist, hair stylist and laundry service. Phone and internet are available.
🛏 US$47–64
🛌 10 bungalows
🅿

SHAWANDHA LODGE
Playa Chiquita, 10km (6 miles) south of Puerto Viejo
Tel 506 750 0018
www.shawandhalodge.com
Across the road from the stunning Playa Chiquita, the French-owned Shawandha Lodge is a luxury complex that oozes comfort and refinement while being totally integrated with the beautiful natural setting. Drawing on a Polynesian inspiration, each bungalow, which is designed in a neo-primitive style, is the height of good taste, constructed with exotic hardwoods, vivid ceramics and thatched palm roofs, and equipped with every requirement. There is a wonderful ambience in the restaurant at night, with dishes created by the French owner/chef. Local tours can be arranged.
🛏 US$109, tropical breakfast included, the seventh night is free
🛌 12 bungalows
🅿

STAYING

PLAYA COCLES

CARIBLUE

Playa Cocles, on the coastal road, between Puerto Viejo and Manzanillo
Tel 506 750 0035
www.cariblue.com

Across the road from the white sand beach of Playa Cocles, the Cariblue resort is one of the most popular choices on the Caribbean coast. Beautiful gardens surrounded by rain-forest contain thatched-roofed duplex bungalows constructed from dark hardwoods, with ceiling fans, mosquito nets and private bathrooms decorated with vivid cracked-tile mosaics. Private porches draped with hammocks complete the relaxed feel. Owing to the great demand, reservations are advised. There is a new swimming pool, snack bar, souvenir shop, bicycles for rent and laundry service. The buffet breakfast is served in the rancho-style restaurant.

🛏 US$85–100, including breakfast
ℹ 20 rooms and bungalows
🏊 Outdoor
P

PUERTO VIEJO

COCO LOCO LODGE

150m (165 yards) from the bus station
Puerto Viejo
Tel 506 750 0281
www.cocolodge.com

In a peaceful spot away from the heart of town, five cabins are woven into a blissfully lush setting. The cabins vary in size, but all are comfortable, spotlessly clean and solidly constructed with hardwood floors, beamed ceilings, bathrooms with hot-water showers, mosquito nets and hammocks seductively draped on each porch. German owner Sabine is extremely helpful and informative and the main lodge reception has magazines, books, games and tour

information. There are good discounts in the green season and for solo visitors.

🛏 US$35–US$50 depending on size of bungalow, buffet breakfast US$5
ℹ 5 cabins
P

PUNTA UVA

ALMONDS AND CORALS TENT CAMP

Punta Uva
Tel/fax 506 759 9057
www.almondsandcorals.com

Some 25km (16 miles) south of Cahuita National Park, and just a five-minute walk from the beautiful Punta Uva beach, this is luxury camping on a grand scale. In a magical jungle setting, the 25 screened wooden cabins have private baths, ceiling fans, night lamps and hammocks. The excellent open-air restaurant serves tasty and filling meals of local dishes and seafood. Many activities are available and elevated walkways lead to the beach. Packages including transportation from San José, accommodation, meals and tours are also available.

🛏 US$257–345 per person, including breakfast, dinner and taxes; 3 nights all inclusive US$432–695 per person
ℹ 25 tents
P

TORTUGUERO

MANATUS HOTEL

Tortuguero
Tel 506 709 8197
www.manatushotel.com

Formerly the rather simple Manatí Lodge, this all-new hotel opened in late 2006 and upped the ante on competing lodges with its sophisticated lodgings. While still offering the standard natural history tour packages, Manatus Hotel has gone straight to the luxury end of the market, with glazed hardwood floors, canopy beds, and spacious modern bathrooms with both indoor and outdoor showers. The open-air public arenas include a pool table, small gym, a pool, and an elegant restaurant that is by far the region's finest, serving creative dishes such as heart of palm sushi, vegetable penne with herb pesto and stuffed roast eggplant (aubergine) with cheese. The restaurant is open

to both hotel guests and non-guests. Kayaks and Aquabikes can be rented.

🛏 US$290 one-night include transport, lodging, and meals, US$375 two-night packages
ℹ 12 bungalows

TORTUGA LODGE AND GARDENS

Tortuguero
Tel 506 257 0766
www.costaricaexpeditions.com

At the northernmost point of the lagoon, the most fashionable choice in Tortuguero is

the Tortuga Lodge and Gardens. Set in 20ha (50 acres), with an awareness of conservation and ecotourism community integration, Costa Rica Expeditions' first lodge has become the most luxurious in their portfolio, following extensive remodeling. Big, bright and breezy rooms are set in a couple of two-floor lodges, each with private bath and a balcony or veranda, complete with hammock overlooking the gardens and the lagoon. The waterside restaurant is à la carte, and there's a wine list worth exploring. On the quiet days you can relax around the free-form pool or wander at will along a couple of trails, viewing poison dart frogs, caiman, monkeys and myriad birds. Be sure to slather on insect repellent, the mosquitos are impossibly aggressive. Expensive, but comfortable, the Lodge has a variety of more economical packages, which include air transportation from San José, accommodation, all meals and tours to the reserve.

🛏 US$99; inclusive package US$328 for two nights
ℹ 24
🏊 Outdoor

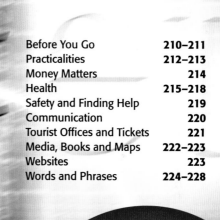

Planning

BEFORE YOU GO

CLIMATE

If your trip is about beaches, blue skies and hot sun go to the north and central Pacific coast between December and April—the high season. This is a clearly defined time with a marked dry season in the Central Highlands and the Pacific regions where almost no rain falls from mid-December to April. Outside these months rain falls steadily, and is heaviest in September and October. On the Caribbean side, east of the continental divide, rain falls intermittently throughout the year. The drier months are February to June, with a small summer (*veranillo*) in September and October.

Outside the high season, rainfall normally occurs in bursts lasting a couple of hours and travel is possible in the vast majority of places. This rainy season has been renamed the green season by the Costa Rican Tourism Institute with good effect. The green season is an increasingly popular time to visit: the country tends to be quieter and discounts are often possible.

A word of warning: some places do close for a break and a few become inaccessible. And many roads are subject to seasonal difficulties such as impassable rivers. Four-wheel-drive vehicles are essential for journeys on unpaved roads, and check road conditions before you set off.

WEATHER REPORTS

The Instituto Meteorológico Nacional in San José provides a five-day weather forecast (in Spanish) on its website: www.imn.ac.cr

WHAT TO TAKE
Clothes

What to take depends on how long you're staying and what you're doing. Starting at the lower altitudes you'll need beach wear, sunglasses and a sun hat—which you'll probably need everywhere—and sunscreen. If you plan to walk on trails, shorts and a light shirt are ideal. In areas where insects are numerous and aggressive, long-sleeved tops and lightweight long trousers are better; some unzip above the knee and become shorts. For the Central Highlands you will need to add a light sweater or jacket for the evenings when there may be a chill in the air. At higher altitudes you'll need something warmer. When preparing for rain it's tempting to take a raincoat, but don't bother unless you plan long treks; buy an umbrella or poncho locally or sit the rain out. You will need comfortable shoes appropriate to your activity, as well as a change when they get wet. Buying large size shoes in Costa Rica is not impossible, but the choice will be restricted.

Costa Rica time is the same as US Central Standard Time, six hours behind Greenwich Mean Time (GMT).

CITY	TIME DIFFERENCE	TIME AT 12 NOON IN COSTA RICA
Amsterdam	+7	7pm
Berlin	+7	7pm
Brussels	+7	7pm
Chicago	0	12 noon
Dublin	+6	6pm
Johannesburg	+8	8pm
Madrid	+7	7pm
Montréal	+1	1pm
New York	+1	1pm
Paris	+7	7pm
Perth, Australia	+11	11pm
Rome	+7	7pm
San Francisco	-2	10am
San José	0	12 noon
Sydney	+13	1am
Tokyo	+12	12am

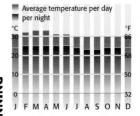

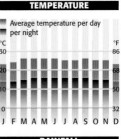

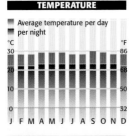

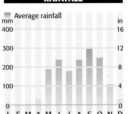

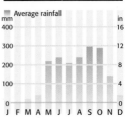

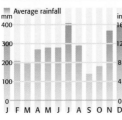

EMBASSIES IN COSTA RICA

COUNTRY	ADDRESS	CONTACT DETAILS
Canada	Oficentro Ejecutivo La Sabana, Edificio 5, Sabana Sur San José	506 242 4400; www.international.gc.ca/sanjose
Germany	Torre La Sabana, Sabana Norte, San José	www.embajada-alemana-costarica.org
Spain	Calle 32, between Paseo Colón and Avenida 2 San José	506 222 5745; www.mac.es
United Kingdom	Centro Colón, Calles 38–40 San José	506 258 2025; www.britishembassycr.com
United States	Calle 120, Avenida 0, Pavas San José	506519 2000; www.usembassy.or.cr

Personal items

If you have personal medical requirements make sure you have enough to last your trip and seek medical advice before leaving home if you have any reason to be concerned. Items worth taking include a flashlight or headlamp, camera and film (it is generally available in Costa Rica, but if you buy in advance you can be certain you have sufficient quantity and quality) or spare memory cards, a water bottle, insect repellent and a universal sink plug (even many mid-range hotels don't have plugs). Glasses or contact lens wearers should take a spare pair or sufficient supplies to last the trip, although it is possible to get most items in Costa Rica.

As ever, specialists will want to take items particular to their activity. A good pair of binoculars is essential for birdwatching. Birders and nature lovers will want to take field guides; they're available in some of the better lodges, but it's better to have your own. Divers and snorkelers might consider taking their own mask. It may be cheaper for surfers to rent a board for a few days than fly their own out.

Pack in a strong bag, the lighter the better, and ideally one that can be locked with a removable padlock. This could then be used on dodgy doors and lockers if the need arises in cheaper hotels. Most mid- and upper-range hotels have safes.

CUSTOMS

The duty-free allowance for visitors coming to Costa Rica is 500 cigarettes and three liters of wine or spirits. No customs duties are charged on personal luggage, including items for personal and professional use as long as they are not in sufficient quantities that suggest commercial use. As with all countries, your bags may be searched by customs officers on entering the country. In the case of families, one declaration can be filled out for the whole family. Never bring banned or illegal goods into the country.

PASSPORTS AND VISAS

Citizens of the US, Canada, Australia, most Western European nations and Japan are permitted to enter Costa Rica and stay for 90 days if they are carrying a valid passport with at least one blank visa page. Your passport should be valid for at least six months after your travel date. People holding valid passports from most Central American and Caribbean countries are allowed to stay in Costa Rica for 30 days without a visa. Citizens of all countries not listed above must obtain a visa from a Costa Rican embassy or consulate before visiting.

On entering Costa Rica, all visitors should be able to show they have an onward ticket to leave the country or proof of sufficient funds to return home or go on to another country. Passport and visa regulations can change at short notice. Always confirm the latest requirements before you travel.

EXTENSIONS

You can extend your stay beyond these limits with a *prorroga de turismo*. These can be obtained at *migración* in San José, on the road from the capital to the airport. For this you need four passport photos, an airline or bus ticket out of the country and proof of funds (for example travelers' checks); you can apply for an extension of one or two months at a cost of US$3 per month. The paperwork can take up to three days but travel agents can arrange all extension and exit formalities for a small fee.

Alternatively, you can leave the country for 72 hours and get a new 30- or 90-day visa when you re-enter. If you enter overland, you may be asked for an onward ticket. A bus ticket can be bought close to the border immigration office; you may get the cost refunded in San José.

RESIDENCY

If you want to take up residency, there are a number of options for individuals seeking to retire or invest in Costa Rica. Essentially you need to prove that you have a regular income or that you are going to invest over US$50,000 to create a regular income. Full details about requirements and the process can be obtained at www.migracion.go.cr. For assistance, contact the Association of Residents of Costa Rica, Casa Canada, Avenida 4 and Calle 40, PO Box 1191-1007, Centro Colón, San José, tel 506 233 8068, www.casacanada.net/arcr

TRAVEL INSURANCE

You should take out travel insurance before your trip. Make sure that it covers medical and dental expenses, and repatriation as well as theft and delay. If you are taking items of high value (binoculars, cameras, videos or laptops) make sure they are covered; some policies do not cover goods over a certain value unless declared in advance. Insurance companies vary in their requirements relating to claims and payments. The bare minimum requirement is a police report (▷ 219). Read the small print in your policy carefully.

PLANNING

PRACTICALITIES

CHILDREN
● Remember that a lot of time can be spent waiting for public transport, so make sure you pack some toys. Nothing beats a GameBoy, unless it's two GameBoys and a link cable. Take reading material with you as it is difficult, and expensive, to find.
● Food can be a problem. It is easier to take food and drinks, with you on longer trips than to rely on meal stops where the food may not be to taste. Avocados are safe, easy to eat and nutritious. A small immersion heater and jug for making hot drinks is invaluable, but remember that the electric current varies. Try and get a dual-voltage model (110v and 220v) or an adaptor.
● Discounted fares apply on public transport, and families will also benefit from reduced fares on sightseeing tours.
● In hotels try to negotiate family rates. If charges are per person, always insist that two children will occupy one bed only, therefore counting as one tariff. If rates are per bed, the same applies. In either case you can almost always get a reduced rate at cheaper hotels. In the better hotels in more commercial resorts, it is quite common for children under 10 or 12 to be allowed to stay for no extra charge if they are sharing a room with their parents.
● Travel with children can bring you into closer contact with Latin American families and generally presents no special problems; in fact the path is often smoother for family groups. Officials tend to be more amenable where children are concerned and they are pleased if your child knows a little Spanish. Moreover, thieves and pickpockets seem to have some of the traditional respect for families.
● Diapers can be difficult to find, so bring a supply with you.

LOCAL CUSTOMS AND LAWS
Costa Rican society is broadly tolerant. The US State Department produce *Tips for Travelers to Central and South America* which can be obtained through the US Government Printing Office, Washington, DC 20402 or via the Bureau of Consular Affairs at www.travel.state.gov

Park life: Costa Rican society is very family friendly

CLOTHING
Most Costa Ricans devote a great deal of care to their clothes and appearance. How you dress is how people will judge you, particularly in the business arena. Even on vacation, smart, clean clothes are always appreciated. In beach communities, wear a sarong and a shirt when walking round town or if you're away from the beach.

CONDUCT
Politeness, courtesy and sometimes ceremoniousness prevails in all situations—even the traffic police give tickets in a rather pleasant manner. Being flustered, rushed and hurried simply doesn't fit in with the way of doing things in Costa Rica, a common trait throughout Latin America. Equally common is the sometimes extended process of introductions. Likewise when departing, take the time to say goodbye.

MAÑANA
Visitors should keep to time arrangements or, as it is known, the *hora inglés*. With just a hint of sadness, the *mañana* culture of "tomorrow" is disappearing from many areas. Tours leave on time, bus services tend to leave promptly and restaurant tables should be taken up punctually.

Get involved with the government and bureaucracy and it's a different world: the sheer amount of paperwork required can be frightening. Stay patient and tolerant if dealing with officials.

DRINK AND DRUGS
Drinking is a part of life, but drunkenness is fairly uncommon. Yes, walking through San José, Limón or other cities and popular areas late on a Saturday you will find a few individuals the worse for wear, but nothing excessive.

Drugs are frowned upon, although their presence is increasing as Costa Rica is used as a transhipment port for cocaine coming up from South America. All drugs are illegal in Costa Rica with a jail term being the likely penalty for possession.

TIPPING
Once a reward for exceptional service, the tendency to tip at the drop of a hat is taking over in Costa Rica. In better restaurants, a 13 percent sales tax and a 10 percent service charge is automatically added to your bill. You are welcome to contest paying the service charge if you wish. The consensus is that bellboys and chambermaids receive tips of between US$0.50 and US$2 per item or day. Generally, taxi drivers are not tipped. Tour guides can be tipped as you see fit—again, the tip should reflect the level of service and attention rather than be an assumed payment.

RELIGION
While 90 percent of Costa Ricans are nominally Roman Catholic, the number that actually attend church on a regular basis is far less. This should not be confused with a lack of respect for the church, which is still very high.

PLANNING

FROM	TO	MULTIPLY BY
Inches	Centimeters	2.54
Centimeters	Inches	0.3937
Feet	Meters	0.3048
Meters	Feet	3.2810
Yards	Meters	0.9144
Meters	Yards	1.0940
Miles	Kilometers	1.6090
Kilometers	Miles	0.6214
Acres	Hectares	0.4047
Hectares	Acres	2.4710
Gallons	Liters	4.5460
Liters	Gallons	0.2200
Ounces	Grams	28.35
Grams	Ounces	0.0353
Pounds	Grams	453.6
Grams	Pounds	0.0022
Pounds	Kilograms	0.4536
Kilograms	Pounds	2.205
Tons	Tonnes	1.0160
Tonnes	Tons	0.9842

ELECTRICITY

Costa Rica runs on 110 volts, 60 cycles AC. Plugs are the US flat-pin style.

WEIGHTS AND MEASURES

For customs the metric system is compulsory. Traders use a variety of weights and measures, including imperial and the old Spanish ones.

RESPONSIBLE TRAVEL

Costa Rica has undergone a change in recent decades from the slash-and-burn deforestation to being one of the planet's leading exponents of nature tourism and what is currently called ecotourism. Costa Rica is indisputably one of the world's most popular nature destinations and tourism, which attracts over 1 million visitors to the country every year, is the country's leading foreign exchange earner. But while there are clearly benefits for both the host country and visitors—employment and cultural exchange—there can also be a downside. Where visitor pressure is high and poorly regulated, adverse impacts on society and the natural environment may be apparent.

Many national parks are partly funded by receipts from visitors. Similarly, you can promote protection of archaeological sites and heritage through your interest and contributions via entrance fees. You can also support small-scale enterprises by staying in locally run hotels and hostels, eating in local restaurants and by purchasing local goods and services.

Increasingly, visitors are keen to be involved in ecotourism—the Costa Rican Tourist Board (ICT) has introduced an environmentally based classification system—Certified Sustainable Tourism— which could help visitors a lot when choosing between hotels. Currently the ICT grades hotels with levels from one to five, awarding Green Leaf signs to certified hotels.

FURTHER INFORMATION

In the US contact the International Ecotourism Society, tel 202/347-9203, www.ecotourism.org for a comprehensive breakdown of the issues. The society has links with several Costa Rican organizations that share an interest in promoting ecotourism. Organizations like Conservation International in the US (01-703/341-2400, www.ecotour.org) and Tourism Concern in the UK (020 7133 3330, www.tourismconcern. org.uk) have begun to develop and promote ecotourism projects. Additionally, organizations such as Earthwatch (US and Canada on 01-800/776-0188, in the UK on 01865 318838, www.earthwatch.org) offer opportunities to participate directly in scientific research and development projects.

While some ecotourism operators' claims need to be interpreted with care, there is clearly demand for this type of activity and opportunities to support worthwhile conservation initiatives.

CLOTHING SIZES

Use the clothing sizes chart below to convert the size you use at home.

UK	Metric	USA	
36	46	36	SUITS
38	48	38	
40	50	40	
42	52	42	
44	54	44	
46	56	46	
48	58	48	
7	41	8	SHOES
7.5	42	8.5	
8.5	43	9.5	
9.5	44	10.5	
10.5	45	11.5	
11	46	12	
14.5	37	14.5	SHIRTS
15	38	15	
15.5	39/40	15.5	
16	41	16	
16.5	42	16.5	
17	43	17	
8	36	6	DRESSES
10	38	8	
12	40	10	
14	42	12	
16	44	14	
18	46	16	
20	46	18	
4.5	37.5	6	SHOES
5	38	6.5	
5.5	38.5	7	
6	39	7.5	
6.5	40	8	
7	41	8.5	

Monteverde has pioneered low-impact tourism in Costa Rica

MONEY MATTERS

CURRENCY

● The unit of currency in Costa Rica is the colón, consisting of 100 céntimos. Coins are minted for 5, 10, 25, 50 and 100 colones. Some public telephones use older silver 5, 10 and 20 colón coins. Notes in use: 1,000, 2,000, 5,000 and 10,000 colones.

● Dollars are widely accepted in cities and tourist resorts, but don't rely on being able to use them outside the most popular destinations. Always have some colones as well.

CASH, TRAVELERS' CHECKS OR CREDIT CARDS?

All three is the easy answer. Each has weaknesses and strengths. Cash should be taken in dollars; they are by far the easiest to change. It is possible to change other currencies, but the rate is normally reduced and you may have to visit several banks.

Travelers' checks have added security, being replaceable if they are stolen or misplaced. Take dollar travelers' checks and make sure they are a well-known name like American Express, Citibank or Thomas Cook. Keep the original purchase receipt separate from the checks; for added security photocopy it.

Credit cards are widely accepted in hotels and restaurants in San José and the more established resorts, but may be difficult to use beyond these areas. Check with hotels in advance when making reservations. The real value of a credit card is for easy cash advances from Automated Teller Machines (ATMs) and banks. Visa and MasterCard are

PRICES OF EVERYDAY ITEMS	
ITEM	PRICE (US$)
Bottle of water	0.40–2
Bottle of beer	0.75–3
Packet of 20 cigarettes	1.50
Tico Times newspaper	1
Cup of tea or coffee	0.25–2
Sunscreen	3–10
Sun hat	5–10
Casado (lunch)	2–10

accepted, with Visa probably having the edge. American Express and Diners Card are accepted in business hotels, but should not be relied upon outside the business setting. However, many businesses apply a surcharge as high as 15 percent if you pay by credit card.

BANKS AND CHANGING MONEY

Getting some first-day money before departure can be difficult. You may be able to get some in Miami if you are catching a connecting flight. There is a bank, just after customs, at the Juán Santamaría International Airport in San José which opens to meet arriving flights so you can change money on arrival if you need to.

Banks are the easiest place to change money. Branches of the state banks Banco Nacional and Banco de Costa Rica are found throughout the country. The core opening hours are from 8.30am to 3.30pm, Monday to Friday. However, some branches are opening for longer; occasionally extending to Saturday morning. Service varies wildly. It can be incredibly slow or surprisingly fast. Be prepared to wait. Banks in areas where processing travelers' checks and credit cards is a rare event may take longer, but this isn't always the case.

Commission rates for changing currency tend to be around one percent.

The black market in Costa Rica has largely disappeared, and the few street money changers that hang around the central area operate illegally. In general it's best to avoid changing money on the street unless you are totally relaxed with the idea. Don't flash large amounts of money around. Check the bank exchange rate beforehand so that you know how much money to expect before asking. While you may show your dollars to the changer in advance, don't hand over the money until you have counted the money you are to receive. Be aware that scams are common.

COST OF LIVING

Budgeting for a trip is always difficult and is dependent on your tastes and mode of travel. Costa Rica is not an expensive country. Income per head of population is around US$4,500.

At the bottom end of the scale you could manage on US$25 to US$40 a day to cover accommodation, meals and travel by bus. As a very rough guideline, bus travel works out at between US$1 and US$1.50 per hour of travel. But this would leave very little for comforts, trips and tours. Comfortable travel is found in the US$45 to US$85 per day range. This should cover reasonable accommodation and pleasant meals based on preference rather than cheapest cost. Beyond US$85 things start to get comfortable with better service, design and decor.

Renting a vehicle will cost from US$350 a week. Tours range in price from US$45 for a day-trip up to US$250 for a two-day all-inclusive white-water rafting or Tortuguero wildlife trip.

Colones are the national currency

HEALTH

Staying healthy in Costa Rica is straightforward. Most visitors return home having experienced no problems at all, except perhaps an upset stomach. However, the health risks are different from those encountered in Europe or the US. Your health also depends on how you travel, and where. There are clear differences between the risks for the businessperson, who stays in international-class hotels and the backpacker.

There are English- (or other foreign-language) speaking doctors in most cities who have experience in dealing with locally occurring diseases. Your embassy will often be able to give you the name of reputable doctors and most of the better hotels have a doctor on standby. If you fall ill and cannot find a recommended doctor, try the Outpatient Department of a hospital; private hospitals are usually less crowded and offer a more acceptable standard of care.

BEFORE YOU GO

Take out medical insurance and ensure it covers all eventualities, especially repatriation to your home country. It is sensible to have a dental check-up, and, if you suffer from a chronic illness, a check-up with your doctor who will be able to provide you with a letter explaining the details of your condition in English and if possible Spanish. Check the current practice for malaria prophylaxis (prevention). Take spare glasses (or a prescription for them), and if you are on regular medication, make sure you have enough to cover the period of your travel.

CHILDREN

More preparation is probably necessary for babies and children than for an adult, and more care should be taken when visiting remote areas. This is because children often become ill more rapidly than adults.

Diarrhea and vomiting are the most common problems, so take the usual precautions. Treatment of diarrhea is the same as it is for adults, except that it should be continued with more persistence. Children get dehydrated quickly in hot countries and can become drowsy unless cajoled to drink fluids. Breastfeeding is best and most convenient for babies, but powdered milk and baby foods are available in Costa Rica. Papaya, bananas and avocados are all nutritious and can be cleanly prepared. Outer ear infections after swimming may be a problem and antibiotic ear drops will help. Wet wipes are extremely useful and sometimes difficult to find, as, in some places, are diapers.

MEDICINES

There is very little control on the sale of drugs and medicines in Costa Rica. You may be able to buy any drug in pharmacies without a prescription. Be wary of this because pharmacists can be poorly trained and might sell you drugs that are unsuitable, dangerous or old. Many drugs and medicines are manufactured under license from American or European companies, so the trade names may be familiar to you. Remember that the shelf-life of some items, especially antibiotics, is markedly reduced in hot conditions. Buy your supplies at better outlets where there are refrigerators and check the expiry date of all drugs. Immigration officials occasionally confiscate scheduled drugs (Lomotil is an example) if they are not accompanied by a doctor's prescription.

VACCINATIONS
Vaccination against the following diseases is recommended. Children should already be properly protected against diphtheria, poliomyelitis and pertussis (whooping cough) and measles. If your child has not had the vaccinations, consider protecting them before you visit Costa Rica. Hepatitis B vaccination for babies is now routine in some countries. Ask your doctor for advice on tuberculosis: the disease is still widespread in Latin America

Yellow Fever
This is a live vaccination, not to be given to children under nine months or anyone allergic to eggs. Immunity lasts for 10 years; an International Certificate of Yellow Fever Vaccination will be given and should be kept because it is sometimes asked for. Yellow fever is very rare in Costa Rica, but the vaccination is usually without side effects and almost totally protective.

Typhoid
A number of new vaccines against this condition are now available: they cause fewer side effects than the old ones, but are more expensive.

Poliomyelitis
Almost everyone in the developed world is vaccinated against this disease as a child. It may be wise to have a booster.

Tetanus
One dose should be given with a booster at six weeks and another at six months and 10 yearly boosters are recommended.

Infectious Hepatitis
This is less of a problem for visitors than it used to be because of the development of two extremely effective vaccines against the A and B form of the

Modern drugs and remedies are widely available

disease. It remains common, however, in Latin America. A combined hepatitis A and B vaccine is now licensed and has been available since 1997; one jab covers both diseases.

OTHER VACCINATIONS
These might be considered in the case of epidemics, for example, meningitis. There is an effective vaccination against rabies, which should be considered by those going through remote areas or if there is a particular occupational risk.

FURTHER INFORMATION
Further information on health risks abroad and vaccinations may be available from a local travel clinic. If you wish to take specific drugs with you, such as antibiotics, these are best prescribed by your own doctor. More detailed information than some local GPs can provide is available from various sources.

In the UK there are hospital departments specializing in tropical diseases in London, Liverpool, Birmingham and Glasgow, and at the London School of Hygiene and Tropical Medicine. In the US the local Public Health Services can give such advice. Information is available centrally from the Center for Disease Control (CDC) in Atlanta, tel 404/639-3534, www.cdc.gov.

The Scottish Centre for Infection and Environmental Health has a website database providing information for visitors at www.fitfortravel.scot.nhs.uk. General advice is also available in the UK in *Health Information for Overseas Travel* (Department of Health) available from HMSO and International Travel and

Health (WHO). Handbooks on first aid are produced by the British and American Red Cross.

ON THE WAY
For many visitors, a trip to Costa Rica means a long flight. The best way to get over jetlag is to force yourself into the new time zone as strictly as possible. The symptoms of jetlag may be helped by keeping up your fluid intake on the journey. The hormone melatonin seems to reduce the symptoms of jetlag, but is not presently licensed in most of Europe, although it can be obtained from health food stores in the US.

On long-haul flights it is also important to stretch your legs at least every hour to prevent slowing of the circulation and the possible development of blood clots. Drinking plenty of non-alcoholic fluids also helps.

STAYING HEALTHY
The thought of catching a stomach bug may worry visitors to Costa Rica, but there have been great improvements in food hygiene and, if you are sensible, intestinal upsets are rare. Diarrhea and vomiting are usually the result of food poisoning, passed on by insanitary food handlers. As a rule the cleaner and the smarter the restaurant, the less likely you are to suffer.

FOODS TO AVOID
Don't eat uncooked, under-cooked, partially cooked or reheated meat, fish, and eggs, especially when they have been left uncovered. Raw vegetables and salads are also possible sources of trouble. Stick to fresh food that has been cooked from raw just before eating and make sure you peel fruit yourself. Wash and dry your hands before eating; disposable wet-wipe tissues are very useful.

Shellfish eaten raw are always risky and at certain times of the year some fish and shellfish concentrate toxins that can cause food poisoning. In that case, the local authorities notify the public not to eat these foods.

Heat treated (UHT), sterilized or pasteurized milk is becoming more available in Costa Rica, as is pasteurized cheese. Matured or processed cheeses are safer than the fresh varieties. Fresh unpasteurized milk can be a source of food poisoning germs. This also applies to ice cream, yoghurt and cheese made from unpasteurized milk.

Tap water is rarely safe outside the major cities, especially in the rainy season. Filtered or bottled water is usually available and safe, although you must make sure that somebody is not filling bottles from the tap and hammering on a new cap. Ice for drinks should be made from boiled water, but it rarely is, so stand your glass on the ice cubes, rather than putting them in the drink. The better hotels have water purifying systems. Drinking water is rarely the culprit in cases of food poisoning. Sea water or river water is more likely to be contaminated by sewage and so swimming can also lead to infection.

The various organisms that give rise to stomach upsets may be viruses, bacteria—for example Escherichia coli (probably the most common cause), salmonella and cholera—or protozoa (such as amoeba and

Healthy flying: drink water and do some exercises regularly

giardia). The diarrhea may come on suddenly or rather slowly. It may be accompanied by vomiting or by abdominal pain; the passage of blood or mucus is a sign of dysentery.

DIAGNOSIS AND TREATMENT

Acute diarrhea is probably due to a virus or a bacterium and/or the onset of dysentery. Treatment, in addition to rehydration, is an antibiotic such as ciprofloxacin; the drug is now widely available and there are many similar ones.

If the diarrhea comes on slowly or intermittently then it is more likely to be caused by an amoeba or giardia. Antibiotics such as ciprofloxacin will have little effect. These cases are best treated by a doctor, as is any outbreak of diarrhea continuing for more than three days. If a doctor is not available then the best treatment is probably tinidazole (Fasigyn). If there are severe stomach cramps, the following drugs may help but are not useful in the management of acute diarrhea: loperamide (Imodium) and diphenoxylate with atropine (Lomotil). They should not be given to children.

Any kind of diarrhea responds well to the replacement of water and salts, taken as frequent sips of some kind of rehydration solution. There are proprietary preparations consisting of sachets of powder which you dissolve in boiled water, or you can make your own by adding half a teaspoonful of salt and two tablespoonfuls of sugar to a liter (1.75 pints) of boiled water. Rehydration is especially important for children.

Paradoxically, constipation is also common, probably induced by dietary change, inadequate fluid intake in hot places and long bus journeys. Simple laxatives are useful in the short-term and bulky foods such as maize, beans and plenty of fruit are also useful.

WATER PURIFICATION

There are a number of ways of purifying water in order to make it safe to drink. Dirty water should first be strained through a filter bag (available in camping shops) and then boiled or treated. Bringing water to a rolling boil at sea level is sufficient to make the water safe for drinking, but at

Stick to fruit that can be peeled, such as papayas and bananas

higher altitudes you have to boil the water for a few minutes longer to ensure that all the microbes are killed.

There are proprietary preparations containing chlorine (for example Puritabs) or iodine (such as Pota Aqua) compounds. Chlorine compounds generally do not kill protozoa (for example giardia).

ALTITUDE

Spending time at high altitude in Central America is usually a pleasure but it can cause medical problems. On reaching heights above 3,000m (10,000ft), heart pounding and shortness of breath, especially on exertion, are a normal response to the lack of oxygen in the air; only the mountains of the Chirripó range reach this height in Costa Rica.

HEAT AND COLD

The temperature in Costa Rica rarely exceeds the 30°C mark (70–80°sF), though the humidity may be higher than you are used to. Remember that tepid showers are more cooling than hot or cold ones. Large hats do not cool you down, but do prevent sunburn. There can be a sudden drop in temperature between sun and shade and between night and day, especially in the highlands, so dress accordingly. Warm jackets or woolens are essential after dark at high altitude. Loose cotton is still the best material when the weather is hot.

INSECTS

These are mostly more of a nuisance than a serious hazard and with a bit of preparation you should be able to avoid being bitten. Some, such as mosquitoes, may be carriers of potentially serious diseases. Sleep off the ground and use an insecticide-impregnated mosquito net or some kind of insecticide. Preparations containing pyrethrum or synthetic pyrethroids are safe. They are available as aerosols or pumps and the best way to use these is to spray the room thoroughly in all areas and then shut the door for a while, re-entering when the smell has dispersed. Mosquito coils release insecticide as they burn slowly. Tablets of insecticide that are placed on a heated mat plugged into a wall socket are probably the most effective. They fill the room with insecticidal fumes in the same way as aerosols or coils.

You can also use insect repellents, most of which are effective against a wide range of pests. The most effective is diethyl metatoluamide (DEET). DEET liquid is best for arms and face. Aerosol spray is good for clothes and ankles and liquid DEET can be dissolved in water and used to impregnate cotton clothes and mosquito nets. Some repellents now contain DEET and permethrin, an insecticide. Impregnated wrist and ankle bands can be useful.

If you are bitten or stung, itching may be relieved by cool baths or antihistamine tablets. Bites that become infected should be treated with an antiseptic or antibiotic cream, as should any sores or scratches.

TICKS AND MAGGOTS

Ticks usually attach themselves to the lower parts of the body often while you are walking in areas where cattle have grazed. They take a while to attach themselves strongly, but swell up as they start to suck blood. The important thing is to remove them gently, so that they do not leave their head parts in your skin because this can cause infections or an allergic reaction some days later. Do not use petrol, Vaseline, lighted cigarettes, etc, to remove the tick, but, with a pair of tweezers, remove the beast gently by gripping it at the attached (head) end and rocking it out in very much the same way that a tooth is extracted. Certain tropical flies that lay their eggs under the skin of sheep and cattle also

You can protect yourself from the strong sun with an umbrella

occasionally do the same thing to humans with the unpleasant result that a maggot grows under the skin and pops up as a boil or pimple. The best way to remove these is to cover the boil with oil, Vaseline or nail varnish, thereby stopping the maggot from breathing, and then to squeeze it out gently the next day.

OTHER ANIMAL BITES AND STINGS

It is a very rare event indeed, but if you are unlucky enough to be bitten by a venomous snake, spider, scorpion or sea creature, try to identify it without putting yourself in further danger. Snake bites in particular are very frightening, but in fact rarely life-threatening—even venomous snakes may bite without injecting venom. Victims should be taken to a hospital or a doctor without delay. Commercial snake bite and scorpion kits are available, but are usually only useful for the specific types of snake or scorpion. If someone is bitten, reassure and comfort the victim frequently. Immobilize the limb with a bandage or a splint or by getting the person to lie still. Do not slash the bite area and try to suck out the poison—this does more harm than good. If you know how to use a tourniquet you will not need advice. If you are not experienced, do not apply a tourniquet.

PRECAUTIONS

Avoid walking in snake territory in bare feet or sandals: wear proper shoes or boots. If you encounter a snake, stay put until it slithers away, and do not investigate a wounded snake. Spiders and scorpions may be found in the

more basic hotels. If bitten or stung, rest, take plenty of fluids and call a doctor. The best precaution is to keep beds away from the walls and look inside your shoes and under the toilet seat every morning.

MARINE BITES AND STINGS

Certain tropical sea fish when trodden upon inject venom into bathers' feet. This can be exceptionally painful. Wear plastic shoes when you go bathing if such creatures are reported. The pain can be relieved by immersing the foot in hot water for as long as the pain persists.

SUNBURN

The burning power of the tropical sun, especially at high altitude, is phenomenal. Always wear a wide-brimmed hat and use some form of sunscreen. Low protection factor sunscreen lotions are not much good; you need protection factor of 15 or above. These are sometimes not available outside tourist areas. Glare from the sun and sea can cause conjunctivitis, so wear sunglasses, especially on tropical beaches.

MALARIA

Malaria is theoretically confined to coastal and jungle zones, but is now on the increase again. There are different varieties of malaria parasites, some resistant to the normal drugs. Consult your doctor and make local enquiries if you intend to visit possibly infected zones and use a prophylactic regime. You can still catch the disease even when sticking to a proper regime, although it is unlikely. If you do develop symptoms (high fever, shivering, headache, sometimes diarrhea), seek medical advice immediately. Opinion varies on the precise drugs and dosage to be used for protection. All the drugs may have some side effects and it is important to balance the risk of catching the disease against the (albeit rare) side effects. It also makes sense to avoid being bitten (▷ 217, Insects).

DENGUE FEVER

This is transmitted by mosquitoes and, as there is no effective vaccination against it, you should try to avoid being bitten (▷ 217, Insects).

SAFETY AND FINDING HELP

SAFETY

In general, Costa Rica is a very safe country. Nonetheless, crimes against tourists have increased alarmingly in recent years. The majority of crimes can be avoided by being aware of the risks. Government authorities have committed to increasing the police presence with the introduction of a Tourist Police Corps in many popular tourist centers. Should you require police assistance call 117, in any other emergency call 911.

PROTECTING MONEY AND VALUABLES

• Leave your valuables in a safe box in your hotel, or with reception if you are happy to trust your hotel.
• If you need to carry cash around, keep it in a safe place about your person, preferably somewhere under your clothing so it is concealed.
• Do not walk around wearing a highly visible bumbag (fanny pack) which invites attention.
• If you are carrying a camera, make sure you have your hand on it or the bag at all times.
• Avoid walking through dark areas on your own at night.

DANGEROUS PLACES

• Bus stops are busy places where first-time visitors can become bewildered: perfect conditions for the bag-lifter to relieve you of your belongings. Remain calm at all times. Try not to appear unnecessarily rushed or lost. If you need to get your bearings, sit down and gather your bags together. If you need to ask directions, avoid leaving one person in charge of more bags than they can hold.
• The Coca-Cola Bus Terminal and surrounding area in San José has a reputation for crime. A police office has opened in the terminal area and some locals say that crime is now falling but nevertheless, take care.
• If you've ever seen a well-organized criminal team work a crowd, you will realize that you have no chance if you have been picked as a victim. Do what you can to avoid being a victim and don't bring anything so precious you can't afford to lose it.

EMERGENCY PHONE NUMBERS

All emergencies
911

Police
117

Fire
118

Ambulance
128

To say there is less creative theft in Costa Rica than in other countries is little consolation once you've had your pockets emptied. Be wary of scams that attempt to distract you. One trick is to throw mud or shampoo on your person, a helper clears it off while a third relieves you of your possessions. Other tricks involve dropping money and asking if it is yours. In the conversation, with your guard dropped, your pockets are pilfered.

DRIVING

Rental cars are commonly the target of theft. The tourist number plates that used to be on rental vehicles, and stuck out like a sore thumb, have now gone. However, your vehicle will still obviously be a rental car. Do not park in the street: use hotel parking or find a parking area. Do not leave valuables in the car, but if you have no choice, put them out of sight. Do not park on the roadside in quiet spots—it will be seen. Organized scams operate in major tourist destinations, such as Tamarindo.

Heed warnings about rip tides

WOMEN

The risks for women visitors in Costa Rica are no different to the risks in your home country. In general, Costa Rica is much safer (in terms of violent crime against women) than the US or Europe, and rape and muggings are uncommon. However, there have been some well publicized incidents in which female visitors have been attacked, and you should exercise the normal caution you would anywhere in the world. If the last few years are anything to go by, violent crime with at times fatal consequences is on the increase, but remains extremely rare. If you are subject to violent crime do not risk your life defending your possessions. Avoid alcohol if you are likely to be on your own, and do not accept alcohol from anyone not in your group. Bear in mind that most people who invite you for a stroll on the beach are not motivated by a desire to practice their English.

SWIMMING AND RIP TIDES

The beauty of some of Costa Rica's beaches hides the very real threat of rip tides—currents that pull you out to sea. If you know what you are looking for, it is possible to see rip currents: They have a noticeable difference in water color, or you may see a gap in the breaking waves or foam and objects floating out to sea. Be sensible and avoid getting caught in a current. Apart from the beaches at Dominical and Manuel Antonio National Park, there are no lifesaving guards in Costa Rica so you will have to depend on local advice. Dangerous beaches popular with tourists are Playa Jacó, Playa Esterillos, Playa Dominical, Playa Espadilla, Playa Bonita and Playa Cahuita.

If you get caught in a rip tide, don't panic; many drownings occur in rip tides when people try to fight the current. Swim at a manageable pace parallel to the shore until you are clear of the current; the waves at either side of the rip tide will take you back to the shore. If you cannot break free of the current, let it take you out beyond the breakers, then swim diagonally toward the shore. Trying to swim against the current will result in exhaustion.

PLANNING

COMMUNICATION

POST
The Costa Rican postal system (correos) is seen as dependably slow and unreliable. Post takes about 10 days to North America, and up to three weeks to Europe. Sea mail, which is generally only used for large packages, can take up to three months. Postal rates are affordable. Packing materials are available at post offices in San José and Limón. Opening hours vary between cities and towns. In San José the post office is open Mon–Fri 7.30–6, Sat 7.30–noon. Courier services are available from San José, see contact details, below.

Mail can be sent to you in Costa Rica via the Lista de Correos of a convenient post office. For San José, the address would be Your Name, Correo de Costa Rica, Lista de Correos, San José, Costa Rica, Central America. There is a nominal charge of US$0.15 for each item.

TIPS
• If sending a package, don't seal the bag before you go to the post office as it needs to be cleared by customs first.
• Parcels often go missing, whether being sent or received, so be wary sending anything of value.

TELEPHONE
Costa Rica has the highest number of land and mobile telephone lines per capita in Central America. Even the smallest towns and villages have at least one phone line, and more lines are being installed. This is all very well if you have your own phone, but the majority of visitors will be subjected to hotel telephones, which can attract a hefty surcharge, or unreliable public telephones. A few public telephones still take cash, and accept small change of 5, 10 and 20 colones (old style silver-hued coins). Simply dial

the number and feed in the money. Rates are cheap but it's a good idea to have plenty of change handy. To get the international operator or to make collect calls dial 116.

PHONE CARDS
Phone or calling cards are very useful. There are three systems: The most useful is Viajera Internacional 199 which permits international and national and calls from any designated public telephone and are available in values of US$10, US$20 and 3,000 colones. After scratching off the security patch, dial 199 and follow the instructions (available in Spanish or English) It can get tedious tapping in the 20-digit security code: To make a follow-on call hit "#". Colibri 197 offers a similar service, but their lines are often busy. The CHIP cards work from blue public phones.

FAX AND CREDIT CARD CALL
In San José you can send and receive faxes (US$0.30 for up to five pages) and make credit card calls from the RACSA Tele-communications Center office at Avenida 5, Calle 1, tel 506 287 0515. They also have a (pricey) internet service. Many hotels, even at the basic end, have fax machines and may allow you to receive faxes for a charge.

INTERNET
Internet access is widely available in Costa Rica and by far the cheapest and easiest way to stay in touch. There is a plethora of internet cafés in San José, and smaller towns usually have at least one café. However, increasingly enterprising individuals and organizations are setting up small offices in out of the way places. Prices vary. Connections are normally slow.

In San José, you should expect to pay around US$1.50 for broadband connection, but in tourist resorts like Tamarindo and Sámara, you may have to pay as much as US$4 an hour. If you intend to use email to keep in touch, make sure you have web-based email such as Yahoo or Hotmail. Some internet companies provide this service already so you will not need to set up a new account.

If you need to set up an account, most internet café owners will happily help. With Hotmail it is possible to make internet telephone calls to the US and Canada which are charged at the internet connection rate—a fraction of the cost of a traditionally routed call.

Public telephones take coins and cards

INTERNATIONAL DIALING CODES	
Australia	00 61
Canada	00 1
Germany	00 49
Italy	00 39
New Zealand	00 64
Spain	00 34
UK	00 44
US	00 1

MAILING RATES			
FROM COSTA RICA (IN COLONES)			
Region	Postcard	Letter	Package up to 2kg
US or Canada	55	70	3,225
Europe	70	90	5,400
Rest of the world	65	100	6,750

INTERNATIONAL COURIERS	
Courier	Contact
DHL	Paseo Colón, Calle 30–32, San José
	Tel 506 210 3838; www.dhl.com
UPS	Avenida 3, Calle 30–32, San José
	Tel 506 290 2828; www.ups.com

PLANNING

TOURIST OFFICES AND TICKETS

TOURIST OFFICES OVERSEAS

The efficient and nationally important Costa Rican Tourism Institute (Instituto Costarricense de Turismo or ICT) has several offices in the US and Europe. There are various ways of getting in touch; the easiest is through www.visitcostarica.com

Alternatively you can telephone them on 506 222 1090, or toll free from the US and Canada on tel 1-800/343-6332, or you can write to PO Box 777-1000, San José, Costa Rica, Central America. Comprehensive sources of information can be found in libraries and in your national press. The country is a popular destination and articles in the press are fairly common.

OPENING TIMES

Generally, shops are open Monday to Saturday from 8am to 6pm. Closing for lunch from 11.30 to 2 is becoming a thing of the past. Opening hours vary between cities and towns. In popular tourist areas such as the beaches of Guanacaste and the Pacific coastline, shops tend to have more extended opening hours. During the week, and in particular on the weekends, curio and handicraft stalls line the streets of the more developed beach towns.

The post office in San José is open on Monday to Friday from 8am to 5pm and on Saturday from 7.30am to noon.

The core opening hours for banks are from 9am to 3pm, Monday to Friday. However, some branches are open for longer; occasionally extending to Saturday morning. Service varies wildly; it can be incredibly slow or surprisingly fast. Be prepared to wait.

TICKETS

Theater tickets can be bought in advance from the ticket offices (Mon–Sat 10–1, 2–5). Ticket prices range from as little as US$2 for a minor national performance at the Teatro Melico Salazar to around US$12–25 at the Teatro Nacional. High profile international performances can vary in price from US$30–70 and usually sell out very quickly, so it is advisable to buy tickets as early as possible.

The Teatro Nacional in Plaza de la Cultura opened in 1897

Other theaters often have workshops, especially for children. There are discounts available for students at most performances and it is always worth looking in the press listings for two-for-one specials, often on Wednesday. Check out the listings in *La Nación* and the *Tico Times* for information on forthcoming events. Seasons for the Teatro Nacional, Teatro Melico Salazar and many others start in March. When it comes to live music, Costa Rican groups generally have a low profile outside the country, except for the group Editus, which won two Grammy awards in collaboration with Panamanian star Ruben Blades. With the exception of pop groups like the Brillianticos there's only a feeding frenzy for tickets when international bands visit. Cinema is a popular pastime and prices vary from US$3–5, often with cheaper tickets before 4pm. Saturday and Sunday afternoon showings are very popular with families and young couples, especially during the rainy season.

ICT TOURIST OFFICES		
	Contact	Open
Next to Museo de Oro Plaza de la Cultura	506 222 1090 ext. 277	Mon–Fri 9–1, 2–5
Central Post Office Calle 2, Avenida 1–3	506 258 8762	Mon–Fri 8–4
Juan Santamaría airport	506 443 2883	Mon–Fri 9–5
Peñas Blancas border crossing	506 677 0079	Mon–Fri 8–8
Paso Canoas	506 732 2035	Mon–Fri 7–10

NATIONAL HOLIDAYS	
January 1	New Year's Day
March 19	Feast of St. Joseph
April 11	Juan Santamaría Day
March/April	Easter
May 1	Labor Day
June	Corpus Christi
June 29	St. Peter and St. Paul
July 25	Guanacaste Day
August 2	Feast of the Virgin of Los Angeles
August 15	Assumption and Mother's Day
September 15	Independence Day
October 12	Columbus Day (and Limón carnival)
December 8	Immaculate Conception
December 24	Christmas Eve
December 25	Christmas Day

PLANNING

MEDIA, BOOKS AND MAPS

NEWSPAPERS

Of the six daily national newspapers the most popular and oldest is *La Nación* (www.nacion.co.cr) which toes— or creates—the establishment line. It also has the best arts and listings section. *La República* (www.larepublica.net) is the main competition, slightly slimmed down in content and style. Bringing up the rear is *Al Día,* which tends to have a frivolous approach to events but good sports coverage. *La Prensa Libre* (www.prensalibre.co.cr) is a good evening paper. *Rumbo* is the main weekly news magazine of the three available; the others are *Triunfo* and *Perfil*. *La Gaceta* is the official government paper.

English-language readers are treated to the *The Tico Times* (www.ticotimes.net) with a gentle mix of national and international issues. They also publish the densely informative *Exploring Costa Rica,* which stuffs everything you need to know about Costa Rica into a few hundred pages. *Costa Rica Traveler* is a free bimonthly magazine found in better hotels and restaurants. Free regional magazines in Jacó (*Jacó News*), Quepos (*Quepolandía*) and Tamarindo (*The Howler*) provide local information. Also look out for the bimonthly *Costa Rica Outdoors,* with good information on outdoor activities (visit www.costaricaoutdoors.com).

TELEVISION

There are 13 local television channels which carry a mix of imported soaps, sport and news. The main station is Channel 7, which competes with cable and satellite services with channels such as the Discovery Channel.

RADIO

Over 100 radio stations are available on the FM band, a few of which broadcast in English. 107.5 FM provides a heady mix of good driving music, and Radio Dos (Doze) on 99.5 FM plays a similar mix of hits.

Once you've had enough of living in the past, explore the wavelengths with the search button. You'll find jazz on Echo 95.7. Outside the Central Highlands reception is patchy.

The national media is independent and boasts several newspapers

BOOKS
Natural history

Les Beletsky, *Costa Rica: The Ecotravellers Wildlife Guide* (1998, Academic Press).
● An overview of the natural wealth of the country, with drawings of wildlife—a good all-in-one choice.

Mario Boza, *Costa Rica National Parks* (1999, Incafo).
● Take the small, handy option, or the glossy coffee table one, both filled with good information and pictures compiled by the founder of the national park system.

Archie Carr, *The Windward Road: Adventures of a Naturalist on Remote Caribbean Shores* (1979).
● A collection of tales about Archie Carr's experiences on the north Caribbean shore and the turtle nesting beaches of Tortuguero.

Daniel Janzen, *Costa Rica Natural History* (1983, University of Chicago Press).
● A glorious weighty book, packed with highly accessible information edited by the grandfather of Guanacaste National Park.

John Kricher, *A Neotropical Companion* (1997, Princeton University Press).
● A detailed guide through the grey area between academic study and keen interest, now available in paperback.

Gary Stiles and Alexander Skutch, *A Guide to the Birds of Costa Rica* (1989, Cornell University).
● The best guide to the birdlife of Costa Rica—accept no imitations.

Travel guides

Christopher P. Baker, *Moon Handbook Costa Rica* (2007, Avalon Travel Publishing).
● A large and detailed guide to every corner of Costa Rica, with detailed maps to both cities and off-the-beaten-path drives.

Lee Eudy, *Chasing Jaguars: The Complete Guide to Costa Rican Whitewater* (2003, Earthbound Sports).

Streetside vendors sell newspapers and magazines

• Comprehensive profiles of 40 of the country's best white-water runs, with maps.

Fiction
Barbara Ras, *Costa Rica: A Traveler's Literary Companion* (1994, Whereabouts Press).
• A much loved collection of 26 stories drawn from across the country.

History
Mark Edelman and Joanne Kenen, *The Costa Rica Reader* (1989, Grove Atlantic).
• A good historical overview of the country, although out of print so difficult to find.

Tjabel Daling, *Costa Rica: A Guide to the People, Politics and Culture* (1998, Latin America Bureau).
• A pocket history and overview of the country, picking up on the main themes that make up modern Costa Rica.

Iván Molina and Steven Palmer, *The History of Costa Rica* (1998, University of Costa Rica).
• A brief, up-to-date and illustrated history of Costa Rica in a highly manageable little package.

Pauline Palmer, *What Happen: A Folk History of Costa Rica's Talamanca Coast* (1977, Ecodesarollos).
• An account of the hardships of life in Costa Rica's southern Caribbean. ("Happen" is a colloquial Creole idiom.)

MAPS
Several companies provide excellent maps of the country. International Travel Maps, published by ITMB in Canada (www.itmb.com), produce an authoritative 1:500,000 travel map which is widely available in stores throughout the country, and internationally in good book stores.
The Instituto Geográfico, Avenida 20, Calle 9–11, at the Ministry of Public Works and Transport (MOPT) in San José, sells good 1:50,000 topographical maps, open 7.30–noon and 12.45–3, from US$2.
But even the best maps should not be completely trusted when you're on backroads in remote regions.

WEBSITES

The amount of information about Costa Rica on the internet is positively daunting. Most hotels and organizations can be contacted by email, many have their own website.

GOVERNMENT AND CONSERVATION
www.visitcostarica.com
The official Costa Rican Tourist Board site, as good a place as any to start your surfing.

www.ticotimes.net
The *Tico Times* website, very useful for catching up on the latest information.

www.costarica-embassy.org
The Costa Rican embassy site in Washington, with useful information and links.

www.usembassy.or.cr
The US Embassy site in Costa Rica with travel information, and some interesting background.

http://costarica.
embassyhomepage.com
The Costa Rican embassy site in London. Good information and up-to-date links.

www.rree.go.cr
The Costa Rican Ministry of Foreign Affairs website with all the information you could need on visas, embassies, residency.

www.minae.go.cr
The Ministry for the Environment and Energy which has overall control for SINAC, the national park program, and energy development.

www.sinaccr.net
The Sistema Nacional de Areas de Conservacion website.

www.inbio.ac.cr
The INBioparques site, with access to the conservation organization's databases.

GENERAL INFORMATION
www.yellowweb.co.cr
Information and links although not always up to date.
www.infocostarica.com
Another good general site.

www.costaricaoutdoors.com
General information and packed

An increasing amount of information about Costa Rica is available online

with snippets of background information and stories.

www.centralamerica.com/cr
Another good base to start looking around.

www.costaricaexpeditions.com
The website of one of Costa Rica's best tour operators, but with up-to-date news and weather which isn't just trying to get you to spend more money.

NATIONAL PARKS
www.chirripo.com
Parque Nacional Chirripó.

www.cocos-island.org
Parque Nacional Isla del Coco.

www.arenal.net
Parque Nacional Volcán Arenal.

www.cct.or.cr.com
Reserva Biolgica Bosque Nuboso Monteverde.

www.ots.ac.cr
Parque Nacional Palo Verde, La Selva Biological Station and Las Cruces Biological Station.

ACCOMMODATIONS
www.costarica.com
A generic website covering all aspects of the country, from travel to business.

www.distinctivehotels.com
The website of Costa Rica's foremost hotel group, representing seven boutique hotels.

PLANNING

SPANISH WORDS AND PHRASES

A little Spanish will make a difference to your visit. Once you have learned a few basic rules, it's an easy language to speak: It is phonetic and, unlike English, particular combinations of letters are always pronounced the same way. When a word ends in a vowel, an n or an s, the stress is usually on the penultimate syllable; otherwise, its on the last syllable. If a word has an accent, this is where the stress falls.

a	as in	pat	**ai, ay**	as **i** in	side
e	as in	set	**au**	as **ou** in	out
i	as **e** in	be	**ei, ey**	as **ey** in	they
o	as in	hot	**oi, oy**	as **oy** in	boy
u	as in	flute			

Consonants as in English except:
c before **i** and **e** as **th**, *although some pronounce it as* **s**
ch as **ch** in church
d at the end of a word becomes **th**
g before **i** or **e** becomes **ch** as in loch
h is silent
j as **ch** in loch
ll as **lli** in million
ñ as **ny** in canyon
qu is hard like a k
r usually rolled
v is a **b**
z is a **th**, *but sometimes pronounced as s*

MAP PHRASES

Ranger Station
Estacíon Guardabosque

Park Entrance
Parque Entrada

National Park
Parque Nacional

Protected Area
Zona Protectora

Wildlife Reserve
Refugio de Vida Silvestre

Biological Reserve
Reserva Biológica

Cloud Forest
Bosque Nuboso

Hot Springs
Fuente Caliente

CONVERSATION

What is the time?
¿Qué hora es?

I don't speak Spanish
No hablo español

Do you speak English?
¿Habla inglés?

I don't understand
No entiendo

Please repeat that
Por favor repita eso

Please speak more slowly
Por favor hable más despacio

What does this mean?
¿Qué significa esto?

Can you write that for me?
¿Me lo puede escribir?

My name is…
Me llamo…

What's your name?
¿Como se llama?

Hello, pleased to meet you
Hola, encantado/a

I'm from…
Soy de…

I live in…
Vivo en…

Where do you live?
¿Dónde vive usted?

Good morning/afternoon
Buenos días/buenas tardes

Good evening/night
Buenas noches

Goodbye
Adiós

This is my wife/husband/son/daughter/friend
Esta es mi mujer/marido/hijo/hija/amigo

See you later
Hasta luego

That's all right
Está bien

I don't know
No lo sé

You're welcome
De nada

How are you?
¿Cómo está?

USEFUL WORDS

yes **sí**	thank you **gracias**	here **aquí**	how **cómo**	I'm sorry **Lo siento**	small **pequeño**
no **no**	there **allí**	when **cuándo**	why **por qué**	excuse me **perdone**	good **bueno**
please **por favor**	where **dónde**	who **quién**	free **gratis**	large **grande**	bad **malo**

morning **la mañana**	tomorrow **mañana**	Monday **lunes**	month **el mes**	June **junio**	Easter **Pascua**
afternoon **la tarde**	now **ahora**	Tuesday **martes**	year **el año**	July **julio**	Christmas **Navidad**
evening **la tarde/ noche**	later **más tarde**	Wednesday **miércoles**	January **enero**	August **agosto**	New Year **El Año Nuevo**
day **el día**	spring **primavera**	Thursday **jueves**	February **febrero**	September **septiembre**	All Saints' Day **Todos los Santos**
night **la noche**	summer **verano**	Friday **viernes**	March **marzo**	October **octubre**	vacation (holiday)
today **hoy**	autumn **otoño**	Saturday **sábado**	April **abril**	November **noviembre**	**las vacaciones**
yesterday **ayer**	winter **invierno**	Sunday **domingo**	May **mayo**	December **diciembre**	pilgrimage **una romería**

MONEY

Is there a bank/bureau de change nearby?
Hay un banco/una oficina de cambio cerca?

Can I cash this here?
¿Puedo cobrar esto aquí?

I'd like to change dollars/sterling into colonnes
Quisiera cambiar dólares libras para colonnes

Can I use my credit card to withdraw cash?
¿Puedo usar la tarjeta de crédito para sacar dinero?

What is the exchange rate?
¿Cómo está el cambio?

GETTING AROUND

Where is the information desk?
¿Dónde está el mostrador de información?

Where is the timetable?
¿Dónde está el horario?

Does this train/bus go to…?
¿Va este tren/autobús a…?

Does this train/bus stop at…?
¿Para este tren/autobús en…?

Do I have to get off here?
¿Me tengo que bajar aquí?

Do you have a subway/bus map?
¿Tiene un mapa del metro/de los autobuses?

Can I have a single/return ticket to…
¿Me da un boleto sencillo/de ida y vuelta para…?

Can I have a standard/first-class ticket to…
Quisiera un boleto de segunda/primera clase para…

I'd like to rent a car
Quiero alquilar un coche

Where are we?
¿Dónde estamos?

I'm lost
Estoy perdido

Is this the way to…?
¿Es esto el camino para ir a…?

I am in a hurry
Tengo prisa

Where can I find a taxi?
¿Dónde puedo encontrar un taxi?

Please take me to…
Me lleva a…, por favor

Please slow down
Vaya más despacio por favor

Can you turn on the meter
Podría poner el metro

How much is the journey?
¿Cuánto cuesta el viaje?

Could you wait for me?
¿Me podría esperar aquí?

POST AND TELEPHONES

Where is the nearest post office?
¿Dónde está la oficina de correos más cercana?

What is the postage to…
¿Cuánto vale mandarlo a…?

I'd like to send this by air mail
Quiero mandar esto por correo aéreo

Hello this is…
Bueno, habla…?

I'd like to speak to…
¿Podría hablar con…?

Who is speaking?
¿Con quién hablo?

What is the number for…
¿Cuál es el número de…?

Please put me through to…
Comuníqueme con…, por favor

Where can I buy a phone card?
¿Dónde puedo comprar una tarjeta de teléfono?

Extension…, please
La extensión…, por favor

SPANISH WORDS AND PHRASES 225

Could you help me please?
¿Me podría atender por favor?

How much is this?
¿Cuánto vale esto?

I'm looking for…
Estoy buscando…

When does the shop open/close?
¿A qué hora abre/cierra la tienda?

I'm just looking
Sólo estoy viendo

Do you have anything less expensive/smaller/larger
¿Tiene algo más barato/pequeño/grande?

Do you have this in…?
¿Tienen esto en…?

This is the right size
Esta talla está bien

I'll take this
Me llevo esto

Do you have a bag for this?
¿Tiene una bolsa para esto?

Can you gift wrap this?
¿Me lo envuelve para regalo?

Do you accept credit cards?
¿Aceptan tarjetas de crédito?

I'd like … grams
Me pone … gramos, por favor

I'd like a kilo of …
Me da un kilo de…

I'd like … slices of that
Me pone … pedazos de eso

This isn't what I want
Esto no es lo que quiero

Can I help myself?
¿Puedo servirme?

bakery
la panadería

bookshop
la librería

pharmacy
la farmacia

supermarket
el supermercado

market
el mercado

sale
las rebajas

NUMBERS

1	6	11	16	21	70
uno	seis	once	dieciséis	veintiuno	setente
2	7	12	17	30	80
dos	siete	doce	diecisiete	treinta	ochenta
3	8	13	18	40	90
tres	ocho	trece	dieciocho	cuarenta	noventa
4	9	14	19	50	100
cuatro	nueve	catorce	diecinueve	cincuenta	cien
5	10	15	20	60	1,000
cinco	diez	quince	veinte	sesenta	mil

HOTELS

Do you have a room?
¿Tiene una habitación?

I have a reservation for … nights
Tengo una reservación para … noches

How much per night?
¿Cuánto es por noche?

Double room
Habitación doble con cama de matrimonio

Single room
Habitación sencilla

Twin room
Habitación doble con dos camas

With bath/shower
Con baño/ducha

Swimming pool
La alberca

Air conditioning
Aire acondicionado

Non smoking
Se prohibe fumar

Is breakfast included?
¿Está el desayuno incluido?

When is breakfast served?
¿A qué hora se sirve el desayuno?

May I see the room?
¿Puedo ver la habitación?

Is there an elevator?
¿Hay elevador?

I'll take this room
Me quedo con la esta habitación

The room is dirty
La habitación está sucia

The room is too hot/cold
Hace demasiado calor/frío en la habitación

Can I pay my bill?
La cuenta por favor

Could you order a taxi for me?
¿Me pide un taxi por favor?

See also the menu reader on page 181.

I'd like to reserve a table for .... people at…
Quisiera reservar una mesa para … personas para las…

A table for …, please
Una mesa para …, por favor

We have/haven't booked
Tenemos una/no tenemos reservación

What time does the restaurant open?
¿A qué hora se abre el restaurante?

We'd like to wait for a table
Queremos esperar a que haya una mesa

Could we sit here?
¿Nos podemos sentar aquí?

Is this table free?
¿Queda libre esta mesa?

Are there tables outside?
¿Hay mesas afuera?

Is there a car park?
¿Hay aparcamiento?

Where are the lavatories?
¿Dónde están los baños?

Can I have an ashtray?
¿Me da un cenicero?

I prefer non-smoking
Prefiero no fumadores

Could you warm this up for me?
¿Me podria calentar esto?

Could we see the menu/ wine list?
¿Podemos ver la carta/ carta de vinos?

We would like something to drink
Quisiéramos algo a beber

What do you recommend?
¿Qué nos recomienda?

Can you recommend a local wine?
¿Puede usted recomendar un vino de la región?

Is there a dish of the day?
¿Hay un plato del día?

I am a vegetarian
Soy vegetariano

I am diabetic
Soy diabético(a)

I can't eat wheat/sugar/salt/ pork/beef/dairy/nuts
No puedo tomar trigo/azú- car/sal/cerdo/carne (de res)/ productos lácteos/nueces

Could I have a bottle of still/sparkling water?
¿Me podría traer una botella de agua mineral sin/con gas?

Could we have some more bread?
¿Nos podría traer más pan?

Could we have some salt and pepper?
¿Nos podría traer sal y pimienta?

How much is this dish?
¿Cuánto es este plato?

This is not what I ordered
Esto no es lo que había pedido

I ordered…
Habia pedido…

I'd like…
Quisiera…

May I change my order
¿Puedo cambiar la orden?

I'd prefer a salad
Prefiero una ensalada

How is it cooked?
¿Cómo está hecho?

Is it very spicy?
¿Esta muy picante?

The food is cold
La comida está fría

… is too rare/overcooked
… está demasiado crudo/ demasiado hecho

We would like a coffee
Quisieramos tomar café

May I have the bill, please?
¿Me trae la cuenta, por favor?

Is service included?
¿Está incluido el servicio?

What is this charge?
¿Qué es esta cantidad?

The bill is not right
La cuenta no está bien

We didn't have this
No tomamos esto

Do you accept this credit card (travelers' checks)?
¿Acepta usted esta tarjeta de crédito (cheques de via- jero)?

I'd like to speak to the manager
Quisiera hablar con el jefe

The food was excellent
La comida fue excelente

We enjoyed it, thank you
Nos ha gustado, muchas gracias

breakfast
el desayuno

lunch
la comida

dinner
la cena

starters
los antojitos/botanas

main course
el plato principal

dessert
el postre

dish of the day
el plato del día

bread
el pan

sugar
el azúcar

wine list
la carta de vinos

knife/fork/spoon
el cuchillo/tenedor/ la cuchara

waiter/waitress
El mesero/la mesara

Where is the tourist information office?
¿Dónde está la oficina de turismo?

Do you have a city map?
¿Tiene un mapa de la ciudad?

Can you give me some information about…?
¿Me podría dar información sobre…?

What sights/hotels/restaurants can you recommend?
¿Qué lugares de interés/ hoteles/restaurantes nos recomienda?

Can you point them out on the map?
¿Me los podría señalar en el mapa?

What time does it open/close?
¿A qué hora se abre/cierra?

Are there guided tours?
¿Hay visitas con guía?

Is there an English-speaking guide?
¿Hay algún guía que hable inglés?

Can we make reservations here?
¿Podemos hacer las reservaciones aquí?

What is the admission price?
¿Cuánto es la entrada?

Is photography allowed?
¿Se permite tomar fotos?

Is there a discount for senior citizens/students?
¿Hay descuento para los mayores/los estudiantes?

Do you have a brochure in English?
¿Tiene un folleto en inglés?

What time does the show start?
¿A qué hora empieza la función?

How much is a ticket?
¿Cuánto vale una entrada?

IN THE TOWN

church
la iglesia

castle
el castillo

museum
el museo

park
el parque

cathedral
la catedral

bridge
el puente

gallery
la galería de arte

river
el río

no entry
prohibido el paso

entrance
entrada

exit
salida

lavatories
los baños

men/women
caballeros/señoras

open
abierto

closed
cerrado

ILLNESS AND EMERGENCIES

I don't feel well
No me siento bien

Could you call a doctor?
¿Podría llamar a un médico?

I feel nauseous
Tengo ganas de vomitar

I have a headache
Tengo dolor de cabeza

I am allergic to…
Soy alérgico a…

I am on medication
Estoy tomando medicamentos

I am diabetic
Soy diabético

I have asthma
Soy asmático

hospital
el hospital

How long will I have to stay in bed/hospital?
¿Cuánto tiempo tendré que quedarme en la cama/ el hospital?

How many tablets a day should I take?
¿Cuántas pastillas debéna de tomar diario?

Can I have a painkiller?
¿Me da un analgésico?

I need to see a doctor/ dentist
Necesito ver un médico/ dentista

I have bad toothache
Tengo un dolor de muelas horrible

Help!
Socorro

Stop thief!
Al ladrón

Call the fire brigade/police/ ambulance
Llame a los bomberos/la policía/una ambulancia

I have lost my passport/ wallet/purse/handbag
He perdido me pasaporte/ la cartera/el monedero/ la bolsa

Is there a lost property office?
¿Hay una oficina de objetos perdidos?

I have had an accident
Tuve un accidente

I have been robbed
Me han robado

Where is the police station?
¿Dónde está la comisaría?

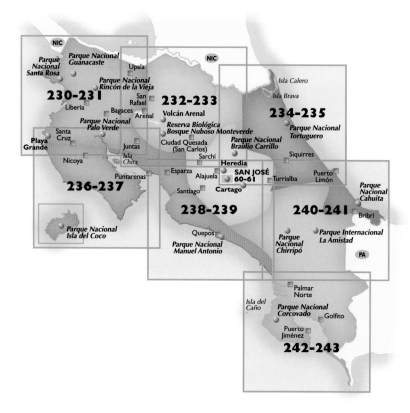

NIC

Parque Nacional Santa Rosa

Parque Nacional Guanacaste

Upala

Parque Nacional Rincón de la Vieja

230-231

San Rafael

Liberia

Bagaces

Arenal

Parque Nacional Palo Verde

Santa Cruz

Playa Grande

Juntas

Isla Chira

Nicoya

Puntarenas

236-237

Parque Nacional Isla del Coco

NIC

232-233

Volcán Arenal

Reserva Biológica Bosque Nuboso Monteverde

Ciudad Quesada (San Carlos)

Sarchí

Isla Calero

Isla Brava

234-235

Parque Nacional Tortuguero

Parque Nacional Braulio Carrillo

Siquirres

Heredia

Esparza

Alajuela

SAN JOSÉ 60-61

Santiago

Cartago

Turrialba

Puerto Limón

Parque Nacional Cahuita

240-241

Bribri

238-239

Quepos

Parque Nacional Manuel Antonio

Parque Nacional Chirripó

Parque Internacional La Amistad

PA

Palmar Norte

Isla del Caño

Parque Nacional Corcovado

Golfito

Puerto Jiménez

242-243

▬▬▬	Motorway (Expressway)
▬▬▬	Interamericana / Pan-American Highway
▬▬▬	National road
▬▬▬	Regional road
▬▬▬	Main road
▬▬▬	Minor road
———	Railway
▬▬▬	International boundary
———	Administrative region boundary
▮	Built-up area
■	City / Town
▨	National park
⌐ ¬	Indian reserve
●	Featured place of interest
✈	Airport
621 ▲	Height in metres
– –	Port / Ferry route
▬O▬	Border crossing
☀	Viewpoint

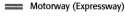

230-243

0   10 km

0   10 miles

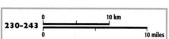

Maps

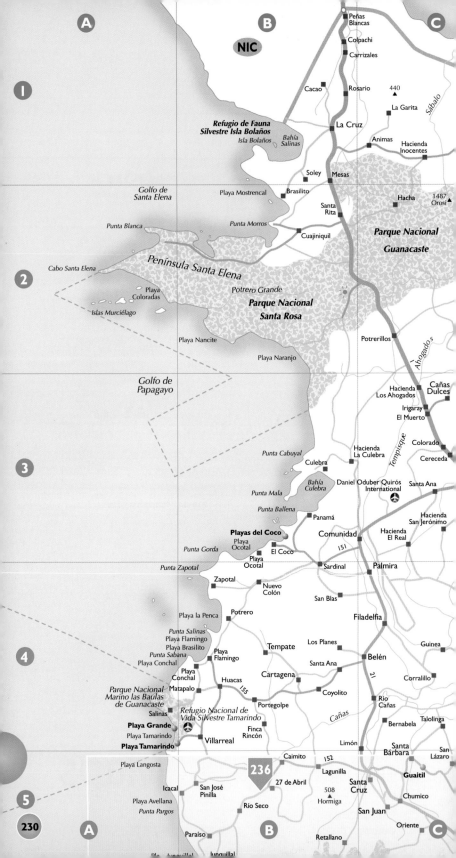

Lago de Nicaragua

D
E

Islas
Solentiname

I

La Virgen

Santa
Cecilia

Orosi

Brasilia

Haciendas

Birmania

Pizote

México

2

4

San José

Delicias

San Isidro

1659
Cacao

Colonia
Dos Rios

Porvenir

Santa
Clara

Upala

Angeles

ALAJUELA

Brisas

Rosario

Colonia
Puntarenas

1806
Rincón de
la Vieja

**Parque Nacional
Rincón de
la Vieja**

San Isidro

Milpas

Canalete

Pital

1916
Santa Maria
**Hacienda
Santa Maria**

Aguas
Claras

Finca
Armenia

Canalete

4

Santo
Domingo

Cordillera

Hacienda Rincón
de la Vieja

2028
Miravalles

Bijagua

232

de

Guanacaste

San Jorge

Curubande

Limonal

Guayabo

Frío

*Zona Protectora
Miravalles*

1916
Tenorio

3

**Parque Nacional
Volcán Tenorio**

Liberia

La Ese

Fortuna

Lago
de Cote

Torno

San Bernardo

1058
Jilguero

142

Aguacate

Liberia

Sante Fé

Paraíso

Arenal

GUANACASTE

Salitral

Hacienda
Tenorio

Tierras
Morenas

Sabalito

*Laguna
de Arenal*

Salto

Bagaces

Montano

Palmira

La Palma

6

Los Angeles

Tronadora

1

Hacienda
Las Ciruelas

*Reserva Biológica
Lomas Barbudal*

Montenegro

19

Tilarán

Hacienda
Asientillo

Corobici

Vergel

**Quebrada
Grande**

4

Hacienda
Tamarindo

Cañas

Jabilla Abajo

Libano

Dos de
Tilarán

Ortega

Hacienda
Mojica

Bebedero

San Miguel

Nube

Hacienda
Palo Verde

**Parque Nacional
Palo Verde**

Quesara

*Reserva
Bosque
Taboga*

Cañas

Barrio Jesús

Sierra

Puerto
Humo

Finca
Lajas

Lajas

Solimar

San Joaquín

Limonal

145

Juntas

Zapote

Tempisque

Porozal

237

Santa
Lucia

18

Palma

Pueblo
Nuevo

Sa

150

San
Antonio

Puerto
Moreno

Huacas

Pozo
Az

Lagarto

231

Guaci

Piave

**Parque Nacional
Barra Honda**

Quebrada
Honda

D

San
Buenaventura

Colorado

E

Tortugal

5

Copal

Yomale

Suac

119
▲
Tortuguero

Tortuguero

Laguna del Tortuguero

334
▲
Parque Nacional
Tortuguero

LIMÓN

Parismina

Parismina

Peje

Pacuare

Reserva Bosque
Matina

San Alberto
Nuevo

Manila

Cairo

Cuatro Millas

Pacuarito

Punta de Riel

Siquirres

Batán

Matina

Boca del
Pantano

32

Estrada

Larga
Distancia

Stratford

Zona Protectora
Pacuare

Corina

Río Cuba

Búfalo

Moín

Portete

Puerto
Limón

BARBILLA

Río
Blanco

Liverpool

○ Isla Uvita

Cieneguita

Blanco

240

Playa Hermosa

Trébol

Westfalia

Parque Nacional
Barbilla

241

Petróleo

Banano

Beverly

María Luisa

Bananito
Norte

Cabeza
de Buey

M

Asunción

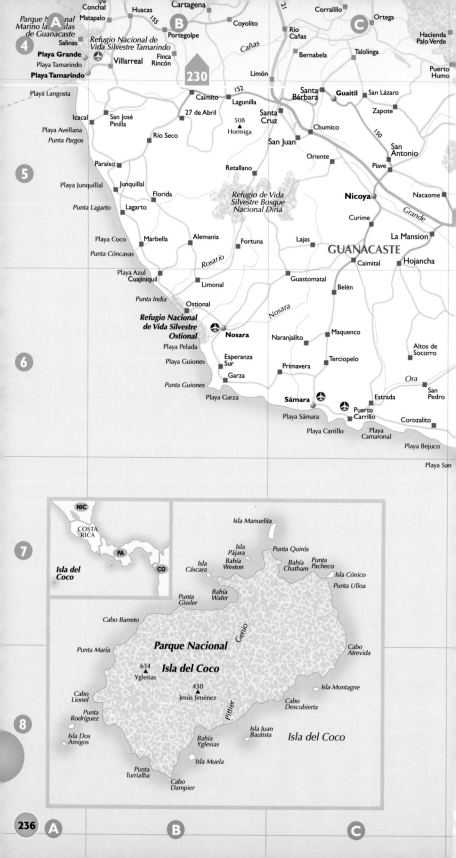

Conchal
Matapalo
Huacas
Cartagena
Corralillo
Ortega
21
Coyolito
Hacienda
Palo Verde

Parque Nacional
Marino las Baulas
de Guanacaste
Salinas
Portegolpe
Río
Cañas
Bernabela
Talolinga
Puerto
Humo

A
Refugio Nacional de
Vida Silvestre Tamarindo
Cañas
B
C

4

Playa Grande
Villarreal
Finca
Rincón
Limón

Playa Tamarindo
Playa Tamarindo

230

Caimito
152
Lagunilla
Santa
Bárbara
Guaitil
San Lázaro

Playa Langosta
27 de Abril
508
Santa
Cruz
Chumico
Zapote

Icacal
San José
Pinilla
Hormiga
San Juan
150
San
Antonio

Playa Avellana
Río Seco
Oriente
Piave

Punta Pargos
Retallano
Curime
Nacaome

Paraíso
Refugio de Vida
Silvestre Bosque
Nacional Diriá
Nicoya

5

Playa Junquillal
Junquillal
La Mansion
Grande

Florida
Lagarto
Curime

Punta Lagarto
Lagarto
Lajas
GUANACASTE

Playa Coco
Marbella
Alemania
Fortuna
Caimital
Hojancha

Punta Cóncavas
Rosario
Guastomatal
Belén

Playa Azul
Cuajiniquil
Limonal

Punta India
Ostional
Nosara

Refugio Nacional
de Vida Silvestre
Ostional
Nosara
Naranjalito
Maquenco
Altos de
Socorro

6

Playa Pelada
Esperanza
Sur
Terciopelo
Ora

Playa Guiones
Garza
Primavera
Estrada
San
Pedro

Punta Guiones
Sámara
Puerto
Carrillo
Corozalito

Playa Garza
Playa Sámara
Playa Carrillo
Playa
Camaronal
Playa Bejuco

Playa San

NIC
Isla Manuelita

COSTA
RICA
PA
Isla
Pájara
Bahía
Weston
Punta Quirós
Punta
Pacheco

7

Isla del
Coco
CO
Isla
Cáscara
Bahía
Chatham
Isla Cónico
Punta Ulloa

Punta
Gissler
Bahía
Wafer

Cabo Barreto
Genio
Cabo
Atrevida

Punta María
Parque Nacional
Isla del Coco

634
Yglesias

Cabo
Lionel
430
Jesús Jiménez
Isla Montagne

Punta
Rodríguez
Cabo
Descubierta

8

Isla Dos
Amigos
Pittier
Isla Juan
Bautista
Isla del Coco

Bahía
Yglesias

Punta
Turrialba
Isla Muela

Cabo
Dampier

*Parque Nacional
Palo Verde*

Bebedero

San Miguel

Tilarán

Cor di llera

Arenal

Nubes

Santa Elena

Monteverde

*Rese
Bosc
M*

Quesara

*Reserva
Bosque
Taboga*

Barrio Jesús

231

Cañas

Finca
Lajas

San
Joaquín

Limonal

145

Sierra

Juntas

Lajas

Solimar

Palma

San Antonio

Porozal

Santa
Lucía

18

Pueblo
Nuevo

Huacas

Pozo
Azul

232

Lagarto

Guacimal

Puerto
Moreno

San
Buenaventura

Colorado

Tortugal

Yomale

PUNTARENAS

Coyolar

Araniu

*Parque Nacional
Barra Honda*

Quebrada
Honda

Coyolito

Manzanillo

San
Gerardo

Rancho
Grande

Cabu

Copal

18

Playa Camerita

Pajaros

247

Barbudal

21

Boca
Letras

Puerto
Jesús

Morales

San
Agustín

Ciruelas

Limonal

*Reserva Biológica
Isla Pájaros*

Chomes

Santa
Rita

San Pablo

*Golfo de
Nicoya*

Pitahaya

Barr

Zapotal

Pavones

Isla Bejuco

Corazal

*Isla
Venado*

Isla Caballo

Puntarenas

17

Chacarita

Carmona

161

Playa Doña Ana

San Ramón

Canjel

Jicaral

Lepanto

Playa
Naranjo

*Isla San
Lucas*

6

Calde

erto C

Cerro Azul

Cuajiniquil

Montaña
Grande

Esperanza

Gigante

*Reserva Biológica
Isla Guayabo*

Protecte

Juan de León

Corra

Península de Nicoya

Jabillo

Zapote

Guadalupe

Quebrada
Bonita

Río Grande

*Isla
Cedros*

Bejuco

Millal

Río Seco

755

Jabilla

Paquera

*Reserva Biológica
Islas Negritos*

Miguel

Guaria

Curú

**Refugio Nacional
de Vida Silvestre Curú**

Playa Coyote

San Francisco
de Coyote

Río Frío

PUNTARENAS

*Isla
Tortuga*

Punta Coyote

Pto. Coyote

Pachanga

Pochote

238

Playa Caletas

Bajos de
Arío

Santa Fé

Tacotales

Tambor

Playa
Pochote

Bahía Ballena

7

Playa Bongo

Cóbano

Playa Tambor

Playa Manzanillo

Santiago

Playa Cocalito

Playa Cocal

Playa Arío

Montezuma

Playa Montezuma

Playa Santa Teresa

Malpaís

Cabuya

*Reserva Natural Absoluta
Cabo Blanco*

8

Playa Balsitas

Cabo Blanco

*Isla Cabo
Blanco*

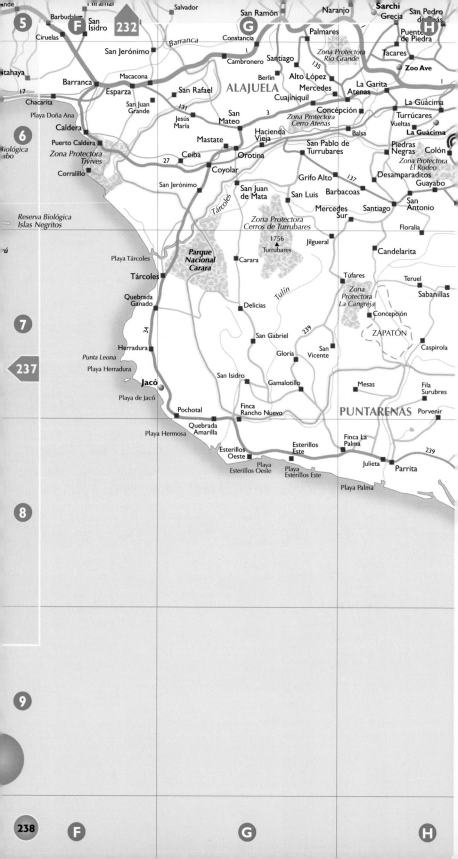

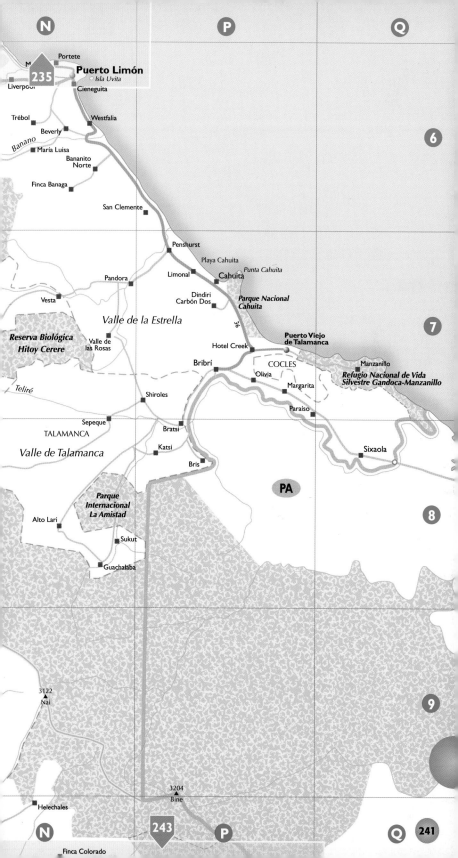

Portete

Puerto Limón
○ Isla Uvita

235

M
Liverpool
Cieneguita

Trébol

Westfalia

Banano

Beverly

María Luisa

Bananito Norte

Finca Banaga

San Clemente

Penshurst

Playa Cahuita

Pandora

Limonal

Cahuita

Punta Cahuita

Vesta

Dindiri
Carbón Dos

Parque Nacional Cahuita

Valle de la Estrella

Reserva Biológica Hitoy Cerere

Valle de las Rosas

Hotel Creek

36

Bribrí

Puerto Viejo de Talamanca

COCLES

Olivia

Manzanillo

Teliré

Margarita

Refugio Nacional de Vida Silvestre Gandoca-Manzanillo

Shiroles

Paraíso

Sepeque

Bratsi

TALAMANCA

Katsi

Sixaola

Valle de Talamanca

Bris

PA

Parque Internacional La Amistad

Alto Lari

Sukut

Guachalaba

3122
Nai

3204
Bine

Helechales

Finca Colorado

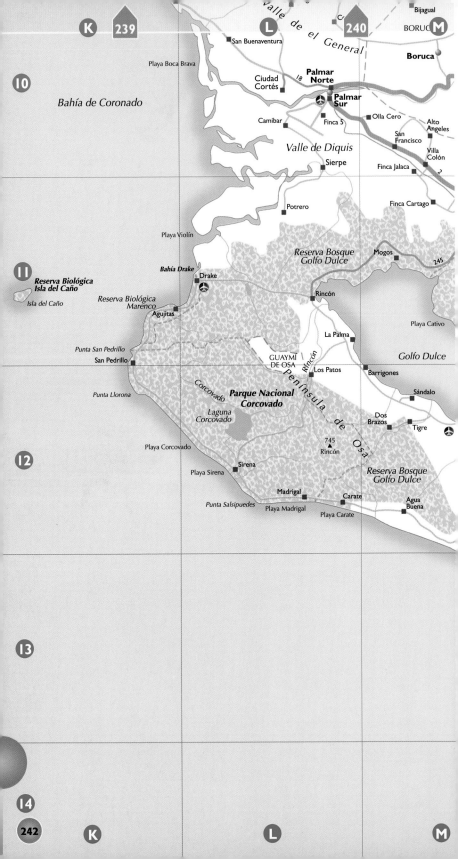

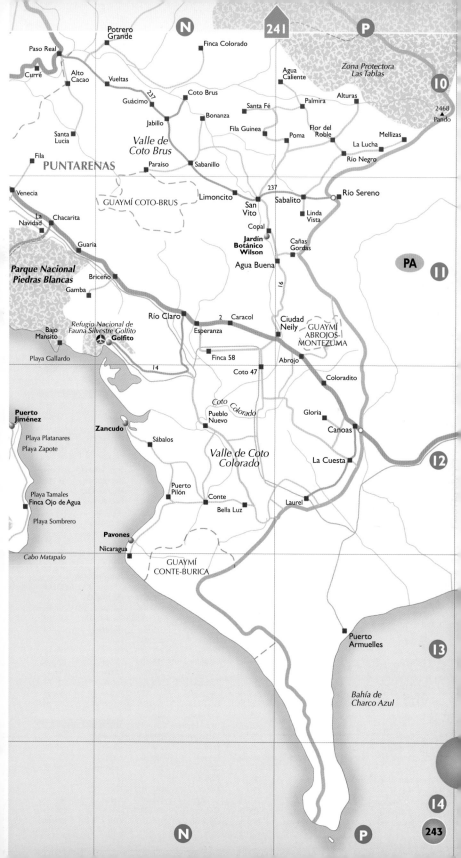

ACKNOWLEDGMENTS

Abbreviations for the credits are as follows:
AA = AA World Travel Library, **t** (top), **b** (bottom), **c** (centre), **l** (left), **r** (right), **bg** (background)

UNDERSTANDING COSTA RICA

4 AA/Steve Watkins; **5cl** AA/Nicholas Sumner; **5cc** AA/Clive Sawyer; **5cr** AA/Steve Watkins; **5b** AA/Clive Sawyer; **7t** AA/Nicholas Sumner; **7cl** AA/Nicholas Sumner; **7cr** Rio Parismina Lodge; **7bl** AA/Nicholas Sumner; **7br** AA/Nicholas Sumner; **8tl** AA/Clive Sawyer; **8tr** AA/Clive Sawyer; **8cl** AA/Clive Sawyer; **8cr** AA/Clive Sawyer; **8cc** AA/Nicholas Sumner; **8cr** AA/Steve Watkins; **8bc** AA/Nicholas Sumner; **8cr** AA/Nicholas Sumner; **9tl** AA/Clive Sawyer; **9tr** Instituto Costarricense de Turismo; **9cl** AA/Clive Sawyer; **9cr** AA/Clive Sawyer; **9cl** Chris Nord/Deep Blue Diving Adventures; **9bl** AA/Steve Watkins; **9br** AA/Clive Sawyer; **10cl** AA/Nicholas Sumner; **10cc** Instituto Costarricense de Turismo; **10cr** AA/Clive Sawyer; **11cl** AA/Nicholas Sumner; **11cc** AA/Clive Sawyer; **11cr** AA/Clive Sawyer; **11b** AA/Clive Sawyer; **13** AA/Clive Sawyer; **14cl** Michael & Patricia Fogden; **14cc** Instituto Costarricense de Turismo; **14cr** Jack Ewing/Hacienda Baru National Wildlife Refuge; **15cl** AA/Clive Sawyer; **15cr** NHPA/Kevin Schafer; **16t** NHPA/Adrian Hepworth; **16b** NHPA/Mark Bowler; **17cl** AA/Nicholas Sumner; **17cc** Jan Csernoch; **17cr** NHPA/George Bernard; **18cl** Tom Vezo/naturepl.com; **18cc** AA/Nicholas Sumner; **18cr** AA/Nicholas Sumner; **19t** NHPA/Jany Sauvanet; **19c** Jack Ewing/Hacienda Baru National Wildlife Refuge; **20l** Michael & Patricia Fogden; **20r** Michael & Patricia Fogden; **21cl** AA/Nicholas Sumner; **21cc** NHPA/Kevin Schafer; **21cr** AA/Nicholas Sumner; **22** Ted Miller/Still Pictures; **23cl** AA/Nicholas Sumner; **23cc** Michael & Patricia Fogden; **23cr** Michael & Patricia Fogden; **24cl** AA/Steve Watkins; **24cc** Instituto Costarricense de Turismo; **24cr** Michael & Patricia Fogden; **24t** Michael & Patricia Fogden.

LIVING COSTA RICA

25 AA/Clive Sawyer; **26/27bg** Sierra/www.divinedolphin.com; **26tl** AA/Clive Sawyer; **26tc** AA/Nicholas Sumner; **26tr** Marianne Coates/www.kidssavingtherainforest.org; **26c** AA/Nicholas Sumner; **26bl** NHPA/Anthony Bannister; **26br** AA/Clive Sawyer; **27tl** AA/Clive Sawyer; **27tr** AA/Clive Sawyer; **27cl** AA/Nicholas Sumner; **27cc** Instituto Costarricense de Turismo; **27cc** AA/Nicholas Sumner; **27cr** Instituto Costarricense de Turismo; **27cc** Michael & Patricia Fogden; **27b** AA/Clive Sawyer; **28/29bg** AA/Nicholas Sumner; **28tl** AA/Nicholas Sumner; **28tr** www.jjphoto.dk; **28cl** AA/Nicholas Sumner; **28cr** AA/Clive Sawyer; **28cl** AA/Clive Sawyer; **28b** AA/Nicholas Sumner; **29tl** AA/Clive Sawyer; **29tc** AA/Clive Sawyer; **29tr** AA/Nicholas Sumner; **29cl** Paul Furlong; **29cc** AA/Steve Watkins; **29cr** Paul Furlong; **29b** AA/Clive Sawyer; **30/31bg** AA/Clive Sawyer; **30tl** AA/Steve Watkins; **30tr** Eye Ubiquitous/Hutchison; **30cr** AA/Clive Sawyer; **30bl** AA/Clive Sawyer; **30br** Instituto Costarricense de Turismo; **31tl** AA/Clive Sawyer; **31tc** New Line/The Kobal Collection; **31tr** AA/Clive Sawyer; **31cl** Studio of Barry Biesanz; **31cc** Studio of Barry Biesanz; **31cr** AA/Nicholas Sumner; **31b** AA/Clive Sawyer; **32bg** AA/Nicholas Sumner; **32tl** AA/Clive Sawyer; **32tc** AA/Clive Sawyer; **32tr** AA/Clive Sawyer; **32cl** AA/Clive Sawyer; **32cc** Gilles Mingasson/Liaison/Getty Images; **32cr** AA/Nicholas Sumner; **32b** AA/Steve Watkins.

THE STORY OF COSTA RICA

33 AA; **34/35bg** AA/Clive Sawyer; **34c** AA/Clive Sawyer; **34cr** AA/Clive Sawyer; **34cl** AA/Nicholas Sumner; **34bl** AA/Clive Sawyer; **34br** AA/Clive Sawyer; **35t** AA/Nicholas Sumner; **35cc** AA/Clive Sawyer; **35cc** AA/Nicholas Sumner; **35cr**

AA/Nicholas Sumner; **35c** AA/Clive Sawyer; **35bc** AA/Clive Sawyer; **35br** Instituto Costarricense de Turismo; **36/37bg** Instituto Costarricense de Turismo; **36t** AA; **36cr** AA/Nicholas Sumner; **36bl** AA; **36bc** AA/Clive Sawyer; **36br** Jacob Silberberg/Getty Images; **37cl** Eye of Science/Science Photo Library; **37cc** AA; **37cr** Nicholas Sumner; **37bl/c** AKG Images; **37br** AA; **38/39bg** AA/Clive Sawyer; **38cc** AA/Nicholas Sumner; **38t** Photodisc; **38bl** Instituto Costarricense de Turismo; **38bc** AA/Clive Sawyer; **38br** Bettmann/Corbis; **39cl** AA/Clive Sawyer; **39cc** AA/Nicholas Sumner; **39cc** AA/Clive Sawyer; **39cr** AA/Clive Sawyer; **39bc** AA/Clive Sawyer; **39br** AA/Clive Sawyer; **40bg** AA/Clive Sawyer; **40t** AA/Clive Sawyer; **40c** Instituto Costarricense de Turismo; **40b** AA/Nicholas Sumner.

ON THE MOVE

41 AA/Clive Sawyer; **42-44t** Digital Vision; **42cr** Digital Vision; **42cl** AA/Nicholas Sumner; **44b** Nature Air; **45t** AA/Nicholas Sumner; **45c** AA/Clive Sawyer; **45b** Cruisewest; **46-49t** AA/Nicholas Sumner; **46b** AA/Clive Sawyer; **47c** AA/Nicholas Sumner; **47b** AA/Clive Sawyer; **48c** AA/Nicholas Sumner; **49c** Embassy of Costa Rica; **50-51t** Nature Air; **50c** AA/Clive Sawyer; **52-53t** AA/Clive Sawyer; **52c** AA/Clive Sawyer; **54-56t** AA/Nicholas Sumner; **54c** AA/Steve Watkins; **54b** AA/Nicholas Sumner; **55b** AA/Nicholas Sumner; **56c** AA/Nicholas Sumner; **56b** AA/Nicholas Sumner.

THE SIGHTS

57 Steve Watkins; Top frieze between **58-126** AA/Clive Sawyer; **59t** AA/Clive Sawyer; **59c** AA/Clive Sawyer; **59b** AA/Clive Sawyer; **60** AA/Clive Sawyer; **61** AA/Clive Sawyer; **62t** AA/Clive Sawyer; **62cl** AA/Nicholas Sumner; **62cc** AA/Nicholas Sumner; **62cr** AA/Nicholas Sumner; **62b** AA/Clive Sawyer; **63t** AA/Clive Sawyer; **63b** AA/Nicholas Sumner; **64tl** AA/Nicholas Sumner; **64tr** AA/Clive Sawyer; **65tl** AA/Nicholas Sumner; **65tr** AA/Clive Sawyer; **65b** Instituto Costarricense de Turismo; **66tl** AA/Nicholas Sumner; **66tr** AA/Nicholas Sumner; **67t** AA/Clive Sawyer; **67cr** AA/Nicholas Sumner; **69tl** AA/Nicholas Sumner; **69tr** AA/Clive Sawyer; **70tl** Instituto Costarricense de Turismo; **70tr** AA/Clive Sawyer; **71tl** AA/Nicholas Sumner; **71c** AA/Nicholas Sumner; **71r** Instituto Costarricense de Turismo; **72t** AA/Clive Sawyer; **72cl** AA/Clive Sawyer; **72c** Instituto Costarricense de Turismo; **72cr** AA/Clive Sawyer; **72b** AA/Nicholas Sumner; **73t** AA/Clive Sawyer; **73c** Instituto Costarricense de Turismo; **74t** AA/Nicholas Sumner; **74cl** AA/Clive Sawyer; **74b** AA/Clive Sawyer; **75tl** AA/Clive Sawyer; **75tr** AA/Clive Sawyer; **76tl** AA/Clive Sawyer; **76tc** AA/Clive Sawyer; **76tr** AA/Nicholas Sumner; **76bl** Ingo Arndt/naturepl.com; **78t** AA/Steve Watkins; **78cl** AA/Steve Watkins; **78cc** AA/Clive Sawyer; **78cr** AA/Steve Watkins; **79** AA/Steve Watkins; **80** Instituto Costarricense de Turismo; **81** AA/Clive Sawyer; **82tl** AA/Clive Sawyer; **82tc** AA/Clive Sawyer; **82tr** Gregory Basco; **82b** AA/Nicholas Sumner; **83tl** AA/Clive Sawyer; **83tr** Instituto Costarricense de Turismo; **83b** Instituto Costarricense de Turismo; **84** AA/Nicholas Sumner; **85t** AA/Nicholas Sumner; **85cl** AA/Clive Sawyer; **85cc** AA/Nicholas Sumner; **86cl** AA/Clive Sawyer; **86cc** AA/Clive Sawyer; **86cr** AA/Nicholas Sumner; **87tr** AA/Nicholas Sumner; **87cl** AA/Nicholas Sumner; **87cc** AA/Nicholas Sumner; **87cr** AA/Nicholas Sumner; **87br** AA/Nicholas Sumner; **88tl** AA/Nicholas Sumner; **88cl** AA/Clive Sawyer; **88cc** AA/Nicholas Sumner; **88cr** AA/Nicholas Sumner; **88br** AA/Nicholas Sumner; **89cl**

AA/Clive Sawyer ; **89cc** AA/Nicholas Sumner; **89cr** AA/Nicholas Sumner; **91tl** AA/Clive Sawyer; **91tc** AA/Nicholas Sumner; **91tr** AA/Nicholas Sumner; **91b** AA/Nicholas Sumner; **92t** AA/Nicholas Sumner; **92c** AA/Clive Sawyer; **93t** AA/Nicholas Sumner; **93c** AA/Nicholas Sumner; **94t** AA/Nicholas Sumner; **94cl** AA/Nicholas Sumner; **94cc** AA/Nicholas Sumner; **94cr** AA/Nicholas Sumner; **95t** AA/Nicholas Sumner; **95cr** AA/Clive Sawyer; **96t** AA/Nicholas Sumner; **96c** Instituto Costarricense de Turismo; **97t** AA/Nicholas Sumner; **97cl** AA/Nicholas Sumner; **97cc** AA/Nicholas Sumner; **97cr** AA/Nicholas Sumner; **97br** AA/Nicholas Sumner; **98t** AA/Nicholas Sumner; **98c** AA/Nicholas Sumner; **99t** AA/Nicholas Sumner; **99c** AA/Nicholas Sumner; **100tl** AA/Clive Sawyer; **100tr** AA/Clive Sawyer; **100c** AA/Nicholas Sumner; **102tl** Jack Ewing/Hacienda Baru National Wildlife Refuge; **102tc** AA/Clive Sawyer; **102tr** AA/Nicholas Sumner; **102c** Jack Ewing/Hacienda Baru National Wildlife Refuge; **103tl** AA/Clive Sawyer; **103tr** AA/Clive Sawyer; **103b** AA/Steve Watkins; **104tl** Jan Csernoch; **104tr** T.Burnett-K.Palmer/V&W/imagequestmarine.com; **105tl** AA/Clive Sawyer; **105tr** AA/Clive Sawyer; **105b** AA/Clive Sawyer; **106t** AA/Clive Sawyer; **106cl** AA/Clive Sawyer; **106cc** AA/Clive Sawyer; **106cr** AA/Clive Sawyer; **106b** AA/Nicholas Sumner; **107t** Instituto Costarricense de Turismo; **107c** AA/Clive Sawyer; **108tl** AA/Steve Watkins; **108tr** AA/Nicholas Sumner; **108b** Instituto Costarricense de Turismo; **110tl** Sierra/divinedolphin.com; **110tc** AA/Clive Sawyer; **110tr** AA/Clive Sawyer; **110b** AA/Steve Watkins; **111tl** AA/Clive Sawyer; **111tr** AA/Clive Sawyer; **112t** AA/Steve Watkins; **112cl** AA/Steve Watkins; **112cc** Instituto Costarricense de Turismo; **112cr** AA/Steve Watkins; **113t** AA/Steve Watkins; **113cl** AA/Clive Sawyer; **113cc** AA/Clive Sawyer; **113cr** AA/Steve Watkins; **114cl** Instituto Costarricense de Turismo; **114cc** AA/Clive Sawyer; **114cr** AA/Steve Watkins; **115t** AA/Clive Sawyer; **115b** AA/Clive Sawyer; **116tl** AA/Clive Sawyer; **116tr** AA/Clive Sawyer; **116b** AA/Clive Sawyer; **117tl** AA/Clive Sawyer; **117tc** AA/Clive Sawyer; **117tr** AA/Nicholas Sumner; **117c** AA/Clive Sawyer; **118t** AA/Nicholas Sumner; **118cl** AA/Nicholas Sumner; **118cc** AA/Clive Sawyer; **118cr** AA/Clive Sawyer; **119** Jan Csernoch; **120t** AA/Nicholas Sumner; **120cl** AA/Clive Sawyer; **120cc** AA/Nicholas Sumner; **120cr** AA/Nicholas Sumner; **120b** AA/Nicholas Sumner; **122t** AA/Clive Sawyer; **122cl** Caribbean Conservation Corporation; **122cc** AA/Clive Sawyer; **122cr** AA/Clive Sawyer; **123t** AA/Clive Sawyer; **123b** AA/Steve Watkins; **124t** AA/Clive Sawyer; **124cl** AA/Steve Watkins; **125l** AA/Clive Sawyer; **125r** AA/Clive Sawyer; **126tl** AA/Clive Sawyer; **126tr** AA/Nicholas Sumner.

WHAT TO DO

127 Instituto Costarricense de Turismo; **128t** AA/Clive Sawyer; **128cl** AA/Clive Sawyer; **128cr** AA/Clive Sawyer; **129t** AA/Nicholas Sumner; **129c** AA/Clive Sawyer; **130t** AA/Nicholas Sumner; **130cl** AA/Clive Sawyer; **130cr** AA/Nicholas Sumner; **131t** AA/Clive Sawyer; **131cl** AA/Nicholas Sumner; **131cr** Instituto Costarricense de Turismo; **132t** Instituto Costarricense de Turismo; **132cl** Instituto Costarricense de Turismo; **132cr** AA/Steve Watkins; **133t** AA/Steve Watkins; **133cl** AA/Steve Watkins; **133cr** Instituto Costarricense de Turismo; **134/135t** AA/Clive Sawyer; **134cl** AA/Clive Sawyer; **134cr** AA/Clive Sawyer; **136t** Instituto Costarricense de Turismo; **136cl** AA/Steve Watkins; **136cr** Instituto Costarricense de Turismo; **137t** Paul Furlong; **137cl** AA/Clive Sawyer; **137cr** Paul Furlong; **138/139t** AA/Nicholas Sumner; **138c** Leonel Gonzalez/Galeria 11-12; **139c** AA/Nicholas Sumner; **140t** AA/Nicholas Sumner; **141-143t** AA/Clive Sawyer; **141c** Paul Furlong; **142c** Image 100; **144/145t** AA/Clive Sawyer; **144c** La Laguna de Lagarto Lodge; **146-149t** AA/Nicholas Sumner; **146c** Rich Coast Diving Co.; **147c** Blue Dolphin Sailing; **148c** Bill Beard's Costa Rica Tours;

150-152t AA/Clive Sawyer; **150c** Dominical Little Theatre; **151c** Del Mar Surf Camp; **152c** La Vela Latina; **153t** AA/Clive Sawyer; **153c** Sierra/divinedolphin.com; **154-156t** AA/Clive Sawyer; **154c** Penelope Mendiguetti/Silver King Lodge; **155c** Rio Parismina Lodge.

OUT AND ABOUT

157 AA/Nicholas Sumner; **158cl** AA/Clive Sawyer; **158cr** AA/Clive Sawyer; **158b** AA/Clive Sawyer; **159t** AA/Nicholas Sumner; **159bc** AA/Clive Sawyer; **159br** AA/Nicholas Sumner; **160tl** AA/Nicholas Sumner; **160tr** AA/Clive Sawyer; **161tl** AA/Nicholas Sumner; **161tr** AA/Clive Sawyer; **161c** AA/Nicholas Sumner; **161b** AA/Nicholas Sumner; **162t** Instituto Costarricense de Turismo; **162b** AA/Nicholas Sumner; **163tl** Instituto Costarricense de Turismo; **163tr** AA/Nicholas Sumner; **164t** AA/Nicholas Sumner; **164b** AA/Clive Sawyer; **165tl** AA/Clive Sawyer; **165tr** AA/Nicholas Sumner; **165b** AA/Nicholas Sumner; **166** AA/Nicholas Sumner; **167t** AA/Nicholas Sumner; **167b** Michael Cannon; **168cl** AA/Clive Sawyer; **168cr** AA/Nicholas Sumner; **168bl** AA/Nicholas Sumner; **168br** AA/Nicholas Sumner; **169t** AA/Clive Sawyer; **169c** AA/Clive Sawyer; **170** Instituto Costarricense de Turismo; **171t** AA/Nicholas Sumner; **171cl** AA/Clive Sawyer; **171cr** AA/Nicholas Sumner; **172t** AA/Nicholas Sumner; **172bl** Instituto Costarricense de Turismo; **173tl** AA/Clive Sawyer; **173tr** AA/Clive Sawyer; **174t** AA/Nicholas Sumner; **174cr** AA/Nicholas Sumner; **174bl** AA/Nicholas Sumner; **175tl** AA/Nicholas Sumner; **175tr** AA/Nicholas Sumner; **175b** AA/Nicholas Sumner; **176bl** AA/Clive Sawyer; **176br** AA/Clive Sawyer; **177tl** AA/Clive Sawyer; **177tr** AA/Clive Sawyer.

EATING AND STAYING

179 Photodisc; **180cl** AA/Clive Sawyer; **180cc** Samasati Nature Retreat; **180cr** AA/Clive Sawyer; **180b** Instituto Costarricense de Turismo; **181cl** AA/Clive Sawyer; **181cc** AA/Nicholas Sumner; **181cr** AA/Clive Sawyer; **182tc** AA/Nicholas Sumner; **182r** AA/Nicholas Sumner; **185c** Justin Henderson; **185tl** Justin Henderson; **185b** Justin Henderson; **189t** Justin Henderson; **189b** Steve Brecht; **190c** Justin Henderson; **190b** Justin Henderson; **191l** Christopher Baker; **195b** AA/Nicholas Sumner; **196t** AA/Nicholas Sumner; **196b** AA/Nicholas Sumner; **197l** AA/Nicholas Sumner; **197r** AA/Nicholas Sumner; **199** AA/Nicholas Sumner; **203l** Steve Brecht; **206l** Casa Corcovado Jungle Lodge; **206** Instituto Costarricense de Turismo; **208r** Photodisc.

PLANNING

211 Digital Vision; **212** AA/Nicholas Sumner; **213** AA/Clive Sawyer; **214** Banco Central de Costa Rica; **216** AA/Clive Sawyer; **217t** AA/Clive Sawyer; **217b** AA/Nicholas Sumner; **218** AA/Clive Sawyer; **219** AA/Steve Watkins; **220b** AA/Nicholas Sumner; **221** AA/Nicholas Sumner; **222t** AA/Nicholas Sumner; **222b** AA/Clive Sawyer; **223** Digital Vision.

Project editor
Robin Barton

Interior design
Keith Russell

Picture research
Alice Earle

Cover design
Tigist Getachew

Internal repro work
Susan Crowhurst, Ian Little, Michael Moody

Production
Helen Brown, Lyn Kirby

Mapping
Maps produced by the Mapping Services of AA Publishing

Main contributors
Peter Hutchison, Caroline Lascom

Copy editor
Jo Perry

Updater
Christopher P Baker

Revision management
Bookwork Creative Associates Ltd

See It Costa Rica
ISBN 978-1-4000-1845-1
Second Edition

Selected text supplied by Footprint Handbooks Limited © 2004

Color separation by Keenes
Printed and bound by Leo, China
10 9 8 7 6 5 4 3 2

A04229
Maps in this title produced from map data:
© New Holland Publishing (South Africa) (PTY) Limited 2004
and © Footprint Handbooks Limited 2004

Relief map images supplied by Mountain High Maps® Copyright © 1993 Digital Wisdom, Inc
Weather chart statistics supplied by Weatherbase © Copyright 2004 Canty and Associates, LLC

Important Note: Time inevitably brings changes, so always confirm prices, travel facts,
and other perishable information when it matters. Although Fodor's cannot accept
responsibility for errors, you can use this guide in the confidence that we have taken
every care to ensure its accuracy.

Fodor's Key to the Guides

AMERICA'S **GUIDEBOOK LEADER** PUBLISHES GUIDES FOR **EVERY KIND OF TRAVELER**. CHECK OUT OUR MANY SERIES AND FIND YOUR **PERFECT MATCH**.

GOLD GUIDES
Built for today's travelers with unique graphics and maps for easy planning and advice on quintessential local experiences, along with Fodor's Choice rated hotels, restaurants, and sights to guarantee an exceptional vacation.

EXPLORING GUIDES
Splendid color photography paired with exquisitely written articles on history, culture, art, and architecture; suggested walks and excursions; and full-color maps allow you to experience a destination like a well-informed local.

COMPASS AMERICAN GUIDES
Long-time resident writers and photographers reveal the culture and character of American cities, states, and regions through intelligently written essays, literary excerpts, and stunning color imagery.

AROUND THE CITY WITH KIDS
68 great ideas for family fun in and around the city, hand-picked by resident parents, with age-appropriate ratings, entertaining trivia, and nearby kid-friendly snack spots.

SEE IT GUIDES
Colorful and practical, these illustrated guides feature smart writing on history and culture, rich photography, *and* practical travel information. Complete dining and restaurant reviews, exact admission fees, kid-friendly ratings, and everything from sightseeing and shopping, to nightlife, performing arts, and outdoor activities.

25 BEST
Compact city guides of must-see sights and the best dining, shopping, and activities; with a detailed, full-size street map conveniently built-in so you can confidently navigate the city.

FLASHMAPS
Easy-to-follow maps perfect for residents or visitors who want to quickly locate restaurants, shops, museums, movie theaters, subway and bus routes, and more.

LANGUAGES FOR TRAVELERS
All the words and phrases you need for greeting locals, dining out, and getting around in a handy phrasebook along with two CDs for pronunciation practice.

Available at bookstores everywhere.
For a complete list of more than 300 guidebooks,
visit **Fodors.com/shop**.

Dear Traveler

From buying a plane ticket to booking a room and seeing the sights, a trip goes much more smoothly when you have a good travel guide. Dozens of writers, editors, designers, and cartographers have worked hard to make the book you hold in your hands a good one. Was it everything you expected? Were our descriptions accurate? Were our recommendations on target? And did you find our tips and practical advice helpful? Your ideas and experiences matter to us. If we have missed or misstated something, we'd love to hear about it. Fill out our survey at www.fodors.com/books/feedback/, or e-mail us at seeit@fodors.com. Or you can snail mail to the See It Editor at Fodor's, 1745 Broadway, New York, New York 10019. We'll look forward to hearing from you.

Tim Jarrell
Publisher